THE RACIAL MOSAIC

RETHINKING CANADA IN THE WORLD
Series editors: Ian McKay and Sean Mills

Supported by the Wilson Institute for Canadian History at McMaster University, this series is committed to books that rethink Canadian history from transnational and global perspectives. It enlarges approaches to the study of Canada in the world by exploring how Canadian history has long been a dynamic product of global currents and forces. The series will also reinvigorate understanding of Canada's role as an international actor and how Canadians have contributed to intellectual, political, cultural, social, and material exchanges around the world.

Volumes included in the series explore the ideas, movements, people, and institutions that have transcended political boundaries and territories to shape Canadian society and the state. These include both state and non-state actors, and phenomena such as international migration, diaspora politics, religious movements, evolving conceptions of human rights and civil society, popular culture, technology, epidemics, wars, and global finance and trade.

The series charts a new direction by exploring networks of transmission and exchange from a standpoint that is not solely national or international, expanding the history of Canada's engagement with the world.
http://wilson.humanities.mcmaster.ca

1 Canada and the United Nations
  Legacies, Limits, Prospects
  Edited by Colin McCullough and Robert Teigrob

2 Undiplomatic History
  The New Study of Canada and the World
  Edited by Asa McKercher and Philip Van Huizen

3 Revolutions across Borders
  Jacksonian America and the Canadian Rebellion
  Edited by Maxime Dagenais and Julien Mauduit

4 Left Transnationalism
  The Communist International and the National, Colonial, and Racial Questions
  Edited by Oleksa Drachewych and Ian McKay

5 Landscapes of Injustice
  A New Perspective on the Internment and Dispossession of Japanese Canadians
  Edited by Jordan Stanger-Ross

6 Canada's Other Red Scare
  Indigenous Protest and Colonial Encounters during the Global Sixties
  Scott Rutherford

7 The Global Politics of Poverty
  in Canada
  Development Programs and
  Democracy, 1964–1979
  *Will Langford*

8 Schooling the System
  A History of Black Women
  Teachers
  *Funké Aladejebi*

9 Constant Struggle
  Histories of Canadian
  Democratization
  *Edited by Julien Mauduit and
  Jennifer Tunnicliffe*

10 The Racial Mosaic
   A Pre-history of Canadian
   Multiculturalism
   *Daniel R. Meister*

# THE
# RACIAL
# MOSAIC

A PRE-HISTORY OF CANADIAN

MULTICULTURALISM

Daniel R. Meister

McGill-Queen's University Press
Montreal & Kingston • London • Chicago

© McGill-Queen's University Press 2021

ISBN 978-0-2280-0870-5 (cloth)
ISBN 978-0-2280-0871-2 (paper)
ISBN 978-0-2280-0997-9 (ePDF)
ISBN 978-0-2280-0998-6 (ePUB)

Legal deposit fourth quarter 2021
Bibliothèque nationale du Québec

Printed in Canada on acid-free paper that is 100% ancient forest free (100% post-consumer recycled), processed chlorine free

This book has been published with the help of a grant from the Canadian Federation for the Humanities and Social Sciences, through the Awards to Scholarly Publications Program, using funds provided by the Social Sciences and Humanities Research Council of Canada.

We acknowledge the support of the Canada Council for the Arts.
Nous remercions le Conseil des arts du Canada de son soutien.

---

Library and Archives Canada Cataloguing in Publication

Title: The racial mosaic : a pre-history of Canadian multiculturalism / Daniel R. Meister.
Names: Meister, Daniel R., author.
Series: Rethinking Canada in the world ; 10.
Description: Series statement: Rethinking Canada in the world ; 10 | Includes bibliographical references and index.
Identifiers: Canadiana (print) 2021028594X | Canadiana (ebook) 20210286059 | ISBN 9780228008712 (paper) | ISBN 9780228008705 (cloth) | ISBN 9780228009979 (ePDF) | ISBN 9780228009986 (ePUB)
Subjects: LCSH: Kirkconnell, Watson, 1895-1977. | LCSH: England, Robert, 1894-1985. | LCSH: Gibbon, John Murray, 1875-1952. | LCSH: Cultural Pluralism—Canada—History—20th century. | LCSH: Racism—Canada History—20th century. | LCSH: Intellectuals—Canada—Biography. | LCSH: Canada—Intellectual life—20th century. | LCSH: Canada—Ethnic relations.
Classification: LCC FC105.M8 M45 2021 | DDC 305.800971—dc23

---

This book was typeset in 10.5/13 Sabon.

*For Alicia and Fenne*

# Contents

Tables and Figures xi
Acknowledgments xiii
Introduction 3
1 Watson Kirkconnell and Scientific Racism 31
2 Robert England and Canadian Citizenship 82
3 John Murray Gibbon and Folk Culture 127
4 Making It Official 171
5 Cultural Pluralism in Wartime 195
Conclusion 234
Epilogue 247
Notes 253
Bibliography 343
Index 383

# Tables and Figures

### TABLES

4.1 Episodes of *Canadian Mosaic: Songs of Many Races* radio program, 1938. 174
4.2 Episodes of *Ventures in Citizenship* radio program, 1938. 179
4.3 Sales and Royalties of *Canada, Europe, and Hitler*, 1939–49. 193
5.1 Episodes of *Canadians All* radio program, 1941. 209

### FIGURES

0.1 *Canadian Mosaic*. Photographed by William (Bill) M. Newton (1914–1970) and published in the *Ottawa Citizen* (18 February 1947), 13. 4
0.2 *Grant's Taxonomy of Mankind.* In Jonathan Spiro, *Defending the Master Race: Conservation, Eugenics, and the Legacy of Madison Grant* (Lebanon, NH: University Press of New England, 2009), 103. 17
1.1 Watson Kirkconnell, ca. 1970. Esther Clark Wright Archives at Acadia University, Watson Kirkconnell fonds, box 13, folder 2. 33
1.2 *Camp Staff*, Kapuskasing, July 1917. Photo courtesy of the Ron Morel Memorial Museum, Kapuskasing, Ontario. 43

1.3  The "negro porter." In Watson Kirkconnell, *Titus the Toad* (Toronto: Oxford University Press, 1940), 59. Illustration by Davina Whitehouse (née Smith) [Davina Craig, pseud.].  78

2.1  Robert England, ca. 1943. Canadian Army photo, courtesy of the John Simon Guggenheim Memorial Foundation.  85

3.1  Detail of John Murray Gibbon, photographed by George Nakash. Library and Archives Canada, Sir Ernest MacMillan fonds, MUS 7, vol. 136.  129

3.2  [Babahamy holding John Murray Gibbon]. Whyte Museum of the Canadian Rockies, Archives and Special Collections, John Murray Gibbon fonds, V225/unprocessed.  131

6.1  "Ma Blushin' Rosie." Photographed by Bill Newton and published in the *Ottawa Citizen* (18 February 1947), 13.  245

# Acknowledgments

I would like to begin by thanking Cuilean Hendra, my high school history teacher, for being an excellent educator and for igniting my interest in Canadian history, and Daniel C. Goodwin for fanning the flames. Dan convinced me to become a history major, supervised my undergraduate honours thesis, encouraged me to apply to graduate school, and specifically suggested that I approach Ian McKay at Queen's University. Much to my surprise, Ian graciously agreed to supervise my master's cognate essay. His feedback was (and is) dauntingly comprehensive but always incredibly helpful, and I am grateful for his continued support. The cognate's second reader was Barrington Walker, and I should like to thank him for taking me on as a graduate student and for supervising the PhD dissertation on which this book is based. Many thanks to the other members of my PhD Committee, Professors Jeffrey Brison, Margaret Little, Laura Madokoro, and Lisa Pasolli, for their much-needed encouragement and for their thoughtful critiques, which directly informed the writing of this book.

Of course, I would like to especially thank those who helped me transform my dissertation into the book that you are holding. At the top of my list is Laura Madokoro, who kickstarted the publication process by introducing me to Kyla Madden, senior editor at McGill-Queen's University Press, and who has supported me throughout. Thank you so much, Laura. Kyla likewise showed enthusiasm about the project from the start and kindly and patiently guided this newcomer through the publication process, offering plenty of encouragement along the way. Thank you! Thanks also to Jeff Brison for sharing his knowledge of the historiography, and to

Lisa Pasolli for her feedback on several redrafted sections. Special thanks to Don Wright for being so generous with his time, editorial suggestions, and all-around support. The press also selected some wonderful anonymous reviewers (A1 and A2). Their encouragement was refreshing and their suggestions were challenging; my sincere thanks to them both. The same was true of my copyeditor, Rachel Taylor, whom I would like to thank for making this a stronger manuscript. I would also like to thank the series editors, Ian McKay and Sean Mills, for accepting this book in the Rethinking Canada in the World series. This is a new and exciting series, and I am delighted to be a part of it.

A portion of chapter 1 was previously published as an article in *Settler Colonial Studies*, and I would like to thank Taylor & Francis Ltd for the permission to reuse that content here. Thanks also to Jonathan Spiro for his permission to reproduce an image from his important biography of Madison Grant. And thanks to all those institutions and companies who granted me permission to reproduce the photographs that appear in the book, including the Ron Morel Memorial Museum and the Whyte Museum of the Canadian Rockies. I would also like to thank the John Simon Guggenheim Memorial Foundation for kindly providing a copy of Robert England's army photograph. I have made good faith efforts to properly acknowledge all reproduced material, but if any errors or omissions are noted after publication, these will be corrected in any future edition.

This book draws on research supported by the Social Sciences and Humanities Research Council of Canada (through a Joseph-Armand Bombardier CGS Doctoral Scholarship). I am grateful for this and all other funding I received as a PhD candidate, which includes the following sources: Queen's University, through an Arthur & Evelyn Lower Fellowship in Canadian History, a Franklin and Helene Bracken Fellowship, and a Timothy C.S. Frank Research travel grant; the Government of Ontario, through an Ontario Graduate Scholarship; and Acadia University, through a travel grant from the Centre for Baptist and Anabaptist Studies. I was also the recipient of a Graduate Student Scholarship from the International Council of Canadian Studies (ICCS), which allowed me to spend several additional weeks in the archives at Acadia University. Thanks to the ICCS for their financial support, the Canadian Studies Network for their nomination, and Stephen Henderson for acting as my sponsor during that time.

# Acknowledgments

A variety of individuals and institutions have helped me with the research that went into this book. I would like to thank the staff of all the archives I consulted, including Sandra Calabrese, Nicki Carter, Helena Clarkson, Suzanne Ell, Elizabeth-Anne Johnson, Kim Geraldi, Patrick Hayes, James Kominowski, Brett Lougheed, Daniel Matthes, Adam McCulloch, Alice Millea, Rick Stapleton, Lewis Stubbs, and Erwin Wodarczak. In terms of debts to archivists, however, I owe the most to the fantastic trio at the Esther Clark Wright Archives at Acadia University. Patricia Townsend, Catherine Fancy, and Wendy Robicheau have answered so very many questions, pulled dozens of boxes, and scanned many, many files for me over the past eight years. It is no exaggeration to say that without them this book could not have been written. The same is true of interlibrary loan staff at Queen's University who hunted down hundreds of obscure articles for me: a huge thank you to them. And I would like to offer special thanks to my research assistants: Alexandra Bowyer for her meticulous online research, and Andrew Lewis for his excellent work at various institutions in the United Kingdom.

After the completion of my dissertation, additional research was completed at the archives of the Canadian Museum of History, where Benoît Thériault's encyclopedic knowledge of the collections made the process a breeze – thanks, Benoît. I also spent an extended research period at the Whyte Museum of the Canadian Rockies in Banff, Alberta, as a Lillian Agnes Jones Fellow. I am grateful to the institution for the opportunity, for the financial support it provided, and for the help that I received from the archivists and staff. Particular thanks are owed to Lindsay Stokalko, who went above and beyond to help me maximize the amount of research I was able to complete.

Although intended as a stand-alone project, the research I conducted at the Whyte Museum helped me to round out the sketch of John Murray Gibbon that this book contains. The historiography on Gibbon is surprisingly scant and, owing to a lack of source material, is heavily reliant on his unpublished autobiography. For this reason, I am immensely grateful to members of his family, Virginia Glover, Alexa Wilson, Fiona Gibbon Taillefer, and Joan Gibbon Vaughan, for providing much new source material as well as invaluable insight into his personal life. They, along with Penguin Random House Archive and Library, gave me permission to view the relevant files held at the University of Reading, for which I am grateful. Special credit goes to Virginia for her early support and for her tireless work in coordinating meetings, and for loans and donations of material. She also transcribed a number of letters and journal entries, as Gibbon's handwriting is often difficult to decipher, and her commentary was far more humorous than any found in the pages that follow. However, I must stress that none of the biographical sketches in this book are in any sense "authorized": the interpretations, emphases, omissions, and mistakes made throughout are mine and mine alone.

I have been shameless about writing various people out of the blue with queries relating to the project and I am thankful for all the helpful responses I invariably received, though I dare not attempt to make a list of all these correspondents. I also appreciate the help and encouragement provided by friends throughout this past decade of study. At Queen's, friends like Sanober and Nick, Sarah and Andrew, Matt, Mike, and Scott all made grad school that much more bearable. Special thanks to Jen F. for her encouragement, support, and comments on multiple complete drafts; for hosting Alicia and me when we came to Calgary; and for her hospitality during my time in Banff. Thanks also to Jenn M. for letting me stay with her during my repeated trips to Acadia University; Ashlee D. for her advice; and Emma and Steve for hosting me during several stints of research in Ottawa.

The hours spent staring (often blankly) at archival documents, books, articles, and the computer screen were draining, and I was repeatedly surprised at just how refreshing an escape into the natural world could be: the sun on my face, the quietness of the fields, the roar of the rivers and creeks, the silence of the lakes, the chatter of the birds, the whisper of the wind, the crunch of the snow, the creak of the ice. All of these lifted my spirits and refreshed me, whether I was in rural New Brunswick; a city park in Kingston, Ontario; a provincial or national park somewhere between Kingston and Calgary; on a tiny island in Eabamet Lake; or standing awestruck in the shadow of the Rockies. For these bits of earth, I am grateful. I am also grateful for my friend of the canine variety, Twig, for his companionship and for his many impositions. He is responsible for my daily exercise, regular breaks from work, and need to perpetually vacuum.

I owe so much to my family, Dobbelsteyns and Meisters alike, who have supported me in so many ways throughout the duration of the project. I am so appreciative of all you have done for me, even if what I was doing or why I was doing it remained unclear (they were not always clear for me either). And I must say that were we not able to eat from the Chef's Table, I can't imagine this book having been completed on time.

Reflecting on an archaeological dig, environmentalist Mark Boyle remarked: "It's all too easy to destroy the present while exploring the past." I think that quote can also usefully describe the experience of studying history at the graduate level and beyond, as it is a time-consuming – and can be an all-consuming – endeavour. This brings me to my final acknowledgment, to the person who sacrificed the most to allow me to passionately pursue this project, my dearest Alicia. Alicia, I have tried writing an adequate acknowledgment of all you have done for me several times, but have failed each one. Without your support, in so many ways but especially emotionally and financially, this book could never have been written. Freeing me up to frantically revise this manuscript – even as we prepared for and adjusted to the arrival of our first child – is a sacrifice I will never forget. I guess all I can say is that I'll try to make up for the ludicrousness of graduate school and a year of "independent" research by talking less about eugenics, race science, and long-dead, nominally white men all the time. (Maybe.)

# THE RACIAL MOSAIC

The study of "race" in Canada's past is not an exercise in assigning blame, but in understanding historical processes from which we are not exempt.

James W. St G. Walker (1997)

# Introduction

On a chilly evening in February 1947, a steady stream of people filed into Lisgar Collegiate Institute in Ottawa. Originally founded in 1843, the elite public high school's name still carries "a weight of tradition and a connotation of excellence." The impressive, Gothic Revival–style limestone building is located just blocks from Parliament Hill, and on this particular evening was dusted with snow. The crowd had gathered to watch the students' annual stage show, a popular tradition that typically saw the auditorium filled to capacity with proud relatives and community members. The program for that year opened with a performance from the student orchestra, followed by the Girls' Athletics group. They presented a piece entitled "The Canadian Mosaic": dressed in traditional clothing from France, Scandinavia, Poland, Scotland, and England, the students performed the dances "of the old countries and then joined in a Canadian reel."[1]

This celebration of a variety of European cultures would have been unthinkable for Canadians just a few decades earlier. While the cultures of the United Kingdom and perhaps French culture would have been acceptable, Scandinavian and Polish cultures certainly would not have been welcomed. In the interwar period especially, as increasing numbers of immigrants arrived in Canada, Polish people were considered "non-preferred" immigrants and the assimilation of all continental European immigrants was considered a pressing and thorny problem.[2] "Should we not, in the interests of the future welfare of this country, try and devise some system whereby we will have some hope of Canadianizing these foreigners who come to our shores?" one Canadian MP asked in 1919, referring

Figure 0.1 Girls' Athletics group performing "Canadian Mosaic," Lisgar Collegiate Institute, 1947.

to the large numbers of "Germans, Austrians, Russians, Poles, and Scandinavians" on the prairies.[3] When it came to such people, the focus was on "Canadianizing" them, not celebrating their cultures.

The metaphor used by the Girls' Athletics group indicated just how much things had changed: indeed, "mosaic" had become one of the most popular metaphors used to describe Canada's cultural diversity. Portraying this diversity as a positive attribute, akin to a beautiful, artistic display, the mosaic metaphor was an expression of a broader underlying body of thought that had developed during the interwar period. This book examines the development and application of this body of thought, or what I call philosophies of cultural pluralism: various expressions of the idea that immigrants to Canada should be allowed or even encouraged to retain some aspects of their cultures. These philosophies, which emerged in the late 1920s and were ascendant through the end of the Second World War, can be considered the ideological antecedents of the Canadian federal government's policy of multiculturalism, which was not introduced until 1971.[4]

Introducing official multiculturalism to the Ukrainian Canadian community, who had been the most vocal advocates of such a policy, Prime Minister Pierre Trudeau declared: "The fabric of Canadian society is as resilient as it is colorful. It is a multi-cultural society:

it offers to every Canadian the opportunity to fulfil his own cultural instincts and to share those from other sources. This mosaic pattern, and the moderation which it includes and encourages, makes Canada a very special place."[5] The images and metaphors that Trudeau employed when talking about multiculturalism – the colourful fabric and the mosaic pattern – are themselves indicators that his was not the first expression of cultural pluralist thought in Canada. This raises a number of questions: Who were the individuals responsible for promoting more pluralist ways of thinking before this period? What were they working towards? And how did they understand their respective efforts and projects?

In order to best understand this history of ideas, *The Racial Mosaic* takes a historical biographical approach and explores the life and thought of three Canadian public intellectuals who were responsible for some of the earliest and most notable expressions of cultural pluralism: Watson Kirkconnell, Robert England, and John Murray Gibbon. Kirkconnell was a Canadian academic, university administrator, and public intellectual best known for his work as a translator, anti-communist, defender of the humanities, and prominent Baptist layman. England was an Irish immigrant to Canada who taught in a Ukrainian school district in Saskatchewan before going to work for the Canadian National Railways (CNR) both in Europe and in Canada.[6] And Gibbon was an Oxford-educated Scot who worked as a publicist for the Canadian Pacific Railway (CPR) in England and in Canada, where he became well known for his best-selling and award-winning book *Canadian Mosaic* (1938).

The chapters that follow examine the intellectual development of these three men and detail how they developed their philosophies of cultural pluralism, in what contexts, and with what limitations, for it is important to note which cultures were included and which were kept off stage, as it were. The results are clear: just as European cultures were the exclusive focus of "the Canadian Mosaic" at the Lisgar stage show, so they were in Canadian society more broadly. The book demonstrates that this focus was the result of a race science that declared European peoples were members of white races, and that these white races were superior to all non-white races. This racism was primarily expressed through exclusion, meaning that only European or nominally "white" peoples and their cultures were defended as worthy of retention and celebration. As a result, the philosophies of cultural pluralism that these three men crafted did nothing to address the prejudice and denigration that peoples racialized as non-white faced. These philosophies of cultural pluralism were also, in some cases, paired with expressions of that same racial discrimination and denigration.

Over fifty years ago, sociologist John Porter demolished the myth of Canadian classlessness and argued that Canadian society was best understood as a vertical mosaic.[7] But not only was Canada's much-celebrated mosaic vertical; it was also self-consciously racial. This vertical, racial mosaic was also intentionally constructed atop another, older configuration of multiple cultures: those indigenous to northern North America. Philosophies of cultural pluralism can therefore be considered an adaptation of the ongoing project of settler colonialism, as these philosophies imagined the Canadian nation as multiracial (containing multiple European races) but ultimately devoid of Indigenous peoples, or else devoid of unassimilated Indigenous peoples. In short, this book argues that philosophies of cultural pluralism were rooted in settler colonialism and limited by racism.

### HISTORICAL BIOGRAPHY

Historian P.B. Waite once argued: "History is about people's lives, from which we make analysis and abstractions at our peril." Yet biography and history have different purposes.[8] In historian Michael Gauvreau's succinct definition, the "standard of successful biography remains the full elucidation and presentation of the subject's self-understanding in the context of his or her society and culture." A work of history, on the other hand, labours to explain that very context: what has happened in the past and, importantly, how and why it happened. Despite these different objectives, there is nevertheless a mutually beneficial relationship between the two research agendas. As two biographers recently suggested, in order to understand the whole "we have to understand the parts, but to understand them, we have to understand the whole. There is reciprocal dependence between these two operations."[9]

Unfortunately, as historian and biographer Barbara Caine has noted, "despite the widespread recognition amongst historians of the importance and popularity of biography, many of them continue to express considerable ambivalence about it." For this reason, biography is slowly emerging, especially in Europe, as a discipline independent from history.[10] Nevertheless, some historians continue to turn to biography.[11] Some have written "classical" biographies, arguing that such works should focus on the life itself, with the larger context discussed only in a limited way.[12] Other historians, by contrast, have employed a biographical approach as a means of addressing a larger historical question or theme, by using individual lives to examine events and processes. Such authors have often employed historian Barbara Tuchman's well-known "prism" metaphor. The idea is that by looking through a life, the historian can reveal previously unnoticed aspects of a historical period or subject. But it is worth remembering that Tuchman was not aiming for a balance. As she put it, her use of biography was less for the sake of the individual subject than exhibiting an age, nation-state, or situation.[13] This has led historian and biographer Donald Wright to rightly question why any biographer would want to see *through* a life. "Lives do not preclude, or even get in the way of, a deeper or new understanding of historical circumstances and historical processes," he notes.[14]

I define historical biography as the process of bringing the tools of the historian to bear on a single life that has passed, combining archival research, wide reading in the secondary literature, and often the use of oral history. However, I also suggest that historical biography represents a particular type of approach – namely, an attempt to chart a middle ground between two predominating approaches: one which foregrounds the life and the other which foregrounds the time (historical context). Historical biography instead alternates its gaze between the subject and their context, exploring the ways in which their stories are interwoven.

This book examines the lives of three men who were recognized in their time as experts on so-called racial diversity and who, in their capacity as public intellectuals, contributed to the conversations and debates about the immigration and cultures of peoples of non-British, non-French, European descent. Of course, in the space of a single book it is impossible to combine multiple comprehensive biographies. The biographical studies that follow can therefore only be described as partial, or sketches, and they focus primarily on the intellectual development of the subjects and their roles as public intellectuals. However, I recognize that their intellectual contributions cannot be studied in a vacuum, and so have tried to pay close attention to the emotional and social factors in these subjects' lives and explore the connections between the two. For to set out only to examine their philosophies of cultural pluralism without taking into account the broader context of their lives would be to construct a false narrative; it would be an example of what historian and theorist Quentin Skinner calls "the mythology of doctrines."

Such mythologies are generated, he explains, when a scholar begins work with the expectation that an author "will be found to enunciate some doctrine on each of the topics regarded as constitutive of [the author's] subject." Much of the past writing on the history of multiculturalism verges on the related mythological assumption that a fully developed ideology was "always somehow immanent in history." This type of assumption, Skinner notes, leads scholars to debate who "anticipated" a particular doctrine or when it "really emerge[d]." He identifies one particular form of this mythology as being created when a scholar focuses on the historical significance of the writer or work instead of seeking to understand what the author was trying to say and do at the time. This point is particularly important, for crafting a philosophy of cultural pluralism was never the life goal of any one of the individuals that this book examines. Rather, their philosophies were expressed at specific times, for specific reasons, and often as a part of larger works, each of which had an intended message and audience.[15]

In examining these works, this book follows Skinner's methodology, namely the version of textualism laid out in his famous essay, "Meaning and Understanding in the History of Ideas." In it, Skinner drew on J.L. Austin's theory of speech acts, which argued in part that by saying something, a person is also *doing* something and therefore *means* something by their utterance. These were what Austin called "illocutionary acts," such as ordering, warning, informing, teasing, and the like. Skinner consequently argued that to understand a statement is to uncover its "intended illocutionary force" – to understand "*how* what was said was meant, and thus what relations there may have been between various statements even within the same general context."[16] Following this approach, when I discuss any of the texts authored by Kirkconnell, England, and Gibbon, whether they take the form of a poem, novel, public address, or nonfiction book, I attempt to examine their purpose and meaning, while also playing close attention to the biographical and historical context.

One question that faces every would-be biographer is why their subject justifies a study, and there is often no easy answer.[17] In this case, the question "why?" may take three different forms.[18] First, why *these* three men? In short, because historians have already correctly identified them as some of the first to promote more pluralist ways of thinking. Only a handful of Canadians were promoting these types of views prior to the Second World War. In an important essay written in 1977, the late historian Howard Palmer identified Watson Kirkconnell and John Murray Gibbon as two of the earliest and most significant champions of this philosophy. Two years later, in a paper about access to ethno-cultural material in Canada, Maltese Canadian author George Bonavia identified Kirkconnell and Gibbon as "pioneers of multiculturalism."[19] That same year, historian N.F. Dreisziger argued that Kirkconnell had "anticipated the concept of government-supported multicultural programmes by some four decades."[20] These claims, and about Kirkconnell's role in particular, have been repeated numerous times in scholarly literature over the last forty years.[21]

Kirkconnell was one of the first Anglo-Canadians to recognize that European immigrants to Canada had cultural and artistic heritages that rivalled those of England and France, and he was perhaps the very first to seek out new expressions of these heritages in Canada. His work with so-called new Canadian literature was unparalleled, and it was in this context that he expressed his culturally pluralistic views. Gibbon, himself an immigrant, was responsible for orchestrating the widely successful CPR-sponsored folk festivals, "pioneering efforts in a North American context, among the first (if not the first) on the continent," and is recognized as "a key figure in the development of Canadian cultural identity."[22] England's two works on the broader subject of immigration, which called for an acceptance of continental Europeans, were widely read and reviewed both in Canada and abroad. While he engaged in the direct promotion of pluralist views for only part of his life, he played a more direct role than the others in putting these ideas into practice, first in stimulating European emigration and later in managing ongoing colonization efforts in western Canada. Though he has received less attention than Kirkconnell or Gibbon, in the 1970s Howard Palmer recognized his importance and interviewed him on several occasions, with the intention of writing an article about his life and thought.[23]

Second, why these three *men*? In part, this is a continuation of the answer to the previous question. Although there were no doubt others who advocated at a local level for the acceptance of European immigrants, few if any others had platforms to rival those of internationally recognized academic Kirkconnell, CPR-backed publicity guru Gibbon, or CNR-backed England. They were not only some of the earliest cultural pluralists but also some of the most successful. Their public recognition as experts on race and immigration meant that when, motivated by the outbreak of the Second World War, the state somewhat belatedly started paying attention to ethnic minorities, officials turned to these three men to help craft programs designed to promote national unity.

However, it is important to acknowledge that the very notion of expertise was gendered. Specifically, expertise was about qualifications and recognition, and Canadian women had far fewer opportunities available for education, employment, and publication. Yet even when women obtained high success in some or all of these metrics, their skills – which might otherwise be recognized as expertise – were often unacknowledged by men in power. The Committee on Cooperation in Canadian Citizenship (CCCC) is a case in point. The CCCC, composed of a dozen members of the public, was created to help advise the government on how it might encourage ethnic minorities to participate in the war effort (its activities are detailed in chapter 5). When it was established in January 1942, it was initially to be composed of nine men and one woman: Margaret Stovel McWilliams. McWilliams was a municipal politician, social worker, published author, and accomplished administrator (founder and first vice president of the International Federation of University Women). However, press reports drafted by the organizers placed the emphasis not on her skillset but rather on her marriage to Roland Fairbairn McWilliams, then lieutenant governor of Manitoba (1940–53). By the time that the CCCC's formation was publicly announced in March 1942, another woman had been added to the roster: Isabel Skelton. Skelton was a published author and historian, but she too was recognized not for her own strengths but rather for her late spouse, Oscar D. Skelton, a well-known academic and civil servant.[24]

When it came to the men of the Committee, however, their expertise was immediately recognized. Multiple officials put Kirkconnell's name forward as a good source of help with issues relating to so-called racial minorities (various European groups), and others likewise suggested England. Gibbon continued efforts to promote cultural pluralism largely as a private citizen but he was later asked to join the Committee as well. His case is particularly telling: press reports made good mention of his book *Canadian Mosaic*, but in it Gibbon fully disclosed that he had not been the first to use the term. The mosaic metaphor was first used in relation to the Canadian prairies in a book by an American travel writer, Victoria Hayward, and was later used more substantially by a Canadian author, Kate A. Foster. Foster's book, *Our Canadian Mosaic* (1926), was based on her study of the "Foreign-Born" or "New Canadians" as the national field secretary of the Young Women's Christian Association (YWCA). Despite an endorsement and foreword from James H. Coyne, President of the Royal Society of Canada, the book garnered almost no press attention.[25] Canadian women had been actively involved in trying to help "Canadianize" immigrants for decades, particularly through organizations such as the YWCA, and it was this type of hands-on involvement that led Foster to deploy the mosaic metaphor as a way of understanding diversity and as a goal to reach towards – a full decade before Gibbon independently arrived at the idea. (Once he found out about Foster's work, he offered to change the proposed title of his book, but she and the YWCA allowed him to go ahead.)

Although Gibbon's book reached a broader audience than Foster's, women's organizations were also partly responsible for its success. Groups such as the Local Council of Women (LCW), the Imperial Order Daughters of the Empire (IODE), the Catholic Women's League, university women's clubs, and various homemaker's clubs, along with the Canadian Authors Association (CAA), reviewed and discussed it and used it for book studies or as the basis for folk pageants.[26] Similarly, women and organizations who had long worked with ethnic minorities in the Canadian west gave Kirkconnell a platform to promote his ideas about the value of immigrant cultures, particularly their literary and poetic efforts. The IODE, the LCW, the Winnipeg Women's Press Club, and the Women's Canadian Club – as well as various women's auxiliary groups, educational associations, missionary societies, and poetry clubs – all hosted his talks and promoted his publications. While Kirkconnell then parlayed this publicity into further high-profile positions, women like Foster, who had plenty of experience with such questions of national unity, were not called upon by the government to assist with the CCCC; their expertise simply was not recognized. So it was, for example, that we find a married woman driving Robert England around the city of London, England (when he briefly worked there for the Canadian Legion) but women were not often seated around the boardroom table with him in Ottawa.[27]

Finally, why these three nominally *white* men? Owing to the racism that structured Canadian society during the period under study, only the views of those people racialized as white were given serious attention. To continue the present example, the federal government only recognized the expertise of men, and specifically men racialized as white. The turn towards social history has meant that, in recent decades, historians have worked to excavate and foreground the experiences of those previously marginalized: women, the working class, and those racialized as non-white. These accounts tell how those people devalued by a majority of people in power actually contributed to the colonization of the lands that became Canada and the building of this new society. These works of history are vitally important, as they work to correct decades of historians' bias and neglect. But, as historian and biographer Barbara Messamore has argued, our ability to obtain a more complete understanding of change is dependent upon understanding both the lives of the "disenfranchised many" *and* the lives of the few who held more institutional power and were able to more immediately shape the course of events in Canadian history.[28]

In this case, examining the thought of some of those individuals most instrumental in shaping the conversations and debates about Canadian immigration, culture, and identity reveals just how deeply race and racism have structured Canadian society. The development of cultural pluralism, a philosophy which suggested that immigrants and ethnic minorities be allowed to retain some elements of their cultures, and that these elements might be beneficial for Canadian society, was arguably a new and unique way of thinking. However, this early pluralism had very real, distinct, and narrow boundaries. And in the philosophies of cultural pluralism that these three "white" men developed, the only cultures that were considered – indeed, that were even deemed worthy of consideration – were European or "white." It is a testament to the depth of the discrimination and racism in Canadian society that this general shift towards cultural pluralism represented a genuine and positive change. But this shift nevertheless was and is distinct from the struggles against ongoing settler colonialism fought by Indigenous peoples and from struggles against ongoing racism, fought predominantly by Indigenous people and also non-Indigenous people groups racialized as non-white.

## RACE, WHITENESS, AND SETTLER COLONIALISM

Because these freighted racial categories of white and non-white are central to this study's analysis, they require some unpacking at the outset. Contemporary studies of whiteness, "Whiteness Studies" or "Critical Whiteness Studies," can be considered a subfield of critical race theory (CRT).[29] CRT began as a study of the relationship between race and the law in the United States. It then grew into a broader theoretical framework for examining the relationships between race, the law, culture, and American society, and has been adopted by scholars working in other fields and in other countries. Similarly, some of the most foundational texts in whiteness tudies are legal in their approach, though the field has likewise grown into a broader theoretical framework used predominantly by social scientists.[30] However, most scholars trace its ideological origins back to African American intellectuals who were writing in the late nineteenth and early twentieth century, such as W.E.B. DuBois.[31] Although "whiteness has no stable consensual meaning,"[32] at its most basic, it refers to a constructed racial identity. Whiteness studies is therefore dedicated to tracing the formation of white racial identities and understanding how they have contributed to the structuring of social relations. But before we can understand the racial category of whiteness, we must understand the underlying concept of race and its history.[33]

From the outset, it is important to remember that the kinds of oppression and discrimination that are now associated with racism have a longer history than the idea of race. In the words of critical race scholar Naomi Zach: "Various forms of clannishness, tribalism, regionalism, and xenophobia can be traced to the earliest days of recorded human history."[34] Racism therefore supplemented, and in some cases replaced, pre-existing logics of domination. As historian Colin Kidd persuasively argues: "Race was not a central organising concept of intellectual life or political culture during the early modern period. White domination did not rest on theories of racial superiority but rather other arguments appealing to religion or 'natural laws.'"[35]

Aside from race, religion, and natural laws, another logic of domination was the European notion of historical development, with its three stages: savagery, barbarism, and civilization. This way of understanding the world was largely the result of work being done in the budding field of anthropology, but this field shifted to racial classifications in the nineteenth century.[36] As the late British social scientist Michael Banton explained, the word "race" was originally used to describe a people of a common ancestry, as in "the race of Abraham," but it was used very loosely, frequently to identify what would be better understood as nations. However, as Europeans began to increasingly recognize the extent of human diversity during a period of increasing exploration, imperialism, and colonialism, they began using this term to refer to distinct divisions of humankind, identifiable by physical characteristics. What propelled race to the dominant way of understanding difference and of legitimating their domination of non-Europeans was its elevation to the category of science.[37]

According to Banton, there was no clear-cut nineteenth-century idea of race. "There were many classifications and theories, and much controversy. But in so far as one simple conception caught popular attention ... it was the doctrine of permanent human types."[38] This doctrine slowly developed throughout the first half of the century and stated that "there is a finite number of races or types ... that the differences are permanent; and that the differences have a decisive influence upon the kinds of social relationship possible between members of different races, perhaps because each race is situated to a particular part of the globe."[39]

Of course, there was no genuine scientific evidence for these claims. Though race continues to be a contested concept, the idea of biological races has been long proven to be a mistaken one.[40] *Racialism* refers to this misguided but not necessarily prejudicial idea (that races are somehow biologically real). *Racism* is the belief that races are a biological reality, *and* that these races can be ranked hierarchically; *and/or* that race is a determinant (of intelligence, behaviour, culture, relations, etc.). *Racialization* is thus a process by which the idea of race is projected – onto people, relationships, practices, and so on.

But racialism, still with humanity today, was not the original or default stance for Europeans. Rather, from the outset races were believed to form a hierarchy, which Europeans used to legitimate their own ideas of superiority. One of the most important signifiers was skin colour, used as a means of identifying a group of people as distinct, as a race that was essentially different from another race.

Racial typologies crafted during this period typically divided the world into three or four main races, identifiable by supposed skin colour: red (Amerindian), yellow (Asian), black (African), white (European). Racializing themselves as white, Europeans considered all the peoples that they racialized as non-white to be inferior.

While the idea of race was being used by Europeans to construct a world order in which nominally non-white peoples were racialized as inferior in order to justify their subjugation,[41] from the outset the idea of race had also been used to explain differences between European nations themselves, and even between members of the same European nations. Europeans racialized themselves as white, but also believed that there were multiple white races that could be ranked hierarchically and that could be identified using other physical features in addition to skin colour, such as head shape, stature, and eye and hair colour. For this reason, theorists refer to whiteness as having two boundaries: one between white and non-white, and another separating grades of whiteness. Whiteness can therefore be conceived of as contingent hierarchies: a ranking of white races in which the order is determined by the dominant racial thinking of a particular historical period.[42]

Around the dawn of the twentieth century, the concept of European races (and their hierarchical arrangement) was primarily debated by two figures: Joseph Deniker and William Ripley. Deniker was a Russian-born French anthropologist who held that there were ten races in Europe, six primary and four secondary.[43] Ripley, on the other hand, was an American economist who "dabbled in anthropology," and in 1899 authored *The Races of Europe: A Sociological Study*. In it, he argued that there were only three main racial groups in Europe: Teutonic, Alpine, and Mediterranean. Northern Europe was home to the Teutons, central Europe the Alpines, and southern Europe the Mediterraneans. Each race was identifiable by distinct physical characteristics. Teutons were tall, long-skulled, and had pale hair, eyes, and skin; Mediterraneans were short to medium in stature, long-skulled, and had darker hair, eyes, and skin; and Alpines were of medium height and were stocky and round-skulled, with hazel-grey eyes and light chestnut hair. According to Ripley, the Teutons were the superior race and were responsible for founding America, and his book was intended to serve as a warning to Americans (presumably those of Teutonic descent) that the country was being flooded with inferior immigrants of the Alpine and Mediterranean races.[44]

Ripley no doubt convinced a number of people that his theories were correct, but his most important convert was Madison Grant. Grant, heir of a wealthy and distinguished American family, was educated as a lawyer but had no financial need or desire to pursue a legal career, so he spent most of his time socializing and hunting. He eventually became a driving force behind many conservation, preservation, and wildlife management efforts, for example the building of the Bronx Zoo. But after hearing one of Ripley's speeches, Grant became passionately interested in physical anthropology. He read Ripley's book, consulted the two thousand additional works in its supplementary bibliography, and went on to write his own book.

Grant's now infamous work, *The Passing of the Great Race* (1916), sold about seventeen thousand copies in the United States, significantly shaped the thought of a number of educated and influential Americans, and helped popularize the basic concepts of scientific racism.[45] Adapting Ripley's taxonomy, Grant argued that humanity was divided into three species: Caucasian, Mongoloid, and Negroid. Of these, the Caucasians were superior and were further divided into three subspecies, or races, namely the Nordics, Mediterraneans, and Alpines. These subspecies could then be further divided into varieties, such as Teutons or Scandinavians, and Anglo-Saxons were thus a subvariety of the Teutonic type.[46] Grant had borrowed the terms "Alpine" and "Mediterranean" from Ripley, but was not comfortable with the term "Teuton," "which he felt had been unfairly expropriated by the nationalists of the Second Reich. So he adopted from Deniker the term *la race nordique*, anglicising it to 'Nordic.'" As a result, this specific version of scientific racism is sometimes referred to as "Nordicism."[47]

While it was almost completely unoriginal, according to his biographer Jonathan Spiro, Grant's book represented the first time someone had brought race science together with eugenics and "presented the whole with such esprit, audacity, and clarity."[48] Francis Galton coined the word "eugenics" in 1883, though his hereditarian theories predate the term.[49] He was cousin to Charles Darwin, accepted his theories, and believed that mental or personality characteristics were equally as heritable as physical characteristics.[50] He noted that by careful selection people could breed animals and plants to have specific physical qualities and, inspired by this idea, asked: "Could not the race of men be similarly improved?"[51] Galton's intention was to improve humanity and he planned to do so by controlling

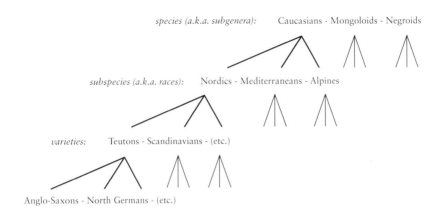

Figure 0.2 Madison Grant's racial taxonomy.

breeding through state regulation of marriage. He eventually abandoned the idea of state intervention but was still interested in how to compel people to "pursue a procreatively eugenic life."[52] Scientists in Britain and in the United States slowly accepted Galton's ideas, and with time eugenics became a global movement.[53] It was never completely unified nor did it have any explicitly defined goals other than to control the evolutionary process. Galton felt this could be done through two different approaches: positive eugenics, or encouraging the fitter elements in society to reproduce, and negative eugenics, or attempting to prevent the unfit from reproducing.[54]

Prior to Madison Grant, eugenicists generally felt that Northern Europeans were superior, but until this time their prescribed programs remained focused on raising the "hereditary endowment of *all* mankind, and hoped that eventually everyone could reach the intellectual level of the upper classes." Grant thus transformed eugenics from a skirmish against individuals who were socially unfit into "a war against groups who were *racially* unfit."[55] It was as if previously only the outer boundaries of whiteness had been guarded, but now sentries were being marshalled to defend the inner boundaries as well.

One insight brought by scholars studying whiteness is that, in the present day, nominally white people often view themselves as not having a racial identity. In his important study of whiteness, photography, and filmmaking, Richard Dyer succinctly describes this mindset: "Whites are not of a certain race, they are just the human race."[56] Since the dawn of racial thinking, however, white racial identity has always been very visible to people racialized as non-white. And historically, people of European descent were far more likely to consider themselves members of a white race and later *the* white race (Caucasian). This fact had been lost on many nominally white American historians, leading Matthew Frye Jacobson to open his important 1998 book on whiteness with a call for scholars to recognize a historical "system of 'difference' in which one might be both white *and* racially distinct from other whites."[57] Historians of whiteness in America have since focused on how whiteness has been constructed, including "how diverse groups ... came to identify, and be identified by others as white – and what that has meant for the social order."[58]

Studies falling into the latter category, such as the numerous works examining how groups such as the Irish gained a white racial identity in the United States, have garnered harsh criticism for their supposed lack of empirical evidence and an alleged reliance on psychohistory.[59] Few comparable studies have been undertaken of the history of whiteness in Canada. This is to our detriment for, as sociologist Steve Garner explains, "the meanings attached to 'race' are always time- and place-specific, each part of a national racial regime. Whiteness is no exception."[60] International, comparative, or so-called transnational approaches are all valuable, but their accuracy depends on the degree to which national particularities have been adequately mapped.

One of the few studies to include the Canadian context is Vic Satzewich's brief analysis of the experience of eastern and central Europeans in North America. Labelling them "peripheral Europeans," and focusing specifically on Ukrainians, Satzewich argues that in the face of discrimination they turned to crafting a political instead of a racial identity. This is unlike the Irish in America, who wilfully adopted racist discourse to assert their whiteness.[61] Ukrainians may not have self-racialized in this way, but they were nevertheless placed on the periphery of whiteness by Anglo-Canadians.

Instead of taking the bottom-up approach of examining how European immigrants self-racialized as white, or claimed a white identity, other studies have examined how the Anglo-Saxon elite in America used race science to construct the boundaries of the racial category of white, determine its inner hierarchies, and defend both its inner and outer borders. One influential example of this type of work is Jacobson's *Whiteness of a Different Color*, which details how whiteness was formed and transformed in America. Jacobson divides the history of whiteness in America into three "great epochs." The first began with the 1790 Naturalization Act, which limited citizenship to "free white persons." Although some eighteenth-century commentators believed that there were multiple white races, their concerns did not make it into the naturalization debate owing to the more pressing legal concerns over slavery and African Americans, racialized as non-white. However, this conception of whiteness as a single category allowed for the massive European migrations of the nineteenth century that filled the nation with peoples whom the framers did not consider desirable. The resulting demographic shift led to a political crisis, a questioning of the underlying racial logic, and ultimately a fracturing of the concept of a unified white race into a hierarchy of white races.[62]

The resulting racial regime marked the second great epoch, which Jacobson refers to as one of "Anglo-Saxonist exclusivity." Jacobson demonstrates that this Nordicist or Anglo-Saxonist regime dominated from the 1840s through the 1920s, though the mindset persisted at "street level" through the 1930s. From the 1920s through the 1960s, whiteness in America was reconsolidated under the umbrella of the Caucasian race; this was the third great epoch. The new perceived racial unity was in response to a number of factors including the passage of a stricter immigration law that limited the influx of supposedly non-Nordic people; increasing African American northward migration; and, later, changes in anthropology and responses to Nazism. In a way, America has never escaped this final epoch, as people continue to wrongly believe that the Caucasian race is a scientific reality.[63]

The main focus of this book is tracing the development and evolution of philosophies of cultural pluralism over time. However, it simultaneously offers some insight into how the boundaries, both inner and outer, of whiteness were constructed and reconstructed in Canadian society. And although Jacobson began his account of the history of whiteness after the signing of the Declaration of Independence, it is importance to acknowledge the colonial roots of whiteness: Canada, a settler colony, began as a project of liberal order that was later racialized.[64]

Settler colonialism is a phenomenon distinct from colonialism, although both are forms of imperialism. In the process of colonialism, whereby one country establishes political control over another, the metropole or home country remains "permanently distinct" from the country they have colonized. In the process of settler colonialism, however, the home country seeks to replicate itself in another land through settlement. According to theorist Lorenzo Veracini, while colonialism was often driven by a desire to harness the labour of an Indigenous population, the primary object of settler colonialism is the land itself. The dominant feature of this project is therefore not one of population exploitation but rather one of population replacement. The logic of this project is, Veracini explains, "a sustained institutional tendency to eliminate the Indigenous population."[65] There is now a scholarly consensus that, in Canada, this attempted elimination of Indigenous peoples and their cultures constituted genocide.[66]

The philosophy underlying the process of settler colonialism in Canada was that of nineteenth-century liberalism. Historian Ian McKay goes so far as to argue that Canadian history – at least from 1840 to 1940 – can be analyzed through "the study of the implementation and expansion over a heterogeneous terrain of a certain politico-economic logic – to wit, liberalism." Liberalism is an essentially contested concept, but McKay takes his definition from historian Fernande Roy and argues that liberalism is fundamentally about the "primacy of the category 'individual.'" It has three core principles: liberty (for the individual), equality before the law (for the individual), and property (the ownership of which defines one as an individual). In different historical periods, these three principles were arranged in different orders of importance, but in its original, nineteenth-century iteration, property was most important, followed by liberty and then equality.[67]

Studying this project, McKay adds, requires attention to those at the core of the project who expressed its values, as well as equal attention to those who resisted and reshaped it. Although liberalism as a theory can be (and in some cases has been) set up as universal and inclusive, it is clear that "actually existing liberalisms" have been exclusionary in practice. However, the connection between liberalism and exclusion is deeper and more foundational, for scholars have also demonstrated how exclusions based on assumptions about gender and civilizational progress were actually essential to the construction of liberalism and its all-important category of the individual.[68]

Of course, when the process of liberal settler colonialism first began in the lands that became Canada, preferential hierarchies existed but scientific racism did not. For example, the French in Canada viewed the fur trade in New France as a tool "to be used in pursuit of a higher goal: the conversion of the Indians to Catholicism." Historian Saliha Belmessous argues that the inclusion of Indigenous peoples in the French colonial project indicates "the absence of an idea of race in the minds of French officials" at that time. Champlain's declaration that intermarriage would allow the Native and French to "form but one people," for instance, suggests that biologically based theories of racial superiority (which explicitly warned against hybridity and miscegenation) did not yet dominate European thinking.[69]

Other groups faced prejudice prior to the arrival of scientific racism. Historian James Walker has shown that from the beginning of their history in British North America, Africans were associated with slavery and thus a subordinate role in society. Indeed, the history of African slavery in pre-Confederation Canada is one that many Canadians have tried, often all too successfully, to forget. This history of slavery resulted in many stereotypes being applied to Africans even after its abolition in 1834. Continuing prejudice, Walker maintains, was in large part influenced by class, as the next four waves of African American migration to Canada were of fugitive slaves who became wage labourers. By the time of Confederation, he suggests, "a colour line had been established in Canada, identifying all blacks as members of a specified class and setting them apart from mainstream society. This line was upheld by attitude rather than by law, justified by convention rather than ideology." While the class status of people of African descent was defined in terms of colour, he argues that it was not yet defined by racial doctrine. Whether or not this was solely about class, as Walker suggests, the broader point here is that race is not timeless and historians have not yet adequately determined when and how ideas about race arrived and spread throughout Canada.[70]

When it did finally arrive in Canada, race science found "fertile soil." Many Canadians accepted the scientific theory of race and, as a result, biases hardened into racism. From roughly the late nineteenth century through the mid-twentieth century, race was a "common sense" idea for most Canadians.[71] This new racist doctrine strengthened the existing practices of settler colonialism. The Canadian federal government's policies intentionally pushed Indigenous people to the periphery of the nation in a physical sense, by dispossessing them of the best agricultural lands and constraining them on reserves, but also in an ideological sense, by attempting to remove or exclude them from the national imaginary.[72] When this was combined with the demographic decline of Indigenous people, owing to settler colonialism, many Canadians came to embrace the myth that Indigenous peoples were a "vanishing race."[73]

Historians have documented the systemic discrimination and racism that marked much of Canada's early immigration policies and Canadians' negative attitudes towards immigrants, and these studies reveal it did not take long for Canadians of European descent to explicitly express their desire for the newly formed nation to become a "white man's country."[74] As a result, the immigration of peoples racialized as non-white was typically made possible only by the most pressing national and corporate interests, which in the case of the transcontinental railway were indistinguishable. In this instance, just over fifteen thousand Chinese men were permitted entrance to work on constructing the railway; they were paid 30 to 50 per cent less than their nominally white counterparts and were often contractually required to buy their supplies from the company stores at inflated prices. Further, they were often brought to Canada by labour agencies that would then garnish their wages for the cost of their passage. Many of these workers were given the most dangerous tasks, and scores died from illness and workplace accidents. Many who survived had not been able to save enough to return to China, as originally planned, and found themselves alone in a nativist country.[75]

Throughout the duration of the project, politicians and citizens repeatedly voiced the opinion that Asian immigrants were unwelcome. Having been advised that without them the project could be delayed by up to twelve years, Prime Minister John A. Macdonald remarked: "It will be all very well to exclude Chinese labour, when we can replace it with white labour, but until that is done, it is better to have Chinese labour than no labour at all." True to form, as soon as the railway was complete in 1885, the federal government, still led by Macdonald, passed the "Chinese Immigration Act" that placed a large head tax on any Chinese person wishing to immigrate to Canada, effectively ending further Chinese immigration. In 1908, the government also reached a so-called "Gentleman's Agreement" with Japan, in order to restrict Japanese immigration "to a number that could be absorbed by British Columbia 'without unduly disturbing' its existing racial balance." And in 1923, the federal government passed a new Chinese Immigration Act that banned virtually all Chinese immigration.[76]

Canadians of European descent may have been clear about who they considered non-white, but it does not follow that for them white was a monolithic, uncontested racial category. Sent from England to investigate the causes of the Rebellions of 1837, Lord Durham in his famous *Report* (1839) declared the problem to be one of race: "I found two nations waning in the bosom of a single state : I found a struggle, not of principles, but of races."[77] The report thus affixed this designation to the English and French colonists in what became Canada, a designation that would last for over a century. As the notion of race developed its modern definition and biases hardened into scientific racism, English and French Canadians were racialized.[78] As a result of this history, whiteness in Canada had clear lines of fracture from the beginning.

The British dream was to have a colony comprised solely of loyal English subjects, but this was impossible on account of insufficient immigration from the home country.[79] Likewise, many settlers would have preferred immigration from Britain alone, but the demands of liberal settler colonialism kept the doors open to people from a wide variety of backgrounds. After Confederation, Macdonald's "National Policy" was crafted in part by the belief that, in order to prevent American expansion, the west had to be settled (i.e., Indigenous people had to be dispossessed and their lands taken). In order to achieve this objective, overall immigration to Canada had to increase. To ensure these goals were met, immigrants from a wide variety of cultural and religious backgrounds were accepted.[80] In America, the racial logic of whiteness changed in response to such demographic, political, and cultural shifts. According to Jacobson, when "white" Americans perceived a stronger threat from undesirable "white" people than from supposedly "non-white" peoples, their focus shifted to the internal boundary of whiteness.

A similar process occurred in Canada. Some Canadians were firmly opposed to the immigration of continental Europeans, while others thought they were necessary in order to colonize the west. From 1896 until 1905, the minister responsible for immigration policy was Clifford Sifton. Sifton's policy was rooted in race, and he was very concerned with keeping out nominally non-white immigrants. His opinion of continental Europeans was more tolerant than some of his contemporaries, which led to bitter disputes, but it does not follow that he did not have a hierarchy. Quite the opposite: he considered southern Europeans (especially Italians), Jewish people, and English city-dwellers all non-preferred. Aside from these groups, he was in favour of largely unregulated immigration of British and continental European farmers, and to this end he orchestrated a wide-ranging promotional program and spent increasing amounts of money recruiting European immigrants. Sifton famously described his ideal immigrant as "the stalwart peasant in a sheepskin coat, born to the soil, whose forefathers have been farmers for ten generations, with a stout wife and half-dozen children."[81]

The firm policing of the outer boundary of whiteness, combined with increasing presence of these so-called "unpreferred" continental Europeans (by 1921, at least 15 per cent of the Canadian population was of neither French nor British origins), led to the expression in Canada of an Anglo-Saxonist sentiment.[82] While in some instances these continental Europeans were racialized as non-white, there is more evidence to suggest that they were racialized as belonging to white races that were considered inferior to so-called Anglo-Saxons.[83] In 1899, for instance, the *Winnipeg Tribune* described the English settler as being "hemmed in by a hoard of people little better than savages – alien in race, language, and religion, whose customs are repellent and whose morals he abhors."[84] These remarks were no doubt made in relation to the various central and eastern European peoples who had been settling in the region, especially Ukrainians. At this time central and eastern Europeans were viewed as a threat equal to that posed by those unequivocally racialized as non-white, and the Anglo-Canadians who discriminated against these supposedly inferior Europeans often made this comparison explicitly. In 1912, for instance, Presbyterian home mission worker Roderick MacBeth argued in his book *Our Task in Canada* that recent immigrants had been "of inferior races and lower civilizations." Just as there was no reason that British Columbia ought to be handed over to the Chinese, he continued, nor should the prairies "be given over to the Galicians."[85]

Sifton's rival, Frank Oliver, acting from personal belief but no doubt also capitalizing on a politicized issue, railed against the supposedly open-door immigration policy and made it clear that the problem was one of race. When it came to Slavic peoples, he argued that they were "an alien race" that threatened Canadian society. As he put it in 1901: "Make no mistake, that there is no comparison between the German who comes from Galicia and a Galician who comes from Galicia, and no man will resent such a comparison more strongly than the German himself ... They belong to radically different races."[86] In 1905, Sifton resigned and responsibility for immigration passed to Oliver, who set to work crafting the new Immigration Act (passed in 1910), which explicitly prohibited the entry of any immigrant "belonging to any race deemed unsuitable to the climate and requirements of Canada."[87] The climate clause was not a value-neutral, scientifically informed policy. Rather, as one influential civil servant wrote in 1913: "It is to be hoped that climatic conditions will prove unsatisfactory [to settlers of African descent]."[88] In other words, such officials hoped the science would provide the rationale for their existing prejudice – and crafted policy as if it did.

Given the heated debate, it was unclear where continental Europeans would ultimately end up in Canada's racial hierarchy. In terms of their role as colonizers, they occupied an equally undefined position. Theorist and historian Robert Young suggests that the term "colonizer" does not adequately describe the position of settler colonists, and so he employs the French term for a colonial settler or farmer, *colon*. Such *colons* were in-betweens, or doubly positioned: they were neither part of the metropolitan centre nor indigenous to the land they inhabited. While *colons* were actively expelling Indigenous people from their land, they were also at the mercy of the metropolis that could choose to protect, oppress, or even abandon them.[89] But *colons* of non-British, non-French, European descent in Canada occupied an even more complex and perhaps liminal space. Although they were in fact settlers, that is, active agents of colonization (reaping the benefits of the displacement and marginalization of Indigenous people by occupying their land), they were also not fully accepted by most of the British or French *colons*. Their status shifted between "preferred" and "unpreferred," depending on the prevailing sentiment and the perceived needs of the colony at the time, but they were consistently understood to be "foreign" elements.[90]

At a national level, it is clear that Nordicist ideas were present in Canada from around the turn of the twentieth century onwards. A preliminary examination of newspapers from the period reveals that Nordicism was most prominent in the 1920s, though support for it was patchy.[91] Likewise, it dissipated slowly and unevenly, but by the late 1920s or early 1930s, many intellectuals came to believe that modern European "races" or nations were no longer racially pure. That is, they believed that there had been much intermixing between these three races over the centuries. So it was that the Nordicist form of racism largely died away, even if a Nordicist racialism lingered on. Some Canadians always believed in a single "white" race, while others experienced an ideological fracturing and reconsolidation of whiteness akin to their American neighbours.

It is unclear how and why whiteness was reconsolidated in Canada, given that the country did not experience the American factors of a sharp restriction of European immigration and internal African American migration. However, most Canadians of British descent retained a belief in the superiority of Anglo-Saxon political institutions, and many intellectuals also continued to believe that an individual's characteristics were determined by their precise racial makeup or heritage. Some more skeptical commentators argued that individuals were shaped by the interplay between their racial heritage and their environment, but both groups shared the belief that Europeans were racially superior to all others. Many of these debates have gone unexamined in the existing literature, as there is no comprehensive work on the history of scientific racism and whiteness in Canada.

However, a number of works have touched on these issues in different ways. Historian Angus McLaren's groundbreaking history of eugenics argued that Canadian eugenicists were deeply concerned about the threat of racial degeneration, but presents the history as if all reformers conceived of a singular "white race."[92] But as this book demonstrates, while Canadian eugenicists and racial theorists would occasionally refer to the Caucasian race, well into the 1940s the focus was on the supposed subdivisions of this race: Nordic, Mediterranean, and Alpine. Historian Carl Berger's earlier history of Canadian nationalism demonstrated how Canadians drew on emergent race science to bolster their own sense of superiority, but few studies have examined how this same science was employed to discriminate against those deemed inferior.[93]

One important work on the construction of whiteness in Canada is Daniel Coleman's *White Civility*. In this work, Coleman – a scholar of Canadian literary culture – set out with the incredibly ambitious goal of determining how the normative concept of English Canadianness came to be established. He argues that at the heart of this norm is a specific form of whiteness based on the British model of civility. The subsequent conflation of whiteness with civility meant that race was not only attached to bodies, but also to conduct.[94] Coleman's is an indispensable contribution to our understanding of the broader cultural logic of whiteness and its expression through English Canadian literature in the nineteenth and early twentieth century.

*In the Province of History*, by historians Ian McKay and Robin Bates, is an equally important work, but one with a different focus. The book provides an in-depth examination of a "particular kind of whiteness," that is, the whiteness at work in shaping what they call tourism/history in the province of Nova Scotia during the 1920s and '30s. They argue that whiteness performed many functions on a symbolic level, especially in helping to construct a singular and "romantic teleological narrative" of the province's past. One particular strength of the book is its nuance in tracing how whiteness, "not a monolithic theme," was grasped in different ways by different people, even as it was put towards this same end. The grasp could be partial and static, expressed in magical terms, or "given a social-evolutionary, quasi-scientific treatment." Throughout, however, the same overriding idea was expressed: that the white races are progressing and that those racialized as non-white were primitive and thus outside the march of progress. Ultimately, McKay and Bates demonstrate how whiteness became a such common-sense idea that a government-issued booklet would confidently explain to tourists that the "Native Types" of the region were in fact "five distinct white races."[95]

Zeroing in on the turbulent period of the Second World War, historian Carmela Patrias addresses the question of how whiteness structured the Canadian labour market. In *Jobs and Justice*, she examines the construction of racial classification by Anglo-Canadian state officials, employers, and workers; the impact of this classification on ethnic minority labourers; and workers' self-identification in response to this racialization. Patrias rightly identifies discrimination against peripheral Europeans as racism. While acknowledging that people of colour have historically been the targets of "the most extreme and overtly state sanctioned racism in Canada," she concedes that "the type of black-white polarization that some scholars place at the core of American racial thought did not develop in Canada." Her work bolsters Satzewich's findings, as she argues colour was not central to the self-definition of central Europeans. She therefore concludes that to suggest immigrants' integration into Canadian society was merely a matter of them becoming white would be to oversimplify complex processes.[96]

Patrias also studied "Anglo-Saxon critics of discrimination," whom she dubbed "Ambivalent Allies." Identifying figures including John Murray Gibbon, Robert England, and Watson Kirkconnell as recognized experts on race during their time, she argues that their definition of race was "often riddled with inconsistencies and contradictions" and that they often continued to be "influenced by racist assumptions." These "confused, even contradictory ideas of race ... [served] to reinforce racist stereotypes and to obscure the full extent and consequences of racial discrimination in Canada."[97] Patrias briefly examines the views of these and a number of other public figures before turning to an examination of the roles of the Left and of the State. However, the brief sketches do not fully examine how these experts on race obtained such expertise, nor do they examine how these experts' views changed over time. These questions are addressed by *The Racial Mosaic* in the biographical chapters that follow.

## CHAPTER OUTLINE

Chapters one through three examine the early life and thought of Watson Kirkconnell, Robert England, and John Murray Gibbon, following the historical biographical approach described above. The fourth chapter argues that official government efforts to promote cultural pluralism predate the Second World War and that they mirror the emphases and exclusions of the experts they consulted. Prior to this time, attempts to promote pluralism had largely been the preserve of private citizens (albeit acting as public intellectuals) with a vested interest in increased immigration. However, as Europe became ever more destabilized, these efforts became increasingly official as governmental agencies such as the Canadian Broadcasting Corporation (CBC) began running programs designed to foster national unity. For instance, Gibbon's famous book, *Canadian Mosaic*, was actually based on a radio program that he designed for, and that was broadcast over, this network.

Official efforts during wartime are explored in the fifth chapter. The federal government, which had until this time employed a security-oriented approach to diversity, enlisted the help of these well-known experts on "racial" diversity. Once retained, these men worked to convince Anglo-Canadians of the loyalty of all European minority groups in Canada. To do so, they developed programs that emphasized Canada's supposed racial uniformity, portraying the country as almost 100 per cent European. They also worked to reassure the population that so-called racial minorities (European ethnic and religious groups) were all loyal to Britain and to Canada. In other words, if the focus prior to the war was on the varied tiles of the mosaic, the focus during the war was ensuring they were cemented into place – and letting Anglo-Canadians know that they were.[98] The conclusion briefly examines the immediate postwar years and points to fruitful avenues for future research, while the epilogue rounds out the biographical sketches of Kirkconnell, England, and Gibbon.

A NOTE ON STYLE

Historians who write about race have been accused of introducing a problem that was not originally there, or of exaggerating it from a minor to a major concern. Writing about race and racism, some critics suggest, is really about indicting "famous men ... who were getting on with their lives" and presuming their guilt.[99] Partly in response to this critique, I have opted to include as much of my subjects' voices as possible (perhaps more than some readers would like), to demonstrate that this is not the case. Race, racialism, and racism were not incidental to their lives and thought; rather, they were deeply integral to these Canadians' thinking about immigration, assimilation, and diversity.

A couple other notes on style are in order. As I make it clear that I use *race* to refer to a specific idea and not a physical reality, I have not placed the word or its attendant concepts in quotation marks. Inspired by critical race scholar Carlos A. Hoyt Jr, I will, however, most often use the term "nominal" when referring to racialized identities.[100] Finally, I have intentionally tried to make this book as accessible as possible by avoiding the excessive jargon and parenthetical (word)play that is all too common in contemporary scholarship.

Over two decades ago, in his book *Multiculturalism and the History of Canadian Diversity*, sociologist Richard Day demonstrated how multiculturalism is sometimes presented "as an *already achieved ideal*." This definition is constructed by conflating Canada's long history of sociological diversity with Canada's more recent policy, portraying the country as a land where diverse peoples have lived in peace and harmony since time immemorial. This false narrative has been publicized by many, including – as Day demonstrated – the federal government.[101] In so doing, Canada's struggle with discrimination and racism, both historical and contemporary, is hidden from sight. But now more than ever, in this age of resurgent racism and xenophobia, Canadians must not slip into complacency by pretending that the country is immune to such forces. As Nzingha Millar has argued: "How we continue to tell the story of multiculturalism in Canada will define our next 150 years."[102] This book is intended as a critical intervention in that storytelling process.

# I

# Watson Kirkconnell and Scientific Racism

INTRODUCTION

In November 1920 a local newspaper in the small town of Lindsay, Ontario, published an unsigned article that named and harshly criticized Canadian census officials for not collecting data on racial origins, and for not correlating such data with other statistics on employment, marital status, family size, income, and age.

> We know little as to the growth and decay of any of the different races and classes in our country. It is well known that, for citizenship in an Anglo-Saxon democracy, races, and even families[,] differ from one another in civic value. The Slav and the Semite are mentally alien to our institutions and are constitutionally unassimilable; the Anglo-Saxon, by whom our civilization has evolved, finds ... [these institutions] natural and vital to his existence. Surely it is important to find out which type is now waxing.

The author continued: New Zealand, Australia, and Great Britain had all appointed Birth-Rate Commissions and found that "their finest Anglo-Saxon stock was, through race suicide, hastening precipitately towards extinction." Canadians, "in a backwater of prudery or indifference," had not even realized the need for "a racial stock-taking" but quickly needed to recognize the clear signs of a similar "racial disaster" in their country.[1]

Despite its prejudicial message, the article drew little criticism from the public, which suggests that many of the locals shared the author's views. However, it did elicit a response from the officials named, who quite naturally were upset with this assertion of their ineptitude. T.J. Begley, the paper's editor, defended the author and maintained that they sought the seemingly unavailable statistics only to "prove or disprove the prevalent belief that the native Anglo-Canadian stock is decaying, in spite of temporal prosperity." He added that the paper's intention in running the article was the "open discussion of problems which we feel are vital to our national welfare."[2] The author of the article was Thomas Watson Kirkconnell (1895–1977), who would go on to become a Canadian academic, university administrator, and public intellectual best known for his work as a translator, anti-communist, defender of the humanities, and prominent Baptist layman.[3] At this time, however, he was an unemployed and relatively unknown Queen's University graduate.

This chapter provides a re-examination of Kirkconnell's life from birth through 1937 and is divided into three parts. The first details Kirkconnell's intellectual development, the second explores how he adopted and adapted a racial understanding of humanity and details how it changed over time, and the final section examines how this racial thought shaped his conceptions of cultural pluralism. As a whole, the chapter argues that Kirkconnell's understanding of human diversity was shaped by societal ideas about race, which hardened into scientific racism as the result of independent study; that this hardline stance softened as a result of intellectual and emotional factors; and that his newfound tolerance was still rooted in scientific racism, was limited to members of nominally white races, and was marked by continued eugenic concerns.

As the following pages will make plain, Kirkconnell's involvement with those he called racial minorities was shaped by specific and deeply held beliefs about race, gender, nationality, culture, empire, and religion. Through an examination of his early years, it will become clear that these beliefs were shaped by his upbringing in a racialized liberal order, in a community largely devoid of ethnic diversity, and in an atmosphere of martial imperialism. Kirkconnell was not unaware of the importance that the community he grew up in played in fashioning his understanding of Canadian culture. As he would later write:

> I was born, a fourth generation Anglo-Canadian, in the little Ontario town of Port Hope. The townspeople were predominantly English, with a garnish of Scotch and Irish. When I was

Figure 1.1 Watson Kirkconnell.

entering my teens, my father moved to Lindsay, and there the population was predominantly Irish, with a seasoning of Scotch and English. In other words, my earliest impression of Canada was of a homogenous Anglo-Saxon country, whose settled way of life I did not question.[4]

The "Anglo-Saxon" as an idealized essence, to which Scots, Irish, and English could aspire, and one upon which a "settled way of life" depended, informed his lifelong patterns of thinking.

### INTELLECTUAL DEVELOPMENT

In 1819, Kirkconnell's Scottish ancestors emigrated to what is now known as Quebec. Nearly thirty years later they moved to what is now the township of East Hawkesbury in Ontario, which at the time was a small and predominantly francophone settlement. Here Thomas Allison Kirkconnell (Watson's father; 1862–1932) was later born. It was likely owing to tensions between English- and French-speaking settlers that when Thomas was eleven years old, the family packed up and moved over seven hundred kilometres away, to a plot of land near Tiverton, a small settlement in Bruce County.[5] Thomas grew up, rejected his future on the family farm and, against his father's wishes, became a schoolteacher. He married another teacher, Bertha Gertrude Watson (1867–1957), in 1889. In 1894 he graduated from Queen's University and was appointed the headmaster of Port Hope High School, and the following year his second child, Thomas Watson, was born.

All the Kirkconnell children were raised in what was in many ways a traditional Anglo-Protestant home in rural Ontario, where they were instilled with the Victorian values of education, Christian religion, temperance, and hard work, as well as a patriarchal conception of gender roles.[6] In 1908, the family moved to Lindsay, where Thomas had been appointed headmaster of the Collegiate Institute.[7] Both Port Hope and Lindsay had few nominally non-white citizens, but whereas Port Hope was mostly composed of people of British origin, Lindsay was mostly Irish, divided into Catholic and Protestant groups. As the town proudly declared in 1924: "The population is almost wholly of British descent, tending towards a citizenship that respects law and order and makes for settled conditions."[8]

Kirkconnell likely grew up knowing little to nothing about the Indigenous peoples in the region, nor did he likely know that for much of his life the family home was on unceded land. The story begins in Ganaraskè, a Cayuga village named after the river that runs through it. The Cayuga ("People of the Great Swamps") are an Indigenous tribe who were part of the Iroquois Confederacy and now are part of the Six Nations of Grand River First Nation in Ontario, the Cayuga Nation of New York, and the Seneca-Cayuga Tribe of Oklahoma.[9] As the French fur traders arrived, the village became an important site for trade, diplomacy, and Christian missionaries. In 1778, a fur trader by the name of Peter Smith arrived, constructed a house, and began conducting his trade. As a result, the trading post became known – at least to other Europeans – as "Smith's Creek." Smith left the region by 1790, but three years later four United Empire Loyalist families arrived in the region, set up white tents, and began to construct log houses. This came as a surprise to the two hundred Cayuga people living in the region, who greeted these brazen colonists with hostility.

Following the War of 1812, increasing numbers of European immigrants came to what was then Upper Canada, including this village, which was renamed Port Hope in 1817.[10] These families were essentially squatters, as they had no legal right to be on the land, and their presence was an aggravation to the Indigenous people there. In 1811, some treaty negotiations occurred at Port Hope, where a spokesperson for the Mississauga complained about the Europeans who had settled in their Islands and cut great quantities of timber without consent. While they agreed to the requested cession of the land, they asked for assistance in "turning the white people away."[11] Their concerns were well-founded: extensive deforestation undertaken to create farmland had resulted in environmental devastation, and from the late nineteenth century onwards would result in flooding, soil erosion, and drought.[12] After 1812, the British increased their efforts to gain title over the land through treaty making. Treaty 20, also known as "Surrender M," covered a little less than two million acres of land from Scugog to the Kawarthas, and was negotiated and signed at Port Hope in 1818. The town of Lindsay, however, was not covered by this treaty – an omission that would not be addressed for over a century, until the Williams Treaties of 1923.

Similarly, Kirkconnell probably had no idea that while he was learning peacefully in school, under his father's dutiful watch, Indigenous children were being snatched from their parents' arms and being sent to residential schools, institutions that tried to assimilate them.[13] As scholars have noted, one of the painful ironies of colonialism is that while the settler society or societies worked to destroy Indigenous cultures, many settlers were themselves fascinated by these same cultures and in some cases sought to appropriate and emulate certain elements of them (or more accurately, settler-colonial stereotypical notions of them). Kirkconnell was no exception, and as a child he would "play indians" [sic] with his friends, each of whom had given themselves "Indian" names (Kirkconnell was "Little Bear"). To prepare for their outings, the friends invented special calls, kept supplies like knives, hatchets, bows and arrows, and an "Indian head-dress," and drew up a map that included places such as the "War Path" and the "White Man's Fort."[14]

But while they could play at having an "Indian" identity in their free time, in public school Kirkconnell and his friends were being instilled with a strong sense of European superiority. Both Port Hope and Lindsay were immersed in an atmosphere of martial imperialism, an impulse that focused on the physical robustness and combat-ready nature of the sons of the British Empire. In his groundbreaking work *The Sense of Power*, historian Carl Berger demonstrated that Canadian imperialism was one variety of Canadian nationalism, strongest in the older areas of Ontario and particularly among the descendants of the United Empire Loyalists. Such was Port Hope, where some of these Loyalists had settled in the late eighteenth century.[15]

Canadian imperialism was deeply rooted in the Victorian belief in progress. In this understanding of the past, Canadian history was not much more than the record of "material growth and the expansion of liberty."[16] This belief in progress was bolstered by racism. Imperialists, Berger noted, associated progress with the British constitution and racial capacity. Indeed, the very capacity for liberty was perceived to be a characteristic of only certain races, most notably the Anglo-Saxon race. That Anglo-Saxons "displayed a special genius for self-government and political organization seemed ... undeniable to many English Canadians," Berger adds.[17] In other words, imperialists believed that certain peoples, due to their biology, historical development, or some combination, literally could not function within a liberal system of governance as they were too immature or ignorant to uphold the responsibilities that accompanied the rights it provided. It is important to note that imperialism was not simply geopolitical, but was a religious, moral, economic, and intellectual movement that permeated various aspects of society in many English-speaking regions in Canada, particularly in Upper Canada or Ontario.[18]

Racial superiority was an explicit part of the imperially oriented school curriculum. The textbook *Ontario School Geography* (1910), for instance, informed students of the faults of the "Yellow," "Red," and "Black" races. Going further, it also judged members of the "White" races, and found British and Scottish to be superior to French and Irish peoples.[19] Militarism was also an essential part of Canadian imperialism, and so in addition to textbooks, physical education and sports were also designed to prepare students for military service in defence of the Empire.[20] (The growing cadet movement that Kirkconnell was involved with throughout his schooling also supported this objective.)[21] Kirkconnell was therefore educated in a system that engendered patriotism to the British Empire and a sense of Anglo-Saxon racial superiority. This type of education was not unique to Ontario, but rather was common throughout the Empire.[22]

The impulse towards rigid order provided by school, church, and cadets would be in perpetual tension with the meandering, whimsical, artistic sensibility present in Kirkconnell's personality from a young age. His childhood habit of building little paths from his house into the woods is suggestive: the paths were neatly graded and meticulously constructed, but wandered off aimlessly into the forest. To this artistic whimsy would later be added a strong sense that whatever he wrote should be published. The combination of these conflicting impulses and the belief in the value of his written material helps to explain his expansive and varied publishing record.[23] These impulses were also evident in Kirkconnell's approach to his university education.

Kirkconnell headed off to Queen's University in 1913 to study the arts. During this period, a student could earn an undergraduate or graduate degree depending on their standing in the classes: first-class standing in honours classes merited an MA, while second- or third-class honours merited a BA. The university advised students intending to earn an MA to allot four or five years for the task, but Kirkconnell completed the degree in three.[24] This would be the last degree he earned by attending an academic institution; the bachelor of letters (BLitt) degree for which he studied at Oxford was not granted and all twelve of his doctorates were honorary.[25] In time Kirkconnell would become one of Canada's best-known linguists, recognized for his translations from a wide variety of languages. When he began at Queen's, however, he had taken a variety of classes in the sciences, mathematics (his best subject), and the humanities. His subsequent decision to focus on classical languages stemmed in part from having dropped to second-class honours in Greek prose composition in his scholarship exams, at which point he stubbornly decided "to major in Greek and Latin as a preliminary to graduate work in English or comparative literature."[26] He ultimately envisioned achieving a comprehensive knowledge of numerous languages and literatures, and obtaining a doctoral degree in comparative philology or literature.[27] With this vision of grandeur in mind, he flitted between serious study of languages for his classes and playful poetic adventures in English and other languages, but the Great War interrupted his plans for further schooling after the MA.[28]

While Queen's laid the foundations for his future career in academia, it also played an important role in reinforcing Kirkconnell's sense of racial superiority. Coming from small-town Ontario, he had been surrounded by people racialized as white, predominately those of Scottish, Irish, or English origins. Queen's did not provide him with a systematic understanding of race science but it was a predominantly nominally white institution, one which was permeated with the racism, xenophobia, anti-Semitism, and misogyny that were so common during this period.[29] For instance, speaking during the First World War, a Professor Mitchell gave an address on the "Future of Canada," which informed students that there were only two types of civilization: Eastern and Western. "Where the Eastern idea finds expression you have despotism and wherever the Western idea is realized you have a commonwealth," Mitchell declared. He then went on to argue that Canada should remain in "organic unity" with the British Empire, which would allow the country to develop "a fine type of democracy" but also to "do her share of the work for the backward races."[30]

Similarly, in 1913 O.D. Skelton, at the time the head of the Department of Political Science at Queen's but later an influential civil servant, addressed the Young Men's Christian Association (YMCA) on "The Yellow Peril." Beginning with an overview of immigration, he reported that 70 per cent of European immigrants to Canada were from Germany, France, Holland, Scandinavia, and the

British Isles. This meant that, unlike in America, "our immigrants are mainly of the same blood, same traditions and same religious beliefs as ourselves and consequently are easier of assimilation than the Southern Europeans." However, immigrants nevertheless brought with them a number of religious, economic, and political issues. "Our most troublesome problem," Skelton declared, "is that of the Jew and the Greek Catholic."

Jews were problematic because they tenaciously clung to their religious beliefs and because of their political inclinations, he explained. "There is a powerful Jewish reform movement in American and Canadian cities," Skelton warned, "particularly where socialism has arisen through sweat-shop conditions." But Jewish people could still be assimilated, so long as Canadians were patient; "we must take the Jew as we find him," he advised, "and interpret his faith in such a way as to get his assent to the broad principles underlying both our faith and his." The Greek Catholic, on the other hand, did not reserve such respect. According to Skelton, this group, composed of Galicians, Ruthenians, and Poles, was simply "poor, unsettled, and ignorant." In calling for the exclusion of Asian people, Skelton shifted the focus from faith back to politics. "Canada supplies the last attempt to work out democratic government. For success in this most difficult form of government we need our immigrants to share our ideals," he argued. It was on this ground that he proposed "the restriction of Asiatic immigration. There is no likelihood of harmony of racial and political ideals. Social prejudice and the lasting faith of the Japanese or the Chinese in his racial ideals forbid intermarriage and general social integration. By introducing Asiatics into Canada without restrictions we would be creating a problem for ourselves worse than that of the negro in the United States." Skelton ended on an upbeat note by encouraging the audience that "assimilation ... will be a great task but one within our powers; and we need not despair of accomplishment."[31]

Other religious and ethnic groups were also singled out, as visiting speakers informed students of the "degrading influence" of Islam and the "idol worship" and "superstition" of Hinduism. Blatant expressions of racism were also acceptable at Queen's during this period. In an issue of the *Queen's Journal* published in 1915, an editor saw fit to print a joke about "a coloured gentleman called Sambo."[32] While it was possibly the only joke of this kind to appear in the publication in the three years Kirkconnell attended Queen's, it is remarkable that there was no recorded opposition to the joke: no letters to the editor, no retraction, no comment at all. Kirkconnell did not object, despite his affiliation with the paper: he was the circulation manager that semester and worked as the arts editor the following fall.

During this period, Kirkconnell's tendencies towards patriarchy and misogyny were similarly reinforced. While he attended Queen's, male students still held most formal positions of power, such as in the student government and the university newspaper (which had no qualms about referring to women as "the weaker sex").[33] Indeed, female education was still discussed by staff and students alike as "a question" that had somehow not yet been fully resolved. At an Arts Dinner held in November 1913, Professor J.L. Morison, of the Department of History, was invited to reply to the toast to "the ladies" but instead "cut loose on women's education." He blamed low university spirit on female students who did not share in sports and argued that women should have their own university in the country, which would provide them with much-needed fresh air and exercise and would reduce the problem of crowded co-ed universities. (This despite the fact that Queen's had only a small residence for women, referred to as "the Hen-Coop.") Women would not have exams, Morison continued, for that would put an unfair strain on their nervous system. Taking his speech beyond education to women's suffrage, he argued that it did not matter if women got the vote or not, because "the addition of a few thousand silly women could not possibly make Canadian politics any worse than they were." Kirkconnell's assessment was that it "was the soundest and most clearly cut speech I have heard in a long time."[34] In his personal life, while Kirkconnell enjoyed interacting with a number of young women at Queen's, he privately recorded in his diary a number of callous remarks about their appearance and their artistic and scholastic abilities. These remarks also reveal his attention to skin colour, as he carefully recorded if his female peers were "alabaster" or "dark."[35]

Kirkconnell's views of racialized peoples and women were being reinforced by his time at Queen's, but his religious beliefs were being challenged. The basic courses in psychology and philosophy he took were found to be "more unsettling than anything else." Although he had abandoned scientific subjects in order to study classics, they soon returned to his "reading and thinking and gnawed away at the roots of [religious] conviction." Caught up in the intellectual currents of the age, he began to feel disoriented and was tempted to abandon his Christian faith.[36]

Eugenics emerged as an alternate belief system during this period. Prior to university he made no references to it, but in an article published in the *Queen's Journal* the year after his graduation Kirkconnell recalled having discussed "empirical eugenics" with his boarding house companions. Informed by the subject, he warned his peers: "If we are to produce men and women of the virile type such as shall guarantee the future of our race and nation let us not adopt measures which will develop aesthetes and exquisites at the expense of red blood and sturdy comradeship."[37] As economic historian Thomas Leonard notes, at bottom, and on a national level, eugenics was based on the fear of inferiority.[38] This fear of inferiority also applied on a personal level, as Kirkconnell was often troubled by his own physical fitness. A sickly child, he was unable to begin public school until the age of seven, and his one youthful attempt at strenuous physical labour resulted in his back giving out and confining him to bed. While at Queen's he complained about a variety of ailments from acne to bad teeth, and after graduating he was found unfit for overseas military service by three successive medical boards. In this way, the unwanted warrior wound up working as a guard in the Canadian internment camps during the Great War.[39]

Perhaps somewhat ironically, given his own health, Kirkconnell's upbringing left him convinced of the superiority of the Anglo-Saxon race and dismissive of those racialized as non-white. Although this was not fully expressed in scientific terminology, he began to be exposed to these currents of thought while at Queen's University and remained interested in these ideas even after he graduated and began working in the military. As such, he began to independently research heredity, eugenics, anthropology, and race science. It was through this period of study that his biases hardened into scientific racism, and that he became convinced of the inferiority of non-Anglo-Saxon races.

### WHITE TIERS

Located in the Esther Clark Wright Archives of Acadia University is the Watson Kirkconnell Room. The reading room for all who wish to access materials from the archives and special collections, it also serves as a shrine to Kirkconnell: the walls are covered with his decorations, medals, farmed diplomas, files, manuscripts, and books. On one pillar of the room is a large brass plaque, unveiled at the room's dedication in 1979, which reads in part: "Apostle of peaceful understanding through his monumental translations from many poetic literatures – Icelandic, Hungarian, Polish, Ukrainian, French. Founder of Canadian multiculturalism. Champion of human freedom."[40] Kirkconnell's connections with European immigrants in Canada were widely recognized in his lifetime, as reflected in the host of honours that were bestowed on him by their home countries, the Canadian government, and various organizations.[41] In his memoirs, he would suggest that his connection with European immigrants began in 1922 during a transatlantic voyage. But Kirkconnell, this "champion of human freedom," actually first became acquainted with Slavic peoples while guarding over them in internment camps in Canada during the Great War.[42]

During the conflict, the Canadian government interned 8,579 "enemy aliens" who were deemed to be a security threat, most of them of German or Ukrainian descent. There was very little genuine threat to security in the country but, as historian Bohdan Kordan argues, internment was really "a policy used to address the core problems of enemy alien unemployment and destitution, as well as the anxiety and resentment of the broader population." The policy also grossly oversimplified the issues of identity, belonging, and loyalty. In Kordan's words: "The security question, in essence, had become racialized: where you came from would determine whether or not you were an enemy." Kirkconnell was dismissive of the prisoners of Slavic descent, writing that they were "ignorant, sullen, [and] inert," and mocking their "thick headed" belief that Austria was going to win the war. His emergent belief in race shaped his recollection of internment. As he would later describe the situation, at the outbreak of the war Canada "found herself at war with Germany and Austria; and awoke also to the presence within her borders of close upon a million descendants of these hostile races."[43]

This emphasis on race had been strengthened while he was working in the internment camps. Kirkconnell first worked as an administrative officer at Fort Henry in Kingston and then, when the camp was shuttered in May 1917, he was transferred to Kapuskasing in northern Ontario. In June 1918, while still at Kapuskasing, Kirkconnell informed his father that he had written to Chicago, Columbia, and Johns Hopkins universities about their post-graduate programs in

Figure 1.2 *Camp Staff, Kapuskasing, July 1917.*

anthropology.[44] One of the first books that Kirkconnell read that sparked his interest in issues of evolution, heredity, and eugenics was titled *Heredity*. Written by Scottish biologist J. Arthur Thomson of the University of Aberdeen, the work was a frequently reprinted and discussed synthesis of much of what was then considered scientific knowledge within the field, and it had inserted hereditarian certainty into the complicated and uncertain early twentieth-century racial theories.[45] Though the Darwinism of his day did not clearly account for how natural selection occurred, this was no barrier to young Kirkconnell, who came to this field passionately persuaded of the permanence of human divisions into types. Fascinated, he discussed the work with his father and continued to read voraciously on the subject, moving from Thomson to other, more explicitly racist authors such as Madison Grant.[46]

As scholar of American literature and culture Ivan Grabovac argues, it is "misleading to think of Grant's nativism as a race-based U.S. nationalism." Noting Grant's handful of references to Canada, he suggests that it is instead a kind of transnationalism.[47] Indeed, Canada was a frequent subject of discussion for Grant and other American activists, who used the country as an example but also tried to steer it in a different direction. One prominent figure in these efforts was Charles M. Goethe. A wealthy American businessman, founder of the Eugenics Society of Northern California, and president of the one-man "Immigration Study Commission of the Americas" based in Sacramento, California, Goethe "spent over a million dollars of his own money to publish scores of racist pamphlets and place hundreds of anti-immigration articles in newspapers throughout the English-speaking world" including many in Canada during the 1920s.[48] In *The Globe* (Toronto), he praised Canada's relative "race purity" and advised them to avoid the "tragic example" of America's race admixture. The next day, the paper reiterated: "That Mr. Goethe's advice is wise, and if it were followed would be in the best interests of Canada – of her immediate and ultimate future – there can be little doubt."[49] In a letter to the more skeptical *Ottawa Journal,* Goethe warned that only one of the five largest nations contributing to Canada's population was Nordic, decried the United States' "non-eugenic immigration policy," and stated that the greatest hope for the future was for citizens of the United States and "the units comprising the British Empire" to gain a clear grasp of this problem. A year later, in the *Winnipeg Tribune*, Goethe lamented the lack of progress: "Where color difference exists you are instinctively alert. In the case of non-Nordic Europe, however, folks are prone to be indifferent. Yet the danger to your institutions is greatest from these."[50]

Clearly not all folks were indifferent: Kirkconnell, father and son, were a rapt audience for the race science that Americans like Goethe and Grant peddled. Thomas and his son had a close relationship, and one that physical distance did not dampen. The two discussed a myriad of topics in their weekly correspondence while Kirkconnell worked in the internment camps. From these letters it is clear that both men believed that heredity determined most of human characteristics, and that both were very concerned with human "fitness" – particularly their own.[51] But while Thomas remained curious of the potential impact of the environment and thought that Thomson had shown hereditarian patterns did not apply uniformly, his son went in the other direction and had become captivated by more deterministic theories as early as 1917.[52] The correspondence also reveals that Kirkconnell's childhood interest in Indigenous cultures had diminished. "I do not fancy spending the rest of my life pottering over defunct Indian tongues," he wrote to his father, "especially when there is no literature connected with them, and their only value consists in a none too certain aid to ethnological classification."[53]

Now actively considering a career in the field, Kirkconnell contacted anthropologist Edward Sapir, who advised him to meet with Franz Boas, Sapir's former graduate supervisor, before making a final decision.[54] In April 1919, Kirkconnell travelled to New York to meet with Boas, who was at that time the head of the Department of Anthropology at Columbia University. In a "candid burst of pessimism," Boas advised him to avoid professional anthropology as it was viewed as a frill by North American universities and would be the first department to have its funding cut. Keen for a prestigious and profitable career, Kirkconnell heeded Boas's counsel and abandoned this choice, though he remained intrigued by the subject.[55]

Had Kirkconnell studied under Sapir or Boas, his worldview would most likely have been quite different. While anthropology was responsible for spreading racial determinism, Boas was among those who worked to challenge these theories that had been so popularized by Grant. Boas had grown increasingly skeptical about the idea of physical "types," and in his landmark work, *The Mind of Primitive Man* (1911), he set forth his alternative. In it, he argued that language and culture had to be separated from race and studied independently of them, and that the idea of Anglo-Saxon superiority was baseless.[56]

But Kirkconnell did not go on to join the group of Boasian antiracists. Instead, having been demobilized, and with alternate plans in place to study at Harvard for a PhD in education, Kirkconnell accepted an offer in August 1919 to work as a transport officer on a ship transporting several hundred German prisoners to Europe for repatriation. What followed was a series of health-related calamities. While in Europe, he fell seriously ill and was unable to return to Canada until mid-November. Then, having barely landed in Lindsay, he moved to Toronto to take voice lessons at the conservatory (intent on becoming an opera singer), but was struck down by the influenza and was forced to return to Lindsay where he spent fifteen months recovering under his doting mother's care. His time in Toronto and Lindsay was not spent idly, however, for he used it to read the work of European and American race theorists and began to study the racial composition of his own country.

As part of his research, Kirkconnell turned to census data for information about race and demography but was disappointed with the information collected. Having recently begun a correspondence course in journalism – this being his newest career ambition – he channelled these frustrations into the article discussed at the beginning of this chapter.[57] The demographic research he was undertaking was part of a larger project, a book manuscript entitled "Anglo-Canadian Futurities."[58] He later described it as a "study of the racial tendencies of the Anglo-Celtic stock in Canada." In reality, it was a eugenic tract aimed at rural Anglo-Ontarians, complete with suggestions for wholesale sterilization of the unfit. The 67-page manuscript was thus a blend of race science and eugenics combined with his sense of Anglo-Saxon superiority, deep antipathy towards French Canadians, and belief in the benefits of a rural lifestyle.

As Kirkconnell would explain, non-white races were "much different" from the three European races. For Nordicists, skin colour was an obvious signifier of difference. However, this did not mean that differences between the European races were invisible; rather, they held that each were phenotypically distinct (that is, that each had discernible and differing physical characteristics). Anthropometry, or the study of the human body's measurements, was therefore an essential component of this racial theory. Due to the historical context in which it emerged, the field of anthropometry was deeply concerned with degeneration, criminality, and identifying typologies, often races. In addition, it drew from earlier scientific streams from the nineteenth century such as phrenology (the study of human skulls) and physiognomy (the study of facial characteristics), both of which lent themselves to racial and eugenic concerns.[59]

Kirkconnell had discovered these important strands of racial and eugenic thought, and was particularly taken with the cephalic index, a measurement of the skull, to the point that he purchased medical calipers and measured his own head and those of his parents. (Indicating the longevity of his beliefs, Kirkconnell would list these measurements in his memoirs nearly a half-century later.)[60] In his 1919 diary, he noted having consulted a phrenologist in Montreal and discussed "anthropometry, phrenology, and applied physiognomistics" with those who called on him while he was convalescing in Britain.[61] And he saw these differences in the world around him. While in England he remarked that "the Limehouse district near the West India docks seemed to bear out its evil reputation by the frequent presence of ugly-looking Chinese, negroes, and degenerate Cockneys skulking in the background like evil genii of the place."[62] Accordingly, within the first few pages of "Futurities" Kirkconnell explained the physical differences between European races. Mediterraneans were long-headed, small, and swarthy, with dark eyes and hair, while Nordics were long-headed, tall, blond, and blue-eyed and had specially evolved nostrils that warmed the cold northern air before it reached their lungs. The Alpine race was physically different from both these races, with its short, wide head, and stocky body "of Asiatic origin."[63]

Kirkconnell then discussed the mental characteristics of each of these white races. The Mediterranean was a kindred stock to the Nordic, but due to migration had a distinct "genius" and excelled in sciences, art, poetry, literature, and philosophy.[64] In the modern world, many seemingly diverse peoples were members of the Mediterranean race, including the ruling caste in India ("the upper class Hindoo"), along with Greeks, South Italians, and Spaniards. The Nordic race was, by contrast, energetic and muscular with an "active and practical" genius for law, organization, and military efficiency. It was this genius, and its related ideals of truth, loyalty, and family life, which had allowed the Nordic race to "carry civilization to higher syntheses." But the Alpine race had "no affinities with the strictly European stocks." They were generally fierce, coarse, and brutal, a "backward peasant people" with no civilization. In more recent history, they had established "the Slav nationalities of the modern world," and represented at least half the populations of Germany, Italy, and France.[65]

It was from these three racial strains that all the modern nationalities of Europe were composed. But Kirkconnell recognized that pure racial groups did not still exist and that instead of being neatly defined by race, national sentiment arose from common religion, economic interests, geographical conditions, history and traditions, and a uniform theory of government.[66] He concluded that despite these cultural commonalities, "racial qualities of mind still exist in full vigour in the individual and these in the exact proportions of his ethnical inheritance."[67] The Anglo-Saxon, however, was a unique subset of the Nordic race that had evolved in isolation in Britain over a period of millennia, without the degrading presence of the Alpine race. Likely owing to the fact that he was Scottish, Kirkconnell gave "Anglo-Saxon" a wide definition: "the racial stocks which have inhabited the British Isles during the past 850 years and the scions of these stocks wherever spread by colonization during the past three centuries."[68]

Kirkconnell's understanding of how races expanded or decayed led him to believe that the Anglo-Saxon stock in Canada was in dire straits. According to his reading, races decayed as a result of climate, food supply, and race suicide. Canada was a northern nation, so Nordics naturally thrived there and non-white races could not, meaning climate was not the problem.[69] As for food supply, Canada was an underpopulated country with plenty of agricultural land, though the increased urbanization that undercut farming was a hazard. The true threat, he thus concluded, was race suicide, or the phenomenon of Anglo-Saxons voluntarily having fewer children. This low natality, combined with the unchecked multiplication of non-Anglo-Saxon stocks, could spell the end of the Anglo-Canadian. Couples needed to have four children each for the population to maintain its current size, he warned, and five or six children were required for any growth.[70]

Perhaps unsurprisingly, given his upbringing and experiences at Queen's, Kirkconnell placed much of the blame for race suicide on women, who he argued were rejecting or repressing their proper biological role. He dismissed outright the idea that birth control would allow for women's greater liberty and development. There might be a handful of cases, he admitted, in which a mother in poor circumstances could be "crushed" by the weight of a large family. But he countered that the main proponents of birth control were well-off women who wanted to be "friends" with their husbands and did not want to be mothers. He defined this type of woman as a familiar nuisance, either too shallow to understand the deeper significance of maternity, or too selfish to care that motherhood was her duty. "The one great consolation presented by these selfish sexual perverts," he concluded, "is that they will exterminate themselves in a generation or two and leave the world to those who do not practise high treason against nature." In another passage, he alleged that the childless woman was "as great a social parasite as the prostitute. Both will perish, racially, and the earth will inevitably be inherited by the offspring of those who are true to sex and type."[71] This overt sexism was certainly not unusual among eugenicists: both Galton and his protégé Karl Pearson were unabashedly opposed to feminism, while others like Havelock Ellis attempted to balance the demands of both eugenicists and feminists (though it should be noted that some feminists were later ardent eugenicists themselves).[72]

In the remainder of the tract, Kirkconnell continued to lay out his gloomy racial interpretation of society. The vigour with which a race exerted itself was a significant factor in its continued survival, he explained, which meant that the increase of unions and the decrease in farm work were also signs that Anglo-Canadian society was imperilled. The pioneer Anglo-Saxon stock, the very stock that had founded Canada (and particularly Ontario), was dying out and being replaced by "either French-Canadians or inferior immigrants from Cockney England or submerged Europe." Though this problem was especially pronounced in rural areas, it was also seen in cities where the "alien immigrant is extremely prolific but the native English-Canadian is found conspicuously wanting."[73]

Historian Angus McLaren has argued that English Canadian fear of French Canadian fertility gave "the hereditarian debate in Canada a particular resonance."[74] Kirkconnell's writing is evidence that the English-French divide not only provided resonance for the movement but also, in some instances, helped shape its contours and give it a specific focus. His manuscript was very intentionally entitled "*Anglo*-Canadian Futurities," and it is possible that he began this independent study partly because of his preoccupation with the English-French "problem," for – as previously mentioned – his family's connection to and relationship with French Canadians was long and strained.[75] In this manuscript, Kirkconnell declared that the biggest difference between the English and French in Canada was not race but rather nationality and religion. Unable to specify French Canadians' precise racial origins, he concluded that "here and there" Nordic traits persisted and as such the French and English Canadians were "of kindred stock."[76] The trouble with French Canadians was that, as in the past, they were steadily multiplying, but he argued that French expansion did not justify hostility. Instead, Anglo-Canadians needed to emulate the French model of having large families, lest they hand over their possessions to "another race."[77]

Kirkconnell may have hedged on French Canadians' racial history but he was certain about nearly every other group. In his opinion, the "Non-Nordic" elements in Canada included people of Austro-Hungarian, Polish, Russian, Bulgarian, Romanian, Italian, Greek, Jewish, African, Indian, Chinese, and Japanese descent.[78] He argued that all these groups had "little or no share in the Nordic blood and the Nordic aptitude for our civilization." Echoing arguments he had heard at Queen's, he added that Asian peoples were particularly damaging to Anglo-Saxon society because of their inherent immorality. This he attributed to their Alpine nature, warning that "to admit them to equality in our civilization is ultimately to corrupt all that we hold most sacred in the moral world."[79] While they might survive in the harsh northern climate, others could not. As he put it in one undeveloped note in the text: "Negro – little chance of growth. Our climate is against his survival. He is out of his proper biological zone."[80]

Kirkconnell was against intermarriage between "widely differing races" (that is, between nominally white and nominally non-white), as these "half breeds" would always die out. Therefore, the threat of such unions was not hybridity but rather the failure of the superior race to maintain its numerical superiority. Such intermarrying should be strictly prohibited, Kirkconnell wrote. "Those who advocate free intermarriage regardless of colour are pernicious fools. In our relationship with backward races, we should not permit free immigration or intermarriage."[81]

In the tract's closing reflections, Kirkconnell remarked that the first step in righting the Canadian situation was "weeding out the possibility of reproduction for stocks bearing serious defects. Criminality, hereditary diseases of the more fatal types, feeblemindedness, and degeneracy should be made bars to parenthood. Wholesale sterilization of the unfit would be the most effective method, though one likely to meet with furious opposition ... Certificates of physical fitness from government medical boards should be made prerequisite for marriage."[82] The second step was to cultivate "respect for maternity and pride in good heredity," and to discourage Neo-Malthusianism (the practice of birth control). Other "positive" eugenic measures, none of them original, included linking salary and tax rate to the size of a man's family. On some issues, such as enlightening the public about their racial duties or facilitating eugenic marriages, Kirkconnell confessed that he did not know how best to proceed. Yet he nonetheless remained confident of the ultimate success of this agenda.

Beyond the specific measures he suggested, Kirkconnell also had a broader vision for the country. He singled out churches and schools as two social institutions that could help shape Anglo-Canadian society. Churches had so far failed by "confining religion to a simple, abstract scheme of salvation and steadfastly disregarding concrete problems," such as race suicide. Kirkconnell wanted them to become eugenic organizations, educating the public at large about their racial responsibilities.[83] Likewise, "the educational systems of this continent have a distinct racial mission to fulfill," he wrote. The purpose of education was to supply each child with "the accumulated knowledge of the race so that he may fit his life into our complex inherited civilization with a minimum danger to himself and the nation in which he lives." In short, Kirkconnell believed that all children had to fully develop their mental and moral capacities in order to transform them into citizens worthy of Anglo-Saxon civilization, that "settled way of life."[84]

Notably absent from the manuscript was any discussion of Indigenous peoples, even though Kirkconnell had learned more about the history of the region through his friendship with Johnson Paudash, Chief of the Rice Lake Mississaugas. Paudash had fought in the Great War as a sniper and afterwards worked in Lindsay as a letter-carrier. "From him," Kirkconnell recalled, "I learned much about the arrival of Mississaugas in Central Ontario in 1740 and about their sternly punitive campaign against the Iroquois that cleared Victoria County for Mississauga settlement."[85] With the help of Paudash and Col. George E. Laidlaw, Kirkconnell mapped fifty-five village sites from the pre-Mississauga period as well as fifteen Mississauga villages, and wrote up these findings in an article entitled "Stone Age Annals of Victoria County" for the local paper.

Scholars of settler colonialism note that the process generally entails the erasure of Indigenous peoples from public memory and history, and this can clearly be seen in Kirkconnell's early works. In them, he acknowledged Indigenous history but presented it as belonging to an extinct people, despite his friendship with the very much alive Chief Paudash. The sites he had visited, Kirkconnell wrote, revealed "evidences of an earlier civilization than our own ... shards of a vanished race." A few of these traces "belong to a people whose diminished descendants still linger on in fenced off corners of *our* land, but by far the greater number must be ascribed to times much more remote and to tribes of somewhat different culture."[86] According to his account of the history, at the time of contact there lived in the northeastern part of North America "two great races of Indians," the Algonquins and the Iroquois (or Huron-Iroquois). The Iroquoian race originally came from the region near the mouth of the Ohio River, he wrote, where they "evolved their typical civilization." Here Kirkconnell relied on his belief in racial essences by suggesting that the civilization was somehow a natural outgrowth of biological race, but also presented Huron-Iroquois culture as fixed, ancient, and ultimately passed.

Kirkconnell dismissively referred to Huron culture as "Strange Works and Stranger Ways." While he acknowledged some accomplishments, he generally cut them down in the same breath. For example, the Hurons led an agricultural lifestyle, "yet their methods were very primitive." They constructed longhouses, but these were so tightly packed with families that the result was a "welter of noisy lawlessness, in which privacy, restraint[,] and decency were inconceivable." They made art in the form of pottery, but their style was unoriginal in that it was mixed with that of the Algonquins. Similarly, they crafted wampum, which he accepted was the equivalent of a written language, but noted that few individuals could still read them. He went on to paint a dreary picture of this early period (roughly the sixteenth through the eighteenth centuries) as an age of "chronic insecurity. Eternal vigilance was the price of existence. Any hour of the day or night might bring the onslaught of a legion of screaming devils." The Hurons also exhibited such devilish behaviour, he suggested, by devouring human flesh "whenever they were fortune enough to capture some of their enemies. There was always a prelude of torture, after which the bodies were divided and boiled in kettles."[87]

Kirkconnell used the rather lurid article as the basis for the chapter on "The Annals of the Red Man" in his *Victoria County Centennial History*.[88] The structure of the book is suggestive of Kirkconnell's firmly colonial interpretation of the history: his history of Victoria County begins when nominally white men arrive; it is not until 122 pages into the text that Indigenous history is briefly touched upon. Instead, the text opens with "a hardy phalanx of Celto-Saxon stock" sweeping away a "wilderness" and establishing "a prosperous agricultural civilization after the manner of that race." It is the story, as one section header puts it, of "A New Domain and a Virile Race." (Statements like these demonstrated his continued belief that race was responsible for the creation of civilizations.)[89]

Throughout the work, Kirkconnell argued that through the scientific study of "physiographical, racial, social, and economic forces" Canadians could "plan for the evolution of a higher economic and social order."[90] He also hinted that eugenics could help plan this evolution: "The most pressing need of the times is a proper medical inspection of all school children," he suggested, in order to identify the healthy and the defective. Eighty-five per cent of defective students were "curable by the simplest kind of a surgical operation," but if these defects were left unchecked the children would be left to live useless lives and would go on to plant "the seeds of incurable disease."[91] Here Kirkconnell may have been subtly suggesting that sterilizations ought to begin once intelligence testing had been completed. Intelligence for him was a clear measure of fitness, and the only solution for incurable ignorance was to stop the afflicted from reproducing.

Kirkconnell had by now applied a racial and eugenic lens to the issues of the Canadian population, census taking, and the history and organization of a local county, but he was not yet finished analyzing the world from a racial and eugenic perspective. After he completed his local history, he applied his framework to a larger problem: unemployment, in the context of international economics. Early in 1921, Kirkconnell contacted Oxford University to enquire about their BLitt program. He was accepted, began in October of 1921, and returned to Lindsay by August of the following year. Despite his background in classics, he chose to study economics because of his planned career in journalism.[92] (The degree normally required a two-year stay, but Kirkconnell used his time in Internment Operations to gain a military exemption for one year. Thus while "enemy aliens" lost their freedom as a result of the wartime policy of internment, officers like Kirkconnell continued to benefit from the policy even after the conflict had ended.) Kirkconnell packed his "Futurities" manuscript along with him to Oxford and attempted to incorporate much of its material in his BLitt thesis. More precisely, he attempted to marry his racial understanding of society with a study of political economy.

It is conceivable that the idea of completing the degree seemed plausible to him precisely because of the possibility of using "Futurities" as the basis for his thesis. Candidates in the program received no "systematic instruction" and were generally left to their own devices, leading one instructor to decry the University's provision for postgraduate work as "an unorganized excrescence on our elaborate tutorial and lecturing system."[93] Given Kirkconnell's interests and the nature of the program, it is unsurprising that the resulting thesis was short on economics but full of racial and eugenic theories. In his estimation, only one-fifth of the book was devoted to "standard analysis." Unsurprisingly, his Oxford examiners denied him the degree, arguing that the original thesis, "though of considerable literary interest and merit, does not show a sufficient amount of independent economic enquiry."[94] Kirkconnell, dejected and out of money, returned home but continued to fight the university for the degree, in part by locating a publisher for the rejected thesis. The protracted battle was ultimately unsuccessful as the university refused to grant him the BLitt. The silver lining in these black clouds, however, was the publication of his thesis as the *International Aspects of Unemployment* in 1923.[95]

The book was not strictly about economics and, in fact, it contains some of his starkest calls for negative eugenics. Kirkconnell argued that unemployment stemmed from imperfections in the organization of the industrial world, which could be divided into two categories: trade fluctuations and imperfections in labour quality. He did offer some suggestions for the former, such as a system of national labour exchanges. This was a common proposal during this era; seven years before this book appeared, John Murray Gibbon called for the creation of national labour bureaus in numerous speeches to Canadian businesspeople.[96]

Kirkconnell, however, put the greatest focus on the second source of imperfection: the quality of labourers. His comments suggest that the unemployed were a separate class of people, and he provided various definitions of subcategories within this class, based on their fitness for industry. As for solutions to the problem that these unemployables represented, Kirkconnell called for the creation of labour colonies where the excess population would be isolated. Attempts would be made to restore those not "beyond salvage," who would then rejoin national industry under strict supervision. Labour colonies were a popular proposed solution during this era, and famed economists had suggested them at various times and as solutions for various problems.[97] However, Kirkconnell believed they were a viable solution because he had concrete experience working in the type of institution he was proposing: wartime internment camps created by the state.

Yet Kirkconnell's newfound understanding of race revealed to him the limitations of such institutions. Owing to his belief in heredity, he warned that such segregation "serves merely to remove a nuisance from the industrial system." Something more had to be done about the "ever-increasing plague of useless and inefficient citizens," and in his mind there was only one solution. These citizens were to "be maintained in life-long segregation ... for the preservation of society; and for the same profound and fundamental reason they should be prevented, through surgical sterilization, from reproducing their worthless kind ... No single act by a modern State could so improve its hopes of permanence and advancement in the social scale."[98] He asserted that the state should be charged with this vital task but since "the plague is international in its activities" a concerted effort was required.[99] Once concerned only with Canada and specifically Ontario, he now advocated eugenic measures – regulation, segregation, and sterilization – on an international scale.

The book was widely reviewed and discussed in Canada, Great Britain, and the United States. Although Kirkconnell later claimed the book garnered "a more enthusiastic reaction than any other book that I have ever written ... a chorus of approval for style and content," an examination of the reviews reveals a more critical reception.[100] While a great majority of the reviews were positive overall, most reviewers agreed that the book contained essentially no new economic theories, that economists and general readers alike would take exception with some of his arguments, and that its value came from its broad perspective on a pressing issue. Many commented on the book's pessimistic tone, but there was certainly no agreement on the style: while some enjoyed how he occasionally thundered "like an Old Testament prophet," one reviewer wished he "would sometimes be less profuse and grandiose with his analogies." Kirkconnell writes "as if he had swallowed the dictionary," another complained.[101]

Kirkconnell's extreme eugenic proposals garnered comparatively little attention, which gives some indication of the popularity and spread of eugenic theories across interwar Europe and North America. Few reviewers even commented on the book's eugenic ideas, and most of them were unconcerned. "His general argument is mildly Malthusian," one wrote. Another found the whole thing amusing: "The objections to his [sterilization] proposal are greater than our author seems to realize, but he is nothing if not thorough-going!" They did, however, concur with the thrust of his argument, concluding in racially charged language that "the inhabitants of an over-populated continent may be obligated to work like galley-slaves for a coolie standard of life."[102] A couple of periodicals argued that he had overestimated the influence of heredity,[103] but only one seriously took him to task for his proposals. An unsigned review in the *Western Daily Press*, a newspaper in Bristol, UK, wrote that the idea of sterilizing unemployed people would "startle even the most extreme of sociologists, and it will tend to the creation of a hubbub of protest ... The elimination of the unfit by these methods would imply the rattling of modern states back to the darkest ages of barbarism." Stunned, the reviewer was left asking if they had correctly understood the author's arguments. "Is it suggested, seriously, that the League of Nations ... should be empowered to enforce, internationally, what is practically the lethal chamber for the elimination of the unfit; or for the extermination of the world's millions of the convicted work-shy?"[104] (Yes, it was seriously suggested.)

There were no such critical reviews in Canadian periodicals. Instead, the book provided the foundation upon which Kirkconnell would build his reputation as a scholar. For instance, a review in the *Winnipeg Tribune* praised the work as a "vigorous tract for the present time," while a glowing column in the *Manitoba Free Press* reproduced praise from international reviews of the book.[105] In order to understand this reaction, it is important to recall that Anglo-American ideas about race and eugenics had long circulated in Canada. As early as 1918 William Moore singled out Madison Grant's book, *The Passing of the Great Race*, as contributing to Anglo-Canadians' sense of racial superiority and subsequent prejudice towards French Canadians.[106] Federal politicians who helped shape the nation's immigration policy were similarly swayed by the Nordicist strain of scientific racism. According to historian Donald Avery, during a 1919 debate on immigration Hume Cronyn (MP for London, Ontario) cited the writings of Madison Grant as justification for excluding "strange people who cannot be assimilated."[107] (A reading of the debate turns up no mention of Grant but does find Cronyn repeating the Nordicist tripartite division of European races as reformulated and popularized by Grant.) Likewise, H.H. Stevens, MP for Vancouver City, owned a carefully annotated copy of *The Passing of the Great Race* and, likely inspired by it, as late as 1921 argued against intermarriage between "Orientals" and white people. And in 1924 Samuel William Jacobs, a Jewish MP serving the George-Étienne Cartier region of Quebec, recommended admitting Swedish immigrants on the grounds that they "belong[ed] to the Nordic race." Illustrating the changing currents in the period, three years later, when Jacobs raised the issue of race in connection with immigration policy, he backed away from the determinist viewpoint he had formerly espoused. "A man may be a scoundrel and come from Scandinavia; a man may be a genius and come from Italy," he suggested.[108] Similarly, only a short while after he had floated some of his most extreme ideas, Kirkconnell too had a change of heart.

### "An Important Lesson": The Consolidation of Whiteness

Late in the summer of 1922, Kirkconnell was at his parents' home in Lindsay, furiously trying to get his book published. Arthur Phelps, the newly appointed chair of the English Department at Wesley College, was vacationing at Bobcaygeon, a small town near Port Hope, when his idyll was interrupted by an urgent piece of news, a wire from J.H. Riddell, president of the college. The telegram informed him that Fletcher Argue, the only other member of the English Department, had quit. (Argue had lived up to his name by getting into a "thundering row" with Riddell and then resigning.) Looking for an emergency replacement, Phelps headed to Lindsay, knocked on Kirkconnell's door, and offered him the job of English lecturer – an offer that Kirkconnell immediately declined.[109] For reasons unknown, but possibly acting on advice from his father (himself an educator), when Phelps called two days later and renewed his request, Kirkconnell changed his answer; he would later look back on this as one of the major decisions of his life.

Kirkconnell was woefully unprepared for the culture shock that the move from rural, ethnically homogeneous Lindsay to urban, heterogeneous Winnipeg entailed. "Western Canada was peopled with a very different ethnic mixture from that of the Anglo-Celtic communities of my Ontario youth or the Ottawa Valley Scotch-French symbiosis of my pioneer ancestors," he would later write. "I found Slavic and Scandinavian names abounding in the class-rolls of college and university ... This was still Canada, but a Canada profoundly different from the little Ontario towns of my boyhood."[110] No doubt it was, for in 1921 almost half of Winnipeg's residents were immigrants and, as late as the Second World War, one-third had been born in another country. Residents of Winnipeg who spoke only English comprised only 54 per cent of the population as late as 1931, and some of the major ethnic groups included Ukrainians, Jews, Germans, French, Poles, and Scandinavians, including many Icelanders. Each of these groups demonstrated various degrees of cultural retention, as evidenced by their newspapers, specialty stores, and political representation. Smaller ethnic groups included Italians, Dutch, Belgians, Hungarians, Austrians, Russians, Czechs, and Slovakians, and some people of Chinese and Japanese descent. Entering a religious bookstore in Winnipeg in 1922, Kirkconnell was astonished to find that the Bible was available in over fifty languages.[111] The years between 1922 and 1926, therefore, marked the first time that he came into close and sustained contact with members of the racialized groups he had been maligning. However, while these experiences may have slowly begun to challenge Kirkconnell's conception of all non-Anglo-Saxons as racially inferior, the process was by no means immediate.

Kirkconnell's immediate focus was getting a grip on the classes he was teaching and getting settled in the city. Although he had done some supply teaching in secondary schools, he had no experience teaching at the university level. As he put it in his memoirs, for the first two years he was "always just one jump ahead of the wolfpack." But even had he known what courses he would be teaching he would not have been able to take the time to prepare, for the book manuscript kept him busy until about four days before college opened.[112] Once the manuscript was off his desk, he plunged into the exciting and emergent literary scene in Winnipeg. Through his involvement in the newly formed Canadian Authors Association (CAA), but especially owing to Phelps's connections, Kirkconnell developed friendships with both established and emerging figures in the Canadian literary scene such as publishers Lorne Pierce and Hugh Dent, novelists Frederick Philip Grove and John Murray Gibbon, and poet E.J. Pratt.[113]

One welcome distraction from the bustle was his impending nuptials. In 1924 he married Isabel Peel, a young woman with whom he had grown up in Port Hope. But their bliss was to be short-lived, for in the early hours of 16 July 1925 Isabel died of complications following the birth of twin boys. She was not quite twenty-three years old and the two had been married only eleven months. The grief devastated Kirkconnell, who sent babies Jamie and Tommy to live with Isabel's parents, packed up their possessions and put them into storage, moved into the men's residence at Wesley (where he would end up living until 1930), and returned to teaching classes. But at night, when he was sitting alone in his room at the top floor of the dorm, listening to the boisterous young men below, the grief and loneliness would set in.[114] Kirkconnell's interest in comparative literature, and specifically European poetry, had been rekindled by the move to Winnipeg and so during these dark hours he turned to translating poems as a way of dealing with the grief. "As these versions accumulated," he later wrote, "an audacious design took shape. I would draw on the elegiac resources of all Europe, ancient and modern, and would marshal these poems, in my own translation, as a memorial to my lost wife." So it was that *The European Elegies* was born, a collection of poems translated into English from about fifty European languages, largely completed by April 1926 but not published until 1928.[115]

The process of writing *Elegies* was what ultimately brought Kirkconnell away from some of the extremes of his scientific racist beliefs, for he was "driven by this bereavement to a profound scrutiny of the fundamental facts of life."[116] A realization of European poetry's beauty and its expressions of emotion doubtless led him to some difficult questions about racial typologies, such as how members of supposedly unfit racial groups could craft such beautiful expressions of the human experience. He would later claim that the translations taught him "a profound lesson."[117] Ostensibly referencing grief, he closed the work's preface with following lines:

The experience which lies behind has been definite, coherent, and profound, but its disclosure is not desired or intended.

Only this I would confess: that the task which was in the beginning an anodyne became an instrument of deliverance and revelation, not in any religious sense normally so conceived, but in the broadest realm of the human spirit.[118]

Kirkconnell never admitted to his former beliefs and this was as close to a confession as he ever made.[119] However, he did not abandon a belief in the scientific reality of race, nor of its influence on the individual. Rather, he simply began to question the notion of racial purity in the modern, "Occidental" (Western) world, and to question whether the mixing of European races was necessarily detrimental. Despite this, he remained convinced that nominally non-white races were inferior.

The clearest explanation of his newfound conception of humanity is found in a speech entitled "Demos and Apollo," delivered to the CAA at their National Convention in 1927.[120] Kirkconnell had always denied that nationality and race were synonymous, with the exception of perhaps Norway and Denmark, but nevertheless maintained that Britain was a unique example due to the historical absence of Alpine stock.[121] In this monologue, however, he argued that the "reality of national characteristics is greatly overrated. Racial qualities are, of course, real enough. Nordic idealism and sentiment, Slavic intensity, and Mediterranean artistry will work through heredity to shape the character of the individual. But virtually all nations are mongrel mixtures of races. France, Germany, Italy, England, Russia – all of the greatest national groups in modern times are vast mixtures of racial strains." He thus still firmly believed in racial inheritance but argued that races did not fall neatly along national boundaries. All that members of the same nation truly shared, he now concluded, was "the sense of a common history during the past five or six centuries, and to a lesser extent ... a sense of common traditions and achievements." In tracing the history of literary movements, he noted "all the great literatures produced by all European nations as nations are assignable to great international movements of thought and art." There was much more intellectual similarity and solidarity amongst the European nations than he had previously thought, and this realization strengthened his embryonic idea that the peoples of the nations might be as similar as their ideas. Kirkconnell had suddenly become one of the writers who saw "the universal in life about them."[122]

Though the process of writing *Elegies* led to a reformulation of his understanding of race, he did not abandon it as a fundamental organizing principle. Rather, this was the moment for Kirkconnell when whiteness was consolidated. The speech was one of the first public indications that he believed a blending of cultures was beneficial, but he still believed race was responsible for shaping personal and national characteristics. After this period, he would occasionally use the term *race* to describe what would now be called ethnicity or nationality. His understanding of the connection between race and nationality is best explained in his address to the Modern Language Association in 1928. In it, he discussed the role of race in literature in the context of analyzing Slavonic poetry. He began by disagreeing with the argument that generalizing about race in literature was dangerous and deceptive. Such criticism could prevent scholars from jumping to hasty conclusions, he countered, but it should not keep them from "affirming what the common man has guessed and the scholar experienced, that nations and races do impress individual qualities upon their literatures." There were international trends in literature, but the fact that each country reacted to these movements in different ways was to Kirkconnell a sign that nations, each shaped by race, crafted distinctive literatures.

European nations were a blend of races, but people groups had particular traits owing to their particular racial makeup.[123] In this case, Slavic peoples represented "a special blending of types. Lacking the Mediterranean element altogether, they are the merging of a broad-headed Alpine majority and an earlier rufous [reddish-brown], dolicephalic [long-skulled] minority with Nordic affinities." The title of his talk was "The Genius of Slavonic Poetry," and here it is important to remember that *genius* referred to the common essence of a race. Similar to his remarks about Indigenous peoples, his description of Slavic cultures was equal parts degrading and complimentary. Slavic people had no "marked originality in literary type" and their literature was "almost wholly derivative," but the genius of their poetry was found in "two transcendent attitudes: universality of sympathy, and a deeply religious attitude towards life."[124] Regardless of his ambivalent treatment of non-British, non-French Europeans, he nevertheless considered them worthy of his consideration; peoples of African, Asian and Indigenous descent continued to be excluded from his scholarly works, for he assumed their racial inferiority. The internal boundaries of whiteness were now deemed to be less important than they had been historically, but the outer ramparts remained as strong as ever.

### The Outer Boundary of Whiteness

A perfect illustration of Kirkconnell's new stance is found in his response to the public activism of the outspoken nativist George Exton Lloyd. Lloyd, the Anglican bishop of Saskatchewan, had been born and raised in Britain before immigrating to Canada, where he studied theology and then joined the militia. He fought in the North-West Resistance, was wounded, and was later decorated for his "bravery" during an unauthorized, unprovoked, and ultimately unsuccessful attack on a band of Cree. He would go on to play a major role in founding the Barr Colony, an all-British settlement. Lloyd's dream was for Canada to remain a colony for British people only, and to that end he engaged in a personal, unwavering struggle for over forty years.[125]

In 1928, the debate over the admittance of "unpreferred" immigrants from continental Europe was raging in the House of Commons and Lloyd was in the midst of a letter-writing spree.[126] One of these published letters clearly provoked Kirkconnell but the article he wrote in response illustrates the nature of his shifting conceptions of race. The article opened thus: "'Yes,' said an American Negro to a companion in peril, 'Us Anglo-Saxons has got to stick togedder.'"[127] Here is one of the first examples of many that illustrate how racism easily coexisted with cultural pluralism. The denigration of those racialized as non-white did not abate even as more tolerant attitudes towards European minorities continued to spread.

The reason Kirkconnell wrote this article, he made clear, was a "hysterical newspaper letter from a Saskatchewan bishop, whose Welsh name proclaims him to be either non-Nordic or a hybrid of Teuton and Mediterranean." This subtle racial slight was then followed by a denunciation of Lloyd's "insolent and un-Christian fulminations," which he suggested were the outcome of "crass ignorance of history and ethnology."[128] Turning again to his self-taught understanding of anthropology, he proceeded to educate the reader that British stock was in fact a "confused blending of dark pre-Nordic types ... with Angles, Saxons, Danes, Norwegians, and Norman-French." He continued: "Purity of British race is a figment of the imagination; yet the blended stock, fused in a national tradition of achievement, has a glorious record." He later clarified which stocks he was referencing: "the intermixture of all *the races of Europe* is not a handicap, but a positive enrichment of national life."[129] Kirkconnell suggested that blending was beneficial because racial qualities were innate and heritable, as evidenced in the Dutch being known for their law, governance, sobriety, and honesty; the Germans for their scientific and musical prowess; the Czecho-Slovaks for their rich culture; and Slavic peoples – "born lovers of the soil" – were known to be "industrious, patient, and progressive."[130]

The article was bracketed with racism, for his concluding argument alerted the reader to the possibility of forceful Asian immigration. "If we restrict this [prairie] territory to so-called Britishers," Kirkconnell warned, "it will remain sparsely settled until opened up by Oriental compulsion a century hence." Immigration might bring a population of Europeans who were poor farm and factory labourers, but they would help "build up a great and richly dowered nation." There were additional benefits as well. Revealing his continued antimodernism, Kirkconnell noted that European immigrants brought with them their own cultural arts "to alleviate both the tedium of a Western farm winter and the deadly uniformity of a Machine age." Their children could also be educated to Western standards and thus contribute to the intellectual life of the nation. Finally, this mass of European bodies would stand as a bulwark against the flood of racially inferior Asian immigrants.[131] Of course, neither Kirkconnell nor Lloyd needed to be worried about Asian immigration: in 1923, just as Kirkconnell was settling in Winnipeg, the federal government used orders-in-council to place a ban on "any immigrant of any Asiatic race" and specifically limited immigration to American citizens and British subjects from certain countries. It then followed up with the Chinese Immigration Act that effectively banned all Chinese immigration.[132]

Despite the racist overtones of the article, largely on its strength Kirkconnell has been hailed as a progressive voice in the immigration debate, and given the admission of "non-Nordic" immigrants to Canada was still a topic of heated debate, this label is not inaccurate.[133] But, as literary scholar Terrence Craig put it, Kirkconnell's stance consisted of countering "the most blatant racism with a less potent strain which ... still insisted on [immigrants'] socio-political subservience to their own established sense of Canadian norms." Craig adds that his anti-racism "only extended as far as the white 'race'" – but for Kirkconnell this was improvement.[134] However, it is important to note that Kirkconnell recommended accepting non-British, non-French, European immigrants not for altruistic reasons but because such acceptance was likely to work to the advantage of Canada's economy and culture, and because it would help keep Canada "white."

Kirkconnell's exclusion of non-Europeans is also made explicit in a volume he published in 1930, entitled *The European Heritage: A Synopsis of European Cultural Achievement*.[135] In its preface, and again drawing on his personal experience, Kirkconnell claimed that intolerance stemmed from ignorance. "Saxon and Slav, Norseman and Celt, all have gifts that have been proven great in the annals of civilization but sincere co-operation ... becomes humanly possible only as men recognize the worth of their fellow-men." The purpose of the volume was therefore to list the achievements of each of the European peoples "in the hope that it may work, even though in a very small way, for interracial respect and admiration."[136] Such a statement suggested that only Europeans were the "fellow-men" of Europeans, that only Europeans were worthy of Kirkconnell's concern.

The opening paragraph of the introduction was similarly a bald assertion of Eurocentrism. "The pre-eminence of Europe in world-history is incontestable. Asia may justly boast of the vast and enduring system of social virtues which has made China great or of the profound spiritual gifts of the Semite and the Hindu; America may acclaim the soaring marvels of the mechanical age; but the record of Europe in art, literature, science, and philosophy during the past twenty-five centuries far transcends the glories of Asia and makes the brief parade of her own transatlantic children seem garish and evanescent by comparison."[137] The entire continent of Africa, it would appear, was not invited to the contest. In fact, no peoples racialized as non-white were thought to inhabit Europe: "The peoples who inhabit Europe to-day are all of white stock," he asserted, "but may be divided into three races: the Nordic, the Mediterranean, and the Alpine."

Kirkconnell then informed the reader that the most convenient way to subdivide and study European peoples was by language. This is interesting in light of his subsequent reference to "an English-speaking negro," who would by his linguistic standard be considered English, yet was held to be "racially unrelated to the Englishman." However, this figure would not make another appearance in the book. Instead, Kirkconnell closed the introduction with an appeal to the reader to "strive to understand something of the infinite diversity [of Europe] within the majestic unity of the whole."[138] Perhaps the only surprising turnabout in this book was that Kirkconnell included some praise for "the race" of Jews. This perhaps reflects the influence of region, for by 1935 the Jewish population in Winnipeg numbered seventeen thousand. (The argument was also new, for in "Futurities," he claimed that the Jews were a single religion but a mixed race.)[139] Despite their inclusion, and his assertion that they "continue to hold a prominent place in the march of civilization," Kirkconnell delved into old, harmful stereotypes, writing of the "financial genius of the Jews" and "its supreme manifestation in the Rothschild family."[140]

Few scholars have since evaluated the work, but historian N.F. Dreisziger sympathetically remarked that it "may not have been a definitive piece of historical scholarship, but owing to its complex nature the work could have required a Herculean effort of decades of dedicated research." More significant for him was the fact that the book "probably succeeded in generating warm respect for things European in the hearts of its readers. Canada's European immigrants stood only to benefit from such feelings."[141] Not everyone would agree. The Canadian branch of the publisher recommended against publication on the grounds that "the expressed purpose of the author" was unlikely to be achieved by "a book that not one in ten thousand of these people [new Canadians] will (or can) ever read with understanding and enjoyment." While overruled by head office in London, the company's reader was not far off the mark. Once published, the book received some harsh reviews. One piece entitled "Canned Culture" suggested the book was useless: "The facts are unassimilated, unrelated – the generalisations futile. Of what use is it to be told that 'The Greeks are heirs to a glorious tradition'? That is the one thing she knows about them ; it is in fact why she has heard of them."[142]

Kirkconnell was undeterred. Perhaps triggered by the ongoing debates and the work of nativists like Bishop Lloyd, he recognized that many other Canadians shared the same mistaken racial beliefs about Europe that he had just shed and sought to reach them. He truly believed that if they could have a similar experience, if they could come to a realization of the beauty of European cultures and literatures (and specifically poetry), they too would embrace all European groups and their descendants in Canada.[143] To raise awareness, he began translating European poetry into English and writing about significant non-British, non-French, European authors.[144]

## RACE AND CULTURAL PLURALISM

Kirkconnell has been repeatedly linked to the development of cultural pluralism and even Canadian multiculturalism. For instance, in his important essay "Reluctant Hosts," historian Howard Palmer suggested that Kirkconnell and John Murray Gibbon were lone advocates for a multicultural society in Canada during the interwar period.[145] Other scholars have made similar assessments, with one going so far as to argue Kirkconnell was "the father of Canadian multiculturalism."[146] But works that suggest multiculturalism represents the end of Canada's history of prejudice towards ethnic minorities present an inaccurate and teleological interpretation of a more complicated history. In the case of Kirkconnell, it is more accurate to say that, in the process of becoming involved with European minority groups and their literatures, he began to express some opinions about their integration into Canadian society. He believed that pride in their cultural heritage would make them better citizens, and he advocated for Anglo-Canadians' acceptance and celebration of these cultures. The statements he made to this effect in the 1930s came in the form of comments on translated European poetry. Continuing to follow Quentin Skinner's textual approach, the remainder of this chapter examines Kirkconnell's purposes in translating and compiling these poems, before turning its attention to the vision for group integration that he expressed within them.

## Early Projects

During the interwar period, English and French Canadians were slowly being exposed to the cultural expressions of people of non-British, non-French European descent, through events such as the CPR-sponsored festivals organized by John Murray Gibbon. In Winnipeg, the "Folk-song and Handicraft Festival" was held in June 1928, and Kirkconnell translated sixteen folksongs from various languages into English for the Festival's programs.[147] Despite the display of artistic talents, Kirkconnell viewed these as vestiges of the Old World and seemed unaware that these groups continued to produce literary and cultural works. Kirkconnell conceptualized culture as a person's national and racial inheritance, one that did not change and evolve but rather was static and bounded. So, while he was becoming increasingly aware of the cultural expressions of so-called new Canadians, his translation efforts remained focused on the classical literatures of Europe.

At least one scholar has suggested that Kirkconnell's involvement with so-called new Canadians was a result of his grief, but the process of his becoming involved with this group was not as direct as it has been made out to be.[148] His initial interest was in the poems and not the peoples of Europe. Indeed, the translations that comprised *European Elegies* had not originally been undertaken with the goal of fostering unity among European nations, although by the time of its publication he expressed hope it would assist in that task. As he put it: "Modern nations are unhappily isolated and estranged by their very loyalties to speech, kin, and faith. But in the presence of the ultimate they may all join hands in community of spirit. Beyond race and creed and language are the fundamental sanctities of human life – love, tenderness, sorrow, fortitude. This little volume is, for the translator at least, a Siloam of these healing waters ... I gain strength from the hope that it may contribute its stream to the ocean of understanding." Judith Woodsworth, a scholar of translation theory and history, suggests that this ideal of reaching humanity through translation was a unique idea in an otherwise ubiquitous introduction.[149] Indeed, his passion to this end should not be underestimated, as it led him to some ambitious projects.

Perhaps in a throwback to his Queen's-era vision of a "comprehensive knowledge of languages and literatures," around 1927 he proposed a colossal volume of *Occidental Poetry*. The book would trace the development of such poetry from its roots in Greco-Roman, Germanic, and Celtic traditions, from the Middle Ages through the Romantic era, and would be illustrated throughout with his own translations. Early on in the project, he contemplated changing from a chronological to a linguistic and regional approach and as a trial run composed a six-part "Outline of European Poetry," published in the widely circulated *Western Home Monthly* in 1927.[150] However, he soon realized that one volume would not be enough, so he eventually concocted his most grandiose scheme yet: a twenty-four volume series entitled *North American Books of European Verse*, which he planned to publish over a period of twelve years.

He originally claimed that the impetus for the project was this desire for unity among European nations. As he wrote to his friend, the author Frederick Philip Grove, "I feel there is in the racial and national diversities in Canada a challenge to the best I have to give ; that I am prepared to devote the best years of my life to interpreting the European tradition to Canada and the peoples of Europe (in Canada) to one another."[151] In the preface to *The North American Book of Icelandic Verse* (the first of the series), he expanded on his reasons for writing. The first was a lifelong interest in languages, and the second was "a compelling sense of great opportunity": to perpetuate the finest elements of the Old World in order to enrich the life of the New World. European immigrants would be better citizens if they proudly drank "from the springs of their ancestral literatures," he suggested.[152]

Kirkconnell was truly motivated to embark on translation projects for three reasons. The first was his deep interest in languages, the second was his goal of promoting understanding and appreciation of European cultures, and the third was to gain personal recognition.[153] One critic, Wilson MacDonald, was particularly vicious in describing this third goal. MacDonald was known for being thin-skinned, but Kirkconnell had for some reason singled him out for fierce criticism. In response, MacDonald retorted that Kirkconnell's motivation for translation could be understood thus: "I must praise Icelandic poetry because the man for whom I have the greatest admiration (Mr. K. himself) has translated Icelandic poetry. In glorifying Iceland I hope to also glorify Kirkconnell."[154]

While there is no doubt some accuracy to MacDonald's critique, Canadians' attention to literature in languages other than English or French during this period was exceedingly rare. Although it is nearly impossible to assess the impact that Kirkconnell's efforts had on Canadians of English or French descent, his works met generally favourable reviews and at least some of his readers were convinced that European literature was of merit. Such readers included members of his own family. After sending her a copy of his "Polish Miscellany" in 1935, Kirkconnell's Aunt Ella wrote to thank him. "It was nice of you to send me a copy of the translations of Polish verse. I had such a queer idea of the Middle European peoples – half savage &c, something like this – 'unwashed, unlettered, and unreadable,' – but [Watson]! 'Matutinal Light' & 'Songs on the birth of Our Lord' have given me quite new thoughts. I cannot recall anything *more* beautiful even by our own people, than the 'Song,' and so fitting to the needs of *our Canada* at this present moment."[155] It is difficult to say how many people held similar views of European peoples, but Aunt Ella's was likely not an uncommon opinion in her community of Port Hope. Worth noting, though, is that she had encountered these poems once they had been divorced from their original context, and that she thought them to be suited to the needs of "our" Canada.

Historian Franca Iacovetta uses the term "gatekeepers" to describe the group of Canadians who, during the Cold War, worked with immigrants with the goal of integrating them into mainstream society, and she included Kirkconnell among them.[156] However, Kirkconnell can also be considered a gatekeeper from a much earlier era. By selecting which literary works he deemed to be of sufficient artistic value, and translating them into English, Kirkconnell established himself as a cultural gatekeeper, a gatekeeper between so-called new Canadian cultures and English Canadian culture. In this capacity, he would decide which writings would be preserved in an accessible, translated format and which would be forgotten.

Kirkconnell was confident of the value of his "Books of Verse" project, and his efforts may have helped convince some people of these cultures, but as a whole it got off to an inauspicious start before descending into disaster. The Canadian branches of two publishers, Macmillan and J.M. Dent, turned down the project before Louis Carrier of Montreal finally accepted it. In the meantime, Kirkconnell kept ploughing his own money into materials. He had spent $750 by the end of May 1929 (adjusted for inflation, this amounts to over $11,000 in 2019).[157]

That this was on the eve of his engagement to Hope Kitchener shows the depth of his commitment. Kirkconnell had proposed to Hope, a young woman from Lindsay who lived on the same street as his parents, in the summer of 1929. He hoped that she would agree, they would marry, and she would return to Winnipeg with him for the start of the fall term. But Hope was aware of the responsibilities she would be taking on, not the least of which included his two young sons, and so she deliberated for a year before eventually agreeing. According to a later friend of the couple, Hope knew she would say yes but wanted "a year in which to read books and attend classes on how to be mother to five year old boys."[158] Whatever the reason, the delay must have stung him, but worse news was yet to come.

Carrier had contracted an American firm for a simultaneous release of the first volume in both countries, and Kirkconnell had an entire manuscript of the second volume (on Magyar Verse) completed. He also had plans to take the book to Iceland in 1930, in time for the millennial year of Icelandic Parliament. Then Carrier went bankrupt. Kirkconnell could have temporarily delayed or even abandoned the project, but he apparently did not seriously consider these options and instead spent more money to have the volume printed and bound.[159] Undaunted, he continued with his translation efforts, and in the next few years turned from an interest in only Old World European cultures to an examination of the literary efforts of Canadians of non-British, non-French, European descent.

Postcolonial theorists argue that Europeans who travelled to "foreign lands" first assimilated information, prejudices, and myths about the land before travelling. After having travelled, they then wrote their own accounts and thereby added new information to and amended the canon. The discourse of discovery therefore involved modes both of imagination and inquiry, and served to organize and categorize the formerly unknown into a "knowable, manageable entity."[160] Kirkconnell's writings about European peoples can be similarly interpreted, as they were yet another example in a long line of works seeking to categorize and manage immigrants to Canada. While not sailing to a "new" land, he was nevertheless scouting out a territory – physical and literary – that the numerically dominant group (racialized as Anglo-Saxon) viewed as foreign.

Previous texts that dealt with the perceived problem of foreign immigrants had constructed precise hierarchies, the best-known example of which is perhaps J.S. Woodsworth's *Strangers Within Our Gates* (1909).[161] Kirkconnell's first approach had been comparatively simple: all non-Nordics ought to be prohibited from coming to Canada. With his slightly revised understanding of race science, he now was in favour of allowing all European immigrants a chance but wanted to ensure they became good citizens. In his mind, this could be done by making such immigrants proud of their racial origins. What was particularly new in this approach was his attention to cultural works being produced by Canadians of non-British, non-French, European origins. Kirkconnell's writings on the subject can be considered part of a discourse of discovery, as he sought to organize, categorize, and translate this body of work in order to convince his fellow Canadians of the humanity of its authors.

Kirkconnell began by collecting many of so-called new Canadians' published works, seeking out biographical and bibliographical information.[162] As always, his interest was particularly in poetry, and his focus on writings in languages other than English or French stemmed from his belief that when first-generation non-Anglo-Saxons tried their hand at English verse the result was nothing better than doggerel.[163] However, he was proud to credit himself with having "discovered" their poetic output written in mother tongues.[164] When pitching an article on Icelandic-Canadian poetry to a journal, he described it as an important and pioneering work but nevertheless prepared for rejection: "This is the by-product of several years of study in the Icelandic literature of Iceland and Canada. It is absolutely pioneer work in the history of Canadian poetry, and its publication may conceivably be regarded as a milestone by our literary historians ... Return postage enclosed."[165] That same year he also published an article about his discovery of "Ukrainian Canadiana," that is, the existence and contents of an extensive library belonging to a prominent Ukrainian politician and educator, Ivan Bobersky, who was living in Winnipeg at the time. He similarly described this to the editor as "spade-work in virgin soil."[166] He felt this literary exploration was of such importance that, in his memoirs, he wagered the one thing he would be remembered for in a hundred years would be that "single-handedly I discovered, surveyed, and recorded in Canada's cultural Registry of Deeds this collectivity of literary achievement."[167]

*Metaphors of Assimilation: Tapestry, Icebergs, Overtones*

Kirkconnell used a variety of terms and metaphors to describe diversity in Canada, including assimilation, digestion, grafting, icebergs (melting), integration, mincemeat, omelette, overtones, salad, symbiosis, and tapestry. This section examines three of his earliest and most commonly used metaphors in order to better understand Kirkconnell's philosophy of cultural pluralism. Each is examined in the context of the publication or publications in which it originally appeared, though some meaning is drawn from the metaphors themselves. Namely, the tapestry implied a careful integration that nevertheless retained some colours of immigrants' home cultures. The metaphor of the melting iceberg, most often used in connection with language, implied a slow and inevitable decline in native language use and as such a degree of cultural assimilation. Finally, the concept of overtones was similar to the tapestry vision, in that it suggested a conscious and intentional blending.

In the preface to his *Book of Icelandic Verse*, Kirkconnell first employed the tapestry metaphor in a passage intended to reassure the reader that his project was not to intended to "Balkanize the New World." He continued: "I do not suggest that fifty linguistic communities be left in uncoordinated isolation, without the integrating influences of an advanced system of education. But I do claim that every effort should be made, especially by the higher educational authorities, to weave into the fabric of national consciousness the brightest threads of European culture." He added that consciousness of great past achievements would be a stimulus to similar achievements in the future. "Mutual knowledge, mutual sympathy, mutual emulation in cultural attainments would surely shape a national life of astonishing richness ... What better gift could North America make to the world than the creation of a society in which cultural catholicity of sympathy and enlightenment was the birthright of every citizen?"[168] Underlying this vision was the assumption that immigrants would gradually lose their original tongue and learn English, and that the state would play an active role in the process of integration, particularly through the school system. European cultures, vestiges of the Old World, were to be preserved in translations to make immigrants proud of their ancestry and to spur them towards similar greatness in Canada. The tapestry would be bright but woven tightly together, and all its strands would be European.[169]

Kirkconnell's analysis of these literatures also employed the tapestry metaphor. In an unpublished paper on "New Canadians in Manitoba," he observed that reactions to the diversity of languages on the Prairies had too often been racial prejudice and intolerance. But, he countered, "while there are genuine dangers in this temporary Babel of tongues and jostling of traditions, there are promises at least worth the risk." The reason for hope was found in his new understanding of race. He explained that "a blending of human strains is normal and invigorating," and that the mixture in Manitoba would eventually result in "a strong unity of loyal tradition embodied in a rich diversity of human elements." He then turned to a discussion of the three main "stocks," "types," or "races" in Manitoba, which he identified as Germanic, Scandinavian, and Slavic. After outlining the achievements of each new Canadian group, he concluded: "In the tapestry of Manitoban history five centuries hence, the threads of 'New Canadian' achievement will form a conspicuous part of the glory of the pattern."[170]

Around this time, Kirkconnell began to grapple with the idea of Canada's national literature, especially as he became increasingly aware of the literary output of these so-called new Canadians.[171] In an address to the CAA on the subject, he argued that Canada did not yet have a national literature, but one way it could develop was if writers became familiar with a wide variety of literatures. For those in Western Canada, this meant exploring literature from a number of European countries.[172] Although he originally referred to English, French, and Icelandic poetry, within a few years he began to speak of a "third Canadian poetry" written in Icelandic, Swedish, Ukrainian, Hungarian, and Italian.[173] Speaking about some of these specific groups in this category, he repeated the same argument: that in Canada the languages would die out with time but that the poetry already written in those languages was valuable. "That such [Icelandic] poetry is only a transient chapter in our literary history,

I am regretfully confident," Kirkconnell wrote in one such instance. The Icelandic language would melt away "in the warmer seas of English speech," and without continued immigration it would cease to be spoken in Canada by the end of the century. However, he argued that the early literature written in Icelandic ought to be translated into English so those of Icelandic heritage could be reminded of the greatness of their ancestors and so English-speaking Canadians could appreciate Icelandic-Canadians' rich cultural heritage.[174]

Kirkconnell later more fully explained this iceberg metaphor while discussing the process of assimilation in the United States. In an article on George Kemény, a Magyar-American poet, he wrote that icebergs melting in the sea were "symbols of European migrants" who came to the United States, where their ultimate destiny was one of assimilation. "On cultural grounds, the loss of their racial identity is greatly to be deplored," he wrote, explaining that it was completely justified for Magyars and others to prize evidence of their "individuality" before they were "absorbed" by broader society. He continued on to argue that, while the extinction of the Hungarian language in America was likely inevitable, its poetry would constitute a priceless record of these early generations' experiences.[175] By introducing the iceberg metaphor in these two articles, Kirkconnell suggested that even in Canada the process for immigrants (whether integration or assimilation) was to include linguistic assimilation and that it was not to be forced but rather was slow, natural, and inevitable.

The year 1935 marked the high point of Kirkconnell's engagement with literature written by Canadians of non-British, non-French, European descent with the publication of an anthology entitled *Canadian Overtones*.[176] As the subtitle explains, the book was a collection of poems "originally written in Icelandic, Swedish, Norwegian, Hungarian, Italian, Greek, and Ukrainian ... translated and edited with biographical, historical, critical, and bibliographical notes." (Kirkconnell had some assistance compiling the volume; Honoré Ewach, a Ukrainian Canadian friend of his, helped by combing the back files of "ethnic" newspapers for poetry, though his work seems to have gone unacknowledged.[177]) In its preface Kirkconnell expanded on his vision for Canada, first expressed five years before in his *Book of Icelandic Verse*. He stated while the published poetry of "New Canadians" exceeded the output of French- and Anglo-Canadians, he was "regretfully confident" this was only a transitory phase. Immigrants typically lost their native tongue and by the third generation spoke only English, and without "continuous reinforcements of new immigrant stock, or a change in the Canadian attitude towards the non-Anglo-Saxon traditions, the impulse towards creative expression in a variety of European tongues will inevitably languish and die."[178] However, he argued, brevity was not an indication of futility and therefore the "newer Canadian poetry" that was truly artistic would remain a cherished possession of those who could appreciate it. Acting as a cultural gatekeeper, he alone would be the judge of what was truly artistic.

Kirkconnell then proceeded to criticize Canadians for their attitude towards immigrants. "Our national attitude towards them has already passed through two ignorant and discreditable phases. In the first, we tended to despise them as European coolies, imported to do heavy work for which our hands had already grown too delicate. In the second and more recent phase, we have been patronizingly interested in their folk-costumes and folk-dances, picturesque incidentals."[179] Here again, even in Kirkconnell's own declarations of tolerance he included racially charged reference, this time to "coolies," indicative of his continued ambivalence for non-European peoples. As for European peoples, he remained optimistic about their futures once they immigrated to Canada. New Canadian poetry could help native-born Canadians develop "a third and much truer attitude towards them [immigrants], as men and women as capable as any amongst us of appreciating the beauties and philosophies of this world."[180] Kirkconnell concluded the preface with a radical suggestion.

> Our constitution is founded on the federal principle. Our nation could not do better than to take "confederation" as its motto in culture and education. Our national holidays might well be given over to such pageantry (including, perhaps, festivals of drama, poetry, and music) as would emphasize the co-operative existence of the distinct racial groups in our population. Our schools might give ample recognition to their history and culture. Our universities might foster their languages and literatures, or even set up an Institute of Cultural Traditions to preserve and encourage all that may contribute to the diversity of our cultural life.[181]

Kirkconnell wanted every Canadian to become aware of their lineage and membership in family, clan, and race, as he believed this "conscious pride in the past" would instil in them a "determination to be worthy of it." Encouraging cultural diversity through the retention of ancestral cultures was therefore designed to create better citizens.

Kirkconnell's vision of pride in one's ancestral past leading to better citizenship is made clear in a later poem. In "The Parson's Tale of the Gimli Prodigal," he wrote about an Icelandic youth, Olga, who turns to a life of crime, is imprisoned, and upon his release finds himself ostracized from his community. However, in a moment of crisis he heads out to his certain doom on stormy waters in an attempt to save an errant boat with three fishermen aboard. Kirkconnell describes Olga's motivation thus:

Out of his far Icelandic past
Heroic impulse now beat purely
To argue him a man at last.
His father, Helgi, once had taught him
His lineage of a thousand years;
And now, perhaps, remembrance caught him
Perhaps that roll-call filled his ears –
...
And in his ear he heard them speaking,
Those generations in his blood;
Dim in his mind he saw them seeking
...
Thus as he stood there in his place
He quenched all thought of love or self
Uplifted on a tide of race
That made him greater than himself.[182]

Kirkconnell made clear that there was still to be a unifying force within a culturally federated Canada. That immigrants should be "speedily integrated into loyal co-operation with our general Canadian population is, of course, of supreme national importance," he wrote, but such integration should not involve the stripping away of past culture.[183] When referring to their literatures, he employed the metaphor of overtones. The term is taken from musical theory and refers to tones not typically observed. As professor of music Ed Sarath explains: "When a note sounds, which we call the *fundamental*, it generates a series of additional tones, called *overtones*, which are generally not consciously perceived by listeners. Usually only the fundamental is heard."[184] In this analogy then, Canadian poetry was the fundamental, while these poems created by so-called "new Canadians" were the overtones. These overtones were not quite Canadian and were not normally perceived, and thus had to be brought to all Canadians' attention in order to "vitalize" citizenship. These were not separate notes but formed part of one national literature.[185]

Yet even *Canadian Overtones*, a text which contains Kirkconnell's most radical ideas for a culturally pluralistic Canada, was marked by racialism and indeed racism that excluded all non-Europeans. Emphasizing the importance of the "racial constitution" of both the individual and the nation, he suggested that "a man's spiritual life" was as "naturally nourished by his racial ethos as a plant by the soil to which ecology has adapted it. Orchids do not flourish on clay nor wheat and barley in a peat bog. It is through recognition of this principle that the newer educational policies in British tropical Africa are seeking to evolve good Africans and not imitation Europeans." Here was the same racially essentialist logic first expounded in "Anglo-Canadian Futurities" some fifteen years prior: African peoples simply could not be "grown" in North America, nor would North Americans flourish in Africa. The passage further suggested that African peoples were not currently in a state to be considered "good" and instead had to be paternalistically and scientifically managed, educated, and ultimately "evolved" by Europeans.[186]

Given their consistent exclusion from consideration in Kirkconnell's writings, it is perhaps surprising to find that his only published children's story included an African Canadian character. Published a few years later, in 1939, the book places the character in a stereotypical role: unnamed, he is simply referred to as the "negro porter." Once introduced, the porter then has the following interchange with Timothy, the protagonist.

"Aren't you sorry that you're black?" said Timothy. "Don't you wish you were white like me?"

"Why no!" laughed the porter. "You see, black is the natural color for people in this world. You white people have been bleached, like celery or potato-sprouts in a dark cellar. You're the freaks and we black people are just the right color."

"I never thought of that," remarked Timothy. "Are you sure that's right?"

"Of course it's right," answered the porter. "Now the conductor calls me the Black Knight. You see nights are always black except when the moon comes up; but I'm still black even then. I'm more natural than night, I am."[187]

Many years later, J.R.C. Perkin, a scholar who succeeded Kirkconnell as president of Acadia University, would point to this as proof that Kirkconnell held no racial prejudice,[188] but this is a doubtful conclusion. The story is populated by "strange figures of the universe of dreams," and the narrator remarks that Timothy "didn't follow all the [porter's] line of reasoning." Given Kirkconnell's other remarks about African Canadians, a more likely interpretation is that the character of the porter is intended as a humorous portrayal of a confused "negro," much like the racist joke Kirkconnell told twenty years before in which an African American soldier confidently declared himself to be an Anglo-Saxon.[189]

Similarly, despite an increasing knowledge of Indigenous peoples and their histories, Kirkconnell continued to exclude them from his consideration. When he moved to Winnipeg, he eventually became aware of Métis peoples and, predictably, the idea of race shaped his perception of them. His 1940 poem, "The Priest's Tale of the Red River Tragedy," begins with one character remarking that in such "blends ... the Indian never seems to pass from sight," but doubting that the "authentic strain" ever came back to the surface. A Métis priest then contradicts him by telling the tale of two young Métis men, Adolphe and Jacques, both rivalling for the love of a young woman named Marie. Kirkconnell first sets the story within the context of ancient times, when Cree supposedly killed humans and placed them in the Red River in order to placate "the grim spirit of the flood." Centuries pass, "Indian fire and arrogance" is "mingled with the blood of France," and the resulting Métis become Christians and forget the requisite sacrifice. Returning to the present, the Priest tells the story of how, catching Marie with Adolphe, Jacques shoots at his rival but accidentally kills Marie. Enraged, Adolphe kills Jacques. Then, in a "primitive" and "pagan" fit, Adolphe scalps Jacques, lets out the "war-whoop of the ancient Cree," gathers Marie in his arms, and jumps into the river.[190] Kirkconnell thereby seemed to suggest that Métis peoples would atavistically return to "purest savage" in the heat of passion.[191]

That his beliefs were rooted in the supposed science of race is confirmed in another poem, in which he wrote that Métis people led

Figure 1.3 The "negro porter" from Kirkconnell's storybook.

"baffled lives" filled with a sense of deep rejection due to "an inner conflict of genetic drives / That strains their living and their lexicons / Unapt in tongue or discipline to be / A perfect Frenchman or a perfect Cree."[192] If Kirkconnell's appraisal is taken as representative, people of non-European descent in Canadian society therefore remained largely, to use David Austin's term, "un-visible": visible but not acknowledged.[193] In his paper on "New Canadians in Manitoba," for instance, Kirkconnell recognized that, as late as 1870, the land had had a majority population of "Indians and half-breeds." However, he did not go on to discuss their history or literature.[194] In a piece written around 1932, Kirkconnell argued that speaking of Canadian poetry required him to consider "at least three poetries – that of the French language, the English language, and the Icelandic language. We could also add the poetry that is mingled in the folklore of the wild Indian races." However, he chose not to examine that canon.[195] Six years later, he was a bit more generous in his description when he spoke of the "fifty Indian and Eskimo languages, many of them rich in oral traditions of legend, myth, and folk-poetry," but again he provided no examples and instead focused exclusively on the other fifty languages "brought here ... by the newer colonists of a pioneer land."[196]

His troubling treatment of Indigenous peoples is best illustrated in another piece in which he described poet E. Pauline Johnson as a "gifted half-breed." The "rhapsodic Romanticism of her style vitiated the credibility of her Indian types," he argued. "Much more convincing has been the firm, quiet work of Duncan Campbell Scott."[197] Kirkconnell did not seem to notice the deep irony of his preference for the "Indian sketches" of the deputy superintendent of the Department of Indian Affairs over the writings of an "Indian." In his mind, the "Indian types" were all the same, and while intermarriage or racial mixing had allowed some writings to emerge, these were incredible—that is, *not* credible. Kirkconnell may have become more accepting of all Europeans but in his mind non-Europeans remained threads that could not and would not be woven into the Canadian tapestry.

Kirkconnell remained convinced of Anglo-Saxons' racial superiority, particularly in the realm of politics, and continued to be deeply concerned about their numerical decline in Canada. In 1937, Kirkconnell contributed a poem to an edited collection of essays published by the University of Manitoba to mark the institution's sixtieth anniversary. In it, he presented two potential futures. One, in a cyclic vision of history, saw the Anglo-Saxons going extinct much like Indigenous peoples supposedly had before them. "The Red Man passes like the lordly bison / That once he slaughtered with exultant cry," one section begins. "Assiniboine and Sioux are vanished faces, / And now the Celt and Saxon likewise wane, / Passing away and leaving other races / To rule the ancient marches of the Plain." The alternative to civilizational decay would see the region, led by leaders shaped by higher learning, "blending the threescore races of our prairies / Into a stream of living nationhood."[198] Ironically, this was the first decade to witness an increase in the population of "status Indians," at least according to the Canadian state's own undoubtedly conservative count. (The figures were released in 1934, three years before Kirkconnell's poem appeared.)[199]

That same year he expressed these fears in an article titled "Thoughts for Dominion Day." Despite repeating the claim that a blending of races resulted in great cultural achievement, he was nevertheless alarmed to find that "elements neither French nor Anglo-Saxon" had increased by 45 per cent in the decade 1921–31. If this trend were to continue, he warned, "the French" would outnumber Anglo-Canadians within a generation, and within a century both would be outnumbered by "the non-English-non-French-group." He then warned: "Ultimately,

Ontario will be French as far west as Toronto, and the Anglo-Saxon stock will be a negligible factor on the far-flung Western prairies ... It is a matter of simple actuarial arithmetic that any racial group that does not average nearly four children per marriage will pass out of existence in a couple of centuries." He continued: "When a racial group, such as the Anglo-Canadian, is not willing to maintain such a birth-rate, it must be prepared to view with equanimity its replacement by other races to whom a normal human family is still a welcome possession." Although a blending of races was "potentially a source of cultural achievement," there first had to be a degree of "conscious integration" in order for Canada to fulfill the ideal of nationhood as defined by French political theorist Ernest Renan: "the memory of great things done together and the desire to achieve still more." The way to achieve such a conscious integration, Kirkconnell suggested, was to recognize that each racial group had a contribution to make to Canadian society. As such, the finer elements of their legacy had to be cherished.

This was the same argument he had been making for nearly a decade, but now he added a disclaimer: it was equally important to "slough off those elements that are inferior." Kirkconnell viewed Canada's racial diversity as making the achievement of national unity a "problem of extraordinary difficulty." One important part of solving this problem was ensuring that the political self-consciousness of each group was "lost in a common loyalty to Canada" while their cultural consciousness was retained. Here was a model of bifurcation in which cultures were to be carefully integrated while politics were to be assimilated. Kirkconnell believed that schools were the institution most responsible for ensuring such a program would be successful. These were Kirkconnell's thoughts for Dominion Day, a stark eugenic warning to Anglo-Canadians. The article marked the continued evolution of his thought and shows that, even before the pressures of the Second World War, he was already returning to his eugenic concerns about the numerical superiority of Anglo-Canadians, the political loyalty of "the non-English-non-French group," and the development of nationhood in Canada.[200]

CONCLUSION

Between 1895 and 1937, Kirkconnell's thought evolved dramatically, from a rather uncritical sense of British superiority as a schoolchild, to a eugenicist and Nordicist of the most extreme sort as a young man, and finally to the culturally pluralistic philosophy – with its "tapestry" metaphor – of his adulthood. The first transition was the result of his independent studies, which drew on the work of Anglo-American scholars and theorists, and is seen in some of his early publications. He never openly acknowledged a transition away from this extreme position, nor did he apologize for it, but it was clearly triggered by an exposure to ethnic diversity and by the emotional experience of loss. Consistent throughout his life, however, was a belief that race was a biological reality that determined individual characteristics. He also clung to the idea of Anglo-Saxon superiority in the realm of governance and retained a related eugenic concern about the numerical decline of Anglo-Canadians. His interest in European cultures was genuine but it was also shaped by his desire for greatness. As chapter 5 details, this desire was realized to some degree during the Second World War, when his expertise on "racial minorities" was recognized and utilized by the state and garnered him a wide audience among the general public.

Kirkconnell's work with semi-official and official government attempts to promote cultural pluralism would bring him into contact with Robert England, another recognized expert on race and immigration. The two had similar philosophies of cultural pluralism but there were some significant differences. Kirkconnell believed that assimilation was a slow, natural, and inevitable process, and suggested that some aspects of immigrant cultures ought to be preserved and celebrated. Much like him, England believed that cultural particularities were in part the result of an individual's racial heritage, though he stressed the importance of the interaction between racial heritage and the physical and cultural environment of the "New World." England was in favour of immigrants retaining some aspects of their culture, but he believed that more active steps needed to be taken to ensure the unity of all racial groups, and therefore suggested a shared notion of Canadian citizenship as the vehicle for ensuring this unity.

2

# Robert England and Canadian Citizenship

## INTRODUCTION

In the summer of 1975, the historian Howard Palmer, who was researching the history of Anglo-Canadian attitudes towards immigrants and ethnic minorities in Alberta, first reached out to Robert England, a retiree, by letter. Despite his name, England (1894–1985) was an Irish immigrant to Canada who, during the 1920s and '30s, had worked to recruit European immigrants for the Canadian National Railways (CNR) and had commented on the issue of immigration to Canada in various articles and books. Palmer was keen to learn more about his life and work and was fortunate that England responded positively to the inquiry. The following March England travelled with his wife to the University of Calgary, where he attended one of Palmer's classes and gave a public lecture. Sometime during the visit, Palmer also took the opportunity to interview him.

Towards the end of the interview, Palmer brought up a quote containing the phrase "better eugenic types," which had appeared in England's book *The Central European Immigrant in Canada* (1929). He explained that the line had recently been quoted in a paper presented at a multiculturalism conference, where it had been used to argue that England believed cultural traits were transmitted racially. "Now are they distorting what you said …?" Palmer asked.[1] "Oh I think so … [that] deduction [is] a long ways off," England stammered. But then his answer got confusing, as he turned to arguing that only physical traits, not cultural traits, were transmitted.

[E:] Some degree of heredity exists. How much is heredity and how much is environment is very, very hard to determine. But there is bound to be [some heredity], otherwise, you wouldn't have any real differentiation at all of ethnic groups ...
P: Do you mean physical or cultural?
E: Physical, [physical in the main].[2] The thing that I maintained was that you were more likely to find what you might call an ethnic characteristic transmitted through the mother than through the father. You'd often find that difference. If you mixed an Indian with an Anglo-Saxon, it's often the mother's characteristics that show up in the sons.[3]

Palmer asked a number of follow-up questions until England finally denied that cultural traits were physically transmitted. Palmer then sympathetically remarked that his statement about eugenics must have been "taken out of context." Yet throughout the exchange, England affirmed some of his older statements about race, all of which suggested a belief in "racial" types and their distinctive cultural traits.

E: What [the author] should have done, if he wanted to check that, he should have taken that whole paragraph there and he'd have found that stated it quite clearly, that "we can never make a German an Anglo-Saxon, anymore than we can make an Englishman, Irish. But if civilization is rich enough ... it will use its [peoples'] various racial traits to advantage." This is quite true. "The recognition that God has written a line of his thought on the cradle of each race doesn't mean any loss of love for country."
P: I guess this "eugenic type" quote, would have some affinity with Nordic, Alpine and Mediterranean strains (traits).
E: That's the general pattern of European immigration and of writers at that time fifty years ago, I don't think that classification would be valid today in ethnology but in the days when I was writing, ethnology accepted the pattern of Mediterranean and Nordic and Alpine ... And that pretty well covered all the white race in Europe at the time. But [mark you] it leaves outside that the [Celtic] groups. Irish and Scots and also Welsh and Cornish. They're not Nordic.[4]

This interchange so clearly demonstrates the staying power of the idea of race and all its attendant confusions. Earlier on in the interview, England had spoken unselfconsciously of Canadian history as a record of the cooperation between "the Anglo-Saxons and the other races who came here." When Palmer eventually pressed him on the question of race, his primary concern was whether or not England believed that cultural (i.e., non-physiological) characteristics were transmitted biologically. While backing away from the terminology of the earlier period, and insisting that race was simply about physical characteristics such as gait, in his response England nevertheless revealed his continued belief that race determined cultural characteristics.

The philosophy of cultural pluralism that emerges from this interview is one in which the state harnessed immigrants' various racial traits to its advantage; it was a vision of a country in which all of God's thoughts were brought together in one racial mosaic. This chapter details how England's particular version of cultural pluralism was formed and changed over time. It is divided into two parts: the first details his intellectual development, from his early life through his studies in Paris. The second part examines the interrelated processes of his continued studies and the direct application of his subsequent theories through his position with the CNR. As a whole, the chapter demonstrates that as an avid student of rural development, psychology, and sociology, England developed his own ideas about integration and assimilation, and argues that these ideas were rooted in a framework of race. Despite this racial framework, he was more sympathetic than some of his peers to immigrants and, in his written works, he stressed the fundamental unity of European peoples. However, in his writings he was also uncritical about the process of settler colonialism and almost always excluded those racialized as non-white from consideration.

## INTELLECTUAL DEVELOPMENT

Robert England was born on 15 September 1894 in Portadown, now part of the city of Craigavon but at the time a town of about six thousand, in Northern Ireland. He was the thirteenth of fourteen children born to Elizabeth (1851–1922) and David England (1851–1910).[5] Once their children reached the age of twelve or thirteen they went to work on the farms of relatives and neighbours and

Figure 2.1 Robert England.

most went on to spend their adult lives in the local linen factory. The town was very Presbyterian and anti-Catholic, and while the family was deeply religious, the Englands differed from the majority as they were Methodists who did not hold the same degree of anti-Catholicism. (A reviewer of his memoirs erroneously gave the family denomination as Presbyterian, to which England wryly remarked, "I think my Methodist upbringing was *not* 'an austere Presbyterian environment,' *not* quite so *grim* as that.") The children grew up with regular church attendance and, at home, frequent readings from the Bible, sermons, and tracts, and repeated warnings against tobacco, liquor, and swearing. In his memoirs, England described his childhood milieu as "an austere environment of patient industry, unremitting thrift, and devout living." The "escape" from this scene, he added, seems to have been almost miraculous.[6]

As a boy, England first escaped to Canada in his mind as he read novels like Ralph Connor's *The Sky Pilot* (1899) and gained a "romantic vision of Western Canada," that "frontier" land, as a place of adventure, romance, and hard work.[7] As a young boy, he looked up to his older brother Nicholas, who rejected the family upbringing early on and turned to adventure and drink. Nicholas was also the first family member to actually visit this often-imagined place, as he made repeated trips to Canada. However, each time he returned to Ireland where he eventually spent three years in the British Army as a member of the Royal Irish Fusiliers. England admitted that while he remained one of the family's "rather exemplary boys," he quite liked Nick's "way with horses, his daring, his love of Canada, and his determination to return there after his three years' military service."[8] England's Sunday school teacher, Jimmy Kellow, stimulated further interest in Canada. Kellow had once visited the country and drew on these experiences in his class, where he taught the children in his class to sing "The Maple Leaf Forever" and "O Canada" and filled their heads with visions of "winter practices and cutters, bob-sleighs, coyotes, and winter clothing and meals. Was there ever such a conditioning for life in Canada for a small boy?" England later wondered.[9]

However, England's move to Canada was by no means inevitable. He first began training to teach elementary school, working as a monitor in the Thomas Street National Schools from 1910 to 1912. At the urgings of his brother Jack, he abandoned these studies and made plans to become a Methodist minister. The church selected young men to attend the Methodist College in Belfast for three years and they often would then attend Queen's University (Belfast) to obtain an arts degree. This was his desired path, but when he took an entrance examination at age eighteen he did so well that the church decided he was ready to be sent out as a probationary minister. According to his memoirs, he did not feel he was mature enough to set out as a preacher, so he opted instead to head for Canada. Sailing in 1914, he listed his occupation as a clergyman, but it is unclear what work he intended to pursue in Canada.[10]

After he arrived in Canada, England eventually ended up in Saskatchewan.[11] "I was schooled in the idea that life on the frontier was hard, tough, romantic, that only the strong could survive, and I wanted to meet the challenge," he later wrote. He worked on farms and at a variety of jobs before deciding to register at Queen's University (Kingston) as an extramural (distance) student in English, Greek, and philosophy. These studies were cut short with the onset of the Great War and his decision in 1915 to enlist. He trained at Camp Hughes in Manitoba, and then went to France as a lieutenant with the 203rd Battalion of the Canadian Expeditionary Force.[12] He fought in the battles of Vimy Ridge, Hill 70, and Cambrai (where he was awarded the Military Cross), and twice was seriously wounded.[13] While recovering from the first injury at a London hospital in 1917 he was attended by a nurse named Amy Marion Hale. Apparently his first words to her formed the question of how soon he might get out of the hospital and on his way to Dublin; the two would marry in February 1919.[14]

The move to Canada and time spent in the military was a period of great change for England. Having escaped the influence of his strictly religious family, he moved more towards the model of his rebellious and adventurous brother Nick and abandoned abstinence from drink and sex.[15] His ideas about people of different nationalities were also shaped during this period. Unlike Kirkconnell, whose biases hardened while he worked in Internment Operations, for England wartime was a period when his tolerance grew as he fought side-by-side with Canadians of various ethnicities. In one instance, his platoon was to cut lanes through the barbed wire in preparation for an attack. His "best help in this was a Russian-born tough member of my platoon, who, impatient with wearing gloves, rolled aside the wire with his bare hands and pulled up stakes." He later would write: "I learnt in the trenches that no race has a monopoly of courage and no race has a monopoly of civic virtue. Each individual is capable of high service *pro patria*." Or, as he later told Palmer: "After that experience, you can't put people down."[16] Of course, England did put some people down, developing a deep ambivalence towards Ukrainians before eventually going on to defend them, but his postwar activities were shaped to a large extent by the conclusions he drew from the conflict. As he put it in an interview in 1921: "Personally, my outlook on social problems has been materially changed since the war and I had become critical of civilization and its institutions. Gradually it is dawning on us that safety lies, not in accentuating racial and nationalistic lines, but in the welding of mankind into brotherhood."[17]

Once the war ended, England was discharged at Regina, Saskatchewan, in July 1919 and immediately went to work on a farm for the harvest season. However, owing to his injuries from the war, mainly damage to his right lung, he could not continue in this line of work.[18] So in October he returned to Queen's University, which he later described as a "place of healing" after the war.[19] Following his continued interest, he studied the Canadian rural west. However, he was unsure what career to pursue once he finished his BA, but eventually he made up his mind to go west and teach.[20] A number of factors influenced this decision. His initial experiences farming in Saskatchewan apparently did little to change his perception of the region, nor did age dampen his susceptibility to romantic literature. He later admitted that one of the books that influenced his decision was the Herbert Quick novel *The Brown Mouse*, in which the hero is a rural schoolteacher who breaks down the isolation between school and community.[21] Later in life he suggested that he wanted to take on a hard task and that his own experience as an immigrant had stimulated his interest. As he put it, the 1920s were years when he "moved as a stranger among strangers. I understood immigrants because I always felt I was in unfamiliar territory myself."[22] Perhaps most important was his postwar opinion that educating so-called new Canadians was "a vital part of that greater work of internationalizing the world."[23]

While at Queen's, England read the latest books on education and immigration such as J.T.M. Anderson's *Education of the New-Canadian* (1918) and C.B. Sisson's *Bi-Lingual Schools in Canada* (1917), as well as the classic *Strangers Within Our Gates* (1909) by J.S. Woodsworth. But his path to the prairies was most influenced by Anderson, another Canadian with an Irish Protestant background.

Anderson had taught school in rural and non-English districts between 1897 and 1911 and during this time learned to speak a bit of Icelandic. Later, while working as a principal, he returned to higher education, earning an MA, an LLB, and finally a doctorate of pedagogy from the University of Toronto. In 1918, he was appointed to a newly created provincial post, director of education among new Canadians.[24]

When it came time to think about employment, England wrote Anderson to ask for a job. Emphasizing his prior teaching experience in Ireland, he specifically requested a position in a non-English and particularly difficult school district. His request was granted and, after completing the BA in 1921, he moved with Amy to the Slawa Rural School. Slawa was located in a Ukrainian district near Hafford, in rural Saskatchewan. The crops had been poor for the four years before their arrival, and England surmised that it was probably one of the poorest districts in the province. The population was approximately 150, the majority of whom were Ukrainian (108), with a handful of Polish (9), German (15), and Anglo-Canadian (18). He later wrote that at the time of their arrival the English-speaking minority was having trouble with the Ukrainian majority.[25]

On their way to Hafford, the couple had briefly stopped in Regina to get their paperwork sorted out. England, an inquisitive, lifelong learner, took that opportunity to pick up a copy of the Foght Report. (Harold Foght was an American educational expert who had been brought in by the provincial government to assess the state of the provincial education system.[26]) England later remarked it was fortunate that he had read the report before he began his duties. Based on his life experience, he agreed with many of the ideas that Foght promoted and Anderson shared, namely "the integration of the rural school with the agricultural economy, the practicalizing of the curriculum, the teacherage, the school garden, the use of members of the district who had skills in schools, and breaking down the walls and isolation of the schoolroom."[27]

England's philosophy of teaching saw education as a work of moulding racial instincts to fit the Canadian environment and culture. As he put it in 1921, "by education is not meant the forcing of Canadian methods, customs and ideals into the lives of these children. Rather is it the development of all that is best in their racial temperament and the blending of their characteristic traits with all that is best in the Canadian." And the best of the Canadian was, of course, seen to be a British inheritance.[28] "I take it that the great ends of all education are health, citizenship, occupation, and leisure," England declared, but he placed the greatest weight on citizenship. For him, Canada was a growing nation that needed nation builders, whose essential qualities were "intelligence, manliness and a capacity for co-operation. These manifest themselves in various ways, which can be stimulated by the right use of leisure; intelligence by a sense of humour, manliness by sportsmanlike behaviour, and co-operation by an interest in team play or the sharing of pleasures in common."[29]

To this end, at the school he implemented a system of "responsible government" for maintaining order. This gendered program saw weekly elections, in which the girls elected a captain to take charge of "inside duty" while the boys' captain took care of "outside duty." Both were responsible for settling disputes and marching pupils in and out of the schoolroom. England's system was also nationalistic, and saw each school day closed with "a very impressive little ceremony." This consisted of the pupils marching from the classroom to the flagpole outside, where they formed a ring. As the flag was lowered, the students stood at salute and sang the national anthem.[30] England was also a firm believer in the importance of extracurricular activities and introduced a Boy Scout troop, wolf cubs, and girl guides, and organized a sports day with other local schools. Sports would not only "promote better physical fitness," he wrote, "but [the students] will develop that characteristic British sense of fair play – the Anglo-Saxon spirit of sportsmanship." An article that he published to draw attention to these efforts closed thus: "Canada will only be a great nation in so far as her rural schools are great schools devoted to the cause of leading out the children into the world about them and, opening up to them the 'spiritual heritage of the race.'"[31]

England thus approached the school and community with zeal and made a number of changes to the school and the grounds. At the convention of the Saskatchewan Educational Association in 1921 he gave a dramatic account of the state of things at the time of his arrival. "The outhousing was a disgrace, and I have seen more sanitary conditions on the front line trenches in France ... Discouragement, disorganisation, and dirt were my first impressions."[32] But he believed in the success of his mission, later paternalistically commenting that the children and their parents gradually "came to appreciate the increasing comfort and cleanliness" resulting from his changes. He was also inspired and encouraged by the frequent visits from Anderson, who came to check in on the Englands within three months of their arrival in Slawa and during the harvest break took England on a tour of other small schools in northern Saskatchewan.[33]

A combination of the press that his efforts were receiving and his growing connections helped England land a Masonic scholarship to further his education.[34] This required him to travel to Saskatoon, where he studied at the normal school and earned his first-class teaching certificate as well as his high school teacher's certificate. (While he was away, Amy ran the school single-handedly for several months.)[35] The scholarship program was a brief stint of formal education, but England had also independently continued his education by reading voraciously from the time he moved to Slawa.[36] Part of the reason for his continued studies was his natural intellectual curiosity, but there was also an aspect of self-doubt. He would later write that in the 1920s he took nothing for granted, and wondered if "an early classical, mathematical, scientific, or ad hoc professional training would have relieved the tensions between a sense of inadequacy and the consciousness of the difficult tasks of my unusual employment."[37] By the spring of 1923, England had become increasingly interested in the work of French sociologist Frédéric Le Play (1806–1882) and was anxious to pursue the topic, so he successfully applied for a Saskatchewan Government Paris Scholarship, and he and Amy moved to France.[38]

While the obvious motivation to accept this opportunity was the desire to study Le Play, England was later vague about the reasons for his departure. In one telling, he remarked that after his graduation from the Normal School he had reached a point where he was developing "perhaps undue zeal in this matter of rural development and rural interest which could easily move into narrow bigotry and fanaticism leading to political agitation." In another account, he wrote of needing the time off to "avoid becoming too much of an evangelist and too interested in political solutions." And in yet another version, he suggested that "having refused offers of more remunerative appointments, I had become a little too like a crusader, the polemical tending to displace the urbane."[39]

The report he prepared as a Masonic scholarship teacher sheds some light on his mindset at the time of his departure. Although by this time England had left his religious faith, he approached teaching with the zeal of a missionary and described his work in spiritual terms. He truly believed that, far from being a mere schoolteacher, he was involved in the crucial and miraculous work of nation-building. By *nation-building* he meant assimilating immigrants into Canadian society, and for him assimilation meant adopting the rights and privileges of Canadian citizenship. Teachers were, he wrote, "priests of a new order, and the school the very temple of citizenship – dedicated to the service of humanity, 'unstopping deaf ears, and making the blind to see.'" Citizenship was not something that could be taught like a course, he explained, but rather was "a spiritual principle, an atmosphere which must pervade all our teachings, inform all our educational plans. Citizenship is a life. Public-spiritedness is its expression."[40]

England was most worried about the assimilation of the Ukrainians and he made it clear that the first step was ensuring they adopted the English language. He recognized that, in a community in which the majority of residents spoke another language, the need for English was rather artificial and therefore had to be created. As he put it: "The word 'propaganda' has always a sinister sound, but propaganda of a healthy nature, inspired by an unselfish motive, is essential in this type of work. In other words[,] we must find ways and means of teaching not only the English language but the *value* of it – creating the need for it." He recognized that convincing the older generation would be most difficult and thus focused most of his efforts on the children. "This is the aim we have set before us here," he wrote. "Teach the children to love English." Through learning English and conversing with English-speaking neighbours, he added, Ukrainians would go on to learn "some of the standards of our western civilization."[41]

This was important, as he believed that Ukrainians were at a lower stage of civilizational development than Anglo-Canadians. For evidence, he pointed to certain behaviours they supposedly exhibited, particularly a lack of honesty. "It would seem that this little trait of deceitfulness is the characteristic of the stage of development," he wrote. "Subterfuge appears to be the natural thing. It goes hand-in-hand with superstition and childishness. The parallel for it is to be found in the 'make believe' lies of children. Children grow out of this period in their lives, but the peasant from South Eastern Europe takes a pride in being able to deceive. It is considered clever." While he acknowledged that a lack of honour was not confined to non-English settlers, he argued that it was nevertheless "an *accentuated* characteristic" among them.[42]

England's beliefs about citizenship and immigration were also shaped by his frustration with the politics in which he was enmeshed, as his work had been hampered by political interference. Though this was the work of local Ukrainian immigrants, he held Anglo-Canadian politicians responsible for the "mercenary" outlook that he believed was behind it.

The older [Ukrainian] people learnt too well our makeshift methods of democracy, and became conscious of power without the restraining sense of responsibility. We neglected them for a decade, except at election time, and when an easy sale was to be made; with the result that they were taught to take a mercenary view of everything. This mercenary view of things makes it difficult to make progress in school matters. School district politics are petty, and the teacher is hampered by the utterly *mercenary* view taken of his work and of the whole educational scheme and aim.[43]

However, he was hopeful that this view was giving way to a "healthier attitude," as Ukrainians had begun to discern between the unscrupulous and the public-spirited English-speaking Canadians, whereas before they had lumped them together "in accordance with their experience of the unscrupulous few."[44]

England argued that formal citizenship, that is, naturalization and enfranchisement, should be contingent upon immigrants' assimilation. Before immigrants were naturalized, they ought to prove that they could read and write in any one language and take an oral exam, proving that they understood the nature and origins of Canada's municipal, provincial, and federal forms of government. (He initially added that immigrants ought to be able to speak English, but then noted in the margins that he had not completely made his mind up about it.) He also added an additional qualification: that immigrants prove that they wanted citizenship by performing some service work, "not for profit but as a sign or outward symbol of inward and spiritual grace." Instead of universal military service, he argued, Canada ought to have "universal civil service." Once this demonstration of public-spiritedness was complete, the immigrant could then be naturalized. Here, too, England had some specific ideas about how it should be done. "The savage tribes of the world can teach us the lessons of the value of ceremony in admitting candidates to the privileges and rights of citizenship," he wrote. During this formal ceremony, which was to be closely linked with the educational system, the new citizen should be issued a certificate of naturalization, signed by a representative of the king. This certificate, he added, would be treasured and would serve as "a token of the greater and more valuable possession," that is, citizenship.[45]

However, because such a formal system was not in place, and because racial assimilation was not proceeding at an adequately rapid pace, England argued that immigration from non-English-speaking countries ought to be restricted until that population already in Canada was fully assimilated. According to him, obstacles to this assimilation included Ukrainians' block settlements; local control of the schools; lack of enlightened leadership; lack of good schools and efficient, qualified teachers; lack of mingling with "good types" of English-speaking settlers; "political jobbery"; and "mistaken democracy in extending use of ballot to unassimilated immigrants."[46]

The idea that immigrants ought not to receive the franchise until they were properly assimilated stemmed from England's experience with the political situation in Saskatchewan. As political scientist Escott Reid noted, for twenty-four years after the formation of the province the Liberal rule over the province was uninterrupted, and for fourteen of those years the Liberals were also the ruling federal party. While this dominance was somewhat unique to the province, patronage was not: it was an essential part of the party politics of the era, and the Saskatchewan Liberals "did not shrink from using [such] corrupt methods." On the prairies, as the non-English, non-French, European immigrant population grew, both federal and provincial politicians tampered their criticisms of these groups and instead began working to obtain their votes by extending patronage politics into these ethnic communities.[47] (For instance, in neighbouring Alberta, even Frank Oliver, an outspoken opponent of continental European immigration, had begun to court Ukrainian Canadians' votes.)[48]

Historian James Pitsula explains that in Saskatchewan, some Ukrainian immigrants had been recruited as organizers for the Liberal Party as early as 1908. One such recruit was Joseph Megas, a former school teacher. Megas helped organize school districts and recruited teachers, ensuring that they were English-Ukrainian bilingual and would teach the Ukrainian language, and that they were "reliably Liberal in their politics." Megas would also accompany Liberal candidates into Ukrainian communities and facilitate their campaigning there. Anglo-Canadians, including members of the Royal Canadian Mounted Police (RCMP), had grave concerns about Ukrainian schools and their teaching of the Ukrainian language. But they could do little, for in Ukrainian-majority districts, Ukrainian Canadians controlled the boards of trustees and would hire Ukrainian Canadian teachers over English Canadian applicants, even those who were more qualified.

England expressed his annoyance with his predecessors in his "Report," where he noted that from 1914 to 1920, with only one exception, Slawa had Ukrainian teachers who were "obviously poorly qualified." In a fiery speech given to the teachers' convention in Regina in 1922, England publicly unleashed his frustration with the system as a whole. Invoking Gresham's Law, that bad coins will drive good coins out of circulation, he suggested that it was the same with poor teachers who were kept in circulation by rural boards, passed along one to another. The solution was for rural communities to keep the good teachers at all costs, and "ruthlessly eliminate the spurious." Exhibiting a clear sense of superiority over Ukrainian Canadians, he also spoke of the need for teachers to be patient in dealing with "the mental infirmities of those whom it is their business to persuade," and the need for local school trustees who would not "resent the superior mental equipment of the qualified teacher." However, few changes were made to the education system prior to J.T.M. Anderson's later electoral victory with the Conservative party in 1929, as the Liberal government relied on Ukrainian Canadians' votes to stay in power.[49]

England's attention to local political matters stemmed from his dealings with the school trustees and the local municipality, which frequently did not pay him for months on end, as well as the local ratepayers who were keen to keep taxes down by any means necessary.[50] His close attention to the broader politics was no doubt also the result of his friendship with Anderson, whose position (director of education among new Canadians) was abolished in 1922 for political reasons. The move backfired, for two years later Anderson became leader of the rather shambolic provincial Conservative party but shortly thereafter led them to victory at the polls.[51]

England's draw to politics was strong enough that at his farewell dinner at Slawa, George Weir (the leader of the Masonic Lodge in Saskatchewan responsible for launching the Masonic scholarship program, and a friend of the Englands) prophesied that England would return to Canada and become a politician. But Amy had firmly told her husband that she would leave him if he entered politics. "I had often speculated as to why through the years she had stuck to this prohibition," England later wrote, "but I suspect in those days she was concerned about my lung wound and the possibility of the extra strain." The couple had to worry about Amy's health too, as she had injured her spine while working as a nurse, seriously enough that "the threat of complete invalidity always remained with her."[52] But Amy's reasoning may not have been so clinical; she may have sensed the dangerous path that England was on. Anderson would go on to win the 1929 provincial election, but with the support of the Ku Klux Klan. While Anderson vehemently denied that neither he nor his party had any formal ties to the Klan, his policies regarding education and immigration aligned with their goals. Late in life, England – no doubt referring to this history – remarked that Anderson might have accomplished more if he had worked harder to overcome "the limitations of his Ontario upbringing," that is, to "scrutinize carefully the attitudes and prejudices developed in youth."[53]

But in 1923, as the Englands were making their sad departure from Slawa, this was all still in the future. The decision to leave Slawa was one that Robert would look back at with disappointment. In an address given over a decade later, he spoke of "the vain regret that I had neither the courage nor the stubbornness to remain in that rural school and build in obscurity without envy or resentment and without the aid of prestige, place or office an enduring thing of dignity and usefulness." He added that the experience of shedding tears while saying goodbye to the community was one that had never been duplicated in any other post. They were, he wrote, "perhaps the only creditable part of my desertion." Such sentiments suggest that, although he was interested in Le Play, he was also driven by further success and prestige. As will soon become clear, this willingness to leave a secure job would be acted upon routinely throughout his adult life, but Slawa would remain his life's "happiest and most fruitful experience."[54]

How England first came to encounter the work of Le Play and how it held such a deep interest for him have not yet been adequately explained, but the link is found in some of the early reading he did while at Slawa. One work that particularly influenced him was psychologist William McDougall's *The Group Mind*, which proposed a theory of mass consciousness.[55] The book's first mention of the Le Playist school comes in two chapters on "The Race-Making Period." Discussing the inability of scholars to account for differences in national character, McDougall argued that "the political differences, which these [other] authors have regarded as the cause of the differences of national character, are really the expressions of a fundamental racial difference ... in short, these authors have inverted the true causal relation." Thus, he suggested, racial differences created national differences, and not the other way around. "I then drew attention to the work of the school of Le Play," McDougall continued, "and especially to its fundamental principle." In his interpretation, this was the idea that while peoples are in a state of "primitive or lowly culture," their geographical or physical environment determines their occupations and social organizations. The resulting modes of occupation and social organization persist over generations and ultimately "mould the innate qualities and form the racial character."[56] That England was drawn to the work of Le Play based on this summary suggests that he already conceived of Ukrainians as possessing a primitive culture and was interested in determining how to ameliorate it through studying and then modifying their social environment. The time he spent studying in Paris would only strengthen these ideas.

England studied at the Collège libre des sciences sociales for a year, attending lectures and spending hours in the library studying monographs of family surveys as well as Le Play's lectures. He eventually submitted a thesis, "The Assimilation of East European Peoples – in the Province of Saskatchewan, Canada (with a specific focus on Ukrainians)," which was examined by a jury of three in a public defence, and for which he was awarded a *certificat d'études sociales*.[57] In this thesis, England attempted to bring together two largely separate bodies of literature. The first was the sociological methodology and studies of Le Play that he immersed himself in upon arrival in Paris. The second body of literature consisted of some of the latest psychological theory, and specifically intelligence studies in the fashion of Alfred Binet (1875–1911).

Le Play was a French metallurgist turned sociologist who founded the Société d'Économie Sociale in 1856 to conduct studies of families. As sociologist Terry Clark puts it, Le Play believed that "studying the family, as the basic cell of every society, would result in a better understanding of social stability," and his resulting monograph series contained a "mixture of conservative Catholicism, praise of patriarchal authority, and modern scientific methods."[58] Binet, on the other hand, was a French psychologist who had a long-standing interest in abnormal child development and who, with collaborator Theodore Simon, created a series of popular intelligence tests. Henry Goddard brought the Binet-Simon test (as it came to be called) to America, where he used it to supposedly establish the hereditarian nature of feeble-mindedness and to advance the cause of eugenics. Other, often overtly racist researchers in addition to Goddard, such as Charles Davenport, also took up Binet's emphasis on intelligence.[59]

In Binet, England saw the development of a new "dynamic" form of psychology overtaking an older, more "descriptive" approach. England greatly respected the work of the respective founders of both schools, writing that Le Play "is to sociology what Alfred Binet is to psychology," but he saw flaws in both bodies of literature.[60] Specifically, he found the work of the Binet-inspired researchers to be more clinical than sociological and noted that they differed from Le Play by their focus on abnormal instead of normal families. Likewise, he found Le Play's works to be more descriptive than dynamic.[61] His thesis was thus an attempt to bring the two movements together, to fuse Binet's dynamic psychology with Le Play's sociology in order to create a "socio-dynamic psychology."[62]

Prior to his departure from Slawa, England had put little weight on racial and hereditary factors, and in his "Report" commented only in passing on general intelligence of the children at his school and the presence of some "feebleminded" parents.[63] His thesis, however, reflects a deeper engagement with these hereditarian theories. "Intelligence tests have demonstrated the importance of heredity," England wrote. "There are, psychologists tell us, children with superior intelligence and, unfortunately, some with an inferior intelligence. We thus learn the strength of the hereditary factor. Man is almost always that which his social environment and his heredity make him. It is therefore the duty of the social psychologist to study the social environment."[64] However, for his own project he proposed studying not the family (like Le Play) or the nation (like Pierre du Maroussem, a student and friend of Le Play who also lectured at the Collège) but rather the community. Studying the community was the ideal way to determine the influence of the social environment, he argued, as it was possible to see in close detail the economic and social organizations and how they influenced families and individuals.[65]

Accordingly, in the remainder of the study he attempted to determine the impact of the social environment.

As discussed in the introduction, the early classification schemes used by Europeans initially marked non-Europeans on a continuum somewhere between savagery, barbarism, civilization, and decadence, based on their supposed level of social development. With the emergence of race science, Europeans instead began sorting humanity into races. However, the lingering influence of this earlier system of classification, compounded by the lack of a scientific consensus on race, meant that the question of whether or not races could improve, progress, or evolve remained unanswered. Recently, scholars have portrayed this as a binary; perhaps most influentially, critical race theorist David Theo Goldberg defined the two positions as "racial naturalism" and "racial historicism." The former suggested that races were unchanging and unchangeable, their differences the result of nature, whereas the latter suggested that races were capable of progress, as their differences were the result of historical development. Goldberg suggests that naturalism was the initial position but that historicism increasingly took hold and countered it from the mid-nineteenth century onwards. Daniel Coleman, a scholar who has studied whiteness in Canadian literature, has similarly suggested that Canadian liberals moved from a naturalist to a historicist position in the late nineteenth and early twentieth centuries.[66]

However, historians must be cautious about placing too much significance on this distinction, for there is evidence to suggest that these viewpoints were not necessarily oppositional but, in some cases, coexisted. That is, some historical figures believed that nature explained racial differences but maintained that supposedly backwards or primitive races could nevertheless improve or literally evolve. Given scholars' imprecise understanding of the history of racial thought, Goldberg and Coleman's portrayal of a shift from a naturalist to a historicist position seems dubious at best and teleological at worst. It is unclear how these strains of racial thought developed, but it is clear that some theorists believed that both history and nature were together responsible for racial particularities.[67] England's thesis took this position: on the one hand, he viewed group differences as being influenced by both social environment and what he called racial instincts, which he plainly argued were the result of heredity. Yet on the other, he portrayed Ukrainians as a primitive, peasant people who simply needed to be assimilated to the more modern Canadian social environment.

His thesis was divided into three parts: the general, the specific, and the conclusion. The first part was comprised of four chapters: "The Problem," "The Country (Saskatchewan)," "The People (Ukrainian)," and "The Means of Assimilation (Rural Schools)."[68] The "problem," as England saw it, was simple. Canada had a double civilization because the French and the English "came together to build a nation." But in western Canada, and Saskatchewan in particular, there were large block settlements of eastern Europeans where "neither English nor French is spoken. The customs, habits, clothing, [and] superstitions remain the same as in Europe. The problem is to assimilate all these peoples to the Canadian environment."[69]

This stark statement overlooked the degree to which he had previously been open to and participated in some degree of cultural exchange: Amy made many friends among their neighbours and, while the couple did not learn to speak Ukrainian, they learned to cook Ukrainian dishes such as *holubtsi* (cabbage rolls) and *borscht* (sour soup), and Amy may have adopted some Ukrainian dress.[70] However, in his thesis he argued that, in their culturally and politically unassimilated state, eastern Europeans presented a threat to Canada's dual heritage, to the democratic principles and ideals that Britain and France fought for in the Great War and that formed the foundation of the Canadian constitution. This threat was grave, he warned: "Within the soul of Canada there are indistinct dreams of the ideals of other nations, embedded in the subconscious. Rome fell because of barbarians from the outside. Canada must find a way of assimilating its different peoples inside, if it wants to live."[71]

In England's view, eastern European immigrants – these barbarians within – were dangerous because they clung to the strife of the old world. The newspapers that arrived in their communities, albeit infrequently, were written "in their native languages and carefully cultivate[d] a love of their homeland, sometimes truly with an air of hostility towards Canada and Canadian institutions." The block settlements were a particular impediment, as they ensured that immigrants did not live in "a Canadian environment, but somehow in an environment opposite to the Canadian ideal." The eastern Europeans had also been exempt from the unifying force of the Great War, and thus continued to "guard the memory of the other countries ... As a result, there are many things to be forgotten and several sacrifices to make so that Canada doesn't miss its destiny," England wrote, neglecting to mention that the reason the war was not unifying for them was in part due to their internment. For him, the threat was racial and perhaps metaphysical. He wrote of the recent discovery of an extensive organization for Bolshevik propaganda among the Ukrainians, holding it to be one "proof of the communication of an almost psychic thought among people of the same race."[72]

In the third chapter, "The People," England provided the following unflattering and essentialist description of the Slavic "race," essentially arguing that all Ukrainian immigrants in Canada were "peasants" who were "invading" the prairies. While the term Slav encompassed a variety of nationalities, he maintained that when it came to physical appearance there was nevertheless a distinctive Slavic type.

> This type is short, thick, and chunky rather than vice versa, neither beautiful nor light in its movements. The face is large with eyes that are far apart and prominent cheekbones, the nose is large and pug-like rather than chiselled and aquiline; the forehead is bent and the expression goes from morose to serene, but it is not often animated or rejoicing. The eyes are a blue-grey, and the hair is blond in childhood but even still they are never truly blond like the Scandinavians. With age the hair becomes dark chestnut. On the whole, the suggestion is one of confidence and a certain heaviness. Nevertheless, excitement or emotion illuminates the faces that are naturally devoid of expression.[73]

England went on to explain that there was essentially no middle class among the Slavs. The middle class in Eastern Europe instead consisted of Germans, Armenians, Tartars, Jews, and Greeks, who worked as merchants, mechanics, bankers, and entrepreneurs. The result, he concluded, was that the "Ruthenians" who came to Canada were "poorly educated, ignorant, and poor. Their assimilation will necessarily take a long time." Using the logic of both racial naturalism and racial historicism (as they have been called), England suggested that Slavs had not been a major force in Europe on account of both racial characteristics and the particularities of their history. "We can ask why this ancient people do not play an important role in the history of the world," he wrote. "This is possibly because of a certain lack of energy and solidarity and of leadership. In addition, their political and cultural development was delayed by the invasion of the Tartars and Turks."[74]

England's warnings about the Slavs were also marked by eugenic concerns. In the second chapter, he explained that in northern Saskatchewan, the majority of the population "is foreign, and it should be noted that this population is always increasing." Even without immigration, he continued, "the growth in the foreign district has always been much larger than in the Anglo-Saxon district. The north of Saskatchewan is thus in the midst of passing into the hands of foreigners." He warned that these foreigners ultimately desired self-governance, which could eventually place "other languages and other customs in power." This was particularly concerning as the north was an area that was ripe for extraordinary development, with its plentiful mineral resources, forestland, and waterfalls for hydroelectric power. England dramatized this threat even further in his conclusion, by presenting the Slavs' supposed desire for autonomy as having the potential to end in civil war. Comparing the situation to that of the United States, he wrote that it was "not impossible that Canada may one day find itself in the face of the same problem – a demand for autonomy on the part of any region. It can save itself now by a discrete policy in seeking to teach its people to live together peacefully." But what would be the basis of this policy?[75]

Perhaps unsurprisingly, given his personal experiences, England's summary of the obstacles to assimilation and his suggestions for improvement both focused on the school. According to him, the majority of the immigrants would never learn English and were illiterate in their native language. Schooling was therefore paramount and would necessarily take time: children, not their parents, would profit from the new country, he argued. Despite having painted a dreary picture of the invading immigrants, he maintained faith in the schooling process. "It is good to remember that the Slav race gave us Copernicus, Huss, Comenius, Tolstoy, and Pushkin," he remarked. "The future depends on education."[76]

The school was the primary means of assimilation, although England also recognized the power of the church; English-language media, including newspapers, magazines, and catalogues; technological innovations such as the gramophone and the telephone; and customs, clothing, and new farming methods. The majority of his suggestions for improvement focused on education, although he also stressed the need for a common language. "Either English or French [must] be used throughout," he wrote (no doubt for the benefit of his French examiners), "but a nation requires a means of communication." As he put it in the opening lines of his conclusion, "Canada, what will it become? A Tower of Babel or a nation?"[77]

This was England's take on the situation in Saskatchewan in 1923. He portrayed it as a land that was passing into the hands of foreign peasants, Ukrainian invaders who were eager to take control. Indigenous peoples were entirely absent from his account, but this omission did not slip by his examiners. Over half of the questions they presented him with concerned the land and its ownership. "How is land granted to immigrants?" they asked, and where did these lands come from? Did the state "take them from the natives, did it buy them?"[78] (Unfortunately, England's answers are not extant.)

As for the colonizers, England believed that immigrants' behaviours were instinctual and stemmed from their race but that, through education, these racial instincts could ultimately be harnessed or moulded to the benefit of the settler society. Quoting literary scholar Jennifer Henderson's work on "race making," Daniel Coleman concurs that in this period "race [was] attached not just to bodies but also to forms of conduct." However, far from simply being *associated* with conduct, race was actually believed to *determine*, to a certain extent, this conduct. This is not an example of the construction of race through discursive practices, but rather demonstrates a reliance on the scientific idea of race as a determinant in shaping theories and practices of immigration and assimilation, particularly in the field of education.[79] Coleman suggests that the English Canadian cultural project of the nineteenth and early twentieth centuries was one of "organiz[ing] a diverse population around the standardizing ideals of whiteness, masculinity, and Britishness." These elements are seen in England's vision for the Slawa school, although his example also demonstrates important nuances. England believed Canada's culture was in large part British, but he emphasized the notion of Canadian citizenship more than membership in the British Empire. Coleman noted the importance of the Scots in inventing English Canada, but here is the important role of an Irishman, and one who presented himself as Canadian and did not dwell on his Irish descent. England was open to some degree of cultural exchange between peripheral Europeans and Anglo-Canadians but he generally disregarded all those racialized as non-white.

## THE RAILWAY AND RACIAL DIVERSITY

The Englands moved to Paris with the intention of returning to Canada, and throughout their time there Anderson kept writing about his developing political career, eventually asking England to join him. Deterred by Amy, England made other plans and, not wanting to be limited to Saskatchewan upon his return to Canada, planned to shift to collegiate teaching.[80] As it turns out, while he would be involved with education in various ways throughout the rest of his working life, England never again returned to the classroom. Instead, immediately after completing his thesis, he was offered the position of continental superintendent with the Canadian National Railways' Department of Colonization and Agriculture. He accepted and was soon recruiting immigrants to Canada. (Illustrating the close connections between the railways and the government in this period, England's boss, W.J. Black, had formerly been the deputy minister of immigration in Ottawa before joining the CNR in 1923 as the head of their new Department of Colonization and Agriculture. England had met Black through a mutual contact several years previous, and Black remembered him and recruited him for the job.)[81]

Both England and the CNR agreed on which immigrants were best. In the report he wrote before leaving Slawa, England had argued that "Scandinavian races are fairly easily assimilated" while "immigrants from South East Europe find it difficult to accept Canadian standards."[82] His employer, no doubt in keeping with the racial hierarchies of the period that privileged Scandinavian peoples, had established offices with the purpose of recruiting immigrants in Stockholm, Oslo, and Copenhagen. These offices reported directly to W.J. Black for the year 1924–25 while the rest of the continent reported to England, who busied himself travelling and establishing a new office in Rotterdam.[83] Black soon realized that the weak link was not in recruitment but in reception and so, despite remaining in charge of Europe, he moved his office from London back to Canada (Montreal) and began planning settlement facilities. This soon became a selling point for the CNR, for they could then promise to look after the immigrants' welfare after their arrival.

One incident discussed by scholar of disability studies Jay Dolmage reveals that England could not escape engagement with the imprecise race science of the era while working for the CNR, for this same race science informed their immigration operations. In the spring of 1927, seven Macedonian immigrants who had been cleared by the CNR in Zagreb were rejected by immigration officers in Canada, on the grounds that they were "of dark type and poor physique." As Dolmage explains, an immigrant could not be rejected for being "dark," yet linking this to "poor physique" created the grounds for exclusion. "This shows just one way in which Canadian immigration linked racial types with insinuations of biological deficiency," he adds.

The CNR officer who had issued the immigrants their certificate back in Europe, F.W. Baumgartner, was blamed for the mistake. To defend himself, he wrote a lengthy letter to England (his boss) as well as to Canada's deputy minister of immigration, explaining his rationale, defending the immigrants in question, and protesting that the "ethnographic conditions" of the regions were "extremely complicated" and as such it was difficult to discern between the desirable and the undesirable types. For their part, the CNR followed up by banning agents from giving certificates to any potential immigrants from the regions of Southern Serbia, or Dalmatia (now Croatia), "or to any immigrant slightly dark in colour." The company also repeated Baumgartner's argument to the Canadian immigration department, maintaining that "it will always be difficult to define precisely the degree of colour which should bar an applicant." England's own boss, Dr Black, suggested that agents might have to examine immigrants' skin under their clothing, to avoid basing their judgement on the normally exposed areas which might be darkened from working in the sun. In Dolmage's words, immigration agents thus "manufactured shades of non-whiteness, using darkness to symbolize genetic inferiority and using the implied inferiority to rescind whiteness. A result was that 'black colour' and 'dark races' became powerful tools for eugenic immigration restriction." In sum, the incident demonstrates that the boundaries of whiteness were still very much in flux in the 1920s, and that questions relating to them had important economic and political implications and a direct bearing on the lives of those living in these figurative borderlands.[84]

Given his penchant for lifelong learning, combined with the need to oversee complex cases such as this one, it is little surprise that throughout his time with the CNR England continued to study independently in a variety of fields.[85] But his primary professional and personal interests remained immigration to Canada, and he would go on to publish numerous works on the subject. The first of these works was a book entitled *The Central European Immigrant in Canada* (1929), which drew together earlier materials, mainly his thesis and the results of the questionnaire that the Masonic scholarship recipients had administered to their communities (and which he had helped craft).

The intention was to use this material in a "thorough study of certain social and national problems pertaining to Rural Saskatchewan," but years later the results still had not been published. The two most likely authors or co-authors of such a report were simply unable to take on the task: Anderson had taken the dive into provincial politics and in 1926 George Weir had taken a job at the University of British Columbia. England, wanting to utilize the survey material, as well as advance a particular argument regarding immigration to and assimilation in Canada (which was still a topic of considerable debate), began work on the book in 1928 and published it the following year.[86] A definite motivation was the ongoing Canadian criticism of continental European immigrants, particularly as to their desirability and ability to assimilate, and, like Kirkconnell, England was inspired to write in part because of Bishop Lloyd's nativist campaign.[87]

Described by its author as a "study of the assimilation in Canada of continental immigrants," and particularly "the more backward non-English speaking districts" in Saskatchewan, England's book was divided into three parts: "A Problem and the People," "The Project," and "The Process and a Policy." Its central arguments can be quickly outlined. The first part argued British immigration to Canada was irreversibly declining and central European immigration was increasing, which meant increased assimilation was necessary.[88] However, the impact of this shift, and the required steps for assimilation, could not be understood without a study of these immigrant groups' backgrounds. England then provided the suggested overview of the religious, ethnic, and national groups involved. The second part of the book consisted of an examination of the non-English school districts in rural Saskatchewan and argued that social conditions were in need of improvement. The primary cause of improvement would be amalgamation into broader Anglo-Canadian society, England argued, but this was not possible without further education. As such, the success or failure of assimilation rested with the rural school, and specifically the teacher, who had to transform the school into a community centre in order to be successful. In the third and final section of the book, England argued that assimilation depended "on the old Canadian as much as on the new" and that cooperation and tolerance were required. He closed by discussing immigration policy and schooling, which he believed were fundamentally linked. As to the former, he defended the present policy but suggested that intelligence testing be added to the medical examination. To the latter, he quoted the Foght Report and made a number of recommendations designed to improve rural schooling.

Scholars since have noted the book's more tolerant vision of assimilation.[89] However, what has gone largely unnoticed has been the framework that underlay all of England's analysis and ultimately shaped his conclusions: race. Unlike his thesis, which unhesitatingly subscribed to hereditarian theories but gave little attention to the specifics of racial theory, the book demonstrates a much greater engagement with and reliance on the literature. He was more influenced by European than American authors, and found Eugène Pittard's *Race and History* to be the "best book on the races of Europe."[90] A respected Swiss anthropologist, Pittard defined race as "the continuity of physical type, expressing affinities of blood, representing an essentially natural grouping," and "abhorred the idea of racial superiority, at least insofar as European races were concerned." Instead, he emphasized that none of the European nations consisted of a single race and that "the achievements of European civilization could not be ascribed solely to the Nordic race."[91] In *The Central European Immigrant*, England explicitly held race to be a biological reality, one that determined whole cultures as well as individual characteristics, a force that had immense staying power throughout millennia.[92] His more tolerant vision for assimilation did discuss the importance of culture, but was nevertheless rooted in and made possible by his particular interpretation of racial theory.

First, England accepted the division of humanity into white and non-white races, with the latter largely excluded from analysis. Unlike other CNR and Canadian government employees, he was far less concerned with the inner divisions of whiteness, and seemingly viewed all Europeans as nominally white. Historian Carmela Patrias argues that to suggest non-British, non-French, European peoples in Canada were racialized as non-white and slowly became racialized as white would be to oversimplify a complex process of racialization. Nevertheless, England directly compared the perceived problem of the assimilation of central European immigrants with

American racial segregation. Although some Canadians envisioned a similar "solution," he reported, its implementation would prove impossible. Further, his discussion of "the negro problem in the United States" suggests a belief, shared by many Canadians during this period, that Canada had no problem with racism against people of African descent because there were simply not many of them in the country.[93]

Secondly, England's classically liberal approach to land ownership and colonialism was married to a racial interpretation of history.[94] "Use is the only equitable title to property," he wrote. "We dispossessed the Indian and there are sound reasons arising from his neglect to build, why this should be so." However, he recognized that colonialism could also result in the extinction of Indigenous peoples. This extinction he explained both in cultural and biological terms. One example he provided was that of the role of dancing in some native societies, which supposedly "stimulated the sexual impulse." The dancing itself was not immoral but Westerners viewed it as such and stopped it, resulting in a decline in the native's population. This was common in places like Australasia, he explained, where "race extinction" was the result of "the disturbance of a race culture." But, he added, this was also happening in North America, especially in America, where the death rate of "Indians" was "alarming." The second example he provided was that of the death rate from tuberculosis among African Americans, which was twice as high as among "white Americans." However, their overall population continued to climb, which to England suggested that they had either psychologically adapted to the disturbance of their race culture or else their survival was the result of "race substitution by the infusion of white blood. We cannot be sure whether it is the hybrid that remains and the pure bred negro dies out," he added.[95]

Finally, England accepted the three-part division of Europeans into the races of Nordic, Mediterranean, and Alpine, and believed that these races determined individual characteristics. "Research continues to reveal facts of the Mendelian inheritance of physical characters, the maintenance of types through thousands of years, and combining in other cases diverse heritages to make of individuals *a mosaic of racial characteristics.* The most notable finding is the persistence of racial types but slightly modified by cross-breeding; it is this which demands the earnest consideration, from the racial as well as the economic standpoint, of those shaping Canada's immigration policy." Here England used the "mosaic" metaphor nearly a decade prior to its popularization by John Murray Gibbon, but in a different sense: he used it to affirm the power of races – even if mixed – to determine an individual's characteristics. Such racial characteristics included introversion or extroversion, preference for rural or urban settings, and a tendency to lead or to follow.[96]

Unlike many of his peers, he rejected the notion of hierarchy among the races, though he did not profess belief in the equality of *all* races. As he put it, he "disregarded extravagant claims as to the inherent race superiority [and] the equally doctrinaire contention of the race egalitarian." He continued: "Since all races are human, differences must be those of degree or quantity, rather than those of kind or quality. There are, thus, differences in average stature, average complexion, average cephalic index, average size of brain, and average mental ability. Such a point of view does not warrant the violent rantings and fantastic claims of [Arthur de] Gobineau, [Lothrop] Stoddard, or [William] McDougall in their well-known works." This last statement should not be interpreted as a rejection of the underlying race science, as his discussion of European races' various temperaments approvingly cited McDougall as evidence. His exception was strictly with racial hierarchies and not with racial determinism, but both are forms of racism. He ultimately concurred with sociologist Frank Hankins who argued that, when it came to immigration, race mixture was not "injurious to quality provided the stock is sound to begin with" but who also maintained "races too diverse may be excluded for social, if not biological reasons."[97]

In accordance with eugenic theories, England also believed that some Europeans were more fit than others. "There are undesirables in South Wales as in Southern Europe," he wrote, adding that immigrants to Canada had to belong to "the better eugenic types."[98] One source of this particular interpretation of race science was Hankins's work *The Racial Basis of Civilization: A Critique of the Nordic Doctrine* (1926), which lambasted eugenicists such as McDougall, Stoddard, and Grant, but nevertheless did not deny the existence of a Nordic race nor contest the imperatives of eugenics.[99] Regardless of the similarities between European races, England believed that their assimilation in Canada was an absolute necessity. "We must incorporate the races who have come to us into *one* people," he wrote, "otherwise, our dominion from sea to sea will perish in strife and anarchy."[100]

A marriage of two beliefs formed the basis of England's vision for Canadian assimilation: first, the existence of universal human instincts; and second, the power of a social environment to temper racial cultures. Common "social instincts" were present in varying degrees in all men, he explained, including "gregariousness, pugnacity, curiosity, acquisitiveness, rhythm, and the instincts connected with sex and parenthood."[101] Alongside these universal instincts were particular racial instincts, but both sets of instincts found a particular expression depending on the cultural or civilizational conditions to which they were subordinated. As he explained: "If we mean by assimilation a process that moulds racial stocks into something else we are flying in the face of what every stock-breeder knows ... No melting pot can make a Slav, an Italian, or Frenchman, an Anglo-Saxon. Racial qualities, vices, and instincts will remain. They may, however, be modified by environment, sublimated into some other form. This is the point at which progress can be made."[102] The process of assimilation thus could not begin until Canadians identified and determined how to make use of the socially important traits that they could expect in each racial group.[103]

Central Europeans' instincts had formerly been subordinated to a pre-modern civilization, England argued, one marked by "patriarchal and ecclesiastical authority, parochialism, attachment to the soil, an inferiority complex through political disabilities, under-privileged women and children, [and] primitive methods sanctioned by tradition allied to all that we regard as picturesque in the peasant – his costume, his customs, his dances, his music, and his mother-wit." Canada, on the other hand, was home to an industrial, modern civilization, one with a quicker "tempo." Assimilation was thus "a task of emancipation," a "challenge and a call to wider perspectives, saner ideals, better habits and customs, but greater responsibility." Similar to many of his peers, including Kirkconnell, his discussion was marked by antimodernism. He specifically decried the increasing environmental destruction, urbanization, industrialization, mass advertising, and rampant consumerism that he saw in Canadian society. Nevertheless, he claimed that, compared to continental Europeans, Canadians were accustomed to "better hygienic conditions, greater mental freedom, [and a] stronger moral fibre."[104]

Lastly, instincts could be repressed, abused, or controlled, and assimilation was all about ensuring that they were controlled or transformed. Pugnacity had to be turned into emulation, curiosity and acquisitiveness had to be refined so as to assist in economic and social progress, and tradition had to recognize the importance of modern efficiency. In short, the immigrant was to be asked to surrender standards, customs, and habits that were below the best in Canadian culture but was allowed to retain "anything that might be helpful to unity and progress." The process of transition thus had to be slow enough to ensure that the best of immigrants' "heritance" was not lost.[105]

In its dismissal of a hierarchical ranking of European races (Nordic, Mediterranean, and Alpine), the book was by no means expressing a majority opinion in Canada. During this period the idea of European races was hotly debated; in 1927, for instance, a long battle was waged in the Letters to the Editor page of *the Globe*, a Toronto newspaper. It began with J.W. Clipsham arguing that if Canada continued to admit "alien races whose social and political ideals are wholly foreign to our Anglo-Saxon ideals," it would weaken the nation itself and the special bond of sentiment to Britain. During this period the terminology was sometimes confused: Nordic races could refer to the "races" of people that lived in Nordic (Scandinavian) countries, while the Nordic race could refer to one of the three subvarieties of the white race. But Clipsham clarified that he did not use the term in the "geographical, but in the ethnological sense," and argued that the Canadian political institutions were "Nordic in their origin and development; our freedom and well-being depend on the[ir] successful workings ... Non-Nordic peoples cannot work these institutions, therefore keep them out." The next month he wrote in to decry the pending decision to allow fifty thousand farmers from "one of the Southern European nations," and repeated his claims that no non-Nordic races were suitable immigrants for Canada due to the racial nature of its system of government. He elaborated that even when other races tried to adopt this system, they failed in the "spirit of co-operation and self-sacrifice" needed to operate it, and thus splintered into factions. He signed off with a blast against the undesirable immigrant who would "mongrelize our blood and ruin the future of our country."[106]

While Clipsham's first letter received no reply, the second aggravated a "British (non-Nordic) Canadian," who wrote back arguing against many of the tenets of Nordicism, including the idea that the British were Nordic, and pointed out that Canada's political system was the result of both British and French settlers. Clipsham steadfastly maintained that there certainly were "three principal racial stocks in Europe, and most of the nations are made up of combinations of two or more of these," denied that his comments were prejudicial, and argued that he was "only concerned with what is for the future good of our country." All successful democracies around the world were "basically Nordic," he added, with perhaps the exception of France.[107] When the "non-Nordic Canadian" responded to Clipsham, they too turned to the authority of race for their argument. The author asserted that he belonged to a real race as he was Scottish, while this Nordic race of Clipsham's was simply mythical. Clipsham retorted by congratulating him on "his derivation from one of the important branches of the Nordic race," and repeated his old arguments about the need to carefully select immigrants.

A "Citizen L. C." also wrote in to contest Clipsham's letter. Seeking to discredit the Nordic myth, they argued that America had very little Nordic stock but was not divided, and that many Italians held prominent places in society. The writer closed by rattling off a long list of supposedly non-Nordic peoples that had made contributions to art and science: "It might be worth his while," L.C. concluded, "to get in touch with the Encyclopedia Britannica." Clipsham may have gotten in touch with the Encyclopedia but not the writer, for he chose not to respond.[108]

England's was a welcome intervention in these debates, as evidenced by the positive reviews, both national and international, that the book received. Berta Hamilton, the assistant director of the Department of Social Service at the University of Toronto, described it as "a much needed contribution to the meagre Canadian literature on the subject of immigration and colonization. The book itself we like tremendously ... It appears to us critical, thought provoking and stimulating." In a later letter she added that "into whatever circle one goes where people are at all concerned or interested in immigration one hears the same sort of feeling about [the book] expressed as I wrote you."[109] As one reviewer accurately summarized, England was "firmly convinced" that the Central European immigrant presented a problem, not of "racial inferiority, but racial differences." The *Empire Review* found the book to be a "valuable contribution to a controversial and important issue" and concurred that "the ultimate solution of the problem of a non-Nordic influx of population depends ... on the capacity for [a] completely successful absorption of new stock."[110]

The *Times Literary Supplement* declared that the book deserved the attention of "all students of sociology and race problems," but found the overall impression to be rather depressing. "We are left wondering whether the low standards of life of these peoples may not prove something of a drag on Canada for a long time to come," they wrote, "unless the problem can be solved through education."[111] Given its treatment of race, the book drew several comparisons to J.S. Woodsworth's *Strangers Within Our Gates* – one reviewer in particular suggested that England's book was more comprehensive and praised it for actually touching on government policy.[112]

One mixed review appeared in the *Morning Post* (London). Entitled "The Bohunk," it consisted mostly of negative quotes about the immigrants, giving the reader the impression that the book and its author, while sympathetic, were opposed to them. This incensed Amy, who wrote a letter to the editor, and her defence reveals that she shared her husband's ambivalence about European immigrants.

> The Central European immigrants whom you class together as "Bohunks," in many cases make some of the finest settlers. They are adaptable, thrifty, and not afraid of work. The type you describe in your article were the ones admitted indiscriminately before the war, and are equivalent to the many undesirables to be found in all countries. As the book points out, those now going forward are very carefully selected types, and will quickly become an asset to Canada ... The term "Bohunk" is particularly offensive to the ear of the immigrant, and was only used by my husband to explain this.[113]

England's assistant, A.R. Milne, wrote a similar letter, although it appears to have gone unpublished. In it, he defended England's book as impartial, and repeated the argument that "the vast majority of the poor types mentioned entered Canada before the War ... The situation now is decidedly different. All immigrants have to conform to high standards as regards to mental and physical fitness and should make good citizens." He added: "Everyone shares your desire that the majority of new settlers entering Canada should be British," but argued that these immigrants were simply not materializing despite the effort and money expended by both the federal government and private interests. He concluded by informing the editor that the book had been "very favourably reviewed throughout Canada."[114]

Given its content, England was initially concerned about the book generating a negative backlash both from the immigrants themselves and from the CNR. However, as it sold widely and received such positive reviews, his boss, Dr Black, and the company president, Sir Henry Thornton, were both pleased.[115] England, now a published author, continued in his role at CNR until March 1930 when he accepted a lateral move within the company and was appointed western manager of colonization and agriculture, based in Winnipeg. The return was a welcome one and the couple quickly became involved in community life.[116]

As a manager of colonization, England remained a firm believer in the benefits of racial heterogeneity on the Prairies. "What would have happened to Western Canada had we been all one race (founded into one mould) anxious to express ourselves in economic and social life the one way?" he asked in an article published in 1933. His answer, likely referring to the economic hardships of the Depression, was that it would have been a far more serious disaster. "But God having written a line of His thought on the cradle of each race," he continued, "let us be grateful for variety – the intangible differences of temperament, the variety of logical processes of thought, almost characteristic racial ways of approaching problems, qualities which are embarrassing at times but are healthy and useful and necessary in the development of the riches of a territory with as great a variety of possibilities as most of Europe."[117]

However, his vision for the future was one in which some blending had occurred. As he put it, the naturalist of the future would identify the "dominant characteristics of race in western fair and on western farm ... noting here and there blonde hair, blue eyes, tanned skin, a high cheek bone, dark eyes, a dramatic power, a practical touch, eyes that dream of the sea, fingers that itch for a violin, little feet that dance, sturdy bodies framed for toil, nervous energy that seeks adventure, tongues linguistically gifted, throats made for song, solemn little thinkers." These children of varied racial origins would grow up and contribute to the building of a nation by contributing to agriculture, resource extraction, art, and literature, he wrote, but would hopefully retain "some of the mother-wit, piety, wholesomeness of peoples bred to the soil."[118] But in order to get to that imagined future, a lot of work had to be done. England viewed integration as requiring work on both sides: Anglo-Canadians had to welcome other racial groups and these other racial groups had to conform to Anglo-Canadian norms to a certain degree. A subsequent program he crafted, the Community Progress Competitions, was designed to address both and was a chance for England to test his socio-dynamic psychology.

The project was the brainchild of Dr Black, who imagined a contest that would span Alberta, Manitoba, and Saskatchewan. To ascertain its viability, he invited England to accompany him on a tour of the west. Shortly afterwards, in May 1930, CNR president Sir Henry Thornton publicly announced the competition's launch.[119] Black passed responsibility for the project to England, who made the focus exclusively rural and drafted the competition's regulations. The contest was open only to communities that were composed of 70 per cent first- or second-generation immigrants from continental Europe. Communities that opted to enter the competition were judged on a score card that examined progress in four areas. The first was education (valued at 275 points), which covered school attendance at all levels, progress being made by students, and the quality of the school and its ground. The second category was agricultural development (275 points), and it covered the layout and appearance of farms, and the quality and quantity of crops and livestock. The third was citizenship, cooperation, and social welfare (300 points), which covered public health, respect for the law, and involvement in community and agricultural organizations. The final category covered arts, handicrafts, and domestic economy (150 points), which included interest in cultural activities such as drama, music, and folk dancing. Communities were given a score out of 1,000, and the top three received prizes of $1,000, $500, and $250, respectively.[120]

The program's purpose was twofold: first, to promote the integration of primarily continental-European districts with provincial services in order to improve their quality of education, health, and agricultural productivity; and second, to raise awareness among the general public about the contributions being made by rural, continental districts – in short, to improve their image. But in England's mind, the competition was ultimately an attempt to harness the power of group consciousness to improve living standards in rural, non-Anglo-Saxon communities. In a 1932 article on the subject, he explained that "pioneer communities" generally developed their agriculture by trial and error and without the benefit of scientific management. Despite widespread extension work on the part of departments and schools of agriculture, many communities remained unreached. Building on the work of the community surveys undertaken by the Masonic scholarship teachers, England hoped to use the competition to stimulate progress. Clearly England still believed in the underlying principle of "Group Consciousness" as described by McDougall, even if he was more agnostic about the details, viewing it as "axiomatic" that "a community [was] the natural and most effective medium for the inoculation of ideas through the force of mass suggestion and imitation." He continued: "It is essential to enlist the underlying racial, religious or cultural motive force in favour of the programme." And while he viewed the differences in terms of "various racial stocks," he now cautioned that "apart from the racial make-up of these communities it is often found that the religious or cultural influence may be a determining factor in the community. We have endeavoured, therefore, to ally ourselves in the community with the leadership that already exists." More than just an example of "corporate-pluralistic objectives," as they have since been described,[121] these competitions were actually a way in which England, drawing on his readings in psychology, sociology, and anthropology, attempted to utilize group consciousness to ensure "non-Anglo-Saxon" communities were modernized.[122] As he put it, the score card was "a weapon" and the scoring was carried out "with definite objectives. The guiding principles are co-operation with the same community, comparison of community achievement and standards with other communities, and competition to reach objects as precisely and simply stated as possible."[123]

Backing away from his earlier views, he stated that a lack of contact with non-English communities in the period immediately following the Great War had led "some of us to believe that racial group settlements were undesirable and such settlements became suspect as being subversive of national unity and unprogressive of agriculture." But he still viewed these criticisms as somewhat valid, given that purpose of the competition was, as he plainly stated, "to bring within the sweep of our Canadian culture and life, the traditional skills, homecraft and handicrafts of our European peoples and to interest them in the services provided by our Provincial Institutions in education, health, and agriculture." Thus, while England later denied that assimilation was one of the project's goals, it clearly was at the time.[124]

The pattern of England's alternating work and study continued in 1934, when he returned to Queen's University to study for an MA in economics and wrote a thesis on "The Colonization of Western

Canada," later published as a book of the same title. In the CNR's Department of Colonization and Agriculture, he was "about the only one that was appointed to a senior position without an agricultural degree," and working with and learning from agriculturalists expanded the scope of his studies and influenced his writing.[125] His second book was thus a sprawling study of conditions in the rural west that paid close attention to the role of the environment and the importance of various crops on the regional economy. "The assimilation of the many European peoples who have settled in Canada has become a question of some controversy," he wrote, "but the problem cannot be understood without a clear understanding of the growth and agricultural development of the country in which they have created large ethnic group communities." No longer satisfied with studying communities in isolation, England was interested in "the ecological adaption of human communities to their environments."[126]

One of England's primary concerns about the Prairie west had long been "large ethnic group communities." More commonly called block settlements, and frequently spelled "bloc," these were regions in which an entire population (or the overwhelming majority) consisted of members of an ethnic or ethno-religious group. As historian Frances Swyripa points out, the term "bloc" was used by academics and outsiders but rarely by residents of these type of settlements. It should also be noted that the term gives the impression it was a singular phenomenon, when in fact it took diverse forms. Group settlements included those that colonists independently formed, those created by federal government colonization programs, and those created by broader sociological or political shifts.[127]

This complexity was rarely noted in the debates of the day, as group settlement was a contentious and politicized issue for Anglo-Canadians, mostly because such "blocs" were viewed as impediments to the necessary assimilation of these groups, and, to a lesser extent, because it hindered individuals from acquiring the land. Despite these criticisms, Clifford Sifton's administration of immigration resulted in the creation of a number of official and unofficial block settlements between 1896 and 1905. With regard to the ongoing project of liberal order, it seems contradictory that vanguards of liberalism, a philosophy which is at its core individualist, would accept and even create block settlements. Particularly jarring is the acceptance of groups such as the Doukhobors, Hutterites, and Mennonites, who practise more communal forms of property ownership. Historian Ryan Eyford, in examining the history of the Icelandic land reserve in Manitoba, puts forth the argument that such settlements were "considered a temporary evil that had to be tolerated to realize the larger goal of extensive western colonization."[128]

England held both of these positions during his life: a strong opposition to block settlements and an acceptance of them as a temporary but necessary step in the colonization of the west. His time in Slawa left him so concerned with the apparent lack of assimilation of Ukrainian Canadians that in his 1923 thesis he repeated Maroussem's claim that non-assimilated colonies were like "cysts" that, in difficult times, could cause "the worst type of complication," and in his subsequent book he described them as a menace. However, in this second book he acknowledged his former views but now pivoted and defended block settlements. "Ten years ago our interest was concentrated on the social problem of assimilation of the non-English settlers of the West," he wrote. "Though interest in this is still marked, our schools, and agencies of social control have changed the character of this problem and some effort now is necessary to conserve the qualities, skills and aptitudes of the fast disappearing older generations of pioneers."[129]

This shift of opinion is perhaps best explained by his employment. As a teacher, he observed life in a rural Ukrainian Canadian community, and was alarmed by its apparent lack of assimilation to Anglo-Canadian norms. But Canadian railway companies staunchly defended Canadian immigration policies, as immigration was a source of profit. Prior to 1925, railway companies recruited immigrants in Europe who then travelled to an urban centre, where they were inspected by Canadian immigration officials. There was a high rate of failure at these ports, meaning that the railways were losing money on these would-be immigrants. As a result, the CPR and the CNR, "presenting a rare united front," attempted to obtain more control over the process. The resulting Railways Agreement was signed by the railway companies and the federal government in 1925 and remained active until May 1930. It dictated that while the federal government retained the power to determine how many people would be allowed to immigrate each year, the responsibility for screening those immigrants would pass to the railway companies. The agreement further stipulated that if immigrants did not find agricultural work within a year of their arrival, they were to be deported at the expense of whichever company had brought them.[130] The Railways Agreement represents a remarkable blurring of state and civil society, as private companies were empowered to exert many of the powers normally associated with sovereign states with respect to the recruitment and retention of citizens; little wonder it has since been called "a stunning abdication of federal responsibility."[131] Much like the federal government was willing to accept the necessary evil of block settlements for the rapid colonization of the west, so too was it willing to hand off responsibility for immigration to private interests.

Perhaps because public opinion towards unassimilated and non-preferred immigrants was so hostile, the agreement also divvied up responsibility for the placement of settlers according to their desirability. Specifically, the federal government – through its Department of Immigration and Colonization – remained in charge of placing preferred immigrants: British, American, and northern European. (They also processed the excluded nationalities who were allowed entrance by special permit only, such as all those racialized as non-white.) The contentious central European immigrants, however, were delegated to the CPR and the CNR. The federal government could therefore rightly claim that they remained focused on preferable immigrants, even as they gave railway companies a relatively free hand to recruit so-called non-preferred immigrants.[132]

The railways were thus incentivized to ensure that their immigrants found success, both to avoid the expense of deporting them and to avoid backlash from Anglo-Canadians, and what better way to guarantee success than to place immigrants in a block settlement where they would face far fewer linguistic and cultural barriers?[133] Officially, during England's time with CNR, the company thus sought to balance the twin goals of increasing successful immigration and ensuring continued assimilation. England, busy working to carry out these directives, defended the diversity of immigrants that the railroads were accepting and argued that diverse character of the population, with "the varied skills, attitudes and aptitudes of so many racial heritages," was an asset to the economy. For one, the different groups had diversified the agrarian economy, and their traditional family structures had also acted as a "shock absorber," taking the edge off the pioneer conditions and the recession-prone western economy.[134] As he explained much later in life, although most sociologists damned the idea of block settlements, he felt they provided that necessary "neighbourliness" or cooperation without which "an attack on the frontier would be almost impossible." The community also provided a needed social safety net during a period when neither provincial nor federal governments provided one.[135]

England now defended block settlements for economic reasons but continued to characterize them as racial in nature, although there was some slippage in terminology. He would occasionally refer to groups as "racial" that would today be considered nationalities, but elsewhere distinguished between the two.[136] However, he remained convinced of the explanatory power of race. In the third part of the book, he provided a description of each of the various "non-Anglo-Saxon" groups that had settled on the prairies. These summaries, while intended to portray each group in a positive light, were deterministic and patronizing. Slavs the world over were marked by "passivity of temperament, peasant psychology and political eagerness" and were also deeply religious, willing to suffer hardship, excellent artists, lovers of colour and hospitality. Those of Teutonic or German origin were marked by order and organization; Scandinavians were easily assimilated, tall, well-built, and intelligent; and Hungarians were also easily assimilated, with the "cheerful temperaments and the vitality of a soil-bred people."[137]

In closing the chapter, he discussed some of the smaller groups and emphasized either their numerical insignificance or their positive attributes. Not many Jewish people had farming experience, he argued, so few remained on the Prairies; Mormons no longer practised polygamy and had a shrewd business sense; Chinese were successful gardeners near cities; and, he noted (perhaps with surprise), there was even "a small negro settlement" north of Edmonton.[138] The references to nominally non-white settlements (Chinese and African) were unusual for England, but it should be noted that they were framed in such a way as to emphasize each group's insignificance as a percentage of the overall population. Nevertheless, and doubtless for company purposes, he concluded that overall, "each group has brought its special interest, its peculiar type of community organization, or its concentration upon some definite type of agriculture, and so has contributed each in its own way to the making of Western Canada."[139]

The next chapter turned to British and French Canadians. England suggested that Anglo-Saxons' heritage of Norse, Norman, Huguenot, and Celtic blood "made the name Anglo-Saxon meaningless," yet maintained that there was "nevertheless a distinctive type that is English," marked by an instinct for fair play, a sense of sportsmanship, political skill, and a practical turn for affairs, albeit with a coldness of approach. As for the French Canadian, "he" was simply "a loyal son of the Catholic Church and a pioneer at all times in the history of Canada." Quebec continued to exert significant cultural influence over French settlements on the prairies, in part through racial characteristics. England explained that French Canadians found in northern Saskatchewan and Alberta retained "the *coureur de bois* characteristics of their forebears – hunting, trapping, love of the outdoors, the gay 'chanson,' the camaraderie and spirit of *bonhomme*. The attitude to the life of the soil is inborn, and the reverence for the church is fervent." However, he reassured the reader that while they held "a totally different creed than their Anglo-Saxon neighbours," French Canadians were nevertheless "a thorough-going product of Canada," and dismissed concerns about "racial rivalries" (such as those expressed by André Siegfried in *The Race Question in Canada*) as "somewhat exaggerated."[140]

Despite the praise of sociological diversity in the book's preceding chapters, in the last section of the book England worked to reassure worried readers that the Prairies remained thoroughly Canadian. One strategy is apparent: despite having only just recounted the long histories of each of these nationalities in Canada, he placed his discussion of British and French-Canadian communities under the section title "The Older Heritage." While he did not label Canadians of non-English, non-French descent "new," he explicitly positioned them as such and stressed that, despite their dispersal, English and Anglo-Ontarian settlers exerted a remarkable influence over all other settlers. "Farm practice, business methods, local governments, all show even in European communities the impress of British institutions, the English language and Anglo-Saxon methods and ideals," he wrote. The heritage was British, but "the heirs are of all races. The heritage includes liabilities as well as assets, but there is every sign that the faith of the fathers will be justified in the children of the prairies."[141]

The parallels between this vision of Canada and the federal government's later description of Canada, as a nation founded by two races but enriched by contributions from other groups, is striking; this kind of thinking both led to and was made official by the Royal Commission on Bilingualism and Biculturalism.[142] In England's account, however, the reliance on race is much more readily apparent.

He remained devoted to the tripartite division of European races and to the power of race in determining individual characteristics. In his mind, racial divisions were natural, whereas other divisions were "artificial." Likewise, in discussing the mark that various races left on an environment, he suggested that northern and central Europeans had, "if there is anything in atavism, the ancestral heritage of the disciplines of Europe, the lessons of Roman order, [and] Teutonic self-respect."[143] The racial history of Europe was thus a source of hope for Canada. "In conclusion," he wrote, "it may be noted that it meant a great deal to Europe that its geometrical centre, Cracow, the original spot where Nordic, Alpine, and Mediterranean races met[,] was early a centre of culture and had a great University. Edmonton, Saskatoon and Winnipeg are natural centres for these rural European communities as they are centres of our Western Universities, likely to become the entrepôts of ideas and ideals."[144] Indeed, he was heartened to see that intermarriage among the "various racial groups" was proceeding rapidly and contributing to their amalgamation and assimilation. Assimilation was a "problem" that was gradually being solved, but there remained several impediments. In particular, England paid close attention to the denominational breakdown of each province, arguing "one of the main obstacles to intermarriage and hence to eventual amalgamation of the various racial stocks is that of religious creed." Nevertheless, he was impressed by the progress and, shifting to a different metaphor than the mosaic, he marvelled at what "a kaleidoscope of races" the West had become.[145]

The significance of England's acknowledgment of ethnic groups racialized as non-white and his warmer attitude towards block settlements as expressed in *The Colonization of Western Canada* should not be overestimated. In other writings from the period, particularly at conferences, his ambivalence towards nominally non-white peoples is clear. In December 1930, he travelled to the semi-annual meeting of the American Railway Development Association in Chicago, where he delivered a paper on "The Contribution of Rural Minded Peoples to Railway and National Development." Discussing the rural and urban distribution of European immigrants in America and Canada, he listed the number of foreign born in a number of American cities. "In all the figures given above," he noted, "the negro population has been ignored, and the figures and percentages relate to the total white population and the white persons of foreign origin." England did not consider African Americans to be foreign or native but instead attempted to erase their presence, along with all those racialized as non-white.[146]

The following year, England reviewed Charles Young's book, *The Ukrainian Canadians: A Study in Assimilation*, which was the first monograph to study this ethnic group.[147] England took exception with Young's treatment of rural Ukrainians and, in his critique, made some revealing comments. Discussing the assimilation of Ukrainians, he questioned whether or not intermarriage was a beneficial process, and again compared central European immigrants to people of African descent. "Has anything been gained by the intermarriage of our Indian, French, and Anglo-Saxon stocks?" he questioned. "A recent writer on racial mixture contends that the mulattoes, composing at present less than twenty percent of the negro population, have produced more than eighty percent of the superior men of the race. Yet is the intermixture a desirable process?" Here England suggested that the infusion of blood from Anglo-Saxons (or nominally white people) was what produced greatness in "mulattoes," but intimated that such unions were ultimately undesirable. Returning to a discussion of Ukrainians, he closed by arguing that even if race and culture were independent, "to concentrate on racial characteristics, while ignoring characteristics which are common to various groups, may well lead to much misconception of the process involved in what has been loosely termed assimilation."[148]

Similar sentiments were expressed a few years later. In 1932, the Canadian Institute of International Affairs (CIIA) invited the Institute of Pacific Relations (IPR) to hold their fifth biennial conference in Banff the following year. The IPR agreed, and so the CIIA began preparing for their arrival. As a part of this process, England was appointed as one of more than forty Canadian members of the conference. In addition, the CIIA's International Research Committee requested that he prepare a paper on Canadian Immigration Policy.[149] The result was a largely descriptive rather than analytical take on the evolution of the policy, but it nevertheless contains some revealing remarks. In it, he explicitly dismissed a hierarchical ranking of nominally white races. Referring to "a dogmatic pseudo-scientific school of thought which justifies and condones the exclusionist policies of the United States," he argued this exclusionism was based either on an economic argument or "on the preservation of some supposed ideal ethnic solidarity, somewhat mythical in its basis, such as Nordicism."[150]

There are no indications that England ever believed there to be inequality among European races. His earliest writings on the subject suggest that he believed each race had its own particular strengths, but that some were more culturally primitive than others. However, England's defence of non-Anglo-Saxons was limited by a racism that privileged those racialized as white; his stance that all European races were equal was not accompanied by a belief in the equality of non-European races. When discussing "Oriental Immigration," England noted that the Continuous Journey Act had "proved extremely effective. By 1909 Hindu immigration received a sudden check which has practically eliminated that source." He was also in favour of the so-called gentleman's agreement with Japan, which had reduced the number of immigrants; as he put it, "the system has worked with satisfaction to both countries." Finally, he spoke approvingly of the Chinese head tax and cited W.G. Smith's analysis, which showed the revenue it provided from 1897 to 1917 had effectively paid for "the cost of the solicitation of Europeans who entered Canada in this period."[151] Perhaps as a result of the narrower vision of tolerance it expressed, he marked the paper "CONFIDENTIAL: *Not for publication.*"[152]

Much like his first book, *The Colonization of Western Canada* received widely favourable press coverage. Economist W.W. Swanson of the University of Saskatchewan praised the book as "one of the more important economic studies written in Canada during the past decade. In its own field it is without a peer." However, he saw through the term "group consciousness" used in the book's second part, instead describing the experiment as one "using racial consciousness as a lever to raise community standards in their economic and social aspects." Swanson concluded that "no serious student of problems of group settlement and racial coöperation can afford to neglect it."[153] The book was not merely an account of the methods of settlement, another reviewer remarked, "but a sympathetic study of the diverse racial elements which make up the population, with special emphasis upon the way in which each group has reacted to its environment."[154] Not all reviewers shared England's vision for cultural pluralism. G.E. Britnell, an economist and political scientist at the University of Saskatchewan, reviewed the book for the *Canadian Historical Review*. He suggested that England's "generous enthusiasm" had led him to "under-estimate the extent to which the Central and Eastern European immigrant has displaced the Anglo-Saxon and native-born farm operator, and to over-estimate tremendously the speed with which assimilation is taking place through inter-marriage." The time has come, Britnell concluded, for Canadians to "count fully the cost of unwise settlement policies."[155] Professor of political economy W.B. Hurd felt much the same, writing that both England's book and C.A. Dawson's similar volume on *Ethnic Communities in Western Canada* left the reader with the impression that "God's in His Heaven and all's right with the West, which, after all, is perhaps a philosophical attitude to assume towards the many gratuitous mistakes of past settlement policies."[156]

CONCLUSION

Throughout all of England's writings, the central idea was that Canada was a growing nation and that the work of assimilating immigrants was in reality about cultivating citizenship. This citizenship required the adoption of the English language and subservience to the Anglo-Canadian legal and educational systems, but it allowed for some cultural difference. As he put it in 1929, "The modern world is more sympathetic to the idea of ethnic individuality. We are beginning to realize that a primitive people has a right to preserve its own cultural background whether it has an aesthetic or not." However, this was not a substantive commitment to diversity. In an address the following year, he added that rural non-English settlements could be made attractive to the urban unemployed by "keeping a little of their national colour and flavour."[157] Nor was this sentiment altruistic; ensuring that the western territory remained attractive to potential settlers was essential to the ongoing work of his department.[158]

His vision of a limited cultural pluralism, however superficial, was also rooted in a particular understanding of race and anthropology. Like Kirkconnell, England was convinced that race determined individual characteristics. He imagined himself to be a social psychologist whose task it was to take into account these racial instincts and then to determine how they might be modified through the social environment. Racial instincts, thus modified, were then to be put to use for the benefit of the local community and ultimately the entire nation. England remained confident that, with sufficient attention to immigrants' social environment, Canada was capable of assimilating various European races – however primitive – to its modern civilization. More than a theorist, however, he put these ideas into practice for the CNR, recruiting immigrants and working to improve the conditions of – and Canadianize – their new settlements.

Like Kirkconnell, who proposed at various times the imagery of a colourful tapestry, melting icebergs in the sea, and musical overtones, England never consistently used a single metaphor to describe Canada's patterns of settlement and diversity, but once referred to the various settlements on the prairies as a kaleidoscope of races. Unlike a mosaic, in which the pieces were fixed, a kaleidoscope could be adjusted to change the colourful patterns for the viewer's pleasure. Similarly, he referred to the supposedly diverse racial heritage of Europeans as "a mosaic of racial characteristics." However, he most often preferred to quote a phrase attributed to Giuseppe Mazzini: "God has written a line of his thought on the cradle of each race." What England, Kirkconnell, and many of their peers had in common was a belief that Canada's diversity was racial in its nature and that an individual's racial heritage to some degree determined their personal characteristics. Yet none of the descriptors they used to try to describe this diversity had any staying power; there was simply no dominant metaphor used to refer to diversity on the prairies or in Canada more broadly. All this changed in December 1938 with the publication of the book *Canadian Mosaic*, written by John Murray Gibbon, a publicist with the rival Canadian Pacific Railway.[159]

3

# John Murray Gibbon and Folk Culture

INTRODUCTION

In the preface to his best-selling book, *Canadian Mosaic*, John Murray Gibbon was upfront with the reader and acknowledged that he was not the first to use the metaphor in this way. Instead, he reported that American travel writer Victoria Hayward used it in a 1922 work to refer to the architectural landscape of the Canadian prairies, and that in 1926 Kate Foster had published a survey of "new Canadians" under the title *Our Canadian Mosaic*. But neither of these works were as successful as Gibbon's *Mosaic*, which was lauded nationwide, garnered the interest of King George VI, and won a Governor General's Literary Award. ("I advise you all to win one of these medals," Gibbon joked to the Canadian Authors Association, "because, if you do, people will read your books.") The press reported that the book was "widely acclaimed by British and Canadian critics for its compelling human interest, sound scholarship, and as an important contribution to the solution of a vital national problem – the problem of Canadian unity."[1]

Within months of its publication, the book and its titular metaphor were spreading across the country. Politicians, activists, teachers, students, ministers, journalists, and editors began deploying the term; women's and young people's organizations began studying the book ("as a guide to studying Canada's nationality problem"); and various groups attempted to determine their place within the Canadian mosaic.[2] And it took almost no time at all before Canada's mosaic was being presented in opposition to America's melting pot.[3] In short, there has never been a more popular metaphor for diversity in Canada than that of the mosaic and Gibbon's book was clearly responsible for its popularization.

For his efforts, Gibbon has been labelled a "proto-multiculturalist" and a "pioneer of multiculturalism," and his book has been held up as one of the first expressions of "full blown pluralist ideas."[4] However, what has been largely overlooked is that this was only the most famous expression of Gibbon's philosophy of cultural pluralism, which had developed over time, been expressed through other metaphors and in different venues, and had been modified along the way. Also largely overlooked has been the fact that, much like in the works of Kirkconnell and England, race was central to Gibbon's analysis: it was how he conceived of human diversity in Canada, it was what defined the tiles of his mosaic, and it shaped the dream of pluralism that he was selling to Canadians.

This chapter examines the development and expression of Gibbon's philosophy of cultural pluralism prior to the publication of his famous *Mosaic*, details its limitations, and argues that these exclusions were rooted in race. The chapter is divided into two sections: the first examines his intellectual development in a colonial context, and the second explores his life and work after his arrival in Canada, with a specific focus on his ideas about immigration, race, and culture. As a whole, the chapter shows that although Gibbon did not study race science to the same degree as Kirkconnell or even England, he too believed that European races had been a historic reality that helped to shape modern European nations (which he also referred to as races) and their individual members. Gibbon's philosophy of cultural pluralism, both prior to and as expressed in his famous mosaic metaphor, was limited by racism. Though he was aware of the presence in Canada of peoples racialized as non-white, he excluded them from consideration.

Prior to the Second World War, Gibbon advocated the acceptance of additional continental European immigrants on the grounds that they were an economic necessity and that they had rich cultural heritages. The policy of integration he proposed insisted that immigrants learn the English language, send their children to school, and obey the law. European immigrants were welcome to retain aspects of their folk cultures, as these would bring a splash of brightness to the nation. Like England, however, Gibbon also suggested that this was a two-sided equation, in which Anglo-Canadians had to welcome immigrants, provide them with the required education, and protect

Figure 3.1 John Murray Gibbon.

them from economic exploitation. This comprehensive vision was expressed through his original metaphor of the garden, in which Anglo-Canadians welcomed the addition of transplanted Europeans and gave them the necessary care and attention, but also carefully pruned them.

INTELLECTUAL DEVELOPMENT

*Colonial Education*

John Murray Gibbon was born in Ceylon, or what is now Sri Lanka. At the age of eighteen, John's father, William Duff Gibbon (1837–1919), had sailed from his native Scotland to Ceylon to grow coffee in the Kandy region. Ceylon had had a long, bloody period of colonial conquest and since 1815 the island had been under the British rule that would last until 1948. Kandy had been an independent kingdom until the British, through brutal tactics, conquered the region and there established the residence of the Governor-General and the island's Legislative Council, on which William Gibbon became quite active (he would later be knighted for his efforts). When the budding coffee industry was wiped out by disease, he switched to growing tea and began employing Tamil labourers from India. Once he had saved enough money he sent for his wife, Katharine G. Gibbon (née Murray; 1842–1916), and their children. On 12 April 1875, John Murray, their sixth child of an eventual eight, was born.[5]

In his memoirs, Gibbon provides a few fond recollections of his time on the island, where he saw little of his father but was looked after by a "Singhalese ayah or nurse called Babahamy," of whom he was very fond. At four years old, he was packed off to Scotland where he and three siblings boarded with a Protestant minister's family in Aberdeen, as his mother wanted to spend most of her time back in Ceylon. Sending children back to Europe for education was apparently a common practice among the colonists there, and in the British Empire more broadly. As historian Adele Perry has argued, in a slightly different context and about children "of color" in particular, this education provided colonial children upward mobility and a way of understanding their place in the world. But even contemporary observers worried about the effect that this early separation from the parents had on the children, especially those of so-called mixed-race

Figure 3.2 Babahamy holding John Murray Gibbon.

marriages.[6] It certainly was difficult on young Gibbon, who was terribly homesick and at one point ran away from home in Aberdeen. When found by a police officer on the docks, young Gibbon told him he was going to sail back to his father in Ceylon, where he would buy him a chocolate with the two pence that he had brought.[7]

Just why was this separation deemed necessary? The rationale, according to Gibbon, was that if children remained in Ceylon much past the age of four "they were inclined to become domineering in their behaviour towards the native servants, and it was thought wise to avoid the cultivation of such habits by having them educated among white people."[8] Gibbon's upbringing was thus shaped by colonial, genteel whiteness. His father profited from the conquest and subjugation of non-Europeans; however, he wanted to ensure that his son did not treat their servants in a way that was considered uncouth, so he shipped him off to gain a European education, which was doubtless considered to be superior to any available in Ceylon. Gibbon attended kindergarten in Aberdeen, then switched to a school run by a French teacher, and finally studied at Robert Gordon's College from 1885 to 1891. He was a bright student, finishing in the top three of many of his classes and then successfully winning a bursary from King's College at the University of Aberdeen, which he would attend from 1891 to 1894.[9] While it is difficult to determine his ideas about race during this early period, the imprint of this colonial upbringing is clearly seen in Gibbon's later portrayals of other places such as Algeria, where he unquestioningly accepted as normal the racialized division between rulers (racialized as white) and subjects (racialized as non-white). Similarly, his early letters show that he was comfortable using racial epithets.[10]

From this period onwards, Gibbon's interest in other European cultures was piqued through art, primarily literature and music. While at Aberdeen he worked on the editorial staff of the college magazine, *Alma Mater*, whose editor-in-chief, William Andrew Mackenzie, stimulated Gibbon's interest in poetry. He also became increasingly interested in music, taking piano and violin lessons and singing in a choir at a number of concerts. As a member of a group of students who used to meet in a private room and sing, he absorbed and enjoyed the music contained in the newly published *Scottish Students' Song Book*. Its international range included translations and parodies of German folksongs, sea shanties, soldiers' songs, and music from America, Austria, Canada, England, France,

Ireland, Norway, Russia, and Spain.[11] He later suggested that it was through music that he "learned to feel a special sympathy" for various nationalities, including Poles, Russians, Czechs, Italians, Austrians, Finns, and Norwegians, specifically through the work of their famous composers. "Music is an international language," the multilingual man concluded.[12]

Convinced by a friend to try for a scholarship at Oxford, Gibbon did not complete his final year at the College. Despite his father's apparent wealth, Gibbon wrote for an "Exhibition" type scholarship, open only to those "who could show that their income was small," with his uncle vouching for his supposed financial hardship. Drawing together his interests in literature and music, he wrote an essay on the relationship between poetry and music that successfully garnered him a four-year scholarship. He studied for a BA in classics at Christ Church, earning second-class honours at the end of his second-year examinations and rising to first-class honours the following year on his final examinations (the dreaded "Greats"). His interest in music and poetry remained strong but he was limited in his ability to pursue these topics. He later recalled being blocked from accessing musical scripts as they had no bearing on his prescribed subjects of study: Latin, Greek, ancient history, and philosophy.[13]

While not a strong athlete, Gibbon played football and tennis and rowed in "Torpids" (a race open to first-year students). In his spare time, he socialized with other Scots, canoed with friends, and spent time with "Paulines" – students from St Paul's school in London, whom he had met while at Göttingen. Most were members of the Fabian Society, a British organization (composed largely of middle-class intellectuals) that advocated socialist reform through democratic and incremental, rather than revolutionary, means. Gibbon was interested enough that he helped them form a branch of the Fabian Society at Oxford. Although at the beginning he had only "vague ideas" about the whole movement, within a year he made the following pronouncement to his girlfriend: "I am now a Socialist ... an out-and-out Collectivist. Somehow or other life in London does bring home the reality to life, and one cannot look upon the poverty and open immorality without feeling that these things lie at one's very door and are due to a great extent to our carelessness and selfishness. The fact is my ambitions are changing now, and I begin to be more and more desirous of being rather a good citizen than anything else."[14] However, he expressed some mixed feelings about the movement in his journal. In one entry, he wrote of his hope that Nancy would "turn Socialist. There's quite a nest of them there [at Somerville Hall], and I'm sure you, who come of good old Radical stock, will get some healthy notions. I'm not sure that I'm a very good Socialist, but I do think that middle class people have a lot upon their heads & hands that ought to be put away. And I want you to join me in helping less fortunate people in getting glimpses of happiness." However, he also critiqued socialists for being insufficiently patriotic and declared his intention to join the volunteer regiment at Oxford. As he put it, "Socialists are apt to be rather out of it where patriotism is required, and in fact merge their patriotism in talk about a universal brotherhood. Now universal brotherhood is all very well, but if your universal brother is going to knock you down you don't bother about words but defend yourself." In a lighter moment, he also wrote that he would "turn a rebel in any Socialist state" that would not allow him to hoard a fire in the fireplace all to himself.[15]

Gibbon had considered joining the British Home Service or the Indian Civil Service, but upon graduating from Oxford in 1898 he was asked by William Andrew Mackenzie (his old editor at *Alma Matter*, back in Aberdeen) to take an apprenticeship at *Black and White*, an illustrated weekly in London. He quickly agreed to the one-year, unpaid position as he felt it would give him "some standing."[16] The possibility of becoming a more active Fabian had also made the move to London attractive to Gibbon. However, these leanings were soon put to an end, not by communal fires nor a lack of martial nationalism but rather by parental intervention: his father firmly insisted that he join the Royal Colonial Institute (now the Royal Commonwealth Society). The institute was a place where those interested in or directly connected to British colonialism could share experiences and research relating the British Empire, and the immersion in this atmosphere solidified Gibbon's adherence to the tenets of classical liberalism, with its overriding emphasis on the individual. Towards the end of his life, he remarked that the meetings of the institute "made me realize that the Empire had not been built up by Socialists, and that countries such as Canada owed their progress largely to individual effort."[17]

In 1900 the apprenticeship ended and Gibbon finally began to receive pay for his efforts. Things were looking up: when Mackenzie fell ill, Gibbon was raised to the position of editor. He was quickly displaced by a more experienced editor but, with the outbreak of the South African (Boer) War, the demand for illustrated news increased, so the new editor spun off the picture pages into a smaller publication entitled *Black and White Budget* and placed Gibbon in charge of the enterprise. Now that he had a steady income, Gibbon finally married Anne Fox (his beloved "Nancy," as he always called her) and the two briefly lived in a basement apartment before moving to a house in the artist colony of Bedford Park.[18]

*Colonial Exploration*

From 1900 to 1910 Gibbon engaged in colonial exploration, sailing to two colonies, Algeria and Canada. The extensive reading that he did beforehand influenced his perception of these locales, and his subsequent comments reveal that his understanding of them was specifically influenced by ideas about race. While his understanding of diversity was racial, he seems to have paid more attention to the white/non-white division and its attendant notions of hybridity than to the idea of hierarchy among white races. After his travels were over, he did not express a desire to return to Algeria, but the number of European "races" that he encountered in Canada fascinated him and stimulated a desire to study the country more closely.

Shortly after moving to Bedford Park, Gibbon was diagnosed with scrofula, which was blamed on the poorly ventilated apartment they had recently vacated. After admitting Gibbon to a private hospital and performing an operation, his doctor then supposedly recommended a treatment of "open air and sun-tanning and rest, preferably in North Africa."[19] Gibbon decided to follow this prescription, despite the steep cost. He would have to take a leave from the paper, and he feared they would take the opportunity to terminate him (they did). He also could not afford the cost of passage, as the surgery had taken his last £200. He decided against writing his father for money and turned instead to Anne's father, who agreed to cover the cost of the trip, so he bade them farewell and sailed for Algeria. He would later drop hints that the trip was not medically necessary and that the doctor's advice may even have been prearranged, but it is unclear why he was so keen to get away.[20]

Gibbon's reflections on Biskra, the Algerian city in which he stayed, reveal that he was already interested in Canada and was also carefully observing the world through a lens of race.

> It was interesting to see how the French, who were the rulers of Algeria, mixed so readily with the native Arab population. There seemed to be almost as many halfbreeds as natives ... I was reminded of what I had read of the *metis* or *bois brulés* in Canada, where the *voyageurs* who were engaged in the fur-trade seemed to have been recruited largely from the children and descendants of French peasants who came out and married Indian wives, rather than roam the woods or prairies as bachelors.[21]

The French situation obviously presented a challenge to his previously held ideas about racial purity, as he found their relations with Arabs to be a curiosity. However, his ideas about race and colonialism in Canada helped him rationalize the number of intermarriages, which he portrayed as a means for peasants to escape bachelorhood.[22]

Gibbon's recovery in Biskra was interrupted by a chill he caught, so on the doctor's orders he returned to England, where he continued his open-air "treatment" in St Ives, an artist colony in Cornwall. From there he travelled to Scotland and Ireland and presumably returned to his life – and wife – in London sometime afterwards. When he "felt sufficiently recovered to do regular work," he began working as a freelance journalist on Fleet Street and began writing a weekly column on parliamentary affairs for the *Illustrated London News*, at the request of his old friend J.D. Symon. Symon was a cousin to Allan Cameron, the Canadian Pacific Railways (CPR) general traffic agent in London, and when Cameron began looking for an advertising agent, Symon suggested Gibbon for the job. Attracted to the good salary and especially the possibility of travel, Gibbon quickly accepted the position.[23]

Hired in 1907, Gibbon's first assignment from the company president was to organize a tour of Canada for the editors of a dozen leading British newspapers (a proud Scot, he ensured one Scottish newspaper was included).[24] The trip was transformative: he was captivated by Canada and particularly by its apparent Scottishness. As always, he had primed himself by consuming a number of books on the subject beforehand, this time on Scottish history, with the result that he saw the influence of Scots everywhere. Further reading made his heart swell with pride: between 1821 and 1886, 171 of 263 commissioned officers in the Hudson's Bay Company were Scottish; a Scot was likely responsible for organizing the Royal Canadian

Mounted Police (RCMP); and Ontario was abounding in Scottish-founded settlements. Of course, the "greatest figure in Canadian history" was a Scot by the name of Sir John A. Macdonald, but he was also happy to learn of the Scottish involvement in the building of the CPR. "To a Scot such as myself the list of names of those who had helped to build up this transcontinental railway in its early stages made me feel as I belonged to the family," Gibbon wrote. "Scottish names were so prevalent among the Canadian people that I felt Canada could not be a foreign country, if circumstances were to turn in favour of making my home in this country."[25]

Upon returning to London he asked his manager to allow him to go on an "educational trip" to Canada each summer. "I felt I must learn to know the Canadian way of life," he later wrote, and "to ride on a western saddle." Indeed, western Canada in particular made a significant impression on him.

I began to realize that the prairies were Europe transplanted – there were not only Britishers and the Canadian born, but there were Germans, Scandinavians, the "men in sheepskin coats" from Galicia and the Ukraine, who, as the saying went, were being hurled by the trainloads at the Canadian prairies.

This trip through the West threw new light on my vocation. I began to realise that the Canadian Pacific was not merely a railway carrying passengers and freight, but through its colonization work helping to build up a new nation. I made up my mind to come out again and make a closer study of this nation-building.

The trip inspired much reading – he ended up spending a full week in Toronto, visiting bookshops and the public library – and ultimately made Canadian history one of his "chief interests, particularly the social history, with its blending of so many racial traditions."[26]

*Colonial Demonstration*

Canada had earned such a close place in Gibbon's heart that when he heard that the country had been shut out of the Scottish National Exhibition being planned for Glasgow in 1910, he suggested a CPR-sponsored pavilion, one that would showcase the work of the Scots in Canada's development, and pitched it to W.D. Ross, a fellow he knew from *Black and White*. Ross sold the idea to the exhibition's organizing committee and Gibbon sold it to the CPR. The result, with its large murals painted by friends from *Black and White*, was so popular that a London publisher approached Gibbon to write a book on the subject. Gibbon accepted and quickly wrote *Scots in Canada*, a 162-page volume that featured the murals as illustrations. Published in 1911, the book sold sixteen thousand copies.[27]

The book was an uncritical celebration of Scottish people's role in the colonization of Canada or, as he put it, the filling of Canada with "a new white population."[28] For Gibbon, the racial history of the Scots was important to understanding their particularities as a group; however, he was seemingly unaware of or uninterested in the Nordicist theory. Instead, he portrayed all European nationalities as white races and gave no indication of any hierarchy among them, though he did take pains to trace racial origins deep into the past. He described the book as "the elaboration of an idea ... the idea of a race movement impelled by the pressure of circumstance and a spirit of adventure, and controlled by a subconscious clannishness, or sticking together." Race for Gibbon was thus an important, inescapable force that shaped global history. The book began with a brief overview of Scottish history, focusing on the blending of Norse, Danish, and Norman strains. The rapid assimilation of Scots in Quebec could later be attributed to race; it was "not so difficult to understand when one remembers that the Frasers at any rate were not Celts but Normans" and the French too were "mostly of a Norman race."[29] The ease with which Scots used canoes was also explained by their racial origins, as such a vessel was fitting for "children of the Vikings," Gibbon wrote.[30] His most grandiose argument, made from the outset, was that Scots were a people who from time immemorial had followed "the North-west trail," making their eventual migration to North America racially predestined.[31]

The process of researching and writing the book, he later remarked, "had a definite influence on my outlook. I ... came to realize how much Canada owed to the Scots ... With this historical background, I became more than ever reconciled to the prospect of making Canada my future home. It would not be a foreign land."[32] Having constructed the narrative of inevitable Scottish immigration to Canada, he now determined to write himself into it. Luckily for him, the opportunity quickly presented itself. In 1913, CPR president Sir Thomas Shaughnessy decided he wanted "the propaganda and advertising of the Company's services in the hands of someone familiar with Europe as well as Canada." Gibbon was thus given the offer to move to Montreal and take the title of general publicity agent, responsible for both advertising and liaising with the press.

Tipped off to the offer half an hour before it arrived, Gibbon came up with the idea to accept on one condition: that he be allowed to travel to Canada by way of the Trans-Siberian Railway. He had been reading about Japan and wanted to see it for himself – much as he had read about Algeria and subsequently arranged to spend his convalescence there. But the company, as he put it, "had a reputation of keeping their employees with their noses to the desk." He pitched the route to Shaughnessy on the grounds that it would give him a chance to see some of the CPR's service to "the Orient" and that he could reach Vancouver just as quickly by the Trans-Siberian as if he crossed Canada on the CPR line. The intrigued Shaughnessy agreed, arranging for Gibbon to first attend a five-day rail conference in Moscow, no doubt to better justify the expense.[33] Gibbon again bade his family farewell and set off on the leisurely trip, which ended in Japan with a curt cable from Shaughnessy that read: "When are you coming?" With that, he boarded a steamship and arrived in Vancouver on 2 August 1913. (Shaughnessy, it should be noted, was a perfectionist whose management style, honed during the CPR's severe financial crisis in the 1880s, consisted of scrutinizing all expenditures, rooting out corruption and waste, and humiliating the perpetrators of even minor transgressions. Given Gibbon's seemingly romantic, meandering approach to work, it seems a small miracle he survived in his position; perhaps this is the best evidence that Gibbon's efforts bore financial fruit.)[34]

### IMMIGRATION AND PLURALISM

Gibbon's work, *Scots in Canada*, helped to pave his way in the country. Though he loved Canada, his first impressions of its CPR offices had not been promising. In 1907, while on the cross-country tour with the British journalists, Gibbon had decided to pay a visit to the office in Windsor Station, Montreal. Vice-president of traffic G.M. Bosworth, an American with notoriously abrupt manners, had greeted him by remarking, "So you are another of those bloody Britishers!" Bosworth died in 1911 but, as Gibbon found out, his spirit lived on in those offices. In 1913, Gibbon was moved to that same station, where he received the cold shoulder from many of the staff. He felt like he was viewed as an "intruder," particularly by those who were Canadian born. As he remarked to a friend at the time, moving to Canada was like "landing on an iceberg." Ironically, it would thaw on account of his British connections. According to his later account, the staff became friendlier when they heard of his invitation to lunch with CPR chairman Sir William Van Horne. Van Horne had been given a copy of *Scots in Canada* and wanted to meet its author, who was obviously "not a mere railway man."[35] By 1914 Gibbon had paid to have a house constructed in Ste Anne de Bellevue, a suburb of Montreal, and had sent for Nancy and their three children, Murray, Ann Faith, and John. Their fourth child, Philip, would be born later that year.[36] In the early years after his family's arrival, Gibbon threw himself into his work, travelling to visit the CPR offices in the United States, but, as always, mixing business with pleasure.[37]

Almost nothing has been written about Gibbon's personal life, in large part because most accounts follow his unpublished autobiography, which itself is silent on the subject ("more a biography of the C.P.R. than of J.M.G.," the would-be publisher complained). For instance, in his master's thesis, Gary Kines suggested that because Gibbon had been separated from his parents at such a young age, he was "emotionally independent," and that this explained his subsequent silence on his wife and family.[38] However, materials still in the family's possession give a glimpse into the relationship between Gibbon and his future wife and reveal a different side. Letters he wrote to young Nancy during the early years of their initially furtive romance express infatuation and paternalism, as he offered her advice on many things, including attire, handwriting, reading material, and politics. Although Gibbon was very lonely at Oxford and felt that he had no friends – and was further convinced that many of his "*so-called* friends" were fonder of him than he was of them – he was besotted with Nancy and felt she was his one true friend. "I always feel as if I could confide in you like a boy but love you like a girl and perhaps that's the best relation one could have," he wrote.[39]

As previously detailed, this lengthy romance culminated in their marriage, but shortly thereafter Gibbon had gone on the long and dubiously justified voyage to Biskra without her. What happened in this intervening period will most likely remain a mystery, but it is clear that afterwards Gibbon poured himself into his work and hobbies.

In 1923, for instance, his family travelled west to celebrate the opening of the Banff-Windermere highway. After the ceremony Gibbon departed for a lengthy trail ride, leaving Nancy and the children at their summer home in Invermere.[40] The prioritization of personal and professional interests over family life is hinted at in an interview in which the reporter, presuming Gibbon was at home on the weekends, asked his daughter how she enjoyed Sunday. "'Sunday?' she remarked. 'Not very much. That's the day daddy writes his novels.'"[41] As he admitted in his memoirs, "I am afraid I have never been much of a family man, though the father of four children, being much interested in reading as well as travel that home was little else than a place to work or to jump from."[42]

Whatever the reason for Gibbon's initial break from married life and his continued independent lifestyle, his eldest son's 1925 breakdown at Oxford, where he was a Rhodes scholar, and subsequent lifelong mental health struggles placed a great strain on the marriage and on Nancy's emotional wellbeing.[43] With time, it became apparent even to other relatives that the couple had grown apart. Gibbon's niece Elizabeth described the two as having a devoted marriage but noted that they had "that deep sadness over Murray always at the back of their minds." Elizabeth also regretfully perceived a lack of communication between them, and offered the following story of how she and Gibbon once went to see a play together. Afterwards, Gibbon remarked that he was glad Nancy had not seen it as it would have upset her, but Elizabeth was "convinced that Nancy would have *loved* it and chuckled like we did at the flippancy."[44]

But in 1913 this was all still in the future, as Gibbon had just arrived in Montreal and was beginning his new job. Essentially cosmopolitan in his outlook, he seems to have been surprised by the need to navigate colonial politics in Canada. Once the ice thawed at the office, however, his outsider's perspective quickly led to some productive changes. One week after Gibbon's arrival in Montreal, CPR president Shaughnessy sent for him and asked if he had any ideas to suggest. Gibbon then provided an astute observation:

> Nearly a third of the population of Canada, and two thirds of that in Montreal, is French Canadian, but the staff in my office is nearly all English speaking … With your permission I should like to make closer contact with the editors of the French newspapers, and ask them to nominate a French Canadian as my

assistant – one of themselves. If they do this, he will have their confidence, and their columns will be more open to what we have to say. This will also make it possible for us to send them any news we should like them to print in French, and save them both time and trouble in translation.

Surprised, Shaughnessy asked if the French press would go for it, to which Gibbon replied that they could at least offer. He then approached Eugène Tarte of *La Patrie*, with the result that Raoul Clothier was nominated to head the French section of the Canadian Pacific Press Bureau.[45]

During the Great War, Gibbon volunteered for the military but was rejected on account of his age and health, and so instead assisted with CPR fundraising efforts in Montreal. After 1916, when the first of an eventual five novels was published, he also worked to strengthen his contacts with the literary world.[46] The latter was facilitated by friendship with B.K. Sandwell, who nominated him for membership in Montreal's Pen and Pencil Club, a small organization for artists and writers. Through family connections, he also obtained membership in the exclusive University Club of Montreal. (During this period membership in both was restricted to men, and the latter did not allow Jewish members until 1960.)[47] Gibbon also began seriously contemplating postwar immigration. On a trip to Chicago, he purchased a number of books "dealing with the racial groups in the United States." The purpose of this study was to understand what was likely to happen in Canada with the postwar influx of European immigrants unable to find free land in America. He soon began making annual trips to western Canada and to British Columbia with the purpose of studying the immigration movement, and within a short time he began publicly speaking on the subject.[48]

In a 1916 address to the Ad Club in Calgary, Gibbon expressed skepticism about the postwar immigration boom that many were predicting. The physical realities of transporting 200,000 soldiers and their family members back to Canada meant that there would be no steamships available to transport would-be immigrants, he argued, and by his estimation this repatriation from Britain and France would take at least a year. Immigration optimists also overlooked economic factors, he continued. "If sentiment and kindly feeling were all that were required ... we would need another Moses to separate the waters of the Atlantic and enable the people to come easily across, for surely there are not enough ships to carry those who want to come." But there had been a movement to control English emigration even prior to the war, and now that so many farmers had died fighting to the point that "their mere absence has forced their womenfolk to work in the fields like European peasants, that movement may very well result in definite restrictions." Gibbon called on the Canadian government to educate veterans and "back to the landers" on farming techniques and financial management, but added that they needed to recognize the need for skilled labourers too. To this end, he proposed the creation of card-indexed national labour bureaus that would list opportunities for skilled and unskilled labour. "These immigrants have travelled perhaps four thousand miles to make their new homes here," he argued. "Give them a square deal."[49]

In an address delivered only a few months later, Gibbon repeated his argument that Canada needed a wiser immigration policy, one that would acknowledge the need for skilled labour, and again called for the creation of a national labour bureau – now adding that if the Dominion or provincial governments were too slow to act, then industries should establish a similar system themselves. He also suggested that for population increase Canada would continue to depend more on natural increase rather than immigration. However, instead of pouring cold water on the idea of English immigration, he now emphasized the likelihood of "an immense volume" of postwar immigration from continental Europe. His opinion continued to change and by mid-1917 he seems to have accepted the notion of an immigration boom, suggesting that the Canadian population (7.2 million in 1911) would number twelve to fifteen million within three years of the war's end.[50]

Like Kirkconnell, many of Gibbon's ideas about Canada's diversity were expressed in relation to literature. In an address delivered in the 1940s, Gibbon suggested that it was through famous literary works that he "acquired a sympathy" for Arabs, Danes, and Spaniards, and "learned to sympathize" with Persians, Belgians, French, Russians, and, later, Ukrainians and French Canadians.[51] At this time, however, he emphasized the notion of unity in diversity. Within four years of his arrival in Canada, he saw the country's racial diversity as a potential source of inspiration for a distinctive national literature. In the winter of 1917, Gibbon gave a talk entitled "Where Is Canadian Literature?" (Having heard he was giving a talk with this title, Stephen Leacock – the most famous Canadian author and humorist of the era – quipped: "I hope to God you will say that there is none.")[52] But a better question was "what is Canadian literature?" or how to define literature as essentially *Canadian*. Gibbon grandly suggested it was the "printed expression of a Canadian state of mind," but this begged the question: what was a Canadian? Canadian did not exclusively mean Canadian-born, he clarified. "If only the writer has lived long enough in the country to catch the Canadian spirit and become in sympathy a Canadian citizen – surely his or her writings can count as Canadian. 'The naturalized alien,' said Joseph Chamberlain, 'becomes your most ardent patriot,' and so the most fervent Canadians are not of necessity Canadian born." Gibbon saw national literature as being derived from a country's geography, social conditions, and history, with Canada providing plenty of fodder for authors. "As for drama – is there no drama in this tide of human souls surging over from Europe into our vacant spaces – Doukhobors, Galicians, Swedes, Belgians, French, Greeks, Syrians, to say nothing of our English, Scotch, Irish and Welsh?" In his mind, "there was never a country so rich in material for the imaginative writer as this ... where the Ruthenian maid in Winnipeg teaches her mistress Ukrainian folklore, where the Chinese laundrymen erect a monument ... to the writer of their own fairy tales."[53] The inclusion of Canadians of Asian descent was unusual but Indigenous people and people of African descent remained absent.

While so many Canadian writers had migrated to the United States, Gibbon remained confident that a distinctive literature could arise, in large part because of the war. The war had stirred the Canadian soul, he argued, and the "pride of race has become a real and tangible emotion instead of something vague, indefinite, negligible, almost to be apologized for." The war had birthed new writers and a new Canadian reading public, and though current writing was unavoidably tinged by the conflict, postwar writing would be distinctively Canadian. For Gibbon, this development was far more important than the concomitant financial benefits for Canadian publishers and authors. Financial success was often an author's worst enemy, he argued, for it inevitably meant a shift from expressing one's soul to trying to meet the publisher's interpretation of the public's appetite. Nevertheless, he paid close attention to the state of the publishing industry, and in his 1917 talk he floated many of the ideas he would later enact as the first president of the Canadian Authors Association

(1921–22), particularly campaigns to urge publishers, booksellers, readers, and reviewers to give preference to Canadian authors.[54]

Gibbon continued reflecting on the state of Canadian literature in 1919, focusing specifically on novels. Novels ought to reflect their times, he argued, and while American and English novels were living up to this criterion, Canadian novels were failing. Their sin was presenting only the lives of farmers, pioneers, or small town dwellers, although romantic American authors were worse still, presenting Canada as little more than "the semi-arctic haunt of Indians, trappers, bad men and mining experts." The dearth of Canadian life in Canadian fiction he blamed on economic reasons, such as the historical lack of Canadian publishers, but he held hope that the tide was turning as a result of the war. Their participation in the war showed the world that Canadians were "a bold, inventive and courageous people, with the result that Canada stands today on the threshold of a new era of nationhood." He concluded that "Canada is still waiting – but will not have to wait long – for her prophet – or more likely her group of prophets who shall interpret her many-sided, but always vigorous, life to her own people and the nations who have accepted her as Come of Age."[55]

Within a year Gibbon was forced to reckon with the fact that increasing nationalism could easily shade into xenophobia. This sentiment had been stoked by both the war, with its internment of so-called enemy aliens, and the Winnipeg General Strike of 1919.[56] "Since the return of peace conditions, the question of the foreign born, particularly in Western Canada, has once more come to the front," he wrote in an article published in *Queen's Quarterly*.

> It has been accentuated by the increased spirit of nationality which has grown out of the war – a spirit which demands that the foreign born shall either accept the ideals and obligations of Canadian citizenship or get out. It has to be faced in view of the possibility of renewed immigration to Canada, particularly from Central and Northern Europe, in view of the renewed demand for imported seasonal labour (such as Italian) which must arise if the pace of construction and development undertaken in Canada previous to the war is to be repeated.

In order to face this question, Gibbon provided "a brief summary of the situation so far as the more prominent racial types of immigrant are concerned." These types included Italians, Germans (and

Mennonites), Scandinavians, "Slav races" (with specific focus on Doukhobors, Ukrainians, and Poles), and Jews. His overview of each typically included the reasons for their immigration, their class, and their stance on education, all with a mind to their "rapid and effective assimilation." Aside from the many novels that he quoted, Gibbon relied heavily on the works of J.T.M. Anderson and J.S. Woodsworth in his attempt to grapple with the so-called problem of the "foreign born."[57] At this time, he expressed a vision of cultural pluralism that called for linguistic and political assimilation but allowed for some degree of cultural retention. When they arrived in Canada, immigrants had a responsibility to conform to the laws, send their children to school, and take an interest and pride in their new country. Canadians, in turn, had to ensure that immigrants felt welcomed, provide them with good and cheap education, and protect them from unfair exploitation. Gibbon saw nothing wrong with these "foreign born" expressing their cultures through folk songs and crafts, which "under more sympathetic treatment are being revived," he noted.[58]

The article exhorted Canada to avoid the mistakes that the United States was making in denying "this flotsam and jetsam of humanity" a home, much less a roof over its head. America was too nativist and suspicious of the foreign born, Gibbon charged, which was resulting in the exodus of immigrants from their borders. He was generally sympathetic to each group, noting that more press was given to the few that committed crimes than to the majority who were trying to better themselves through schooling and hard work, and commenting on each group's openness to education. He praised the "'New Canadian' movement in Saskatchewan" under the leadership of Dr Anderson. He believed the education of "new Canadians" was crucial, for without knowledge of the language (English), immigrants were "readily exploited" by employers, landlords, and political agitators. Seeking to assuage fears about immigrant's left-wing tendencies, he went on to claim that 80 per cent of immigrants involved in the Winnipeg strike were "inarticulate" (illiterate?) and had therefore been exploited by Bolshevist leaders. When newcomers were properly educated, he countered, "any tendency to Bolshevism will automatically die."[59]

Despite its generally tolerant message, the article contained more than a hint of anti-Semitism. Gibbon claimed that due to their familiarity with overcrowding, Ukrainians "were therefore easily exploited by the Jew landlords of Western cities and towns like Winnipeg." Jews themselves were "the element which every nation in history has found the most difficult to assimilate," he argued. Part of this was due to their "city fever," or tendency to head for already overcrowded cities, which in turn was due to the fact that "the Jews (so far as they are not de-Hebraized) are tied down by their need of 'Kosher' food and the Synagogue to places which support a Jewish colony. The social culture of the strict Jew is so closely identified with his religion that this is evidently the chief barrier to his assimilation with the Canadian race."[60] Anti-Semitism marked Gibbon's writing about Jewish people from the late 1890s through the 1920s, though his attitude towards Jewish people changed over time. Gibbon spent the summer vacations of 1893 and 1894 in Gottingen, Germany. During this time, he attended a service at a synagogue and remarked that it was "wonderfully interesting and well worth seeing." And when the owner of the home he was staying in received a "half-threatening" note, chastising her for shopping at a Jewish-owned store and stating that no true German woman would deal with Jews, he wrote to his girlfriend (and later wife), Nancy: "What brutes these Anti-Semites are ... There aren't Philo-Semites here but this is just a little too much."[61]

However, Gibbon later flirted with anti-Semitic theories during his coverage of the Dreyfus Affair (1894–1906). This charged political scandal, surrounding the wrongful conviction of a French military officer of Jewish descent named Alfred Dreyfus, involved forged documents, the suppression of evidence, multiple trials and convictions, the acquittal of the true criminal, and Dreyfus's eventual exoneration. Ultimately, it served to lay bare the anti-Semitism that marked French society. In an article written in 1899, Gibbon prefaced his report by remarking that, "like most Britons, [he] had considerable sympathy for Dreyfus, and believed him to be innocent ... [and] that his sufferings were due mainly to the machinations of a corrupt General Staff," but made sure to later clarify that he (Gibbon) was "not a Jew." Sitting through the court proceedings, Gibbon "realised for the first time the true French attitude – that it was not a question of one man's innocence or guilt, but a question of Jew and Frenchman. It was not the fight of individuals but the fight of races that we were watching." And in his opinion, both races were using dirty tactics. When addressing the question of whether there had been some bad faith on the part of some of the "more obviously flamboyant Dreyfusard [Dreyfus-supporting] correspondents," he pointed the reader to an article in another publication that contained the "significant explanation that 'Les Agences télégraphiques sont toutes aux mains des Juifs' [The telegraph agencies are all in the hands of Jews]. These questions can be sifted by those more qualified to judge than myself," he added, closing the article with the suggestion that the prosecution was moving forward with "racial instinct" to defend "the honour of France."[62]

A few years later, in 1909, Gibbon selected for inclusion in his collection of fairy tales for children the anti-Semitic story of "The Jew in the Bush."[63] His prejudice was also baldly expressed in his third novel, *The Conquering Hero* (1920), released a few months after his article on "The Foreign Born." As Terrence Craig put it, in the middle of this "otherwise conventional and mediocre novel, Gibbon unnecessarily inserts a scene of powerful anti-Semitism quite unrelated to the plot." The book also racialized Jews as non-white. "The English-Canadian hero, when asked if his friend the Polish princess is Jewish, replies bluntly: 'No, white.'"[64] Craig's dismissive appraisal of the novel unwittingly downplays the influence it may have had, given it was extremely well received by the press.[65] That Gibbon's tentative defence of European immigrants continued to be tinged with his ambivalence towards certain "racial" and religious groups is evident in the first paper he presented to the Royal Society of Canada.

## *The Garden Metaphor*

Sir Edward Beatty, the president of the CPR, had a rule that "no official of the railway may join any outside organization without first obtaining his leave." So when University of Toronto president Sir Robert Falconer offered to put Gibbon's name forward for fellowship in the Royal Society, Gibbon asked him to wait and then dutifully brought the request to the president.[66] Beatty expressed surprise, explaining that he understood the Society to be composed of professors, that he "could not see the connection between practical railway life and membership in such an Academic society," and that he knew of no other CPR officials who were members. Further, Fellows were expected to produce research papers for the Society's *Transactions*, so what did Gibbon intend to write about? "I said that since I was an immigrant myself, I thought it might be interesting to find out the contributions which the various groups of immigrants into Canada had brought with them. They weren't all peasants," Gibbon replied. Beatty apparently found this answer sufficient, acquiesced, and Gibbon was made a fellow in 1922.[67]

The following May, Gibbon delivered a paper entitled "European Seeds in the Canadian Garden," which was intended to counter the attitude that European immigration was hindering the development of a distinctly Canadian culture. He began by accepting the premise that "literature expresses the idiosyncrasies of racial thought" but argued that the experiences of America and Britain showed that immigrants might develop first-rate literature. "Is our wholesale immigration of the twentieth century bringing any such human seeds from Europe into the Canadian literary garden?" Gibbon asked. In an attempt to answer this question, he explored the Germans, Russians, Ukrainians, Scandinavians (Swedish, Norwegian, Danish, Icelanders, and Finnish), Jewish, Polish, Rumanians, and Greeks in turn. Inching away from outright anti-Semitism, his brief treatment of Jewish people consisted of making an ambiguous remark ("the eagerness of the Jew for education when he can get it, and his ability to make use of it[,] is notorious"), naming two well-known Canadian Jewish authors, and noting the influence of the Yiddish theatre on American drama.

Gibbon concluded that while most of the European immigrants were lower class or peasants, they were quickly becoming educated, showed great promise, and might "add richness and colour to the present somewhat monotonous Canadian literary garden." Revealing the reason for his talk, he remarked: "I trust this brief review will help to dispel any fear lest our Continental European immigration will set back Canadian culture." Like Kirkconnell and England, Gibbon also expressed antimodernist sentiments, and concluded his talk by countering that the real danger was that "materialism and prosperity-worship" rampant in North America would ultimately "destroy the poetry and the artistic impulse which so many of these immigrants bring with them."[68]

Gibbon's conception of new Canadians continued to evolve, and in November 1923, when he gave a different version of his "European Seeds" talk to the Empire Club in Toronto, he was convinced by their secretary to use the title "Canadian Letters and the New Canadian." This version of the talk focused more on the question of immigration, and in it he acknowledged that his was not a universally held opinion: "There are some who contend that the influx of these Continental Europeans into Canada is not a desirable thing, but threatens to weaken the bonds which unite the British Empire, as they know nothing of and would not properly value the great heritage of English literary tradition associated with the name of Shakespeare. Viewed in this light, the question resolves itself into whether these New Canadians are worthy of receiving or capable of appreciating this heritage of English literature." However, he quickly turned the question on its head. Pointing to the rich cultures of European immigrants' home countries, he suggested the "question is not so much whether the immigrant is worthy of the heritage of Shakespeare, but whether we ourselves are the worthy heirs."[69]

Gibbon then made an increasingly common argument, namely that the British were themselves a mix of a great number of groups but what kept them stable was the "Anglo-Saxon ideal of simplified Self-Government and Individual Freedom." Their composite character had not hindered British literary development but had enriched it, he maintained, adding that Canada's relatively welcoming immigration policy was in keeping with British tradition, just on a larger scale. "England has never known an immigration of foreign-born so varied in racial origin as Canada has experienced in this Twentieth Century, or so large in proportion to its previous population." Looking to America, a country that had experienced heightened immigration thirty years prior, he found that "the immigrant races" had positively influenced the development of their literature and suggested that the same was taking place in Canada. He offered a large number of examples of American immigrant authors, as well as a number of Canadians, including those of French, German, Scandinavian, Slavic, Russian, and Jewish origins.[70]

Gibbon was, despite ignoring all non-white immigrants, remarkably tolerant for his era. Indeed, as historian Stuart Henderson notes, this speech was "fraught with anxiety over his unfashionable views on the value of immigrants."[71] However, there was still a clear sense of British superiority, for it was the Anglo-Saxon ideal alone that made any sort of "composite" population possible. Gibbon concluded his talk by explaining its original title.

> This summer I found in a hitherto neglected corner of my garden a beautiful cluster of hollyhocks. Where they came from I do not know – I did not plant them – their seeds may indeed have been dumped into that corner in the most unromantic way, hidden

in a load of manure. But there they were, and by pruning off superfluous leaves and giving a little attention, they grew to be the most beautiful flowers in that garden. Now in the immigrant races we have the possibility of just such flowers in the Canadian literary garden – people who in their own country even though they were illiterate peasants enjoyed the possession of rich treasures of folk-lore and folk-song, peasants who in their arts and crafts show a deep feeling for harmonious form and colour, men and women and children eager to learn the language of the country that has given them refuge from the tragic circumstances of Europe, and surely ready some day to express their thoughts and aspirations in language which shall not perish.

European immigrants to Canada then, even if they came as in a load of manure, could still bloom and become beautiful citizens, furnishing the nation with colourful folk arts.[72] So long, of course, as they learned the imperishable language (English), all that these newly replanted folks required was a little pruning and a little attention.

Gibbon's garden metaphor was natural given his wife was an avid gardener (one of the first groups Nancy joined upon moving to Canada was the Ste Anne de Bellevue Horticultural Society) and, as his comments suggested, he too dabbled in gardening.[73] However, the garden metaphor is also notable for its eugenic overtones. In her recent study of sterilization in Alberta, Erika Dyck noted that eugenicists often described their campaigns using such organic metaphors including that of a garden and worried that "Canadian gardens seemed more susceptible to foreign weeds." Here they followed their British counterparts such as Havelock Ellis, who wrote: "In these matters, indeed, the gardener in his garden is our symbol and our guide."[74]

Some scholars have argued that certain passages in Gibbon's novel *The Conquering Hero* reveal "sympathy for eugenics," but his other remarks about eugenics during this period complicate this interpretation. In his earlier novel, *Drums Afar*, a character by the name of Kelly is questioned by Viola, his romantic interest, on his "past moral and physical history." "I want to be the mother of worthwhile children," she tells him, "and I've been taught enough to know that I can't be that unless my husband has lived cleanly." Recounting the story the next day to his pal Charles, he expresses exasperation. "Honest to God, I have led a clean life ... But these New Woman notions are the limit. I'd rather go again before the

State Bar Examiners than face Miss Mainwaring again in that canoe. Well, I guess she had a perfect right, only what she said didn't seem to fit in with the moonlight and the stars. Regular eugenics fan." Here eugenics is dismissed as an extreme, unnecessary movement, one that women are interested in but for which men have no use.[75]

In *The Conquering Hero*, the character of the doctor is described as having been celebrated in his day as "a pioneer in the science of eugenics, that is to say, in the theory that only the physically fit should be allowed to marry." He takes his daughter, Stephanie, on an overseas trip in an attempt to prevent her from marrying a prince of fine pedigree who is unfit due to illness. They return to find the prince has married but his wife has taken his money and left him to die alone. The doctor advises Stephanie to let him suffer, but she "was less cold blooded," and carries the prince off to Africa to attempt a recovery. There the prince eventually dies, but afterwards Stephanie gives birth to his child, "whose very existence was fatal to the Doctor's propaganda for eugenics. If he could not prevent his own daughter from bearing children to an incurable, how could he hope to persuade the world at large? For her part the Princess became profoundly cynical and careless of gossip." While the passage suggests some sympathy for the basic idea of "negative eugenics," it is also presented as a heartless and generally futile effort.[76]

Gibbon's apparent ambivalence towards eugenics had dissipated within two years of the publication of this novel. In a popular and widely reported satirical address entitled "Book Birth Control for Authors and Book Eugenics for Publishers," Gibbon argued that Malthusian principles should be applied to the overproduction of novels, and specifically that novelists should be discouraged from producing more than one book every two years. As for "certain publishers," he recommended "the eugenic plan of segregation in alternate years in a penitentiary where the cell should be furnished with a radio broadcasting set at which poets would be permitted to recite verses twenty-four hours a day." In his published version of the talk, he went even further in mocking eugenics: "Let me emphasize that I am advocating book-birth-control and not eugenics, for authors. To advocate eugenics would be to recommend that authors, like the feeble-minded, should be forcibly segregated from their fountain pens or typewriters, or be incapacitated by an operation from writing books, or be compelled to produce a certificate that their parents were successful authors before they themselves were permitted publication, or be able to satisfy the Ku Klux Klan that they are normal 100 per cent Americans." Gibbon's injunction was generally received favourably, although one newspaper editor wryly pointed out that "it may be assured that he believes his own books are good enough to be born and brought up; but with his general contention most people will agree."[77]

When it came to the Canadian garden, Gibbon would focus not on pruning the lilies as a eugenicist, but rather giving them attention as a publicist. He did so by continuing to give variants of this talk for about a year, notably to Jewish audiences, which suggests a continued and intentional movement away from his past anti-Semitism. (For instance, in February 1924, he gave a talk entitled "Canadian Literature and the Foreign Born" to the Baron de Hirsch Book Club, and the following month gave a similar talk to the Temple Emanu-El Brotherhood.) Aside from public lectures, Gibbon soon created a larger project that would draw attention to Canadians of European descent and their contributions to Canadian culture.[78]

## The Folk Festivals

Gibbon had long been a lover of folk music. Back at the University of Aberdeen in the 1890s, he sang folk songs from the *Scottish Students' Songbook*, and while he was enrolled at Oxford he learned more folk songs during summer vacations in Germany. On his first trip to Canada in 1907, the group of journalists he was accompanying were taken on a tour of the harbour in Quebec in a pilot-tug with Liberal MP Jacques Bureau at the helm. Much to Gibbon's surprise and delight, Bureau was perfectly comfortable "serving ginger ale in his shirtsleeves" and "singing the French-Canadian folksong 'En roulant ma boule roulant.'" Gibbon later remarked: "I imagined the kind of letter that some English Colonel would write from his Club to the London *Times* if a British Cabinet Minister were to have done anything of the kind." He was equally as fascinated with the politics in "the new country" as he was with the songs themselves, some of which he had known from the book *French Songs of Old Canada* (1904).[79]

Gibbon learned more of what he called the "charm" of French folksongs from his wife's former classmate, Margaret Gascoigne. Gascoigne was an excellent musician who played the organ and had recently opened a school for girls in Montreal, and it was at her instigation that Gibbon convinced the manager of the Chateau Frontenac hotel to issue a booklet of French folksongs. He felt that they would especially appeal to American tourists, as they were "so different from the negro spirituals and from Stephen Foster." (Foster was an American songwriter known for his minstrel songs, such as "Oh! Susanna.")[80] The result was *Chansons of Old French Canada* (1920), edited by Gascoigne and her friend and fellow teacher Ethel Steath, along with anthropologist Marius Barbeau and James Kennedy.[81]

In January 1926, fire destroyed the Riverview Wing of the Frontenac, one of the oldest parts of the hotel, causing damages in the range of $1.5 million (the equivalent of over $22 million in 2019). The CPR opted to rebuild and the new wing was scheduled to open by June, so Gibbon was tasked with publicizing the grand reopening. Recalling the success of the *chansons*, he suggested a dinner party for leading Canadian and American newspaper editors, at which the score would consist of traditional French folksongs.

After receiving the go-ahead, Gibbon called up the manager of a French radio station and asked him for the name of the best folksinger. "Charles Marchand," the man replied.[82] When Gibbon approached the singer, he was shocked that Marchand refused the offer on the grounds that he would only sing such *chansons* before a sympathetic audience. The newspapermen, Marchand said, would not understand the meaning of the songs and they would probably be patronizing. He disliked singing for urban French Canadians too, as they were "apt to look down on these folksongs as 'habitant' stuff – 'peasant' stuff." When Gibbon proposed that he sing translations, so that the audience would understand, Marchand replied that he had never found any suitable translations. Undaunted, Gibbon asked for time to translate some himself before Marchand made a final decision. He then "wrote several versions in plain, colloquial English, following so far as [he] could the sound of the French." To Gibbon's relief, Marchand found them suitable enough that he agreed to perform at the event.[83]

According to Gibbon, the songs were a hit, although the event seems to have had a greater impact on Canadians than on American tourists. On the train back from the event, Fred Jacobs of the *Toronto Mail and Empire* remarked that "if Ontario were to hear these songs there would be much better understanding of Quebec in that Province" and urged Gibbon to complete a book of translated songs. Gibbon then asked Marchand for his thirty most popular songs and translated them. The resulting manuscript entitled *Canadian Folk Songs (Old and New)* was published in 1927.[84]

In the book, Gibbon tried to address the issue of class that had led to *chansons* being treated with disdain by wealthy, urban French Canadians. His novel idea was to argue that folk songs sung by *Canadiens* had their origins in troubadour songs originally sung in royal court in France. "One must avoid the common error of thinking that all French Canadians are of 'habitant' or peasant stock," he chided. "There was blue blood in plenty among the early settlers."[85] Anthropologist Marius Barbeau, in a critical yet restrained review of the book, refuted this origin story. While not denying that the two had some contacts and interchanges, he nevertheless argued that "the troubadour and folk-song *repertoires* ... hardly ever coincide at any point of their independent evolution. The art of one was both aristocratic and academic, and it was the direct outcome of medæval Latinity. The other, the folk song, was, on the other hand, and has remained, essentially oral and democratic."[86] The book was also not free of the patronizing and essentialist conception of French Canadians that its author sought to counter; the reader was informed that French Canadians were "a sociable race" and that the folk songs offered a window into their temperament and mentality, revealing "a simplicity and charm which can hardly be duplicated." None of these faults hindered its success; the book was reprinted yearly until the outbreak of the Second World War and reissued afterwards.[87]

While Gibbon was in the midst of writing the initial draft, the general manager of the Chateau approached him for help creating an early spring attraction for the hotel. Naturally, Gibbon suggested a "Folksong and Handicraft Festival" with "spinners and weavers at work, and with fiddlers and dancers of country dances." The addition of handicrafts stemmed from his realization that many folksongs were work songs, meant to accompany specific forms of labour. The festival was classic Gibbon: collaborative, expensive, extensive, and successful.[88] His main collaborator was Barbeau, who worked closely with him in making the arrangements. The handicraft exhibit was assembled by the Canadian Handicrafts Guild, Holt Renfrew, the provincial government, and the National Museum at Ottawa; and the folksongs were led by Marchand's own quartet, the Bytown Troubadours, with the assistance of Barbeau and the Toronto Conservatory of Music.

One unique aspect of the festival was the inclusion of Indigenous people. This was no doubt the result of the CPR's past success in utilizing Indigenous cultures to promote tourism. One of the most prominent examples is that of the "Indian Days" festival held in Banff. This event has sometimes been included in the list of CPR festivals organized by Gibbon in the 1920s,[89] but the reality is more complicated. In 1887 Banff National Park was created at the insistence of the CPR, who then constructed the Banff Springs Hotel. When it was completed in 1888, it was one of the most luxurious in North America. In 1894, a spring flood washed out a section of the railway lines, stranding some guests at the hotel. Local guide Tom Wilson had the idea to travel to nearby Morley to convince a group of Stoney (Nakoda) people to come and stage an event for the tourists. So began "Indian Days," though they were not actually established as an annual independent event until 1911. The event began as a single day affair but, as they grew in popularity, this was increased to two days in 1912 and three days in 1928. Once formally established, the event was sponsored and publicized by the CPR, though it continued to be largely organized by local entrepreneurs such as Tom Wilson, Norman Luxton, and Jim Brewster.[90] The event was particularly remarkable due to the fact that Stoney (Nakoda) peoples had been intentionally excluded from the park since its creation. However, owing to their long history of gatherings in this region, "many Nakoda peoples do not consider Indian Days an event with a distinct starting point or as separate from previous gatherings and established cultural practices."[91] The Banff region thus had a long and somewhat unique history of settler engagement with Indigenous people and their cultures.

Early on, Gibbon made note of the commercial potential of Indigenous cultures and began working to publicize "Indian Days." In late 1922, and in collaboration with publisher Hugh Eayrs, Gibbon convinced Barbeau to write a book about the event, one intended to "create a popular interest in the Indians." He then supplied Barbeau with research materials about the Stoney (Nakoda) peoples from the CPR library and from private sources, gave him a working title, and carefully edited the draft. These changes included shortening the manuscript, cutting Barbeau's criticism of missionaries, which he feared would cause grave offence, and introducing some subtle plugs for CPR facilities (mentioning, for example, that some attractions were "within walking distance of the comfortable hotels at Banff"). The resulting volume – Barbeau's first book – was published as *Indian Days in the Canadian Rockies* in 1923. For the "enormous amount of study" he put into the work, Barbeau received compensation valued at $400 from the CPR.[92]

Gibbon also began trying to include Indigenous people in additional events.[93] In July 1923, for instance, there was a notable Indigenous presence at the official opening of the Banff-Windermere highway. On that occasion, the official party departed from the CPR's Banff Springs Hotel in the morning, stopped at Kootenay Crossing for the official ribbon cutting and a luncheon, and then descended into the town of Invermere where, the press reported, "Kootenay Indians, dressed in their glory of color and war paint, greeted the two lieutenant-governors," Dr Robert G. Brett of Alberta and Walter Cameron Nichol of British Columbia. Chief Paul addressed the crowd through his translator, John Long Time Star, and the officials expressed their appreciation and promised to attend the evening's powwow. That night, five tribes of the Kootenay gathered at Lake Windermere for the celebration and were welcomed in their language by Lieutenant Governor Nichol, who also donated prize money for the stampede.[94]

Inspired by these past successes, when he began planning his Folk Festival at Quebec, Gibbon worked to include an Indigenous component. As he later put it: "Indians from the neighbouring village of Lorette added colour by contributing Huron Indian songs and dances, as well as the Christmas carol 'Jesous Ahatonnia,' taught to them 300 years ago by the Jesuit Father Brébeuf."[95] The inclusion of Huron-Wendat people was thus premised on the idea that their hymn could mark a connection to the colonial period, and was thoroughly marked by assumptions about their supposedly assimilated state. For instance, the sketch of the "Hurons of Lorette" (the Huron-Wendats of Wendake) provided in the festival's "General Programme" described these participants as "the half-breed descendants of the ancient Hurons and Wyandots discovered by Champlain and Sagard." It continued on to explain that "most of them are more like Europeans than Indians," though they still "cherish their racial affiliation with the early Hurons of prehistoric times. They have lost their language and much of what is really ancient. They still remember a few of the native songs and dances, and some of the canticles taught them in Huron by the early Jesuits."[96] Not all Indigenous content was provided by Indigenous people themselves, nor did all the content relate to cultures that were geographically near: Canadian soprano Juliette Gaultier de la Vérendrye also performed "Eskimo, Nootka, and Kootenay songs."[97] Overall, the Indigenous component was not intended to displace the emphasis on French folk culture, given that the festival was advertised abroad as a celebration of "The First White Man's Music in America."[98]

The festival ran from 19 May to 21 May 1927 and was opened by the arrival of the lieutenant governor. It drew so many more people than expected that Gibbon was embarrassed: hundreds were turned away owing to lack of space. The eight o'clock performance in the Concert Hall was so popular that when he first saw the crowd that had gathered by seven thirty, his first thought was "Great Heavens – is this a fire?" A special CPR train had brought in prominent American critics, and visitors from the neighbouring towns of Trois Rivières and Chicoutimi had "flocked in by every available means of transportation to hear the traditional French music performed by such talent" and stood waving dollars in the air, trying to buy tickets. The hall was already so full that Gibbon had to lock a section of the loft to ensure his special guests from Toronto would have seats. Some of those turned away were undaunted and, rather than going home, waited outside in hopes of catching some of the songs.[99]

The English and French press alike were effusive. *La Presse* declared the festival an extraordinary success, one that had attracted thousands of tourists to Quebec, reflected "our entire national life," and had been "an extremely fruitful initiative."[100] "How grateful we must be for the Canadian Pacific to have made such an event possible," Eugène Lapierre wrote in *Le Devoir*. "Is it not admirable to see an English company ... be an instrument for maintaining our traditions? ... Our race can only profit from such commendable enterprises."[101] The English-language *Gazette* declared the festival to have been of national importance, one that had brought forth "something dormant, a wealth of national culture, that has been buried under an oppressive weight of materialism ... It has stimulated the craving for something beyond the standardized ideas of modern life in North America, and the consensus is that a most lofty and national object has been attained." The article added that given the popularity, the festival would likely be made an annual event.[102] What a coup! The festival was not interpreted as a mere publicity scheme for the CPR but rather was hailed as a balm for the very modernity that the company represented. Gibbon had discovered for himself the selling power of culture.

Others quickly saw the light. The CPR's general manager of hotels, in Gibbon's words, "had been converted by the experience at Quebec to the efficacy of music as a drawing card," and asked him for an idea to fill the Banff Springs Hotel just before Labour Day, when many guests started to move out. His solution was a Highland Gathering and Scottish Music Festival, held from 3 September to 5 September 1927. "I never was so happy as when authority was given to arrange this Highland Gathering," Gibbon later wrote. "After all I was a Scot myself, and though not a Highland Scot, I had visited and been thrilled by Highland Gatherings at Braemer, when I lived in Aberdeen, and had some idea of how they should be run." This was another large undertaking, involving bagpiping, Gaelic singing, a Hebridean choir, and an open-air service on Sunday. And, as before, Gibbon relied on Indigenous people to bring some "colour" to the proceedings. "With the help of Duncan Campbell Scott, Deputy Minister of Indian Affairs, we secured sixty Peigan Indians from the foothills of Alberta," he later recalled.[103]

CPR president E.W. Beatty, pleased by the success of the festivals, authorized a repeat of the folk festival at Quebec City. Seeing "the better understanding created by this movement," he asked if something similar could be done in other parts of Canada "among other racial groups with similar intentions." According to his later account, Gibbon then "suggested we should try out something of the same kind among the so-called New Canadians – the Poles, Ukrainians, Germans, Austrians, Hungarians, Czechoslovaks, Swedes, Norwegians, Danes, Icelanders, Italians and Hebrews, who were pouring into the West and providing real problems of assimilation. I knew that they all had their traditions of folk-music and handicraft, and the Canadian Handicrafts guild was prepared to cooperate." Beatty agreed, "his only stipulation being that they should be identified with Canadian Pacific hotels, so as to justify the appropriations that would be required." The festival, "designed to promote more mutual understanding among immigrants on the prairies," was thus planned for 19 June to 23 June, not quite a month after the second festival at Quebec City.[104]

The second festival in Quebec differed from the first in that the Indigenous component was eliminated on account of mixed reviews. Although one syndicated review by American critic Pierre V. Key noted simply that the performers from Lorette were unique, popular, and "quite civilized in their every-day costumes," Barbeau fretted that another American critic, Oscar Thompson, had dismissed both the children's round dances and the performance of "the halfbreeds of Lorette" as "concessions to local requirements."[105] Gibbon, who viewed musical critics as "a necessary evil," brought in only to create wider interest in the festivals, advised Barbeau that not too much weight should be put on any individual critic. Yet although he defended the children's round dances, he expressed agreement that the "half-breeds of Lorette were certainly poor."[106] Writing to Juliette Gaultier, Gibbon explained the change in programming thus: "We have kept out the Indian and Eskimo music from Quebec this year because there are so many more folk melodies available, and our time is limited. The few Indians last year were generally considered to be disappointing, and without their participation, there is no longer the same excuse for introducing Indian music. The Eskimo music has also lost the charm of novelty at Quebec."[107]

While there were apparently no domestic objections to the initial inclusion, and then exclusion, of Indigenous people in folk festivals, the same could not be said about so-called new Canadians. Returning to Winnipeg after the second festival at Quebec, Gibbon ran into a roadblock: significant opposition to the planned New Canadian festival had arisen from critics who argued that the CPR "had no right to encourage these immigrants to be anything but good Canadians." According to Gibbon, this sentiment was "largely due to a book." In 1909, Presbyterian minister C.W. Gordon, writing under the penname Ralph Connor, published *The Foreigner: A Tale of Saskatchewan*. The novel tells the story of Kalman Kalmar, a young Ukrainian immigrant, and it contains what Gibbon called "a realistic and not very flattering picture of the Slav quarter in Winnipeg" and further described Ukrainians as "dirty and heavy drinkers." Released when Connor was at the height of his popularity, the book was a top-ten bestseller in both 1909 and 1910 and was made into a movie in 1922. As one illustration of the novel's popularity, in the early 1920s the Toronto Public Library had seven hundred copies of the book yet still had difficulty keeping copies available. As such, although blaming a nearly twenty-year-old novel for Anglo-Canadian attitudes towards Ukrainians at first seems unlikely, perhaps Gibbon's diagnosis was more accurate than it first seems.[108]

To fix the problem as he saw it, Gibbon called up the author and invited him to the concert as his personal guest. Connor had been involved with a previous festival, having led the open-air church service at the Highland Gathering at Banff, and had thoroughly enjoyed himself. He thus accepted Gibbon's invitation, attended the concert, where he especially enjoyed the performance of the Polish National Dance, and afterwards went to meet the dancers. Upon returning to his seat, he remarked to Gibbon: "Do you know, these are some of the finest, most cultured people I have met since I have come to Winnipeg. But I have something on my conscience – I feel that I have done them an injustice." Referring to his book, in which he suggested immigrants were "lousy and drunken," Connor now declared a desire to make amends and asked Gibbon for advice. Gibbon replied that he ought to call all his friends and tell them that the show was the best in town. "That change of heart did us a world of good," Gibbon later wrote. The criticism evidently died down, and the final concert had standing room only.[109]

Again, at first glance it seems improbable the idea that Connor's intervention alone could be responsible for such a dramatic change, but his enormous fame should not be underestimated. Daniel Coleman suggests he may have been "Canada's first celebrity author," and recounts how he was recruited by the federal government to tour the United States to help convince the country to join the Great War. Even there he was met with immense interest: so many people converged to try and get his autograph that the police had to be called for crowd control.[110] However, it is also important to look beyond Gibbon's own interpretation – which foregrounds his intervention – to other accounts, as contemporaries specifically pointed to notions of racial superiority as the reason for the initial opposition. For example, journalist E.L. Chicanot reported that "what has been termed Canada's Nordic complex produced a very apathetic attitude toward the festival at first," before word of the "unique entertainment" spread and interest eventually grew.[111]

The publicity surrounding the New Canadian Festival emphasized its racial diversity. One advertisement loudly announced that four hundred performers from "15 Racial Groups" would be displayed "in picturesque songs, dances, and costumes, assisted by distinguished soloists."[112] However, all fifteen of these racial groups were European. Given that Gibbon was familiar with non-European cultures, this must have been a deliberate choice. Recall that he was born in Ceylon; toured Japan and found it to be a country of "extraordinary interest"; convalesced in North Africa; and was familiar with Chinese poetry.[113] Also, as a frequent traveller across Canada and the United States, he had no doubt been assisted countless times by porters of African descent. (When Van Horne took the reins at CPR in 1881, he imported the Pullman sleeping car service from America. African Americans traditionally staffed the Pullman sleepers, so Van Horne copied this aspect as well. According to historian Sarah-Jane Mathieu, by 1900, regular runs from Montreal to New York and from Toronto to Chicago featured sleeping and dining cars staffed exclusively by railroaders of African descent.)[114]

Indeed, through constant travel and immersion in popular culture, Gibbon was fully aware of racial minorities and common stereotypes about them.[115] This is best illustrated in a letter to anthropologist Marius Barbeau in which he critiqued a draft script of a radio program Barbeau was working on. Musical interest had become incidental to an overall goal of melodrama, Gibbon charged, and the script writer seemed to need advice not from someone knowledgeable about music but from the editor of *Boys Own Companion* (a paper featuring adventure stories with sensationalized plots). Then, as if acting in the role of the latter, he sarcastically proposed some farcical changes to the plot. One included the mounting of an expedition against some Indigenous people who are suspected of scalping. "The Indians," he suggested, "are [then] discovered to be a lost tribe of Pullman porters who have strayed out of one of [American playwright] Eugene O'Neill's masterpieces and are practising voodoo rites in the intervals of kidnapping."[116] Despite his knowledge of and perhaps even annoyance with common stereotypes about racialized peoples, Gibbon made little effort to counter them: in his Festivals, Indigenous people were included for "colour" and then excluded for failing to please the crowd, and Canadians of African and Asian descent were completely excluded from the outset.

Though most scholars have commented on Gibbon's racial exclusions, they have struggled to explain his understanding of race.[117] At the Winnipeg Festival, for instance, the Scandinavian nations were grouped together in two distinct shows, leading historian Stuart Henderson to suggest that "this apparent segregation of the Scandinavian Folk suggests a quiet racism at work in the construction of the New Canadian Festival."[118] Up until this point, Gibbon had not made any explicit statements in print outlining his understanding of race. He sometimes used the term to mean something more akin to "nationality," but he also used it in a quasi-biological sense. His exclusion of African and Asian peoples from his festivals and writings were undoubtedly race-based exclusions, but it is important to note that he also privileged some white "races" over others, specifically the Scandinavian or Nordic races. For instance, and much like Robert England, he presented them as the most promising settlers, writing in 1920 that "the Scandinavian immigrants into Canada have presented little obstacle to rapid and effective assimilation." Three years later, he repeated the same argument and provided its underlying logic: "Coming from countries in Northern Europe where climatic conditions are not unlike that of Canada, the Scandinavians have readily adapted themselves to Canadian life."[119]

In Henderson's interpretation, "the Northern 'races,' always treated with more respect by Gibbon, are held together in the construction of the festival program, separated from the eastern and southern Europeans; the implication is that the Scandinavian nations are stronger, more unified in their shared beliefs, cultures, and histories. They are, one might infer, like Britain in this regard."[120] Yet it seems more likely that Gibbon was influenced by the racial ideologies of his period, in which Scandinavian countries were "like Britain" not because of their strength or cultural unity but rather due to their common racial heritage. Henderson argued that race "was employed by Gibbon in a somewhat more complicated way than many of his contemporaries. His understanding of race, while framed by his reliance on the four principal categories (white, black, red, yellow), was complicated by his view on the different strata within the first, primary race. The category 'white' was divisible and could be hierarchically organized; the other three remained more monolithic, less synthetic."[121] Instead of being a more complicated way of understanding race, however, this was in fact a more common understanding of race than Canadian historians have recognized.

Gibbon believed that, at least historically, Europeans had evolved from three distinct biological races, although he maintained that modern racial groups were a blend of types. In his unpublished tract, "Anglo-Canadian Futurities," Watson Kirkconnell had noted the power of the environment in shaping races, though he paid much more attention to the hereditary power of race. Gibbon also believed that the power of climate in shaping racial groups was significant, hence the *Canadian Mosaic*'s subtitle: "The Making of a *Northern* Nation." However, he had not been as convinced of the hereditary power of race. He therefore focused on the cultural differences between racial and national groups, and was concerned with identifying those traditions that might be beneficial to the future Canadian race that he believed was evolving, both physically and culturally.

The race-based exclusions that kept Canadians of African and Asian descent from being welcomed as part of this and subsequent New Canadian festivals demonstrate the limits of Gibbon's tolerance. He was fully aware of the "colour" that their cultures might have brought to the event but he chose not to include them.[122] This discrimination was commonplace, if uneven, across the country during this period, but it was by no means inevitable. Montreal's Chinatown is one of the oldest Asian communities in North America but, as Kwok Chan argues, "the kind of racism the Chinese in Montreal have been subjected to is a systemic, institutional, collective one." Chinese immigrants who arrived in Montreal during the late nineteenth century had often been those who had worked to build the transatlantic railway for the CPR. Once it was complete, they faced such racism in British Columbia that thousands headed east. Wherever they went, their labour was, due to discrimination, largely confined to the laundry and restaurant industries. By 1900, the Chinese community in Montreal numbered nearly a thousand and it was already fighting against that discrimination. For instance, laundry workers unsuccessfully petitioned the city to make their establishments tax exempt, arguing that the high annual licence for operating laundromats was specifically designed to drive them from the city. (The licence was $50, or about four months' wages.)[123]

Likewise, African Canadians of the period were actively fighting discrimination and attempting to cultivate a race-based collective identity.[124] While efforts such as the launch of newspapers like *The Dawn of Tomorrow* were centred in Ontario, the fight against discrimination was ongoing in Gibbon's home of Montreal. The CPR had made the city its general employment centre and many African Canadians from Nova Scotia subsequently moved there to work for the company. Most lived in the "Little Burgundy" district, but the city as a whole was generally unwelcoming. In Sarah-Jane Mathieu's words, "Blacks in Montreal spent much of the interwar period wrestling hostile city councilmen, fighting police harassment, and fending off deportation." They also faced denigration and exclusions. In 1921, Loew's Theatre notified the public that African Canadian patrons "would be segregated in 'Monkey Cages,' the opera house's upper balcony." When the Coloured Political and Protective Association of Montreal sued, the Supreme Court of Quebec sided with the theatre.[125] A combination of rulings like these and discriminatory social customs led many African Canadians to identify Jim Crow–style racial segregation as a continental rather than exclusively American phenomenon.[126]

The CPR contributed to this set of circumstances. The company was perfectly content to hire Chinese workers to complete the railway only to cut them loose when it was completed, and to break immigration and labour laws and bring in foreign African and West Indian labourers (knowing that they would be excluded from the railroad union, which was limited to workers racialized as white),[127] but no African or Asian cultures would be represented or celebrated at company-sponsored festivals. Early pluralistic efforts such as these were therefore limited by a racism that positioned European cultures as the only ones worthy of celebration.

Yet this limited pluralism represented positive change in this era. Although the festivals "often betrayed limited perspectives on the non-British ethnic groups in question," historian Gillian Mitchell contends, "they were groundbreaking in their efforts to exhibit pride in multi-ethnicity during a period in which cultural intolerance of immigrants from non-British backgrounds was optimal." Indeed, it was during this period that the Ku Klux Klan moved into Canada. Although it would gain its greatest foothold in the province of Saskatchewan, the Klan established a branch in Montreal in 1921. While the KKK definitively stood for "White Supremacy," there were fewer people of African descent in Canada than in America, so their concern shifted to Jewish people, members of the Roman Catholic Church, and ultimately those they considered non-Anglo-Saxon. As historian James M. Pitsula puts it, their mission was "Keeping Canada British."[128]

Although the Klan did not spread as successfully in Manitoba, there was nevertheless an underlying sentiment of xenophobia in the province, as evidenced by the opposition to the New Canadian Festivals. Gibbon may have pushed past some initial opposition to hold the event, but ambivalence and distaste were clearly expressed at its close. One writer in the *Winnipeg Free Press* described the festival thus: "Blazing in colours, the hotel rotunda presents a motley scene. Garbed in seemingly grotesque clothes of many bright hues, the European mingles with the conservatively clad westerner. The new Canadian seems perfectly at home in this setting, for it is that of his native land. But the westerner is bewildered, there are many things that arouse his interest."[129] Nevertheless, the Festival may have convinced some English Canadians that European immigrants had something of value. Some, like Rev. Gordon, may have had a change of heart. Gibbon was confident that they did, though it is largely impossible to determine.

Even if the festivals had mixed success in combatting prejudice against European minorities, they fulfilled their mission to drive tourism to such an extent that other provinces and municipalities began to request them. A month after the New Canadian festival, a second Highland Gathering in Banff was held. Closing out the year was an English Yuletide Festival at the Empress Hotel in Victoria, British Columbia (BC), at the request of the province's lieutenant governor, followed by a Sea Music Festival in Vancouver in January. At the request of Premier James Gardiner, Saskatchewan got its own New Canadian festival (the "Great Western Canadian Folksong, Folkdance, and Handicraft Festival"), held in Regina in March 1929. A third Highland Gathering was held that August, followed by an English Music Festival at the Royal York Hotel in Toronto. The year 1930 saw an additional five festivals: a repeat of the Sea Music, Great West, and Canadian Folksong and Handicraft festivals, along with a fourth and final Highland Gathering. Taken together, it is clear that the CPR-sponsored festivals were a commercial enterprise that were just as much about English and Scottish cultures as they were about European ethnic minorities: fully half of the sixteen events were dedicated to one or both of the former.[130]

At the end of October 1929, Gibbon travelled to Toronto to deliver an address to the Empire Club. As the English Music Festival was opening at the city's Royal York Hotel a few weeks from then, the talk was presumably intended to drum up interest. Entitled "The Music of the People," it reveals some of his thinking about the role of the festivals in the integration and assimilation of European immigrants. Gibbon first established that folk singing was a thoroughly English tradition, arguing that if Canada was going to keep its doors open to "British immigration and to British ideas and British civilization, we are going to have a revival of these old English country dances here, because the immigrants that are destined to come here are dancing these dances to those folktunes, learning them in their schools and keeping on dancing when they grow up." Next, he challenged the idea that folksongs in Canada were the preserve of French Canadians. "As a matter of fact every racial group coming from Europe to Canada is bringing with it a wealth of folkmusic in song and dance," he countered, "and this should be preserved as a most precious asset instead of being allowed to disappear through neglect, indifference or hostility." Gibbon argued that folk music was an asset to Canadian culture, but more importantly it was a way of quickly assimilating immigrants. Folk music was the most intimate thing in the life of a people, so recognizing its value was about recognizing their humanity. It was like telling a new mother "that [her] baby is the most beautiful baby you have ever seen," he explained. "You will gain their confidence in a way that is surprising." Once this confidence was won, and mutual trust had been established among the "various racial groups," their rapid assimilation was assured, he argued, to which his audience responded, "Hear, hear!"

He closed his speech with the final argument that welcoming and fostering the "artistic instincts of the New Canadians" was a British tradition, for English culture had been "greatly enriched by the children of naturalized aliens." Providing some recent statistics, he informed the audience that of the top six English composers, four were of continental European stock. "They are names of which England has a good reason to be proud, even though their stock may not be of Anglo-Saxon origin," he declared, to applause.[131] In this address, the tension between wishing to preserve individual European cultures and wishing to meld them into a singular Canadian culture was ultimately unresolved, but the act of welcoming immigrants' cultures was presented as an English, and therefore an acceptable, tradition. Looking beyond the folk festivals to another one of Gibbon's hybrid hobby/publicity innovations – this time a trail riding club – reveals some of the intentions behind his tolerance and indeed its limitations.

Gibbon had routinely gone horseback riding on trails in the Canadian Rockies since 1909. In July 1923, he and a number of other riders set out on a trip to visit the spectacular Wolverine Plateau. Upon arriving at the site, some of the riders, including Gibbon, decided to spend some additional time there, while the others continued on to Banff. However, a blizzard set in and his group was unable to leave the Plateau for three days. In his autobiography, Gibbon claims that on the third morning he got the idea to start an "Order of the Trail Riders of the Canadian Rockies." He suggested that the qualifications for membership would be based on buttons that indicated the mileage of trails one had ridden, on the grounds that "Americans love buttons." The group liked the idea, so Gibbon drafted a Constitution. After he returned to Banff, he consulted the well-known guide and successful businessman Jim Brewster and "a number of old-timers." Finding them all in favour of such an organization, he formed a committee to get other members, and served as its secretary. Thus began the Trail Riders of the Canadian Rockies, an organization that exists to this day.[132]

The original constitution that Gibbon drafted declared that membership in the Order was "open to all, irrespective of age, sex, creed, colour or profession." However, he later explained that there were "special reasons" for some of the articles.

> The "irrespective of age" was put in because I knew an old lady who was a trail rider and who proposed to continue as such till she died. The "race" was inserted because I wanted to have at least one Indian Chief in our membership. "Creed" was there in case anyone like Father de Smet who pioneered through White Man's Pass should want to join us. "Colour" was intended to cover the case of the negro butler whom Dr Charles Walcott, Secretary of the Smithsonian Institution, brought with him every summer from Washington to do the catering on his geological camping trips and had 1500 miles of trail riding to his credit.[133]

Gibbon's approach was non-discriminatory yet it was not intended to be anti-discriminatory; the underlying hierarchies remained intact and unquestioned. First Nations Chiefs would be a draw for tourists and the ability to bring along African American butlers would be convenient for wealthy American tourists who, given his remarks about buttons, seem to have been a target group. (By 1952, the group had over two thousand members, roughly half of whom were American.)[134] The normative member was a white Protestant male, but membership was ostensibly open to all. The creation of the organization also cannot be disentangled from Gibbon's commitment as a CPR employee to drive the company's revenues. Thus in 1934 Gibbon was fine to convince the king of Siam (now Thailand) to join them for a trail ride, but he also knew full well that their decision to ride longer than first planned "meant $500 a day more to the hotel for the rent of the Royal Suite" (with inflation, that amounts to roughly $9,300 per day in 2019).[135]

And yet it is worth remembering that not all were so welcoming during this period. Another one of the CPR's publicity schemes was a program whereby popular artists were invited to the hotel at Banff to paint the Rockies. A local history recounts the following anecdote involving one of these artists, the well-known German-born American wildlife painter Carl Rungius. In 1931, while making final preparations for a show of four local artists, the artist "curtly dismissed from his presence a young man whom he took to be one of the Japanese bellboys ... Only later did Rungius learn that the man had been an emissary from the Queen of Siam, then visiting the hotel, who wanted to ask for a special showing for the Queen. The Queen never did visit the show."[136]

## CONCLUSION

In 1919, Gibbon was waiting for prophets to interpret Canada's "many-sided" life to other nations and to its own people; within a decade he had become one of those prophets. In his final years, Gibbon portrayed the arc of his life as a transition "From Scot to Canadian" (or, for his more discerning Scottish audience, "From Aberdonian to Canadian"). While he was proud to be a Scot, he viewed himself as having fully become a Canadian. But what did it mean to be a Canadian in the first decades of the twentieth century? In 1929, he declared: "If you can weave a good story around it, you can sell anything." His day job was to sell the transportation and recreation provided by the CPR. But he made the job into one of selling Canada, and he sold a particular version of Canada not just to people in other countries but also to Canadians themselves.

The story that Gibbon saw as genuinely Canadian, the story that he chose to weave around the nation, was one of immigration and diversity. He portrayed Canada as a racially diverse nation that was welcoming to immigrants and their cultures. For Gibbon, however, all of these races were European or white, a category that he initially viewed as excluding Jewish people. Although he was open to some degree of cultural retention, the philosophy of cultural pluralism that Gibbon developed called for immigrants' linguistic and political assimilation. The metaphor he first developed to express this vision was that of a garden, in which Anglo-Canadians accepted European transplants but carefully positioned and pruned them, with the goal of crafting a visually pleasing arrangement. Excluded were all peoples racialized as non-white, with Indigenous people like potted plants: not a part of the garden but occasionally brought in for an additional splash of colour and novelty.

His later mosaic metaphor openly assumed the erasure of Indigenous cultures and called for a careful arrangement and even outright construction of the individual European cultures that made up the whole. Less invested in race science than some of his peers, he nevertheless believed that with enough time Canadians would begin to resemble a unique race, with distinctive physical characteristics and a specific culture. The tension between plurality and singularity inherent in this vision ultimately remained unresolved, just as it would in the federal government's later notions of unity in diversity. Regardless of the paradoxical nature of this vision, the increasing attention paid to Canada's diversity meant that Gibbon's ideas became increasingly popular and he, along with Kirkconnell and England, would soon find himself called on by the state to help manage the problem that this diversity was believed to represent.

# 4

# Making It Official

## INTRODUCTION

From the mid-1920s through the mid-1930s, only a handful of private individuals developed philosophies of cultural pluralism and actively worked to promote them. These ideas were, in turn, taken up by some private organizations. There was a notable absence of state involvement throughout the first decade of pluralistic ideas, but this began to change in the late 1930s. The literature on the history of multiculturalism as official government policy, insofar as it has been sketched, has focused on the role of the federal civil service and how the Second World War triggered the "rise of a bureaucracy for multiculturalism."[1] However, a closer examination of the late interwar period complicates this interpretation. This chapter examines two Canadian Broadcasting Corporation (CBC) radio programs that aired in 1938, Robert England's *Ventures in Citizenship* and John Murray Gibbon's *The Canadian Mosaic*. It demonstrates that, with regard to the promotion of cultural pluralism in Canada, the boundaries between the state and civil society had begun to blur by 1938, as state-run institutions began to draw upon the resources of private individuals and organizations in order to broadcast a message of toleration and unity. Further, it argues these programs reveal the importance and longevity of conceptions of race in Canadian discussions of diversity, assimilation, and citizenship. Official attempts to promote cultural pluralism may have resulted in slightly more inclusive programming, but they also sanctioned and continued the existing racial exclusions of public intellectuals upon whom they relied.

## GIBBON'S MOSAIC

Expressed in talks and brought to life through the folk festivals sponsored by the Canadian Pacific Railway (CPR) during the 1920s, Gibbon's vision of a culturally pluralistic Canada was spreading. By 1929, he intended to cap the other folksong and handicraft festivals, which he believed "had done so much to create mutual understanding among the many racial groups in Canada," with an English Music Festival. He apparently considered the festivals' stated goal of mutual understanding to be accomplished and was ready to move on to other things. There were also more practical considerations at hand. Given the pressures of the Great Depression, by that fall the future of the folksong festivals was uncertain. The Banff Highland Gathering was such a success that it avoided the axe that year, but the writing was on the wall. Gibbon was therefore relieved by the CPR's subsequent shift into radio broadcasting. The final festivals were held in 1931, and that same year Gibbon headed to London to learn about radio broadcasting from Gladstone Murray of the British Broadcasting Corporation (BBC). However, the CPR's incursion into radio was short-lived. With the creation of the CBC in 1936, CPR president Beatty "decided to avoid the risk of political complications, and to step out of the field except as a telegraph transmission company." Relations with the CBC remained cordial, and Gibbon wrote and read the scripts for a number of programs until finally he was informed that some of his listeners found his accent too Scotch. He was replaced by – in his own words – "professional announcers who spoke with more of a Canadian accent."[2]

Before he was ushered away from the microphone, however, Gibbon produced an important Canadian folk music series. On a train headed for Ottawa, Gibbon found himself seated next to Leonard Brockington. Brockington (1888–1966) was born and raised in Cardiff, Wales. He emigrated to Canada in 1912 and, once he arrived, made his way to Edmonton and then Calgary. In 1913 he married Agnes Neaves Mackenzie, who was essential to his later success. (In 1924, Brockington was diagnosed with rheumatoid arthritis and the disease became increasingly debilitating. Agnes took care of him, their two children, and the household while he pursued his varied career.) Within a short time after his arrival in the city he trained as a lawyer and began work as the city solicitor in Calgary, a position he would hold for over a decade. During this time, he also became a well-known public speaker. In 1935, he moved to Winnipeg to work as general counsel for the North West Grain Dealers Association and the following year was appointed chairman of the CBC's Board of Governors. According to his biographer, Brockington "envisioned public programming that would unite the country" and devoted a great deal of time and attention to what was supposed to be a part-time position. His desire for equal access to programming across the country brought him into conflict with the federal minister responsible for the CBC, C.D. Howe, who accused him of being more concerned with "the mechanical operation of broadcasting stations" than with developing additional programming.[3]

Little wonder then that when he found himself next to Gibbon, probably the most well-known publicist in Canada at the time, Brockington asked for suggestions for future content. Gibbon responded by reminding him of the Calgary folksong festival, to which Brockington had contributed by organizing a choir of Welsh coalminers, and suggested that the CBC "could find no better method of creating mutual understanding among the various racial groups of Canada, particularly in newly settled districts," than by organizing a folk music series. Brockington had firsthand knowledge of many of the groups likely to be involved, and not just because of the folk festivals. He had moved to western Canada on a train filled with immigrants from "Galicia and Ruthenia," and later had routine dealings with people of all backgrounds in his position as city solicitor, where he was apparently particularly sympathetic to Indigenous people.[4] Naturally inclined to approve, Brockington ran Gibbon's idea by CBC general manager Gladstone Murray, who evidently approved. (The Canadian-born Murray had been with the BBC in Britain for over a decade before returning to Canada to lead the CBC.) The two then asked Gibbon to submit some scripts. Drawing on materials he had gathered for the folksong festivals, Gibbon quickly submitted the requested drafts and the series was approved. Entitled *Canadian Mosaic: Songs of Many Races* and intended as a sequel to the festivals, the program was designed with the same goal: "to create a better understanding of the contribution made by the various racial groups in Canada."[5]

The half-hour show aired on Sundays for thirteen consecutive weeks and was quickly described as a "radio treat," one that was "genuinely artistic and very informing." Gibbon's involvement was a clear draw, with the *Ottawa Citizen* remarking that, with him in

Table 4.1 Episodes of *Canadian Mosaic: Songs of Many Races* radio program, 1938

| Date aired (1938) | "Racial group" discussed | Notes |
|---|---|---|
| 2 January | French | |
| 9 January | Scottish | |
| 16 January | Irish | |
| 23 January | Scandinavian | Discussed Norwegian, Swedish, Danish, and Icelandic groups |
| 30 January | Germanic | Discussed German, Dutch, and Austrian groups. Featured Elie Spivak, Harold Sumberg, Cecil Figelski, Leo Smith, and Louis Crerar (pianist) |
| 6 February | English | |
| 13 February | Ukrainian | Featuring "Hymn for New Canadians," based on the music of Sibelius's "Finlandia," with original words by Gibbon |
| 20 February | Polish | Music from Paderewski, Chopin, and Boccherini |
| 27 February | Welsh | Elie Spivak, violin soloist. Songs included "Men of Harlech," "The Farmer and His Wife," and "the Dove." Frances James sang six songs for which Gibbon had written lyrics: "David Thompson," "Governor Simcoe," "Fathers of Confederation," "Come Sing of a Miner," "The Mountie," and "Hiking Song." |
| 6 March | Russian and Hebrew | Louis Crerar, pianist. Music included "Songs of an Immigrant," "In Modo Antico," "River in Spring," "Volga Boat Song," "In the Forest," "Hotikvah," "It Now Is Law," "The New Canaan," and "Quartet in G." |

Note: Table compiled using information found in newspaper coverage of the series; see the articles cited in the notes for this chapter.

charge, "a high standard of entertainment might be expected." In the introduction, Gibbon "quietly, naturally, with distinct enunciation of every syllable and beautiful diction," explained that Canada was a mosaic, with each group contributing their culture to the "enrichment of the life of the nation which is evolving."[6] Publishers John McClelland and George Stewart heard Gibbon's series and were interested in its underlying concept, so McClelland called and invited Gibbon to a meeting in Toronto. There Gibbon was then asked to turn the series into an illustrated book, and he quickly agreed and set to work.[7]

Released in December, *Canadian Mosaic* was greeted with glowing reviews: it was "a joy to read and a pleasure to behold," one gushed. Robert England, writing for the *Winnipeg Tribune*, unsurprisingly suggested that the book was a reminder that "God has written a line of His thought on the cradle of each race."[8] Gibbon made sure to send copies to politicians and civil servants, including Prime Minister Mackenzie King and Undersecretary of State O.D. Skelton. King replied that he had "heard much commendation" of the radio series and had hoped for it to be published in that expanded format "with some account of the racial backgrounds from which this music has developed." (With typical self-absorption, he added that he was pleased to note the book's several references to his grandfather.) In his reply to Gibbon, Skelton replied quite frankly that he was afraid "we have not made much progress lately in a better understanding of the New Canadians, and not the least value of your book will be the stimulus it will give in this direction."[9]

Someone reading *Canadian Mosaic* would quickly grasp that, in order to understand "New Canadians," they had to understand race. In the book's first chapter, Gibbon set out to understand the racial classification of humankind. He went back as far as possible and discussed the "Crô-Magnards," but he was disappointed to report that scientists had not found enough of them to divide up into races. He therefore moved along to the next stage in his survey, that of taking the "white-skinned Europeans known as Caucasians, and classify[ing] them by their size, the shape of their heads, faces and noses, and the colour of their hair and eyes." The result "has given us the division into three classes," he continued, namely the Nordic, Mediterranean, and Alpine. But these were historic races, he argued, "familiar mostly to scientists or to the Nazis, whose plan it is to make all Germans Nordic." In his view, Nordicism was still science but one that few laypeople (except the Nazis) were currently interested in. The *Encyclopedia Britannica* could not help him in his quest to understand race, for it merely defined race as a "tribe, breed or group of individuals descended from a common ancestor," and this was far too broad for his liking. Turning to the Canadian census monograph on the "Racial Origins and Nativity of the Canadian People," written by W.B. Hurd, he found a more suitable definition: race was a "sub-group of the human species by ties of physical kinship." Modern national groups were thus mixtures of various "racial strains."

Gibbon hedged on whether any European peoples had, in the past millennium, "evolved biological types which could appropriately be termed 'races,'" concluding that it was a "matter for debate." He then offered up his own definition of race. "Man ... is an animal that uses tools. The tools he uses to get along with his fellow-men are chiefly language, customs, costumes, art[,] and music. If people live long enough together, say five hundred years, in family groups that intermarry, and if they use the same kind of such tools, they begin to become recognizable as a Race."[10] This definition mirrored the census's insistence that race combined both biology and culture, given that intermarriage was seen as an integral part of race making. Gibbon continued on to argue that the Canadian people had "not yet been blended into one type. Possibly, in another two hundred years, Canadians may be fused together and standardized so that you can recognize them anywhere in a crowd."[11]

Canadians had not yet attained a shared physiognomy, but it was clear that they would share one skin colour. As he put it: "This Canadian race of the future is being superimposed on the original native Indian races and is being made up of over thirty European racial groups, each of which has its own history, customs, and traditions."[12] From this statement alone, it is clear that Gibbon believed the Canadian mosaic was to tile over Indigenous peoples and that he felt no qualms about it. In reality, this would be like tiling over an existing mosaic. For, as Gibbon surely knew but failed to acknowledge, Indigenous peoples were – and are – equally diverse, in that each group has its own history, customs, and traditions. But Gibbon's future mosaic was instead to be composed strictly of Europeans, or what he called "foreign white stock."[13]

Running through the book was tension between an assimilatory drive to meld all peoples into a single race (a distinctive type) and a desire to maintain distinctive European cultures as tiles in a mosaic.

And while the mosaic was about maintaining distinctive cultures, it was not necessarily about preserving existing cultures as they were. In the book's preface, Gibbon wrote of the need to "collect and separate *and perhaps ourselves fabricate* the tesserae or little slabs of color required for what the artist has in mind as a mosaic."[14] The mosaic would therefore be arranged in such a way that it was pleasing to the Anglo-Canadian eye, even if this required the alteration or outright fabrication of the tiles (that is, the ethnic communities and their cultures). In this sense, the underlying philosophy remained the same as when he expressed it using the language of gardening, and it was this philosophy that had shaped the arrangement of the folk festivals. Thus, whether in a Canadian garden or a Canadian mosaic, the inclusion and exclusion of peoples and their cultures was based not on geography, relationships, or input from the various groups. Rather, the mosaic was determined by Anglo-Canadians' aesthetic tastes.

ENGLAND'S *VENTURES IN CITIZENSHIP*

Gibbon successfully popularized the idea of a Canadian mosaic to such an extent that, within only a few months of the radio program, many people and organizations had adopted its use. But the results were not merely discursive; rather, his efforts to a large extent paved the way for additional folk song programming over public radio. In January 1938, the same month that the *Canadian Mosaic* radio series began, the well-known Nova Scotian folklorist Helen Creighton met with Gladstone Murray in Ottawa. Like Brockington, Murray was keen for more original programming, and so Creighton left the meeting having agreed to create a twenty-episode series on the folk songs of Nova Scotia. While regional in its subject matter, it nevertheless was broadcast nationwide and received fan mail from listeners from across Canada. The folk programming was so successful that the CBC ordered a second series, which aired in 1939.[15] Creighton was not the only one tasked with creating a new radio program in the wake of Gibbon's success, as Robert England was soon called upon to contribute to the CBC's efforts.

Despite England's upward trajectory at the CNR, in 1936 he had made the unexpected decision to take a job at the University of British Columbia (UBC) as the director of extension services and associate professor of economics.[16] The appointment may not be as random as it first seems: in his role with the CNR, England had increasingly come to see the importance of agricultural and technical extension work and had said as much in several publications.[17] As UBC was only just establishing their Extension Services department, the Englands took the summer of 1936 to tour universities in Canada, the United States, and Europe to gather information about adult education. His first year was marked by a focus on public lectures, panel discussions, seminars, and library resources, and he frequently spoke to a wide variety of groups about the department's mission.[18]

Owing to the need to reach a wide audience, during his short time with UBC England had become increasingly involved with radio work. He was apparently so well known to the CBC that, in the spring of 1937, Gladstone Murray (with Brockington's backing) offered England a job. He turned it down on account of its low pay, but that did not mean he was keen to stay at the university.[19] Indeed, despite the challenging nature of the position, England was still not content. According to his later account, the time spent in Germany the previous year had convinced him that war was inevitable, and that when it arrived both he and Amy would want to do their part, but he also realized that their finances were limited. With these considerations in mind, he accepted the better-paying and more stable position as the economic advisor to the Winnipeg Electric Company in September 1937, where his annual salary would nearly double, starting as it did at $9,000 (the equivalent of $157,000 in 2019).[20] Beyond the financial gains, the return to Winnipeg was personally rewarding. The Englands were greeted with favourable press coverage as they resumed their former lives, both returning to volunteerism: Amy with the Manitoba Handicrafts Guild and Robert with a variety of committees.[21]

Now that both the Brockingtons and the Englands were living in the same city, the two couples became good friends. One day in 1938, Brockington asked England to undertake a series of radio programs about the various groups in the Canadian west and to base the series on Winnipeg. England agreed to the proposal on the conditions that he remain unpaid, that he be given a free hand in crafting the series, and that he be given a clerical assistant, as well as the assistance of dramatic and musical producers. Brockington and Murray agreed, so England put together a series entitled *Ventures in Citizenship*, which aired over thirteen weeks beginning on 28 September 1938.[22] The series was first promoted as an attempt to "present the musical and cultural background of various New Canadian groups," and later coverage described the series as portraying, "in an artistic and

Table 4.2 Episodes of *Ventures in Citizenship* radio program, 1938

| Date (1938) | Topic/title | Guests |
| --- | --- | --- |
| 28 Sept. | What is Involved in Canadian Citizenship | |
| 5 Oct. | Second Generation New Canadians | |
| 12 Oct | Viewpoints of a Mixed Family | The Dubienski Family |
| 19 Oct. | Ethical Life | Rabbi Frank, Rev. C., and Father d'Éschambault |
| 26 Oct. | Adjustment to Canadian Political Life | |
| 2 Nov. | A Celebration of Citizenship | Watson Kirkconnell |
| 9 Nov. | The Hebrew Contribution | |
| 16 Nov. | The Mennonite and German Contribution | |
| 23 Nov. | The Ukrainian Contribution | |
| 30 Nov. | The Spirit of Scandinavia | Esse Ljungh and Stanley Hoban |
| 7 Dec. | The Polish Contribution | W.J. Rose |
| 14 Dec. | The French-Canadian Contribution | Father Antoine d'Eschambault |
| 21 Dec. | Christmas Party | (Various choirs) |

Note: Table compiled using information found in newspaper coverage of the event and the files found in Library and Archives Canada, R5347-0-1-E, box 6, folders 4 and 5.

entertaining manner, the characteristic contribution to Canadian citizenship of the various ethnic groups in western Canada."[23]

Instead of utilizing real personalities, England opted for fictionalization in order to make for a "sharpened, brighter script." The all-male cast of characters consisted of Mr Brown, a "typical Canadian," and his English friend Mr Willoughby, who is visiting the west. Accompanying them is Mr Wood, "a skeptical, practical sort of person," and Professor MacAlistair, "a pedant who nevertheless has some very sound ideas." Brown quickly offers to take Willoughby around to visit the various communities, "and so begins a cultural odyssey which lasts throughout the series." CBC producer John Kannawin declared that the remaining episodes were "going to take us into some strange places, and bring us up against some strange ideas. But we are shirking nothing. The issues will be faced and discussed without fear – though always with moderation."[24] The program was no doubt inspired by a need for national programming and by the success of Gibbon's series. However, the rise of racial nationalism in Europe was likely a contributing factor. (For instance, in the first episode, Willoughby remarks: "race and nation ... have become so important in post-war, European propaganda.")[25]

The first six episodes of the series were introductory, followed by six episodes on the contributions of specific groups, and a concluding "Christmas party" episode. According to England, the opening broadcast was a discussion of "citizenship, race and ethnic differences, and the problem of integration and assimilation." The next episode, entitled "The Second Generation," saw Brown and Willoughby visit the home of a Scandinavian friend named Ljungh, who is entertaining three friends: a German, a Russian, and a Czech.[26] The third episode followed the same format and saw the duo visit the home of Mr and Mrs Dubienski, described by the press as an "actual Canadian family, representative of several racial stocks." Mr Dubienski was a native of Poland, while his Ontarian-born wife was of Scottish-Canadian descent, and the episode was structured in such a way as to draw a contrast between Mr Dubienski's old home in Poland and his new home in Canada. Continuing the theme of the previous week – and in keeping with England's emphasis on the second generation – the "modern, thoroughly Canadian outlook of the children" is another main subject of discussion.[27]

The fourth episode departed from the pattern of the initial three. Entitled "Ethical Life," it features a dramatized discussion among a Roman Catholic priest, a Jewish rabbi, and a Protestant minister. Brown and Willoughby listen but do not participate in the debate, which is not about religion but rather "the ethical life of Canada ... the ideals towards which Canadians must work, and what ends have already been achieved in forging a new country."[28] "Political Life," the fifth episode, featured several guests and was widely advertised across the country.[29] It depicted schoolroom scenes showing training in citizenship, and the "ritual of a citizenship ceremony" led by Justice Dysart.[30] The episode also featured a reenactment of a debate in the Manitoba legislature over a motion to abolish the office of the province's lieutenant governor. Marcus Hyman (MLA, Labour) played himself and delivered the same speech he originally gave opposing the motion.[31] Episode six, the final introductory broadcast, was a "Celebration of Citizenship" (discussed below).[32]

The second half of the series consisted of five episodes dedicated to the contributions of specific groups to Canadian citizenship. The groups examined were Jews, Ukrainians, Scandinavians, Poles, and French Canadians, in that order.[33] Episodes typically featured a speaker and music from the group, often with a special guest or choir. The final episode took the form of a Christmas festival, and similarly featured English, French, German, Icelandic, and Ukrainian choral groups from Winnipeg. Each group sang some of their traditional carols before uniting, with the backing of an orchestra, for a rendition of the "Hallelujah Chorus" from Handel's Messiah.[34] (That the series ended on a triumphantly Christian note is odd in that it excluded at least one of the groups they had featured, Jewish people.) A listener could therefore easily think that the only people groups in western Canada were European, given the series' omission of Canadians of African and Asian descent, as well as Indigenous people.

The series powerfully demonstrates the centrality of the question of race in discussions of Canadian loyalty, unity, and citizenship. Its essential message, crafted by England, is found in the introductory episode.

> Charles Lamb, once, in speaking to a friend, said of another man, "I hate that man." "But," said his friend, "you don't even know him." "Of course, I don't," said Charles Lamb, "how could I hate him if I knew him." That has been the thought behind the planning of this series of broadcasts. The aim of these programmes will be to tell in part of the contributions being made

to Canadian life and citizenship by our neighbours of varied racial origin ... God has written a line of thought on the cradle of each race. To obliterate these lines would be irreverent, unnecessary and would blot out some of the funded wisdom, mother wit, genius and achievements of humanity. Our Canadian experiment in human understanding stands for cultural differentiation without the disintegration of Canadian loyalty.

This "great venture" was thus one of "seeking unity while shunning uniformity" and "of combining freedom and order."[35]

According to the press, the scripts were compiled from material supplied by a "committee from the various racial groups" and were arranged and written by the CBC's John Kannawin in collaboration with England's assistant, Harry Darracott. England retained only one of these scripts among his papers, the introductory episode intended to be "a discussion on citizenship, race and ethnic differences, and the problem of assimilation and integration." The premise of the episode is that Mr Willoughby comes to visit Winnipeg, where he meets up with his friend Mr Brown and is given a tour of the city. They then join Brown's other friends, Mr Wood and Professor MacAlistair, for a private lunch, where the talk quickly turns to the city and its residents.[36] Right away, they ask the visitor if he has ventured to the north end of the city, where Wood alleges there are groups of European immigrants who have not yet been "assimilated into the main stream of our Canadian life" and who are "isolating themselves into communities."

The two friends disagree on how central diversity is to the city's identity: Wood thinks too much emphasis is placed on it, while MacAlistair counters that it is good for visitors to learn about "the extraordinary mixture of races" found in the whole of the west. He continues on to argue that fictive portrayals of the west have been misleading, with their focus on "Red Indians; Cowboys; Two-Gun Pete; blizzards; [and] homesteads." None of these scenes have depicted the real life of the Canadian West, he declares, for none "showed the various racial groups, settlements and communities." North of the St Boniface Bridge is culturally different from the area to the south but all its inhabitants are Canadians, he adds.[37] This brief passage demonstrates that, from the outset, Indigenous peoples' real presence was denounced as fictive, race was established as a normative category, and assimilation was raised as the primary consideration with regard to diversity.

What is most notable about this script, which set the tone for the entire series, is its fixation on race. Though "race" is repeatedly challenged throughout the episode, even its opponents continue to use the term. At one point in the conversation, MacAlistair suggests that it is "unfortunate" to confuse race and nationality given they are not synonymous terms: "The scientist's conception of race ... is purely biological; and while the races of men were differentiated before the end of the old Stone Age, the basic unity of the human race is now generally accepted." He quickly clarifies that he is speaking only in regard to Europe, where there are no longer "pure races," and later advocates for the use of the term "ethnic group." However, this term is used in such a way that it combines culture and biology, and so is merely race by another name. In his definition, ethnic groups are characterized by both physical elements, including "colour of the skin, details of hair, formation of nose," and social elements such as language, government, religion, and arts.[38] (Recall that these were the same features that Kirkconnell had originally used to forcefully argue for the existence of the Nordic, Mediterranean, and Alpine *races*.) MacAlistair later forgets his own repeated injunctions about terminology, remarking that the way young people of all (European) "races" play together gives him hope for the future. Although the characters make various attempts to jettison the terminology of race, the notion of biological determinism remains.

It is this belief in biological determinism that makes the characters' debate about assimilation so heated. Early in the conversation, Wood sympathetically remarks that a visitor might well wonder what type of people would emerge in the west. "You know, the question of racial assimilation is a very important aspect of community life," he adds. MacAlistair, who has only just finished speaking of the racial mixture of the west, then jumps in: "You don't mean to tell me you're advocating the theory of racial purity which is taken so seriously in many parts of Europe today?" Wood replies that he most certainly does not, but that Canadians "like to remember that we are a British Nation" and "should try to retain the definite characteristics of our people." Would future generations in the west eventually lose "the British way of looking at things?" Willoughby wonders. To this Brown replies:

> Suppose they do. If by absorbing all these racial traits into our people we are able to evolve something better, it seems to me to be all to the good. Take the English themselves. The Englishman

has been described by Arthur Weigall as "God's Glorious Mongrel." I venture to say that if the ancient Briton had been left to himself to develop without any outside influence, he would be as pure-blooded today as a South Sea Islander – and about as advanced culturally. It was the influence of the Dane, the Norman, the Teuton, [and] the Roman on ancient Britain – the contribution each of these races made to the blood of the Briton – that made the English people as we know it today. Even the Arab left his trace on British people. It is something to be proud of, not because of its purity, but because of its mixture. And so it is with Canadians.[39]

Here racial theories similar to those held by Robert England are seen quite plainly. The underlying belief was that each race had distinctive strengths, and that racial purity was related to delayed cultural development. Progress was not attained through the blending of cultures. Instead, racial mixing was what made richer cultures. England's belief that a common language (English) and a strong school system would aid assimilation was also put into the mouths of several characters. "Unity of language is often the basis of a successful state," Brown remarks at one point, adding that English is a powerful factor in the process of "welding the new-comers among us into a Canadian people."[40]

But to what were newcomers supposed to be assimilated? According to the radio series, they should assimilate to "the British scheme of things," that is, British ideals and institutions in Canada. The skeptical Wood, having grown impatient with the "scientific way of looking at it," admits his fear that Canada is unlikely to make "one people" out of all the various groups. He adds that they are "bound to develop their own racial characteristics," which would go on to threaten Canada's Britishness. "You mean that certain races are incapable of carrying on the British tradition?" MacAlistair asks. "Certainly," Wood replies. To him it is a fact that "British institutions, having been created by British people, are congenial to them, and probably quite unintelligible to others." This is the same argument that Kirkconnell had made in his 1920 article (though he specifically named Slavic and Jewish peoples as being unassimilable) and that England had long fretted about in his own writings.

The only path to Canadian unity, MacAlistair concludes, is through racial intermixture. But some groups are unlikely to intermarry, and this is cause for grave concern. As he puts it, "if you can't amalgamate the races, what chance is there of a Canadian citizenship?" Besides, even with some intermixing, racial characteristics, those "hidden influences," would eventually "spell disaster."[41]

MacAlistair counters that society, government, and industry together will eventually "mould these people into a more North American pattern ... the differences in temperament and certain psychic tendencies can contribute to a more balanced community." He also proposes that citizenship is an attitude, and the others rally around this idea, which he then expands in alliterative fashion. Citizenship in democracy, he enthuses, is about consent, conservation, contribution, and co-operation, all made possible by courtesy "and perhaps a dash of Christianity." He then critiqued the method of assessing immigrants' level of assimilation by ranking groups based on criminal statistics, inter-marriage rates, and literacy. (This strategy was common during this period, used many times in the works of Kirkconnell.) "Men are good or bad citizens independent of what group to which they belong," MacAlistair counters. Instead of trying to mould all the various groups into one, Canada should rather set these people to work creating that very mould, he concludes.[42] Brown, apparently converted at last, concedes that "we are not simply taking over British traditions in Canada; but ... accepting these various peoples with all that they have to give us – and are combining their characteristics with those of the British and the French – with a resultant something that is distinctly – Canadian."[43] Ultimately, the listener was left with the impression that, although Canadians would not form one singular "race" or ethnic group due to barriers of tradition and religion, through the cooperative model of citizenship, something (or someone) uniquely Canadian was being formed. This was not about fashioning a mosaic with distinct subgroups; rather, this was about Canadians collectively deciding what their national identity would be, though it was obviously to be a blend of British, French, and various other European traditions.

Indigenous cultures and traditions were conspicuously absent, and the sixth episode of the series drove home this settler colonial narrative. It took the form of a Hayward Celebration, a technique that the press declared was believed to be "absolutely new to radio."[44] Dr F.H. Hayward, an English schools inspector and educational specialist, had designed "Celebrations" as a form of secular liturgy, with one person leading a group through prepared script.[45] The idea of using this format was England's, but he had Watson Kirkconnell design this particular script for the series, and it aired with the title "A Celebration of Citizenship." According to Kirkconnell, it was "designed to pay honour to the pioneers of Canada of all races, first in terms of their general labours, and then in terms of the pioneer record of specific groups."

The celebration begins by praising the European "pioneers," thus erasing Indigenous peoples from the story and instead telling a narrative of colonial progress. The script then turns to a series of spokesmen (and they are all *men*) representing Canadians of French, British, German and Dutch, Scandinavian, Slavic, and Jewish descent respectively. Each spokesman provides a brief sketch of his group and, while intended to be complimentary, these sketches are nevertheless simplistic and deterministic. French Canadians are described as having a record of "piety and devotion." And, in the script's only hint at the existence of Indigenous people, Kirkconnell describes French missionaries Jean de Brébeuf and Gabriel Lalement as having "steadfastly faced martyrdom and unspeakable torture at the hands of savage men."

The English are described as fearless explorers and creators of Canada's political structure; German and Dutch are less spectacular settlers who nevertheless have contributed deep religious faith and persevering honesty. The Scandinavians are positioned as the racial forebears of both the British and the French ("We are the Vikings, the purest Nordic stock of Europe ... our blood has coursed in British veins since the days when Sweyn and Canute ruled the British Isles. Even in the Canadians of Quebec, colonized from Normandy, the race is predominantly ours"). Scandinavian nations are also portrayed as having balanced individualism with social justice and communal welfare ("Our highly educated nations are born individualists, but they have come to look beyond raw liberty to social justice and communal welfare").

Slavs are described as "an old race" but "the newest of Canadians," whose dream of freedom has been denied for a millennium. However, Kirkconnell's sketch implies that their loyalty is conditional and their integration destined to be only partially complete. If their political liberty and social justice could be assured then they would be "unfailing" in their loyalty, he writes; left unanswered is the question of what might happen if these assurances are not met. Slavs would also never fully assimilate, Kirkconnell suggests, as their "love of vivid color and design" and "fondness for song and dance and drama" would not be denied.

Jewish Canadians are described as intellectual luminaries who are small in number but would provide a proud – yet unidentified – contribution to Canada. The seventh and final spokesman represents all the groups not yet named: "Hungarians and Estonians and Finns, Greeks and Italians, Letts and Lithuanians and Albanians, Syrians and Chinese and Japanese." While the inclusion of several of these nationalities is unusual, the treatment of this entire group is different than the others. Lumped together, no positive attributes are listed for each. Instead, their representative recites the following simple lines: "We come from a score of lands, each with its achievement in human history, each with its possible contribution to Canadian life. Out of the blending of our races will come a richer synthesis. Our racial threads will add an intenser [sic] colour to the tapestry of national life." However, some threads are still missing: people of African and Indigenous descent remain excluded. Emphasizing the theme of unity, the celebration concludes with all the groups singing "O Canada" together.[46]

The series was popular from the beginning. "Continuously jangling telephone bells in the CBC offices greeted the conclusion of the opening broadcast of Ventures last week. Some listeners were critical, some enthusiastic. All were keenly interested," one columnist reported.[47] It was later described as "a remarkable experimental series" that "hit the air with a bang," and was considered "one of the season's great successes."[48] Denny Brown, radio columnist for the *Winnipeg Tribune*, wrote that it "should go down as one of the all too few examples of what can be done in Canadian radio. Almost every program has sustained an enviable record for production and originality, and the series was one of the few successful attempts to combine education with entertainment."[49] It would not be the last, for it had set the tone for future efforts to promote unity while praising diversity. Some of the hallmarks of this approach included the erasure of Indigenous people and people of African descent, a debate about the precise nature and role of race, and an emphasis on the creation of a distinctly Canadian culture or people.

### WATSON KIRKCONNELL AND POLITICAL LOYALTY

Kirkconnell would be one of the first public intellectuals to be drawn into official attempts to promote unity in Canada during wartime and he would do so with one additional qualification. He had been invited to lecture on Hungarian poetry at the Stephen Tisza University at Debrecen during the summer session of 1938, and it was also announced that he would be receiving an honorary doctorate from the university. The degree would give him the designation that he so craved; he would finally become Dr Kirkconnell, a title he would consistently use afterwards without ever noting its honorary status.[50]

Watson and his wife Hope sailed for Hungary in July, toured a number of European countries, and upon their return in September he immediately began speaking about the situation in Europe, chalking up some forty-one addresses in two months. He later estimated that he averaged one hundred public addresses per year from 1938 to 1941, most of them on political issues and "in defence of the European-Canadian communities in Canadian life." Some were analytical and others trivial but all were met with interest.[51] While his focus remained on the situation in Europe, others had begun to wonder about European groups in Canada. Returning from a meeting of the Canadian Institute of International Affairs (CIIA) held in Winnipeg in March 1939, the organization's national secretary, John Baldwin, wrote to Kirkconnell, urging him to tackle "the problem of a study on Canada's foreign language groups." Baldwin wanted to check into the work of Robert England, but he asked Kirkconnell to nevertheless give "serious consideration to this possibility of a study on central Europe of a more general nature."[52]

Another project was the last thing that Kirkconnell needed at this point. The stress of his workload as a professor, coupled with a low salary and a growing family, had taken its toll and the already slim man had lost a significant amount of weight. Reaching such a low point, he had come to the inevitable conclusion that he needed a higher-paying job and had begun hunting for one.[53] Yet in the midst of this turmoil, he could not resist Baldwin's entreaty and quickly responded, dismissing the idea that Robert England's work would suffice. "I do not know that anyone has yet ventured to discuss these groups as political actors, with definitive and incisive views, especially in the field of foreign affairs," he wrote. With the letter he enclosed a manuscript proposal for a book that would essentially be based on his ongoing review of the non-English-language press for the *University of Toronto Quarterly*, expanded to cover forty newspapers in fourteen languages and with a specific focus on politics.[54] With the rumblings of war, and the push from Baldwin, Kirkconnell's focus thus shifted from promoting appreciation of translated poetry to assessing each of the various European minority groups in order to determine their loyalty to Canada and the degree to which they had assimilated. This adjustment is put most plainly in one of his notes from the period, which reads: "100% loyalty needed ... Need of cultural tolerance, but political Loyalty."[55] This emphasis on political loyalty would soon become a mainstay of the federal government's official programming during the conflict.

The CIIA was interested in Kirkconnell's pitch and supplied him with a grant of $100 (or the equivalent of around $1,700 in 2019), which he used to pay for the additional newspapers. He continued to work on the book manuscript throughout the summer but, as ever, was low on funds, so he sold a series of eight articles on "Canada's Minorities and Hitler" to the *Winnipeg Tribune* and the *Ottawa Citizen*, which appeared in November. The introduction declared that Anglo-Canadians were now an "actual minority in Canada," with French Canadians numbering at over 3.5 million, and over 2 million Canadians of "other European stocks." "In times of crisis, it is important to know something of the attitudes of these people towards the major issue at stake," Kirkconnell wrote, and his survey of their press revealed that "the vast majority of these European-Canadian groups are unquestionably loyal to the Dominion," despite surprising divisions and shades of opinion on what should be done about the European situation.[56]

Informed by Baldwin that the CIIA was stopping action on all existing book manuscripts but that a pamphlet would be welcomed, Kirkconnell shifted gears and proposed stitching these articles together with a more extensive introduction, adding that it could be done in a matter of days. Baldwin again expressed interest, but in the end the pamphlet was never published. The CIIA, after having located a publisher for Kirkconnell's larger book manuscript, backed out of supporting it too, citing its polemical nature.[57] Nevertheless, Kirkconnell's old friend Bill Clarke at Oxford University Press persevered. In fact, Clarke's own concern about Canada's racial composition led him to push additional edits. He wrote to Kirkconnell that he wanted the book to have "strong conclusions on the necessity of immigration from Anglo-Saxon stock to counter-balance the rapid increase of non-Anglo-Saxons" (a strategy of immigration that Kirkconnell personally did not believe was a viable option), and added that it ought to stress "how closely the preservation of our democratic institutions is allied to and depended upon our connection with Great Britain." The resulting book, entitled *Canada, Europe, and Hitler*, was published in November 1939, just three months after the outbreak of the war.[58]

The reason for the work, according to its preface, was to "clarify some of the issues, both national and international, that confront Canada in the present war." A close reading of the text suggests that Kirkconnell's purpose in writing the book was actually to convince English Canadians of two facts: first, that Hitler posed a threat to the entire world and that Canadians therefore needed to support the war effort; and second, that so-called new Canadians and French Canadians were loyal to Canada. To achieve these aims, Kirkconnell employed a variety of rhetorical techniques and lines of argumentation. He was keen to demonstrate his unparalleled understanding of European sources, including *Mein Kampf* in the original German, and the book has the air of extravagant, authority-boosting empiricism. (In the preface, Kirkconnell admitted that he had availed himself of the help of three collaborators, but emphasized that this was only done for purposes of speed and that he alone was responsible for the selection and analysis of the materials gathered and translated.) This apparent linguistic expertise sits alongside references to race science, brought in to add historical depth and analysis. To a present-day reader, the combination is jarring, but this was not at all the case in Kirkconnell's mind, as he confidently stood by his dated, narrow interpretation of the contradictory and confused literature on race.

Kirkconnell's entire analysis was based on the assumption that the Anglo-Saxon (or Anglo-Canadian) was the normative model to which racialized others could be compared, including French Canadians. No Canadians of non-British, non-French, European descent were truly citizens in the way that Anglo-Canadians were, for all others lacked, by blood, affection for Britain.[59] "The two greatest obstacles to our national unity will have been surmounted," Kirkconnell argued, "(1) when Anglo-Saxons in Canada realize the fundamental fact that loyalty to Canada need not (and for more than half the population of Canada cannot) include *filial* affection for Britain and (2) when European-Canadians *as sons by adoption* share from the affection and admiration for Britain that springs from a fair appraisal of what Britain has accomplished and could accomplish for world peace."[60] Thus while the true or filial affection for Britain could only come through the Anglo-Saxon bloodline, an adoptive affection could be cultivated. This affection was built on the realization of Britain's (and therefore Anglo-Saxons') global power, which would thus encourage loyalty to Canada, a proud member of the British empire. Although Kirkconnell still believed that so-called new Canadians should be allowed freedom of cultural expression, his focus was now on ensuring that they had the prerequisite affection.

During the war, Kirkconnell's eugenic fears once again came to the fore. He interpreted the French Canadian birthrate as "fecundity ... unremittingly winning for itself an ever-widening empire from the Canadian wilderness." By contrast, he warned, "British-Canadians are at less than half of the country's total and are losing ground at an alarming rate." He blamed Anglo-Canadians, and especially Anglo-Protestants, for failing to multiply at the adequate rate of four children per family, which was necessary for "the survival of a race or group." Kirkconnell admitted that "the Anglo-Canadian," and by this he undoubtedly meant himself,

> can nevertheless scarcely view with equanimity the rapid replacement of his own stock by that of alien groups. The Anglo-Saxons, who have displayed the greatest political genius of any age or people, have bequeathed to Canada the master-principles of responsible government and federalism. As heirs of that tradition and still the largest of the many national groups in Canada, the Anglo-Canadians naturally hope for the perpetuation of their blood and institutions in this land. For the former, our Anglo-Canadian birth-rate is no longer adequate, and immigration from the British Isles ... has been relatively unsuccessful since the War. Unless we are prepared to take parenthood as a serious duty, *la revanche du berceau* [revenge of the cradle] will speedily submerge us in both East and West – and that deservedly, when the potential mothers of our race mistake comfort for civilization.[61]

The text served as a racial warning with a eugenic focus and as such shows the continuity of Kirkconnell's thought. A belief in the political genius of the Anglo-Saxons – and therefore the Anglo-Canadians – was a hallmark of his earliest Nordicism, as was a fear of French fecundity and an insistence on blaming women for the supposed problem of low natality. Kirkconnell would continue to make such eugenic claims throughout the war, for instance remarking in 1942 that Anglo-Canadians had "chosen present comfort at the price of racial extinction" and were "addicted to race suicide."[62]

In his discussion of Canadian minority groups, Kirkconnell's standard tactic was to detail the size of the group; their character, measured by their crime rate, acquisition of English, and political leanings (among other factors); the percentage of their population that had been born in Canada; and the general level of integration. The purpose of the second half of the book, consisting of his overview of the European-Canadian press, was to reassure Anglo-Canadians that all the so-called new Canadian groups were in fact politically loyal and would support the war effort. As he put it in his conclusion: "From the foregoing seventy pages there thus emerges a most variegated mosaic of European-Canadian opinion, which shapes itself nevertheless into a pattern of quite astonishing unanimity on the issue of supporting Canada."[63] This is perhaps the first time that, in a nod to Gibbon's book, Kirkconnell used the famous "mosaic" metaphor in a publication, but note he used it in reference not to the variety of people groups in Canada but rather their opinions.

Kirkconnell's own vision for Canada remained that of a tapestry made of bright European threads. As he argued: "All the values of civilization are not summed up in the Anglo-Saxon. To weave into the Canadian fabric the multi-coloured threads of all of Europe's cultural legacies ought, if it were possible, to produce in the end a civilization of unusual richness. In the ancient Greek world, it was Athens, the most miscegenated in blood and culture, that led in all artistic and cultural achievements, while Sparta, which kept its Nordic stock relatively pure, was left far behind in everything except the art of war."[64] (This was the same reasoning that Robert England had provided in his book *The Central European Immigrant in Canada* a decade prior.) The reason for the acceptance of European minorities was therefore not altruism, but rather its likeliness to benefit Canada's culture and its admittedly "miscegenated" blood. In order to turn immigrants into better Canadians, it was necessary to accept part of their own cultures, Kirkconnell argued. "A man is more likely to become a better Canadian, and to make a more confident and valuable contribution to Canadian life, if he *is led to feel* pride in his own national past and to realize that his fellow-Canadians, because they admire and respect his national tradition, expect great things from him."[65] Accepting immigrants' cultures was not about their inherent worth but rather was a

Table 4.3 Sales and royalties of *Canada, Europe, and Hitler*, 1939–1949

| Date | Free copies | Sales: Canada | Sales: England | Sales: combined | Royalties |
| --- | --- | --- | --- | --- | --- |
| 21 Nov. 1939– 31 Mar. 1940 | 142 | 1,012 | 300 | 1,312 | $163.58 |
| 31 Mar. 1940– 30 Sept. 1940 | 28 | 136 | 300 | 436 | $36.90 |
| 30 Sept. 1940– 31 Mar. 1941 | 7 | 92 | 0 | 92 | $13.80 |
| 1941–1942 | 6 | 47 | 51 | 98 | $8.50 |
| 1942–43 | 1 | 27 | 13 | 40 | $4.53 |
| 1943–1944 | 7 | 74 | 0 | 74 | $11.10 |
| 1944–1945 | 0 | 26 | 0 | 26 | $3.90 |
| 1945–1946* | 0 | 8 | 0 | 8 | $1.20 |
| 1946–1947 | 0 | 1 | 0 | 1 | $0.15 |
| 1947–1948* | 0 | 5 | 0 | 5 | $0.75 |
| 1948–1949 | 0 | 2 | 0 | 2 | $0.30 |
|  | 191 | 1,430 | 664 | 2,094 | $244.71 |

Notes: Table compiled using the annual royalty statements found in the Esther Clark Wright Archives of Acadia University, Watson Kirkconnell fonds, box 6, folder 7. Annual sales ran 31 March to 31 March unless otherwise noted; for the year 1945–46, a defence tax of 5% was levied on the royalties; and years with missing statements are denoted by asterisks (*).

strategy to ensure that immigrants felt an expectation to become good Canadian citizens.

The book sold briskly and received positive reviews, with influential Canadian public intellectual B.K. Sandwell declaring it "the best short history of recent international relations in Europe up to September 1939 that has yet appeared."[66] Surprisingly, it seems to have been well-received by the French-language press as well. Edmond Cloirier, manager of the newspaper *Le Droit*, was generally pleased with Kirkconnell's treatment of French Canadian opinion, critiquing him only for not having differentiated between French people living in Quebec and francophones living in English provinces. He later successfully sought permission to reprint the entire tenth chapter (concerning the Anglo-Saxon and the French), along with an introduction, and distribute it to some five hundred professionals and businessmen as a Christmas booklet.[67]

## CONCLUSION

The roots of the federal government's official promotion of cultural pluralism can be traced as far back as the late interwar period, when the new national radio corporation began to broadcast series that encouraged the toleration of European "racial" minority groups and their cultures. The radio format proved to be successful in combining entertainment and education and in drawing on the expertise of private individuals. This model provided a foundation for future efforts and, as the next chapter demonstrates, would be replicated during the Second World War. However, these efforts were limited to European "racial" groups, typically ignored Canadians of African, Asian, or Indigenous descent, and were expressed in a racialist discourse. In the case of Kirkconnell, such efforts were also marked by long-lasting fears about Anglo-Saxon numerical superiority, the French Canadian population, and the adequate assimilation of so-called new Canadians. As it will quickly become clear, others in government and federal civil service shared these ideas and concerns, which meant that wartime efforts to promote "unity in diversity" were similarly exclusionary.

# 5

# Cultural Pluralism in Wartime

## INTRODUCTION

During the Second World War, the Canadian state's overall involvement in promoting cultural pluralism was limited. Reaching Canadians of non-English, non-French, European descent was simply not a high priority – with the exception of those classified as enemy aliens, and then with radically different intentions. This chapter examines how the early cultural pluralists began to tailor their efforts to the wartime context and how their expertise was appropriated by the state. Official attempts to ensure national unity were fragmented, sporadic, and ill-supported. They are best understood not as an effort directly coordinated by the state so much as the results of the interplay between a few determined individuals within the civil service and the handful of private experts on "racial diversity" they engaged. The federal government, concerned about the loyalty of some particular groups, eventually initiated some attempts to promote unity among them by soliciting the help of public intellectuals. Drawing on the prewar model, these efforts continued to employ radio broadcasting, supplemented with the mass distribution of printed materials. The federal government concealed its involvement in the earliest ventures; but, whether branded as official or not, the resulting efforts reproduced and reaffirmed racial categorizations, were limited to people of European descent, and were fraught with anxiety about particular "racial" and religious groups. Much like the efforts that preceded it, this was a cultural pluralism limited to peoples racialized as white, now further constrained by an increased focus on security, unity, and citizenship.

In order to best understand domestic policy during Second World War, it is first necessary to understand the person at the helm during those years, Prime Minister William Lyon Mackenzie King. Particularly relevant to this chapter are his ideas about race and assimilation, and his leadership style and subsequent approach to public information. King's political career had been built in part on Anglo-Canadian racism, especially one event during his time as a deputy minister in the Department of Labour: the Vancouver Riots. In September 1907, approximately ten thousand of Vancouver's Anglo-Canadian residents, angry about increasing immigration from Asian countries, rioted for three days. Parading through the streets, they smashed windows, assaulted people of Asian descent, and attempted to destroy businesses that they owned. Historian Patricia Roy notes that these riots were unsurprising given the city's traditional hostility towards Asian peoples.[1] The uprising was connected to similar riots that occurred in the United States around the same period; historian Erika Lee argues that while these events were not internationally coordinated, they represent "the most public, violent, and extreme manifestations of an interconnected anti-Asian racism gripping the Pacific coast." Further, scholars suggest that, in response to these events, Canadians and Americans began thinking about "the 'Oriental Problem' ... as a global issue that united 'white men's countries' together against 'the yellow peril.'"[2]

The riots were worrisome for the federal government on account of Britain's alliance with Japan, leading then prime minister Wilfrid Laurier to swiftly apologize to the Japanese government and to create a commission to assess the damages and issue compensation. Laurier dispatched his minister of labour, Rodolphe Lemieux, along with Secretary of State Joseph Pope, to Japan to attempt to work out a mutually acceptable emigration scheme.[3] He also sent Mackenzie King to Vancouver to head up the promised commission. King would ultimately complete three major reports relating to the riot. (This research he parlayed into a PhD from Harvard University, making him the only Canadian prime minister to date to hold a doctorate.)[4]

King was a believer in white racial superiority and preferred racial segregation when possible, confiding in his journal after a trip to India a few years later that he found it "impossible to describe how refreshing it is to be again with people of one's own colour. One becomes very tired of the black races after living among them. It is clear that the two were never meant to intermix freely."[5] King believed that nominally non-white races were unsuitable for Canada on account of the country's climate, but he also viewed European immigrants as unequal in desirability owing to differing levels of assimilability. Historian Robert Harney notes that King preferred American, British, French, Belgian, Dutch, Swiss, German, Scandinavian, and Icelandic settlers as he felt these groups were most easily assimilated, and that this view remained remarkably consistent throughout his life. But assimilation did not guarantee acceptance; in his diaries, King described non-British, non-French people of European descent residing in Canada as "foreigners" or "foreign elements," seemingly without regard to their citizenship status.[6]

As historian N.F. Dreisziger puts it, though King "undoubtedly considered himself a man of humanitarian outlook, he was ... – beyond doubt – an anti-Semite and, by instinct, also a racist."[7] Historians Irving Abella and Harold Troper note that King and his cabinet were ultimately responsible for keeping Jewish people out of Canada throughout most of the 1920s and again from 1935 onwards, even as the situation deteriorated in Germany. His obsession with national unity in wartime was used to cloak his anti-Semitism, as he argued to Cabinet that Jewish refugees ought not to be admitted as they would cause riots and undermine provincial-federal relations. In his words, there was no point in "creating an internal problem in an effort to meet an international one."[8]

Prior to the Second World War, King had stubbornly refused to make plans for the possibility of a future conflict, despite having been pressed to do so since 1935. It was not until 1938 that a number of inter-departmental committees were formed in preparation. One of these was to deal with the treatment of so-called enemy aliens, in this case, Germans, Italians, and Japanese.[9] In his assessment of the period, Dreisziger divides politicians and civil servants into two categories: those who advocated rigid control of enemy aliens (marked by internment); and those who advocated for a flexible and more humane approach, one that sought "to alienate as few ethnic groups as possible in order to co-opt most of them into the Canadian war effort and the mainstream of national life." However, this distinction only holds up when aliens of European extraction are considered. As Dreisziger himself notes, many of the same officials who pushed for a flexible approach towards the Germans and Italians were openly discriminatory towards those racialized as non-white, especially Japanese Canadians.[10]

Indeed, there was an obvious discrepancy in treatment between Japanese Canadians and German and Italian Canadians from the very outset. The preliminary report of the interdepartmental Committee on the Treatment of Aliens and Alien Property, submitted in September 1939, presented European aliens as benign and recommended that each individual be judged on a case-by-case basis. As for the Japanese group, which they referred to as "Asiatic," the Committee argued that it might be necessary "to recommend the internment of nearly all the [Japanese] enemy nationals, since it is recognized that public feeling ... might render this course necessary, not alone to avoid danger of espionage and sabotage, but also for the protection of the person and property of enemy aliens."[11] Evidence such as this demonstrates three important points: first, the recommended course of action was described as internment, not "evacuation"; second, this internment was presented as a necessary course of action owing to concerns about both state security *and* the security of Japanese people because of racism on the part of nominally white Canadians; and third, Japanese immigrants and Canadians of Japanese descent were subjected to far more harsh treatment both during the war and immediately afterwards. A number of Canadians of European descent were also interned, including over 600 of Italian descent, over 800 of German of descent, and around 130 people deemed to be Communists.[12] But for the nearly 22,000 Japanese Canadians that were interned, the government took the additional step of dispossessing them of property, land, and goods, which were then sold off, often at prices that were well below market value. In total, 3,964 Japanese Canadians were also deported back to Japan, despite the fact that over 60 per cent of them were Canadians by birth or naturalization. Ian Mackenzie (MP for Vancouver Centre) made it clear that the selling of property in particular was about more than wartime security, promising his constituents in 1942 that it was his intention to "see they never come back here."[13]

Aside from security concerns, the other main way in which the federal government engaged with ethnic minorities during the war was through public information. The prime minister's approach to public information no doubt mirrored his approach to the press. As journalist and historian Mark Bourrie explains, King was a former reporter, and throughout his political career he employed no press advisor and held no press conferences, viewing them as perilous. Instead, he cultivated personal relationships with select members of the tiny Parliamentary Press Gallery. The chosen few were each led to believe that the relationship they shared with the Prime Minister was unique, when in fact he gave this treatment to several others, all of whom were selected on the basis of their perceived trustworthiness, deference, and discretion.[14] So too did King seek to personally manage – even micromanage – public information during the war. Describing the plan that he settled on, historian William Young remarks: "It was all very complicated but, in King's mind, prevented the possibility of anyone becoming a Canadian version of Dr. Goebbels. No one but the Prime Minister would serve a co-ordinating function."[15]

Immediately prior to the outbreak of the war, King was insistent on limiting Canadian involvement in the conflict. When the war broke out, King similarly sought to minimize the government's role in public information as much as possible. To this end he tried to avoid creating a dedicated infrastructure and instead carefully oversaw these operations himself. In his mind, he and Cabinet would decide what information the public should receive and a cabinet committee could handle the details of dissemination. By September 1939 this ad hoc arrangement had proved inefficient so King proposed creating a permanent organization under the leadership of Leonard Brockington, who would report directly to him. Encountering opposition from newspaper publishers who objected to an outsider holding the post, he backed away from appointing Brockington. King still hired him as an assistant, but the role was ill-defined and the fit poor: Brockington sought to change Mackenzie King's image, polish his speeches, and move beyond a reliance on newspapers to include radio broadcast and public speeches as well. King wanted none of it, later remarking: "I thought I was getting a cart horse, but I found I got a race horse." Brockington made it clear he intended to resign but King attempted to keep him, employing much flattery. ("He covered me with whipped cream and bullshit," Brockington later complained.) Brockington would eventually break free, but before he departed in 1941 he was involved in coordinating some of the earliest and most discreet public information projects, ones which involved the assistance of public intellectuals.[16]

In November 1939, the same month that Kirkconnell's book *Canada, Europe, and Hitler* appeared, Deputy Minister of Justice J.F. MacNeill wrote a long memo to the prime minister on the need for messaging targeted at recent immigrants and suggested that the government hire one or more persons to help with this effort. Heading into the conflict, King's main obsession had been maintaining national unity, which he saw primarily as a question of harmony between English and French Canadians (no doubt remembering the conscription crisis of the previous conflict that had bitterly divided the country). However, he was becoming increasingly aware that national unity now involved ethnic minorities as well, so he responded that the memo contained an excellent suggestion and asked his staff to follow up.[17] The next month, King created the Bureau of Public Information (BPI), though little was accomplished during its early existence.[18] A month later, in January 1940, Kirkconnell published a two-part article entitled "War Aims and Canadian Unity" in the *Winnipeg Evening Tribune*. In it, he argued the essential thesis of *Canada, Europe, and Hitler*, namely that national unity depended on the recognition that all national groups shared the fundamental ideals of life and that these ideals were being threatened by the Nazis. These ideals, according to Kirkconnell's Christian liberalism, were freedom of the individual, freedom of national groups to develop their own national character and tradition, and "liberty of Christian faith." Beyond winning the war, he added, Canadians' profound desire should be to build a "co-operative world in which peace shall endure" (presumably under Britain's able leadership). However, he noted that only the government could issue "an official statement of national policy."[19] He was clearly hoping the government would issue a policy and most likely was angling to make himself a part of the process. Whether or not the article was the reason, he was soon called upon to assist the federal government's war aims.

THE UKRAINIAN CANADIANS AND THE WAR

In his memoirs, Kirkconnell claimed that following the publication of his article "War Aims and Canadian Unity," "Mackenzie King, who usually worked by indirection, then asked me through a personal emissary, Leonard Brockington, to write a substantial pamphlet." Kirkconnell and Brockington met in Ottawa at the end of February and the two began discussing the publication of a pamphlet aimed at minority groups.[20] After the meeting, Kirkconnell drafted an outline for a work entitled "War Issues for Canada"; but further discussions between Brockington and Kirkconnell's friend and publisher, Bill

Clarke, led the group to wonder if a publication directed at Ukrainian and German Canadians would be more effective.[21] It would therefore appear that the federal government perceived these two groups as posing the greatest threat to national unity.

The Germans were a fairly easily contained threat, having been subject to internment since 1939, but the Ukrainian Canadians were a completely different story. In terms of sheer numbers, those of Ukrainian descent constituted "the second largest non-British, non-French ethnic group in Canada," and many Canadians viewed them as an internal security concern.[22] Initially, the Royal Canadian Mounted Police (RCMP) was much more concerned about left-wing (communist) groups in Canada than right-wing (Nazi and fascist) groups, a concern amplified by the non-aggression pact that Germany and Russia signed on 23 August 1939. This preoccupation with left-wing radicals turned the government's attention on the Ukrainian-Canadian community, as the strong leftist tradition within the community had prospered in the interwar years.[23] At the outbreak of war, Ukrainian Labour Temples had fifteen thousand members dedicated to "improving the circumstances of workers and farmers in Canada and around the world, and preserving and expressing Ukrainian cultural traditions in their adopted Canadian homeland."[24] In addition, many Ukrainians were strongly nationalistic and desired an independent state back in Europe. Left-wing Ukrainian Canadians were thus perceived by the state as a threat because they resisted ideological assimilation to the liberal order. As a whole, Ukrainian Canadians were viewed as a genuine threat in wartime as it was unclear whether certain factions would side with Hitler if he promised them a European homeland. The government had begun expressing concerns as early as April 1939, when O.D. Skelton of the Department of External Affairs wrote to RCMP commissioner Stuart Wood, requesting a report on all Ukrainian Canadian political organizations. Wood replied that the information had already been collected but that more time was required for analysis. Mackenzie King was also aware of the situation and continued to receive updates on the Ukrainian community throughout 1940.[25]

It was in the context of these concerns that Clarke asked Kirkconnell to draft a pamphlet aimed at Ukrainian Canadians. This represents the first instance of government intervention in ethnic communities that were not identified as "enemy aliens." In early March 1940, Clarke provided Kirkconnell with an update on the situation from Ottawa. He reported that Brockington felt the government should be involved in distributing the pamphlet, would make " a very strong case to the Prime Minister, at the proper time," and in fact had "already discussed our tentative plans with Mr. King, and had found him more than casually interested, to say the least." In closing, he asked for a copy of the draft so he could submit it to Brockington, who would "use it to get some scheme under way as quickly as possible," and raised the idea of a Ukrainian collaborator for the sake of representation.[26]

Bringing in a collaborator was not a bad idea. Kirkconnell was a latecomer to Ukrainian literature, having more knowledge of Hungarian and Polish, though he presented himself as an expert on all things European. Perhaps unsurprisingly, he found that as a result of his initial lack of engagement with their community, Ukrainian Canadians were suspicious of him.[27] However, his subsequent engagements with Ukrainian communities remained more literary than political. While not as evident to Anglo-Canadian readers, Ukrainian reviewers had noted *Canada, Europe, and Hitler*'s neglect of Ukrainian sources and over-reliance on Polish and Hungarian ones, which they argued had skewed Kirkconnell's analysis. Ukrainian nationalists in particular were angered that Kirkconnell did not argue for the creation of an independent Ukrainian state in Europe; one particularly aggrieved nationalist published an entire pamphlet dedicated to exposing Kirkconnell's alleged errors and contradictions.[28]

Working as an intermediary between the federal government and Kirkconnell, Clarke seemingly had no knowledge of how bitterly contested Kirkconnell's previous work had been in some quarters of the Ukrainian Canadian community, and innocently inquired about getting "some outstanding Ukrainian" to collaborate with Kirkconnell on the proposed pamphlet. Kirkconnell agreed that a pamphlet tailored to a specific group would be most effective but dismissed the idea of a Ukrainian collaborator, ostensibly on the grounds that the Ukrainians were split into five factions and there therefore could be no single representative. "You will realize from this just how the Ukrainians are the most baffling of all our minorities," he added. The pamphlet was originally to be released only in Ukrainian, but in the end both the English text and the Ukrainian translation, completed by the long-suffering Honoré Ewach (who had assisted with the research for *Canada, Europe, and Hitler*), were published by mid-1940.[29]

Kirkconnell later described the work as "an attempt to set forth the war aims of Canada and Britain in terms which would appeal to the loyalties of Ukrainian Canadians both as Ukrainians and as Canadians, and would encourage them to sink their differences in a common Canadian war effort." In reality, however, the first half of the pamphlet was aimed at convincing Anglo-Canadians that Ukrainian Canadian loyalty was guaranteed. As he put it, Ukrainian Canadians, "despite their recent settlement and alien traditions," were standing firmly by the side of their fellow Canadians. Much like Robert and Amy England had portrayed the earliest Ukrainian immigrants as somewhat undesirable, so too did Kirkconnell divide Ukrainian Canadians by generation. The first generation, he argued, had been largely military-aged men aligned with the Austrians, and their own "rash utterances" were to blame for their internment. Unlike them, the second generation viewed themselves as Canadians first and Ukrainians second, he suggested. The result was that at the outbreak of this second war, nearly all Ukrainian Canadian organizations had pledged loyalty to the war effort. He returned to this theme in his conclusion, arguing that Anglo-Canadians could soundly put their faith in second-generation Ukrainians.[30]

Seeking to assuage Anglo-Canadian fears that Ukrainian Canadians were insufficiently assimilated, he dealt with a number of these arguments before turning to nationalism, which he believed had the potential to unsettle Ukrainian unity and peace. Nationalism, "within certain limits, is perfectly natural and perfectly legitimate," he suggested, in that its two main impulses were attempts to preserve Ukrainian culture in Canada and an interest in Ukrainian's political future in Europe. Kirkconnell had long defended the first effort, and here he reiterated his argument: "A Canadian of Ukrainian extraction is a better Canadian if he realizes that the stock from which he comes has a fine past, incorporated in literature, music, handicrafts, and religious faith. It will give him pride of origin, helping to restrain him from conduct unworthy of his people, and it will at the same time give him confidence in his own ability to accomplish worthy things." Linguistic assimilation was, however, a necessity; but Kirkconnell again reassured the reader that "on a continent where English is the speech of 130,000,000 people, the economic compulsion to acquire the dominant language is overwhelming." He also defended the existence of Ukrainian cultural organizations, not simply for helping to keep Ukrainian traditions alive, but rather for providing a bridge between Ukrainian traditions and "the Anglo-Saxon tradition," particularly for youth who might feel in limbo between the two. As was his usual rhetorical strategy when discussing any and all European minorities, he argued that the war was actually strengthening unity amongst the various Ukrainian "factions" (which he enumerated and briefly described) as well as between Ukrainian and Anglo-Canadians. For the benefit of Ukrainian readers, he also provided an overview of Nazi rule and argued that Slavic peoples should not expect Hitler to give them freedom but rather "brutal extirpation" and horror.[31]

Kirkconnell's treatment of the so-called Ukrainian question, or the question of a European homeland, displayed a patronizing tone and a transactional view. If Slavic citizens in Canada were sufficiently appreciative of "liberty and democracy" and appropriately unified throughout the war, thus convincing Canada of their "political maturity," then their case for "their European kinfolk" would be more convincing after the conflict ended. In other words, while a Ukrainian homeland might or might not be possible after the war, until then Ukrainian Canadians – led by the second generation – ought to sit tight, quietly work to preserve their culture, maintain unity, and openly support the war effort. Much like England, Kirkconnell viewed Ukrainians as being behind Anglo-Saxons on the scale of civilizational advancement, and he expressed this clearly: "[Ukrainian] leaders realize that mere patriotic zealotry is not enough and that what distinguishes a mature nation from people such as the Afghans and the Berbers is not the fervor of its tribal consciousness but the capacity it can show for civilized conduct and co-operative institutions and its ability to create and cherish a rich and satisfying national culture."[32] In this way, Kirkconnell implied that first-generation Ukrainians were not truly Canadian citizens, and while the second generation was made up of good prospects, they remained, to borrow historian Ian McKay's term, "probationary liberals."[33] The pamphlet thus served to try to convince Canadians of Ukrainians' loyalty, but also had ominous overtones for the Ukrainian Canadians. If they failed to recognize that they were Canadians first, and if they failed to exhibit the traits of civilization, they would remain an immature ethnic group, comparable to inferior races – and perhaps they would be treated as such.

The federal government's coercive organization of consent, by distributing a supposedly privately written and independently published tract, was only an acceptable tactic when Ukrainians represented a minor threat. When the perceived threat level escalated – when some Ukrainians remained firm in their leftist persuasions, breaching the terms of the probation, as it were – strict coercion was required. In May 1940, the Canadian government, "responding ostensibly to the deteriorating military situation in Europe but acting more immediately on the advice of the RCMP and the Minister of Justice, E. Lapointe," banned the Communist Party of Canada and related organizations. This included the Ukrainian Labour Farmer Temple Association (ULFTA), and as a result forty Ukrainian communist leaders were interned. In order to decisively eliminate the supposed threat, the government went further and appropriated properties owned by these banned organizations, including ULFTA community halls, and suppressed the left-wing ethnic press.[34]

Around the same time that this seemingly unofficial pamphlet appeared, the news became public that Kirkconnell was resigning his position at United College to take the headship of the Department of English at McMaster University in Hamilton. While the College's Board of Regents accepted his resignation with "great regret," Kirkconnell was happy to move on. His new salary, he later wrote, was "so enhanced that my wife's martyrdom and my own stomach ulcers were things of the past." (His starting salary is unknown, but in 1941 it was approaching $4,000 a year, or the equivalent of $62,000 in 2019.)[35] The next month was a whirlwind of farewell receptions, including one from the Ukrainian community. One of the final events was the presentation of gifts and a bound volume of letters of farewell from the various Polish and Hungarian organizations in the city.[36]

Kirkconnell's engagement with so-called new Canadians had shifted from an interest only in their "Old World" literatures, to an interest in the poetry they were writing in Canada, and finally to a wartime investigation of their politics and defence of their loyalty. The move to Hamilton changed the dynamic again, as the city was less ethnically diverse than Winnipeg. In addition, Kirkconnell was becoming increasingly fixated on the threat that he believed communism posed to Canada, which resulted in his translation work grinding to a halt. As he remarked to a friend: "Since coming to McMaster University eighteen months ago, I have been very busy with new courses and administration, and have likewise carried a considerable burden of war work. In such circumstances, my work in East European languages has virtually come to a standstill." Additionally, he became less associated with individual community groups than with integrating agencies like the Council of Friendship and the Canadian National Unity Council.[37]

While defending Canadians of non-British, non-French, European descent against charges of disloyalty, Kirkconnell simultaneously continued to repeat the eugenicist and assimilatory message of *Canada, Europe, and Hitler* in subsequent publications as the war progressed. In "A Canadian Amalgam," a brief three-page article written around July 1940, he acknowledged the linguistic diversity of Canada, especially the presence of nationalistic French Canadians, but immediately warned the reader that Anglo-Canadians were declining as a percentage of the population. "The precarious balance between the French and the Anglo-Saxon communities in Canada has been complicated further by large-scale immigration from Europe," he wrote. He then listed the population of each group, focusing on the Europeans. "Asiatics and Indians total fewer than 200,000. Negroes are negligible, at fewer than 20,000," he wrote, dismissively, adding that such figures revealed "a formidable problem in nation-building, full of dangers and yet pregnant with splendid possibilities."

Instead of viewing their population decline with "angry dismay," Anglo-Canadians had to remind themselves of which of these possibilities could be achieved if they provided "sane leadership of what is still politically the dominant group ... The very diversity of Canadian elements is the condition out of which (granted a unity of allegiance) a vital national life may well emerge." In other words, unity in diversity was possible, but only so long as Anglo-Saxons remained in charge. Kirkconnell went on to warn the reader that the formation of a united Canadian nation was by no means guaranteed. "It was vaguely assumed by the Anglo-Canadians, into whose provinces the great bulk of the newer European immigration flowed, that these strangers would soon be assimilated to the Anglo-Saxon tradition and would help to maintain a non-French majority in the Dominion. The results have been a little disconcerting," he admitted. European immigrants were slowly learning English, but were maintaining their own cultural organizations, and sometimes they retained their animosities towards other European groups. With the onset of war, however, most had rallied behind the war effort and were proving loyal. "There is thus a possible silver lining to the present storm-cloud of war," he concluded: that the conflict would serve as a unifying force.[38]

Both articles reveal that for Kirkconnell, a "multi-national" society was one in which Anglo-Canadians maintained numerical majority and political dominance, and French Canadians remained a minority. Further, in his dream state, all European immigrants had given up their cultural exclusivity, bitterness towards other European groups, and interest in the politics of their European homelands. The resulting ideal Canadian nation, built on a fraternity of English-speaking Canadians of various ethnic origins, would cleave to British tradition and leadership and resist the influx of American culture. As he put it in an address around the same period, Canada's problem was "to maintain a common political loyalty, while preserving all possible variety of culture and tradition." He continued: "The problem is not a simple one. It calls for a fine balance between rights and duties." Canadians should not try to "force an Anglo-Saxon pattern on all our citizens," he cautioned, but should instead embrace "a spirit of tolerance and understanding in which our differences can be harmonized (but not homogenized) in a common political loyalty."[39] This vision of cultural pluralism, retooled for wartime, was a far cry from the more radical idea of a cultural federation that he had been calling for only five years previous, but it was certainly more easily stomached by the equally cautious individuals involved in the federal government's attempts to reach minority groups during wartime.

The government seemingly considered ethnic minorities a regional problem specific to the west, as the newly formed Department of National War Services (DNWS) dispatched a recent British hire, Tracy Philipps, on a speaking tour of western Canada. However, much as the government hid its involvement in Kirkconnell's pamphlet, so too did the DNWS shield its involvement by arranging to have Philipps's salary paid by the Canadian Clubs, which were in turn subsidized by government grants. His three objectives were to interpret the background of the war in talks at Canadian Clubs, build up "Canadianism and unification" among "Eastcentral European peoples" for war purposes, and determine the possibilities of counteracting communism. Accompanying him on this trip or mission was Vladimir J. Kisilevsky, later known by the Anglicized surname "Kaye."[40] The government, through the efforts of unofficial agents such as Kirkconnell, Philipps, and Kaye, eventually succeeded in uniting the non-leftist Ukrainian factions to some degree, and by November an "all-inclusive 'Ukrainian Canadian Committee'" was formed.[41]

## FASHIONING CANADIANS ALL

Around this same time, in October 1940, a senior bureaucrat recommended the launch of radio broadcasts aimed at foreign-language groups, but their suggestion was countered with a preference for print media. Robert England was recommended as the best candidate, but he was not taking on permanent positions (ostensibly on account of his health), so Kirkconnell was recommended for the job. Despite the suggestion being passed along to the DNWS, there were no immediate results.[42] Kirkconnell, for his part, continued to independently declare the loyalty of Canada's minorities. In early November 1940, he travelled to the Canadian Club in Toronto and gave an address entitled "European Elements in Canadian Life," in which he supposedly pressed for the creation of a "committee to deal with the foreign element in the Canadian population," an idea first expressed in "War Aims and Canadian Unity." This caught the attention of another sympathetic civil servant, Thomas Davis of the DNWS, who began lobbying for the creation of such a committee or department.[43]

Before this committee was established, the government again made use of Kirkconnell's services, this time in a more transparent fashion. In November 1940, Davis suggested to DNWS that the BPI "undertake some very specific and targeted efforts 'to create good feeling among the people who have come to Canada from foreign lands.'" The Bureau in turn contacted V. Béatrice Belcourt, public relations officer with the Canadian Broadcasting Corporation (CBC), to write a report on "the available talent among new Canadians" and whether it would be advisable to use any such talent in a radio series. She concluded that there was available talent and that the government should proceed with a series, adding that "if Professor Kirkconnell's services are available he should be used in an advisory capacity ... as he is loved and respected by [new Canadians]."[44] The first project of this new initiative was a radio program and accompanying booklet, both entitled *Canadians All*.[45] The radio series consisted of thirteen weekly broadcasts that ran from 27 February until 21 May 1941. Each episode provided an overview of one minority group and described their cultural traditions, ethnic character, and contributions to Canada, and featured musical or dramatic performances intended to showcase their talent.[46]

A spokesperson for the Dominion, usually a man of business, legal, or academic standing, introduced the group of the week. Then

Table 5.1 Episodes of *Canadians All* radio program, 1941

| Date aired (1941) | Topic | Notes |
| --- | --- | --- |
| 26 February | Ukrainian Canadians | Address: Lieut.-Gov. R.F. McWilliams of Manitoba, speaking on democracy. Soldier: Capt. Michael Syrotuck, battery commander in the Royal Canadian Artillery. Music: Constance Stefanik (soprano); Donna Gresco (12-year-old violinist); John Meinyk (pianist and composer); and a Ukrainian choir. Broadcast from the Ukrainian Reading Hall in Winnipeg. |
| 5 March | Icelandic Canadians | Address: John W. Dafoe. Music: Icelandic Male Voice choir, directed by Ragnar H. Ragnar; Mrs Lincoln Johnson and Alex Johnson (soloists), and Gunnar Erlandsson and Frank Thorolfson (accompanists). |
| 12 March | Netherland Canadians | Address: University of Toronto president Dr H.J. Cody, on "Education in the Democratic State." Soldier: Sgt. August Strodyk (RCAF). Music: Cornelius Ysselstyn (distinguished cellist); Samuel Hersenhoren (conductor). Broadcast from Toronto. |
| 19 March | Hungarian Canadians | Address: J.M. MacDonnell, K.C., president of the National Trust Company (Toronto), "Individual Freedom in the Democratic State." Music: a "Hungarian gypsy orchestra" directed by Joseph Oriold; a male choir; and songs played on the cimbalon. Broadcast from Toronto. |
| 26 March | Swedish Canadians | Address: Sidney Smith, president of the University of Manitoba. Soldier: Lieut. C. Moberg, an officer at the infantry training centre at Fort Osborne. Music: a Swedish choir conducted by Arthur Anderson; Freda Simonson (pianist and soloist); and Florence Forsberg (13-year-old soprano soloist). |

*cont.*

Table 5.1 (cont.)

| Date aired (1941) | Topic | Notes |
|---|---|---|
| 2 April | Finnish Canadians | Address: Sir Ernest MacMillan, on "Unity in the Democratic State." Soldier: William Arthur Erikson (RCAF). Music: a Finnish mixed choir of 26 (directed by either K.G. Assiala or Samuel Hersenhoren); and Usko Kalervo Ollikkala (bass-baritone). Broadcast from Toronto. |
| 9 April | Czech Canadians | Address: Edward Anderson, K.C., LL.D., chairman of the Winnipeg Electric Company. Music: a Czech mixed choir, directed by Josef Zajicek. |
| 16 April | Polish Canadians | Address: Justice A.K. Dysart. Soldier: Flight-Lieut. J.T. Gultray (RCAF). |
| 23 April | Belgian Canadians | Address: Judge Joseph Bernier. Soldier: Corporal Claude Vermander (Royal Canadian Corps of Signals). Music: a Belgian choir and Frank Simons (harpist). |
| 30 April | Italian Canadians | Address: Watson Kirkconnell. Soldier: John Lago (RCAF). Music: choir of the St Agnes Church, with Tito Fandos as soloist. Broadcast from Toronto. |
| 7 May | German Canadians | Address: Dr. J.W. Clarke, M.C., of Winnipeg. Soldier: Con Schmidt (Royal Canadian Engineers). Music: a German Canadian choir, with Victor Klassen (tenor soloist). |
| 14 May | Norwegian Canadians | Address: Prof. Arthur L. Phelps. Music: Norwegian Glee Club of Winnipeg, a male chorus, directed by A. Hoines. Broadcast from Winnipeg. |

*cont.*

Table 5.1 (cont.)

| Date aired (1941) | Topic | Notes |
|---|---|---|
| 21 May | Final Program | "A Tribute from the Dominion at large to national groups" in which "Canadians of English and French descent ... salute[d] the citizens of other lineages." Address: Prime Minister Mackenzie King. Music: concert orchestra from Toronto, directed by Reginald Stewart, and vocal music from the Alouette Quarter of Montreal. Broadcast from Ottawa, Toronto, and Montreal. |

Notes: Table compiled using information drawn primarily from the radio columns of the *Leader-Post* (Regina), *Star-Phoenix* (Saskatoon), *Montreal Gazette*, *Vancouver Province*, *Vancouver Sun*, and the *Winnipeg Tribune*; and also the following sources: "Canadians All, New C.B.C. Series," *Star-Phoenix* (24 February 1941), 5; "Opening Address by Dr. Watson Kirkconnell, Professor of English in McMaster University, Hamilton, for the 'Canadians All' Programme," 30 April 1941, Esther Clark Wright Archives of Acadia University, Watson Kirkconnell fonds, box 6, folder 20; and Gibbon, *The New Canadian Loyalists* (Toronto: Macmillan, 1941).

a male member of the group currently serving in the Canadian armed forces gave a brief address, followed by musical selections.[47] According to early newspaper coverage, the series brought representatives of non-English, non-French, European groups "to tell, in song or drama, of the contributions each is making to the life of this country" and to present their "views on Canadianism."[48] Anglo-Canadians welcomed European minority groups, who in turn were expected to pledge their loyalty to the British Empire and to the Dominion of Canada. During the first broadcast, for example, the lieutenant governor of Manitoba provided a "short review of the history of the Ukrainian race and a tribute to its culture." (Surprisingly, he then went on to chastise the majority population for, "with characteristic English insularity," having shown little inclination to learn about Canadians from other European countries.) Captain Michael Syrotuck then took to the microphone to declare that Ukrainian Canadians were "first of all Canadians," and that Canada had offered them a safe haven in which their cultural development was encouraged and where they were free to preserve their traditions and customs. In closing, he reminded English Canadians that the Ukrainian Canadian enlistment rate was "proportionally far higher than their population would suggest."[49]

Similarly, the introduction to the Dutch episode by Dr Cody, president of the University of Toronto, was an assertion that Netherlanders would "maintain here their forefathers' love of freedom and loyalty of truth." It was followed by Sgt Strodyk's message that Dutch Canadians were prepared to make "whatever contribution may be required ... even our property and lives, in defence of the British Empire which is fighting so valiant a battle for the upholding of democracy and the maintenance of the freedom we in Canada enjoy."[50] The final program brought in the ultimate Dominion spokesman, the prime minister, who delivered a three-minute address. In it, he gravely asserted that the freedom of Canada relied on world freedom, the very freedom that was at stake in the present war, and exhorted European Canadians to serve in the military. "Never has there come to men of any race an opportunity to render like service to the ill-fated brothers of their native lands. No higher hope could be given to the enslaved peoples of Europe, than the knowledge that Canada's call to service is being answered by free men of their own race," King declared.[51]

The reception to *Canadians All* reveals much about how Canadians who thought themselves to be more tolerant actually conceived of minorities and the relationship between foreign- and native-born. Irene Baird, a columnist for the *Vancouver Sun*, congratulated the CBC on the series. "Recently I read a letter from an indignant Canadian who felt that for the duration of the war all foreign language groups should be suppressed as far as possible. This spirit seems to typify all that is narrow and dangerous," she wrote, "it breathes the same intolerance, the same obsession with master-racehood that has made dictatorship so noxious, inhumane and blind." In this interpretation, intolerance was a foreign and not a Canadian spirit. However, tolerance of other cultures was not a project of altruism but rather was part of a reciprocal relationship between the host country and its immigrants. "Just as surely as our foreign-born citizens owe a debt to Canada for her hospitality towards them, so we owe them a debt for their share in our industry and culture," Baird concluded.[52]

Further inspiration, and controversy, would come from the publication of the pamphlet that was intended to accompany the radio series. Early in the year, Kirkconnell had travelled to Ottawa, where he discussed the project with the BPI and agreed to write the booklet and provide a brief preliminary introduction of the new series on-air.[53] On 20 February, W.B. Herbert, assistant to the director of the BPI, wrote Kirkconnell to congratulate him on the "very good job" he had done introducing the series the previous day and to inquire as to the progress of the writing. While the *Canadians All* booklet was originally intended for high school students, Herbert informed him that the program continued to expand. "It is our plan," he wrote, "to make this [booklet] available to citizens who listen to the 'Canadians All' programmes." Kirkconnell delivered the initial draft of the *Canadians All* to BPI director G.H. Lash on 12 March 1941, and it entered publication in English in June and in French in July.[54]

"In this booklet," the foreword read, "the authoritative pen of Prof. Watson Kirkconnell tells the story of the peoples of Canada, and points to a road for us to follow towards permanent unification of all our groups into one strong, resolute nation."[55] The entire work was marked by Kirkconnell's own conceptions of race, nationality, and cultural pluralism, most of which had not significantly progressed beyond the views he had developed in the late 1920s. His understanding of the threat of war, Nazis, and the Communists, and his notion of national unity, which he had been expressing since 1938, shaped the rest of the content.

The first section of the booklet was an essay by Kirkconnell, largely made up of material recycled from previous publications, which stressed the same arguments he had been making for several years: Canada was mainly composed of groups of transplanted Europeans; no one European group predominated; there was great commonality among Canadians of all backgrounds; and that unity, not uniformity, was necessary.[56] He also argued against the conflation of nationality with race, arguing that in Europe there were just three "main subspecies of the human race, namely (i) the tall, fair-haired, long-skulled Nordic, (ii) the short, dark, long-skulled Mediterranean and (iii) the stocky, broad-headed Alpine type." He added that each nation was a mixture of the three, and that this intermixture was beneficial.[57] Kirkconnell also informed the reader that Nazism and Communism were twin world conspiracies that threatened civilization, and part of their agenda was to create "minority problems" where none existed. Ideology, not ethnicity, was the enemy and therefore Canadians should never assume, Kirkconnell argued, that "our fellow-Canadians, of any origin, are *by nature* unworthy of our sympathy, respect, and good will."[58] He stressed that while there had been some enemy penetration of ethnic groups in Canada, the vast majority remained loyal to Canada.

The second half of the booklet was entitled "Racial Origins," the introduction to which argued that the "nature and extent of the ultimate contribution of each group to our national life may be gauged both by the previous achievements of the group and by the instalments already rendered to Canada." The remainder of the section contained brief summaries of these achievements for twenty-five groups of Canadians: Anglo-, Asiatic, Baltic, Belgian, Bulgarian, Czech and Slovak, Danish, Finnish, French, German, Greek, Hungarian, Iberian, Icelandic, Italian, Jewish, Jugoslav, Netherlands, Norwegian, Polish, Rumanian, Russian, Swedish, Swiss, and Ukrainian Canadians. There was no concluding section, as the BPI had rearranged the booklet so that the catalogue of races would come last. They feared that readers, finding their interest lagging in the midst of the long section on racial origins, would stop reading and "miss the vitally important message" of the essay.[59]

The second section of *Canadians All*, the list of groups in Canada by racial origin, has since drawn comparisons to J.S. Woodworth's *Strangers Within Our Gates* (1909). Woodsworth, a Methodist minister living in Winnipeg, wrote his book with the intention of providing

Canadians information about the various newcomers to Canada so they could be "processed and assimilated into British-Canadian ways of life." According to Daniel Coleman, the book's "taxonomy of immigrants" by their racial or national origins established "what John Porter (1965) famously later called the *vertical mosaic* and what [sociologist] Richard Day has more recently called the Great Chain of Race classification." This hierarchical ordering of races, Coleman writes, closely resembles "the Enlightenment teleology of civilization's single timeline." Day argued that *Strangers Within Our Gates* followed this Chain from pinnacle to base, with a listing of racial groups in descending order from most to least desirable. Desirability in this case indicated not only level of civility but also suitability as immigrants, by which Woodsworth meant how easily they could be assimilated to the British-Canadian way of life. His list, in his own words, was as follows: immigrants from Great Britain, immigrants from the United States, the Scandinavians, the Germans, the French, Southeastern Europe, Austria-Hungary, the Balkan States, the Hebrews, the Italians, the Levantine races, the Orientals, and the Negro and the Indian.[60]

Day contended that in *Canadians All*, Kirkconnell followed Woodsworth's lead by first providing population and immigration statistics to prove the existence of diversity in Canada. The difference was Kirkconnell's emphasis on equality, which he first expressed by focusing on the various groups' contributions to Canada. The other sign of equality was what Day sardonically dubbed Kirkconnell's "egalitarian innovation": the alphabetical ordering of the racial groups.[61] However, in the original draft Kirkconnell had the Anglo- and French-Canadians come first (his ordering of the other groups is unknown), and the idea of alphabetizing the list was not Kirkconnell's idea but was the suggestion of BPI officials Lash, Herbert, and Claude Melançon (associate director); the three feared "jealousies as between the groups."[62] Kirkconnell was likely somewhere between his early conception of race and nationality, in which certain nations by nature of their racial history were inferior, and his later view that assumed Anglo-Saxon superiority but accepted that all other European national or racial groups were on equal footing with each other. In either case, it is clear that he believed European races to be far superior to any non-Europeans.[63]

While historians such as Dreisziger have praised the King government for its role in fostering ethnic tolerance in Canada, however haphazard it may have been, it is clear that the creation of *Canadians All* was motivated by the much more pragmatic goal of wartime unity and that any newfound tolerance only extended so far. The government needed to convince supposedly older Canadians (i.e., Anglo-Canadians and French Canadians) that ethnic groups were not the enemy. This would remove the threat of civic unrest stemming from ethnic tensions and ensure that so-called new Canadians did not encounter a degree of intolerance that might cause them to question or even change their allegiance. In order to accomplish both these aims, the government first had to ensure that these groups were in fact firm in their loyalties. Wartime cultural pluralism was therefore about making European minority groups "feel that they belong."[64] The *Canadians All* program exhibited many marks of this strategy, and its exclusions reflected the prejudices of its creators.

Firstly, Belcourt's original report on "new Canadian" talent available for a radio program was extremely paternalistic. In it, she noted that ethnic groups were pleased with the "slightest attention," and they were "particularly flattered *when made to feel* that they are helping in the War effort." She later added: "We should not forget that these people need probably a little more nursing than we older Canadians and I feel that they sometimes get not only less but the reverse." As such, the BPI had to accept whatever these groups had to offer to the "program and, even if they were comparatively modest, the "content should be *viewed* as a contribution and not as a condescension on our part."[65] Such statements suggested that Anglo- and French Canadians were doubtful that these other groups had much to offer but had to be careful to ensure that these sentiments were not obvious. The publicized reasons for the program were much more grandiosely patriotic. A letter written by Lash and distributed to the BPI's mailing list declared that the radio broadcasts featured Canadians of "various racial origins" demonstrating their "adherence to and support of the Canadian way of life." National unity was crucial, Lash argued. "A study of the Nazi technique of penetration and domination will prove that the first step always is to create a minority problem. In Canada where no racial group (and that includes Anglo-Saxons) has a numerical majority, the opportunities for the employment of such tactics are obvious. Nothing is more important today than we should achieve a measure of national unity we have not known." He added that the bureau had enlisted "Professor Watson

Kirkconnell, the leading authority on the racial groups of Canada," to write a booklet to accompany the broadcasts.[66]

Secondly, Herbert noted that if the booklet was published in Quebec it would be "pioneering ... in trying to create a favourable interest in the foreign-language Canadians." In short, to his knowledge, there had never been any interest in trying to foster unity among the ethnic groups in Quebec; perhaps it was assumed that Quebec remained an enclave of French monoculture. In any event, Melançon sensed that Quebecers were not prepared to accept so large a publication. Instead, he and Herbert recommended that the French version contain only the first section of the booklet, and that the "Racial Origins" material be released in newspapers in a continuing column.[67] Belcourt's suggestion was that the French-Canadian section of the radio broadcast be portrayed as part of the old culture and not lumped in with "the other new Canadians," which made perfect sense as they were not "new Canadians" (though many of the other groups were not so new either).[68]

Thirdly, Herbert questioned Kirkconnell's treatment of the Jews, noting that it was different from his treatment of the other groups in that he repeated and then refuted some common charges made against them.[69] This not only gave the charges currency, he argued, but also gave the appearance that the government was making a special defence of one group over others. Herbert's reservations on this matter were fuelled by the doubt and suspicion – if not outright anti-Semitism – of others in the BPI. "Mr. Melançon tells me," Herbert wrote, "that certain Jews share in control of the Montreal and District Savings Bank – and that this is a point which would be seized upon to disprove your defence statements."[70] Even those in the government's employ promoting ethnic tolerance harboured their prejudices, which in this case led them to shy away from refuting anti-Semitic charges. (Kirkconnell's own attitudes towards Jewish people during this period were mixed. In May 1939, he decried the Nazis' brutal anti-Semitic policies, but at the same time was not ready to join in "a wholesale condemnation" of the Nazi regime. By 1943, however, he had become aware of the extent of the persecution that Jewish people faced and published a poem on the subject, entitled "The Agony of Israel." However, this appears to have been the extent of his activism. As his anti-communism became increasingly vocal, his habit of identifying communists and their leaders by ethnicity or religious identity would lead some critics to accuse him of being an anti-Semite.)[71]

Finally, the pamphlet omitted the original inhabitants of the land that later became Canada: First Nations and Inuit. The BPI, it would appear, was prepared to back Kirkconnell's dismissive appraisal that despite "a few Indian survivors, a few Asiatic immigrants, and some negroes brought in from Africa," Canadians were "at least 98 per cent ... transplanted Europeans."[72] This was Kirkconnell's only reference to any of these groups in the entire first edition of the booklet, and it suggests that he assumed the eventual extinction or assimilation of Indigenous peoples.

In fact, it took a missionary's letter for the bureau to consider including Indigenous peoples in future editions. Rev. R.B. Horsefield, who was living at the Devon Mission in The Pas, Manitoba, commended the booklet but decried its grave defect: "It totally ignores the real Canadians, the Indians and Eskimo." In keeping with the theme of accomplishments and contributions, he noted that "these races have played an indispensable part in the development of the country, teaching the pioneers the art of existing and travelling under its rigorous conditions," and implored the director to "devote a page to them in future editions."[73] (While this stance – that Indigenous peoples were only important insofar as they helped the colonizers – has its own problems, it is remarkable that Horsefield was apparently the only person to object to Indigenous peoples' exclusion from the pamphlet.) Herbert forwarded the letter to Kirkconnell and asked what he thought of it, and included his own unconcerned thoughts on the matter: "We are receiving a tremendously favourable response ... There have been a few kickers – as was to be expected; but on the whole the comments are unusually complimentary." He also noted that a second edition would likely have to be published owing to the success of the first.[74] (Sometime in the fall of 1941, Kirkconnell prepared a revised second edition, which included a section on "Eskimos" and "Indians" and reflected Russia's newfound status as an ally.)[75]

Public reaction to the pamphlet was more mixed than Herbert suggested. Several letters came from religious quarters, including one from a pastor who planned on making it the basis of his next sermon, yet wrote to express his dismay that the booklet focused on artistic and scientific but not religious contributions. Another pastor, this one with the United Church in Hamilton, also wrote to personally thank Kirkconnell for his "fine contribution to Canadian unity." Schoolchildren also wrote requesting a copy for the classroom, and one adult even wrote what they considered to be a "rather successful pageant" based on the work. Many wrote to request additional copies of the booklet or for additional information, with letters coming from as far away as England and Brazil.[76] At least one person wrote to thank him for the publication and especially for his inclusion of the Jews, others to congratulate him on the publication and his work in promoting unity, and still others noted similarities between his work and Gibbon's *Canadian Mosaic*.[77]

Some Canadians, however, were not so pleased with the publication. One letter writer challenged Kirkconnell's statistics on the Jewish community and declared that the booklet was "full of deliberate misrepresentations." Another wrote to take exception with Kirkconnell's claim that one of the most aggressive communist leaders was Scottish. Yet another complained that while the description of the British people as a racial mixture was accurate, no Canadians would believe this until the education system abandoned the myth of British racial unity and began teaching along similar lines. A subsequent letter proved this point: an angry response came from the director of Protestant education in Quebec who, in a letter marked "personal," declared that "the importance attached to the different racial origins is certainly out of proportion." In particular, he was upset that the Germans had more space than the French, felt that the Czechs and Slovaks had far too much space, and was dismayed that Anglo-Saxons had fewer lines of text than the Irish, Welsh, or Scotch. Clearly, Anglo-Canadian notions of superiority stubbornly persisted throughout the war years.[78]

The biggest blast of disapproval came from within the government itself, particularly from the Communist MPs in the House of Commons, as Kirkconnell's aggressive anti-communism antagonised increasing numbers of politicians.[79] The federal government had gladly accepted his help in building unity among Canadians of non-British, non-French, European descent, and had found no problem with his racially exclusionary publications, but his anti-communism soon became a major issue for them. With Russia's midwar switch of allegiance, anti-communist views were politically unpalatable and the federal government feared that Kirkconnell (along with Tracy Philipps) was destabilizing recently and tentatively unified groups such as the Ukrainian Canadians.

In 1943, Kirkconnell gave an address to the Ukrainian Canadian Congress in Winnipeg. Intended to affirm the loyalty of Ukrainian Canadians to the war effort, the lecture nevertheless contained many attacks on Canadian communists. It clearly got under the skin of some federal leaders, as afterwards Prime Minister Mackenzie King "asked, not so innocently, whether an order under Defence Council Regulations could be issued restraining Kirkconnell from writing and public speaking."[80] King was apparently so concerned about national unity that he was prepared to silence the voice his government had only just appropriated. That Kirkconnell's address coincided with the Canadian-Soviet Friendship Rally in Toronto, which King chaired, likely contributed to this sentiment.[81] But King never took action, so Kirkconnell continued to take every possible opportunity to speak out against communism.

Kirkconnell's crusade against communism led to the frequent accusation that he was a fascist or a Nazi, that he was somehow supporting Hitler by criticizing Russia. At first he was nonplussed, writing to an acquaintance: "I have tried to steer a clear but vigorous course between the Right and the Left in politics, and have been damned by the extremists at both ends ... Perhaps I am somewhere near a sane centre." Or, as he more memorably put it a few months later: "You have perhaps heard me sometimes described as a 'Fascist'. You will soon see that I am merely a Mid-Victorian Liberal on the rampage." But the hate mail continued to arrive, accusing him of being a "DIRTY FASCIST SON OF A BITCH."[82] After receiving death threats, he "avoided shortcuts through back alleys after dark" and purchased an automatic pistol for protection.[83] His less ideologically driven colleagues like Gibbon attracted far less controversy.

PUBLICIZING "NEW CANADIAN" LOYALTY

Much like Kirkconnell, Gibbon's private efforts brought him to the attention of civil servants who wanted the federal government to engage with ethnic minorities. *Canadian Mosaic* had sold so well that a reprint was planned but, due to the increased cost of book production in wartime, the publisher postponed these plans. However, in 1941 publisher Ellen Elliott asked Gibbon to author a brief work "on 'New Canadians', that is the Canadians of European origin especially, and the war," to be published as part of the Macmillan War Pamphlets (Canadian Series).[84] This appeared as the cleverly titled *The New Canadian Loyalists*, in which Gibbon tied the patriotism of so-called new Canadians to the storied legacy of the United

Empire Loyalists, the British subjects who sided with the British Crown during the American Revolution / War of Independence and then chose to move to British North America after their loss.

Gibbon opened by praising the United Empire Loyalists, noting that through the end of the nineteenth century they were viewed as "the cream of English-speaking Canada." Canada simply would not have been the same without them and their "adherence to British ideals and traditions." Clarifying he meant this group no disrespect, he expressed his intention to use the title for new Canadians whose immigration continued and who, he argued, were "proving to be just as loyal to Canada as the United Empire Loyalists were to the British flag." Historian Norman Knowles has shown that there was never a consensus on the defining characteristics of the Loyalist tradition but rather that it has been constructed and contested by various groups since the eighteenth century. Gibbon's invocation of this heritage was therefore not an unprecedented appropriation, but it was certainly a novel application of the term. Ever the publicist, Gibbon fully intended it to be somewhat controversial. As he told the publisher, "I have used the title 'The New Canadian Loyalists', as I think this would make people read the book."[85] (Kirkconnell copied this strategy, seemingly without acknowledgment, for a 1943 pamphlet entitled *Our Ukrainian Loyalists*.)

*The New Canadian Loyalists* was like a small *Mosaic* recast for wartime. Whereas Kirkconnell's *Canada, Europe, and Hitler* focused only on European Canadian groups' loyalties as expressed in their press, Gibbon provided a brief sketch of each group's history in Canada, drawing wherever possible a direct lineage to the United Empire Loyalists; commented on their ongoing assimilation; and noted their particularities, expressions of loyalty to the Britain, and contributions to the war. However, both texts shared the same overall goal of convincing Canadians of English and French descent of the loyalty of all other European Canadian groups.

As always, highest praise was reserved for Scandinavians, the first group to be examined in the pamphlet, who Gibbon argued "presented the fewest problems in regard to assimilation." This was evidenced by their lack of demands for exceptional treatment like pacifism or bilingual schools, their lack of left- or right-wing extremism, and their high rates of intermarriage with "those of British stock." Gibbon conceded that their ease of assimilation was partly attributable to earlier residence in America where they were "broken in to the North American mentality."[86] However, this argument does not signify an absence of a racial logic in the work. Like its antecedents (*Canada, Europe, and Hitler* and *Canadians All*), Gibbon's pamphlet drew on race science and was expressed using racial terminology. All groups were described as racial, even groups more accurately classified as religious, like Jews and Doukhobors. Additionally, Gibbon provided more details about certain groups, such as the physical features of Ukrainians and the tendency of Jewish Canadians to not "intermarr[y] much with those of Aryan races." There was also the omission of a number of groups racialized as non-white, including Canadians of African descent, some of whom were part of that original wave of Loyalist immigration.[87]

Structured like *Canadians All*, the pamphlet opened with a brief essay before turning to a look at the individual groups. In this case, Gibbon's first few pages outlined five factors that he claimed governed the immigration and assimilation of new Canadians. First, whatever the push factor, immigrants were attracted to Canada with the belief that it was a new democracy in which they could enjoy more land and more freedom than in their homeland. Second, when they arrived, they would not be content unless they could find profitable work on a farm or in industrial work. Third, they needed to be greeted with friendliness, and luckily many Canadian organizations were doing this work. Fourth was the role of education, such as pioneered by J.T.M. Anderson. The final factor was freedom of conscience and of religion. Unlike in England's works, in which he clearly stated that integration was a two-sided affair, Gibbon's introductory section rather weakly tried to suggest that Canadians of English and French descent needed to be tolerant of and even friendly towards so-called new Canadians, as it would help them assimilate to a satisfactory level.[88]

Gibbon tried his best to ensure the success of the pamphlet, first priming the pump by working the title into an address to the Canadian Authors Association (CAA) in August. "I call them the new Canadian loyalists. They are more patriotic than native-born Canadians. That's one thing the war has done for Canada – it's brought the European intelligentsia here, and already they are enriching our music, arts and literature with their contributions," he suggested. Once the pamphlet was published in mid-September, he then purchased some three hundred copies for distribution. He also obtained a list of "foreign language newspapers" from Michael Petrowsky, a Ukrainian

Canadian employed by the RCMP's Intelligence Department, and had the Canadian Pacific Railway (CPR) press department send each of these editors a copy in hopes of getting reviews.[89] He also sent copies to smaller periodicals that the company was associated with, as well as signed copies to friends such as the famous author Charles G.D. Roberts (who "devoured it" and judged it to be "most valuable and important to us all ... intrinsically so lucid and interesting"). Finally, he gave an address on the subject at the Toronto Book Fair in November and arranged to have copies of the pamphlet for sale at that time. These efforts led to some success, as the book was mentioned in the *Montreal Gazette*, the *Globe and Mail*, the *Vancouver Province*, and several non-English-language papers. The publisher was delighted, noting that it was the first pamphlet to receive treatment in a newspaper editorial. Similar to his *Mosaic*, though to a lesser degree, the pamphlet and its title were taken up by private groups and were discussed by several women's organizations.[90]

### THE CCCC

The year 1941 saw the federal government make additional efforts to reach nominally white ethnic minorities in Canada. In June, and in keeping with his racial hierarchies, Prime Minister Mackenzie King appointed Joseph T. Thorson, an Icelandic Canadian MP from Winnipeg, as minister of the Department of National War Services. The move surprised many, elevating as it did a low-profile politician to such an important post, but King cynically intended the move to "please those of foreign extraction in the country" and bolster their support for the war.[91] That fall, senior bureaucrats finally agreed on the need for a committee to advise the minister of national war services, as well as any other federal department, on the question of foreign language-speaking groups in Canada. It was not until 1942, however, that the Committee on Co-operation in Canadian Citizenship (CCCC) was formally established. Shortly thereafter an additional body was soon created, the "Nationalities Branch," which was intended to provide administrative support to the CCCC. England and Kirkconnell had been approached about leadership positions in these new appendages of the BPI but both declined: England because he did not want a permanent position and Kirkconnell because he feared the position would cost him his ability to freely speak out against communism. However, the two agreed to sit as members of the dozen-strong CCCC, which was ultimately led by Professor George Simpson of the University of Saskatchewan.[92]

The rather convoluted history of the CCCC and the Nationalities Branch has been detailed elsewhere, although the focus has often been on the mysterious figure of Tracy Philipps, a British intelligence officer who worked in Canada for the DNWS and the RCMP.[93] But as historian Stephanie Bangarth, a reviewer of the most recent work on the subject, asks: "Are we so much further ahead by knowing so much about Tracy Philipps?"[94] This skepticism is warranted, for the focus on Philipps has obscured important aspects of the development and implementation of wartime policies and practices relating to ethnic minorities. This section thus looks beyond him to the roles played by the other experts: Kirkconnell, Gibbon, and, to a lesser extent, England.

The scope of the CCCC's activities was limited from the outset. Despite all the initial dithering about what the Committee should be named, so as to avoid "the idea of racial or political particularism," it was clear from the outset that only European groups were to be considered. During their first meeting, the idea of preparing a pamphlet to overcome prejudice against foreign-sounding names was being discussed when H.F. Angus asked about their terms of reference. Angus was a professor of economics at the University of British Columbia who, since 1934, had campaigned for the enfranchisement of second-generation Canadians of Asian descent. According the CCCC meeting minutes, Angus "wished in particular to know whether this Committee would concern itself with the *Japanese* and the Chinese in Canada. He pointed out that, if the Committee concerned itself with this problem, it should realize that its general viewpoint might be found at variance with the attitude of the present Government of British Columbia." Simpson confessed he did not know but would seek clarification from the minister, whose later answer was that "for the present the Committee's activity shall not concern itself with the Japanese and the Chinese in Canada."[95]

In the Committee's fourth meeting, Angus returned to this question, this time inquiring if the Nationalities Branch touched on "Jewish groups." Tracy Philipps deflected, arguing that he doubted that Jewish people wanted to be included in the category served by the branch but added that they had routine correspondence with them. (This, of course, ignored that fact that some of the other groups did not want to be included either. Only a few weeks before the meeting, a Ukrainian Canadian had written to the editor of the *Montreal Gazette* decrying the Nationalities Branch as an insult to all "New Canadians.") Angus pressed on: was Jewish Canadians' recent European origin in doubt? The discussion that ensued was not recorded in the minutes. In the end, however, Philipps sidestepped the apparently still unanswered question by declaring that the lack of clarity on this point "had never stopped the Branch from doing all it could for them." However, the only examples he could offer were his participation in the Jewish Charities Drive and the "appreciative letter" he had sent them.[96]

It appeared that the usual limitations, racial and religious, would apply. But what about content? Would a focus on folk culture and translations suffice during wartime? The committee waffled on this point. During the first meeting, Simpson asked if the committee ought to concern itself with arts and crafts. Gibbon proposed that they were best left to "regional spontaneity." (The reply is rather ironic, given the most prominent folk music and handicraft festivals in Canada had been the result of his careful planning and not any regional impulse.) England, on the other hand, emphasized that such exhibits took an enormous amount of work and rather pointedly added that "the time had come for stressing practical utilization." In a later meeting, Gibbon drifted in this direction by recounting his experience with folk festivals but the Committee responded that during wartime no new folk festivals should be encouraged.[97]

During this initial gathering, however, Gibbon had a different type of plan to propose. Stepping squarely into what Kirkconnell no doubt considered his territory, Gibbon unveiled his idea for a massive translation project entitled "A Secular Bible for a New Canada." This "Secular Bible," he explained, would consist of translations of selections from "the literatures of all the Continental races" – over twenty, he noted – who had migrated to Canada. Gibbon wanted it to be a work of perfection: only the best works would be selected and translations would be done by the finest scholars and most accomplished writers. As a means of ensuring this excellence, Section II of the Royal Society of Canada ought to be brought in to help identify the proper texts and linguistic experts. The project would take years, Gibbon admitted, so he also pitched a temporary plan that would pave the way for this ideal volume. The first step would be to compile already-existing translations into a huge series that he called a "four-foot library shelf." The series would consist of two sets of forty volumes each, subsidized by the Canadian government – perhaps with assistance from the Carnegie Fund – so as to ensure wide sales.[98] (The term "Secular Bible," much like his previous use of the title "Loyalist," was no doubt designed to attract publicity – and it succeeded with at least one person. After Gibbon had the idea published in the *Proceedings* of the Royal Society of Canada, one reader of the offprint wrote to him: "My Presbyterian conscience revolted a bit at its startling heading. But now, having read and re-read it, I can appreciate its value and timeliness.")[99]

The Committee agreed to put it on the agenda for the next meeting, and in the meantime asked Kirkconnell to prepare a report on the literary merits of the proposal and Gibbon to make further enquiries as to the financial aspects.[100] In his report, delivered at the CCCC's next meeting, Kirkconnell reported that he subscribed enthusiastically to the theory underlying the proposal: "that translated masterpieces [could] be a potent force in bringing about a sympathetic integration of our diversified peoples into a single nation. I question, indeed, whether any other single plan could contribute more to 'co-operation in Canadian citizenship.'" However, he added that the process of education through literature "ought to work both ways," with the targeted groups also learning something of the English and French literatures. "What we want to achieve is not just an amiable Anglo-Saxon awareness of a 'European-Canadian tradition,' still less any trend towards a separate political consciousness on the part of the European-Canadians," Kirkconnell warned. "It is rather the realization by every group of a common Canadian tradition to which we can all make a worthy contribution."

But defining this "common Canadian tradition" was a difficult task. In terms of culture, and for Kirkconnell, it meant that the series required a volume on literature from England, Scotland, Ireland, and Wales. And, he was forced to admit, the series would also require a volume on France, for "who indeed is a Canadian if the 'Canadien' is to be omitted?" Somewhat in defiance of this complexity, he concluded: "Regardless of cultural dualism or pluralism, I like to think of Canada as one nation." Ultimately, he supported both the single- and multi-volume projects Gibbon had pitched, while identifying a number of additional issues with them.[101]

When these reports were presented at the second meeting of the CCCC, the project received mixed reviews. Given the amount of work that Gibbon and Kirkconnell had put in, and despite the fact that the committee could not reach a unanimous decision, the chair proposed that a separate committee be formed to prepare a memorandum on the project for the minister of the DNWS.[102] Afterwards, Kirkconnell recorded that the primary criticism was "that the scheme was not actual and direct enough in the present war crisis." Gibbon's more detailed report to Simpson summarized the four criticisms of the project: the inclusion of works by enemy nations, the desire to cover all "racial groups," the inclusion of overly highbrow titles, and the unsuitability of the project during wartime. To address these issues, Gibbon proposed lowering the number of groups covered by eliminating enemy nations, including the Germans, Italians, Hungarians, and "Roumanians" until the war's end.[103]

This was not simply a cost-cutting measure for Gibbon. After hearing Rex Stout, an American author and wartime propagandist, tell a Canadian audience that the Germans had to be beaten both in the war and in the years afterwards, without sentimentality, compassion, or compromise, he sent a brief telegram to Kirkconnell remarking that he would "go further and make German one of the dead languages after Greek and Latin."[104] The sentiment shaped another of his projects, a song-folio entitled *Brahms and Schubert Songs Transplanted* (1944), in which he sought to keep the tunes alive but eliminate the German lyrics by replacing them with new English ones. He planned to present the completed works to the Vancouver and Mainland Branch of the CAA with the help of soprano Frances James and later to air them over the CBC, and proposed that they call the collection "Killing the German Language." James refused to go ahead with the series and her decision essentially ended their twenty-year friendship. His sometime musical collaborator, Murray Adaskin, also felt Gibbon had crossed a line, later telling an interviewer: "At the beginning of the war, [Gibbon] got really worked up about the German language business, because he took all of the most beautiful of German songs, Mozart and Schubert and Schuman and this, and wrote what he considered were Canadian words to this ... German music[,] that was alright, but not the German language. And this is where – he went a step too far really, it was unfortunate."[105] Presumably on similar grounds, and despite his earlier fascination with Japan, Gibbon opposed the country's inclusion in a volume on "Asiatic" literature.[106]

When Gibbon wrote to Simpson proposing that enemy groups be omitted from their series, he had sent a copy to Kirkconnell, who in turn responded with alarm. He quickly wrote to Simpson and sent

Gibbon a copy of the letter, in which he charged that the proposed change had a "fatal demerit."

> It sends to Coventry precisely those groups that we need to handle most sympathetically to keep them from being soured and alienated by ill-treatment. I know something personally of the heart-break of young Canadians of Italian and German origin through the contumely and discrimination shown them by ignorant or headless fellow-Canadians. To have that discrimination made the basic principle of a Government publication would be worse still ... If Anglo-Canadians are too intolerant to accept an all-inclusive Heritage series, I think we had better defer it; for the limited series would simply confirm them in their intolerance towards the omitted groups, and the effect on the latter would be calamitous.[107]

To this Gibbon replied that he knew Simpson was taking the idea up the ladder, where recommendations needed unanimity lest they be "turned down on an excuse." Pushing back against Kirkconnell's suggestion for the expansion of the series, he added that given the CCCC's mandate was Canadians of non-British and non-French origins, they could eliminate the possibility of including books on the literatures of Great Britain, as well as those on English and French Canada.[108]

Thorson, the Icelandic Canadian minister of the DNWS, expressed enthusiasm for the project but had reservations regarding funding. As for the debate over which groups should be included, the chair of the CCCC, Professor Simpson, sided with Kirkconnell and affirmed that the project had to be all-inclusive. Sensing the impossibility of the larger project, he proposed a smaller-scale undertaking, namely a school reader that would contain extracts of the best European prose and poetry. Kirkconnell seized on this idea, telling both Simpson and Gibbon that he thought it had real merit and could possibly pave the way for a full size "Secular Bible," but he was particularly enthused because he felt he could handle most of the translation work himself.[109] Gibbon countered that Section II of the Royal Society of Canada (RSC) should appoint a committee to edit the readers, and set about preparing an address to deliver to their annual meeting.[110]

Gibbon's description of the proposed talk reveals much of the assumptions behind the project and its aims. "One of the major handicaps militating against the ready assimilation of over 600,000 of the Canadian population is the lack of mutual understanding between the various racial groups, not only the newcomers but also the older groups," he wrote. "We are still paying the penalty for the building of the Tower of Babel ... We might sympathize more with each other's mentality and traditions if we knew more about each other's literature."[111] In the resulting lecture, the project was pitched less as one of assimilation and instead one contributing to the "successful reconstruction and better integration of the Canadian people" in peacetime.

He believed that this work of integration was a vital but overlooked task, and suggested that, as an immigrant himself, he had special insight into the situation: "As one who came to this country thirty years ago from a well-settled land with only minor racial distinctions left in a population drawn from many sources, and as one whose business has involved constant travel across Canada, I have perhaps had more occasion to be impressed by the lack of racial cohesion in the Canadian people than those who were born here and have not travelled much in Canada." Canada, he continued, was "still half a country of immigrants, still racially in a state of flux which has kept being stirred into a whirlpool and swollen by new streams of immigration." After the Great War, various organizations promoted commonality of feeling among "the foreign-born," but generally Canadians took a laissez-faire approach. This was a mistake, Gibbon charged, for if racial groups were left in isolation they would "form minorities with an inferiority complex."[112]

The main venue for promoting national cooperation was the schools, but this education did not reach the older generation. It was also quite culturally limited, meaning that the Anglo-Canadian student learned nothing of the traditional cultures of the European immigrants "who are so often his classmates or neighbours." It had been through exposure to their literatures that Gibbon had gained "sympathy" for a variety of people, including Arabs, Danes, Spaniards, Persians, Belgians, French, Russians, and, later, Ukrainians and French Canadians. Based on this personal experience, Gibbon was convinced that Anglo-Canadians needed to be exposed to the cultures of new Canadians and that this was possible only through translation.[113]

Gibbon further argued that language was one of the major hindrances to national unity, as the "thought and tradition of a race are for the most part expressed in its language." He argued that Canada was constitutionally bilingual but cited statistics that showed new Canadians were showing a preference for English, "the language of Shakespeare" and "the language which they say is the best for doing business on the continent." As such, there was no need to waste time translating their cultures into French. In fact, he portrayed Canada as unilingual (Anglophone) and Quebec as bilingual, remarking about the western schools that they were doing their part in teaching "a common language (or in Quebec two common languages)."[114] This, of course, ignored the existence of Francophones in the rest of the country and the history of French schooling in both Ontario and Manitoba.

The CCCC had already failed to produce a concrete translation project owing to the grandiose ideas of its members, an inability to decide which groups deserved inclusion, and also some internal competition between Kirkconnell and Gibbon. Gibbon hoped that his pitch to the RSC would help tilt the scales in his favour, as he assumed they would agree to establish an Editorial Committee and begin recruiting scholars to the project. Indeed, Gibbon was well known for his success in spearheading projects; as publisher Henry Button once put it, "When J.M.G. gets on the 'warpath' he usually gets what he wants – 'or a reasonable facsimile of the same'!"[115] But this time he would be sorely disappointed: the RSC instead opted to form a committee to evaluate the project's viability.

With this latest bureaucratic setback, Gibbon came up with yet another iteration of the plan after talking to CBC producer Rupert Lucas. The two bumped into each other on a train trip, and Gibbon came out of the conversation convinced that the dramatization of European plays over the CBC would be a great opportunity to build up a quarter of the "Secular Bible" without any initial cost. "The broadcasts would not interfere with your school readers," he assured Kirkconnell, "and would reach an adult audience which the school readers would not touch. They can be started this winter, and not have to wait till the end of the war." Gibbon then took the idea to Brockington, but it never got off the ground.[116]

The RSC did not appoint a committee until the end of July, and when it did it consisted of three men, Arthur Woodhouse, M.A. Buchanan, and Kirkconnell (chairman), who were not given formal instructions until early August.[117] However, by December Kirkconnell could advise Gibbon that the Committee felt the scholars necessary for the project were "fatally preoccupied with other work." Kirkconnell was already busy at work on his own version of the project, the "All People's Readers" (based on already translated materials), and hoped to get a draft to publishers by January 1943. His rejection of the "Secular Bible" was no doubt motivated by a number of factors, perhaps including a desire to avoid further translation work, knowledge that such a project – like his own former endeavours – was doomed to fail, and even jealous turf-guarding.[118]

The RSC Committee's report, written by Kirkconnell, advised the translation would involve a minimum of twenty-five languages, but could be extended to a maximum of forty. It also subtly suggested the elimination of non-European groups, noting that if "Asiatic, Eskimo and Amerindian languages" were added in order to cover all groups, the total could reach as high as sixty. However, the presence of William White, a scholar of China and a former Anglican missionary, ensured that these groups remained a part of the tentative plan.[119] The committee's ultimate verdict was that while the proposal had great promise, it was "scarcely feasible as an immediate undertaking." They also poured cold water on the radio drama proposal, stating that based on their inquiries the undertaking would be too difficult for a variety of reasons, such as finding "non-contentious, vivid, modern and representative" works and scholars capable of completing the translations. Unsurprisingly, the committee concluded that Kirkconnell's "All People's Readers" were the "most immediately practicable enterprise," and advised the Committee remain in existence for another year while the work continued.[120]

Gibbon refused to lose hope. In his reply, he remarked that the report was "very interesting" and requested a number of additional copies, adding that he was glad the committee's term had been extended for another year.[121] However, after a brief summary of the RSC's report was presented at the fourth and final meeting of the CCCC in November 1943, the ill-fated "Secular Bible" disappears from the record, as do all its variants: the Heritage Library, the "All Peoples' Readers," and the radio dramas.[122] In all likelihood it was a casualty of the CCCC's disintegration: England resigned in 1943 and Kirkconnell followed suit in 1944. While both members were replaced, the committee never met again. It was officially disbanded in January 1945.[123]

CONCLUSION

The federal government's official efforts to promote cultural tolerance were designed to maintain stability on the homefront and ensure near-universal support of the war effort. Given this was a completely new venture, the government turned to experts on European minorities (known then as racial minorities). All of them were men racialized as white who had fashioned philosophies of cultural pluralism in the interwar period. Even before being pressed into government service, these men had retooled their philosophies of cultural pluralism for the conflict. Specifically, they shifted from simply celebrating various European cultures to interrogating and then emphasizing the political loyalty of European minority groups in Canada. As a result, the goals of the cultural pluralists and those of the state initially aligned. However, European minorities remained a distinctly low priority for the federal government, which for the duration of the war lacked a cohesive policy and an effective apparatus for engaging with them.

This chapter's examination of the fragmented efforts made during this period reveals the limitations of what amounted to official federal government attempts to promote cultural pluralism, and indeed, limitations of the philosophies of cultural pluralism themselves. All of the minority groups that these programs discussed were racialized as white. Indeed, the predominating strategy was to emphasize Canada's racial homogeny by arguing that the country's "diverse races" were all European, each of which had something to contribute to Canadian culture. Groups racialized as non-white were written off as demographically negligible and no attempt was made to recognize their loyalty or contributions to the war effort. The programs that the experts developed were also, in some cases, limited by civil servants' continued prejudice towards certain racial or religious groups, most notably Jewish people. Ultimately, government-sponsored efforts to ensure national unity were born of a particularly narrow, racialized vision of who constituted the nation. Ironically, these efforts to combat the racial hatred of the Nazis were often rooted in but a different interpretation of the same underlying race science.[124]

The ideological tension between celebrating diversity and emphasizing national unity had a direct influence on wartime policy. The body that was belatedly created to advise federal departments on questions relating to minority groups, the CCCC, seems to have never been utilized in its intended manner. Instead, the smaller executive group, the Nationalities Branch, became far more active, with its paid staff actively monitoring the so-called ethnic press (presses that were publishing in languages other than English or French). When George Simpson, the head of the CCCC and the Nationalities Branch, stepped down in 1942, the position was not immediately filled. So it was that Tracy Philipps, whom officials never intended to have "any administrative duties," assumed the role of acting director and made decisions as he saw fit.[125] However, his anti-communism brought him into conflict with numerous departments and officials; "practically every agency of Government with whom I discussed the problem had somehow been unable to co-operate fully with Mr. Philipps," England later reported.[126]

The initial purpose of an interdepartmental effort to engage with minorities was ultimately unsuccessful owing to a lack of political will, a subsequent lack of dedicated resources and personnel, and the ideological divide between the federal politicians navigating the complex wartime alliances and the fervid anti-communism of at least two of the advisers that they had retained. Unexpectedly, after the troublesome anti-communist staff and advisers such as Philipps and Kirkconnell were jettisoned, the bureaucracy itself was retooled yet again for peacetime.

# Conclusion

## PLURALISM AND CITIZENSHIP

*The Racial Mosaic* has detailed the development of cultural pluralism in Canada, but what of official multiculturalism? The exact path from 1945 to 1971 has not yet been well traced. How did the philosophies crafted by three public intellectuals end up influencing Canadians' thinking about diversity in the postwar era? Did these ideas affect public policy? Specifically, what connection, if any, is there between the work of these early cultural pluralists and the later official policy of multiculturalism? In order to adequately provide a history of Canada's official policy of multiculturalism and to answer to these important questions, additional research is required – research that I am in the midst of conducting.[1] However, an examination of the immediate postwar years offers some insights.

As the previous chapter concluded, the situation in 1944 was grim and it seemed highly unlikely that either the Committee on Cooperation in Canadian Citizenship (CCCC) or the Nationalities Branch would continue their work after the conflict ended. When deputy minister of the Department of National War Services (DNWS) Thomas Davis departed Canada for Australia, one of his final recommendations was that the Nationalities Branch be closed down. His boss, the newly appointed General LaFlèche, instead decided to let the branch continue its work. But LaFlèche recognized that the Branch needed help and so he put his new deputy minister, C.H. Payne, on the job. Payne, in turn, asked Robert England to assess the Branch and prepare a report. Arriving back in Ottawa in April 1944, England worked with his usual efficiency and delivered his recommendations by June.[2] His report's specific proposals notably focused only on Canadians of European descent, relied on a number of essentialist stereotypes about their supposed "folk" cultures, employed the terminology of race, and compared prejudice against European minorities in Canada to anti-African American racism in the United States.

England had long promoted Canadian citizenship, by which he meant more a civic ideal and less a category of belonging, though for an equally long time he had advocated naturalization ceremonies with plenty of pageantry to further instill a sense of belonging in newcomers. His subsequent report proposed reorganizing the Nationalities Branch into a Citizenship Division, creating a citizenship training program, inaugurating a citizenship ceremony, and providing a "clearer and more adequate definition of a Canadian citizen, or a Canadian national."[3] Two years later, England's dream came true when Paul Martin Sr announced the Canadian Citizenship Act.[4] Introducing the Bill for its first reading, Martin remarked: "Our 'new Canadians' bring to this country much that is rich and good ... They should be made to feel that they, like the rest of us, are Canadians." Much like the culturally pluralist programming of the Second World War, the "main objective of the bill" was to foster national unity. "For the national unity of Canada," Martin added, "it is felt to be of the utmost importance that all of us, new Canadians or old, have a consciousness of a common purpose and common interests as Canadians; that all of us be able to say with pride and say with meaning: 'I am a Canadian citizen.'" As a result of these and other similar comments, historians have interpreted the Act as being intended to "eliminate some of the ethnic and racial tensions" that had been aggravated by the Second World War.[5]

On 1 January 1947, the new Citizenship Act came into effect. The first week of the month was declared "National Citizenship Week" and citizenship ceremonies were held all across Canada. The very first was a carefully rehearsed national ceremony, sponsored by the new Citizenship Branch of the state department, held on 3 January at the Supreme Court in Ottawa. In a radio address broadcast nationwide by the Canadian Broadcasting Corporation (CBC), Prime Minister Mackenzie King declared that, while in the past "divergent racial origins have repeatedly been a source of division," the new conception of citizenship being inaugurated was "designed to bridge the gaps created by geography and by racial descent." To immigrants, he continued, Canada represented "a homeland where nationhood means not domination and slavery but equality and freedom."[6]

Yet a mere four months after this speech, in which he praised "the idea of equality among men" as the foundation for Canadian nationhood, King would stand in the House of Commons and argue against large-scale immigration from "the orient" on the grounds that it would "change the fundamental composition of the Canadian population" and give rise to social and economic problems.[7] Clearly, in the eyes of its politicians, postwar Canada was not intended to be a homeland free of discrimination for all. This racial discrimination was not limited to the political sphere, but also permeated Canadian society more broadly. Indeed, sociologists David FitzGerald and David Cook-Martín have demonstrated that one of the ties between racism and liberalism has been democracy. Democracy was "a channel for the rise of racist policy from below," they explain, as greater public participation in politics led to the promotion of racist policies.[8]

## THE IMPERIAL THESIS

But what of the supposed brotherhood of British imperialism? There is a strand within the scholarly literature, slender but present nonetheless, which suggests that cultural pluralism and indeed the eventual policy of multiculturalism in Canada have their roots in Britishness.[9] This argument was probably first made in the 1970s by historian J.M.S. Careless, who suggested that although Canadians of British descent may have wanted to see immigrants assimilate, "their own imperial heritage brought them, at policy levels, to affirm the mosaic ... Imperialism consequently also pointed towards multiculturalism in Canada." He specifically argued that British-Canadians were already in many ways "multicultural," in that they encouraged religious tolerance and had allowed the British and French to retain their heritages; therefore, allowing other ethnic groups to retain their own cultures was but an expansion of this ideal.[10]

However, Careless's argument is deficient in at least four ways. First, it uncritically celebrates an imagined British-Canadian tolerance of all immigrants while ignoring the broader context of settler colonialism. Second, it understates the very real pressure Anglo-Canadians exerted on immigrants to assimilate to British-Canadian norms. Third, it portrays the British-Canadian group as homogeneous and ignores how British immigrants were judged differently based on particular aspects of their identity, specifically whether they came from an urban or rural area and whether their work experience was in agricultural or industrial settings. Finally, the argument does not take into account the role of race and racism in shaping philosophies of cultural pluralism.

While there was slow and begrudging acceptance of non-British immigrants, British and continental European immigrants alike were all active agents in the process of settler colonialism in the lands that became Canada. Careless discussed the colonial histories of Canada and America but only insofar as to compare their common British past, and maintained that Canadians were more welcoming of diversity than Americans in part because Canada had no clean break from its British imperial past. Colonies that begin anew, he continued, often then fervently push a unitary culture, with no one feeling this pressure more strongly than minority groups.[11] However, the flip side of this coin is that many Anglo-Canadians did not feel a pressing need to invent a specific Canadianism precisely because they viewed their country as a British colony, which led many to insist that newcomers assimilate to British-Canadian norms – linguistic, political, legal, and cultural.

Many English-speaking Canadian elites voiced the opinion that it would be best if only British people immigrated to Canada. Yet those intimately familiar with the spadework of imperialism, as historian Sarah Carter has called it, were more concerned with getting the right kind of immigrant, meaning immigrants that showed aptitude or potential for farmworking, and not necessarily those belonging to a particular European nationality.[12] In fact, English immigrants from urban areas were viewed as unwilling and incompetent agricultural workers, leading in some cases to "No English Need Apply" disclaimers being added to employment advertisements.[13] Therefore, the acceptance of continental farm workers was not an outgrowth of British imperialism but rather was a result of the demands of settler colonialism more generally. And, as this book has shown, far from being universally accepted, this specific and limited form of cultural pluralism was bitterly contested.

But both groups (those who wanted more restrictive immigration policies, and those who wanted the doors open to all European farmers) held one belief in common: that people racialized as non-white were unfit to settle in Canada, regardless of their farming skills. Many Euro-Canadians and their organizations petitioned the federal government to ban the immigration of people of African descent. Far from promoting tolerance, the people and organizations furthering British imperialism were in fact pushing for racist exclusions. In 1911, for instance, the Imperial Order Daughters of the Empire (IODE) in Alberta held an emergency meeting to express their alarm at the "continuous and rapid influx of Negro settlers." (In fact, only approximately one thousand African Americans immigrated to the entire country between 1905 and 1912. During this same period, some 1.9 million people total immigrated to Canada.)[14]

Of course, *ideas about* Britishness did influence the development of philosophies of cultural pluralism: first, the idea of Britain as a historically multiracial nation; and second, the idea of British liberty. Early cultural pluralists such as Kirkconnell, England, and Gibbon consistently argued that European immigrants had to assimilate to Anglo-Canadian legal and political norms, and that this framework alone was capable of holding together such a racially diverse population. Both inclusion and exclusion turned on this point: a common argument in the early twentieth century was that Asian peoples in particular were fundamentally incompatible with the Anglo-Saxon system of governance. However, this system could maintain a diverse collection of European races because British people (Anglo-Saxons) had themselves descended from a number of prehistoric European races. This argument was made to CBC listeners during the *Ventures in Citizenship* broadcast, to the Empire Club of Canada in Gibbon's 1923 address, and in many of Kirkconnell's publications.

Yet it is worth noting that none of these men could themselves make strong claims to the Anglo-Saxon identity: England was Irish, Gibbon was Scottish, and Kirkconnell was nominally Scottish but his lineage was more complex. Hyper-aware of his diverse European origins, Kirkconnell stubbornly maintained that he was Anglo-Saxon and always gave this term an expansive definition so as to include himself.[15] Gibbon claimed he was Scottish, not Anglo-Saxon, but that he had become Canadian. And while England occasionally reflected upon his Irish origins, he seems to have identified more with the nascent Canadianism that he worked to boost and less with a sense of Britishness. Perhaps because British institutions were seen as the heritage of Anglo-Saxons, these intellectuals rarely used the term "Anglo-Celtic," even when it would have been more accurate. As Daniel Coleman reminds us, Scottish people were leaders in formulating a pan-ethnic notion of Britishness.[16] Similarly, Scottish immigrants (and in this case, at least one Irish immigrant) in Canada played an important role in helping to develop a pan-ethnic notion of Canadianness. Again, however, this culturally pluralistic identity was not a defining feature of British imperialism but rather was developed almost in spite of it.

Whether pushing for a culturally British or a culturally pluralistic nation, Anglo-Canadian intellectuals faced one complication to their arguments: Quebec. During his lifetime, Kirkconnell moved from a hatred of French Canadians to a more ambivalent stance, offering some tentative defences (and one collaborative work of translations), but staunchly maintained that Anglo-Saxon political leadership was required in order for Canada to survive as a culturally or racially diverse nation.[17] Robert England paid lip service to French language and culture when required, such as in his thesis defence and in his books on immigration. However, in these same books he presented a caricatured view of French Canadians, his conception of Canadian citizenship stressed British traditions, and he was fixated on immigrant children being taught English. Gibbon, a politically astute businessman working in Quebec, nevertheless considered Canada to be an essentially English-speaking country. His efforts at cultural promotion in the province focused on bringing French folk culture into the public eye, and – notably – he did not attempt to celebrate any other European cultures in Quebec. It would appear that no one else did either; recall that the federal government's Bureau of Public Information determined that their *Canadians All / Tous canadiens* program was the first effort to foster unity among ethnic groups in Quebec.

In short, from the interwar period through the end of the Second World War, cultural pluralism was primarily an English-language project aimed at European minority groups, which made French Canadians an awkward fit. European minority groups – that is, non-British, non-French European minorities – were referred to as "new Canadians." Confusingly, however, this term was used both to refer to recent immigrants and to the communities themselves, many of which were not new at all. As the earliest colonizers in what became Canada, French Canadians could hardly be lumped in with so-called new Canadians, yet many English-speaking Canadians were as ignorant of French Canadian culture as they were of Ukrainian or Polish culture. And in wartime, Anglo-Canadians were similarly suspicious of Quebec's loyalty. This quandary was the result of Canada's colonial past, but British imperialism did not offer the early cultural pluralists a path forward.

A variant of Careless's broader argument, that Canadian multiculturalism has its roots in British imperialism, is also made by historian Peter Henshaw, who invokes the case of John Buchan. Buchan was a British novelist and civil servant who became the fifteenth governor general of Canada, a position he held from 1935 until his death in 1940. (Prior to Buchan assuming his position in Canada, he was made a peer, with the title Baron Tweedsmuir being created for him in 1935. As such, he is often referred to as Lord Tweedsmuir.) Since his death, academic discussion concerning his legacy has been remarkably polarized. On the one side, Henshaw has argued that Buchan was a progressive "champion of multiculturalism" – a claim which is, of course, hopelessly anachronistic. On the other, critics have repeatedly questioned the content of his novels and declared him to be a racist and an anti-Semite, and others have drawn attention to his administration of racially segregated concentration camps in South Africa.[18] The inability to reach a consensus on Buchan's attitudes is more a reflection of scholars' intentions and not the man himself. Previous accounts have not tried to understand the development of his thought, but rather to present Buchan as either an irredeemable bigot or a prescient progressive, a truly "model governor general."[19]

In the midst of this fruitless debate, the reality that people can and do change over time seems to have escaped notice. Even without considering the attitudes expressed in his novels, it is irrefutable that Buchan held anti-Semitic beliefs until at least the 1930s.[20] However, his views seem to have changed somewhat during that decade: in 1934 he publicly denounced Hitler's anti-Semitism and he became an increasingly ardent Zionist.[21] Similarly, there is no doubt that Buchan was familiar with and subscribed to racial theories that held Europeans to be superior to non-Europeans, even if he believed the latter were capable of improvement. Although Buchan apparently worked successfully to lower the death rate in the concentration camps in South Africa, he never doubted the necessity of the underlying colonial project: he was a firm believer in nominally white people's dominance over peoples racialized as non-white.[22] As Dan Freeman-Maloy observes, Buchan "heaped praise on the Boers as 'one of the greatest colonising forces in the world' and insisted that the British Empire would need to rule in close co-operation with them if 'the plateaux of our Central and East

## Conclusion

African possessions are to be permanently held by the white man.'"[23] Buchan's imperialism did not dissipate with age, although his experiences in Canada may have helped him to consider the possibility of racially integrated colonial societies. (In Buchan's final novel, the posthumously published *Sick Heart River*, the protagonist finds in the Canadian arctic a society based on "the brotherhood of all men, white and red and brown, who have to fight the savagery of the North." This seems to be drawn from his own reminisces of his travels there, when he wrote: "In the face of a harsh Nature human beings seem to have acquired a keener sense of responsibility towards each other. I cannot imagine a more pleasant or wholesome society.")[24]

Similarly, while Buchan later exhorted Ukrainian immigrants to remain Ukrainians, it is unclear what Buchan thought their contribution to Canadian society could be – if anything at all. Consider this argument, made in his very first speech in Canada:

> There are other cultures in the world, each with its own value for its own people. On them I pass no criticism, except to say that they do not mix well with ours. There is a good deal of anarchy in our art and letters today, caused by permitting alien elements – Slav, Mongol, Negroid – to intrude into a sphere which they have no place. These elements have their value, no doubt, but that value is not for us.[25]

If his later comments are interpreted generously, as suggesting that Ukrainians retain their cultures for the benefit of Canada as a whole, this too represented a shift in Buchan's opinion about immigrants and about Slavic people in particular.

Henshaw's essay does not deal with these questions in all their complexity – the speech quoted above is curiously absent – but instead conflates racism with assimilationism. Henshaw opens the essay by admitting that due to the "distasteful generalizations about race and ethnicity" (more accurately termed racism and anti-Semitism) that appeared in his novels, Buchan "has been labelled a racist, an anti-Semite, and a reactionary defender of the British Empire." But then he pivots:

> What, then, should we make of such assertions as this one to a 1936 gathering of Ukrainians in Manitoba: "You will all be better Canadians for being also good Ukrainians"?

It might be thought that someone like Buchan would have been less concerned about promoting non-British cultures and identities in Canada than about encouraging the assimilation of all Canadians into a dominant "British" identity. It is true that throughout his life Buchan championed the cause of imperial unity ... It is also true that Buchan believed in a hierarchy of peoples or nations ... in which British and other "northern" races were at the top. Yet Buchan did not believe that his mission as governor general was to promote a homogenous British identity in Canada.[26]

(This is a rather curious way of saying that Buchan believed in a racial hierarchy in which nominally *white* races were at the top and that nominally non-white races were all below them; and that, despite this, he was open to white immigrants in Canada maintaining some elements of their original cultures.)[27] But it was not the either-or situation that Henshaw suggests. As this book has shown, it was entirely possible for people to believe in the superiority of nominally white people and to believe that the complete cultural assimilation of European immigrants was unnecessary. In fact, this stance was growing increasingly popular throughout the interwar period.

Although Henshaw exaggerates the role Buchan played, it may be that in his later years he, like Kirkconnell, England, and Gibbon, held a philosophy of cultural pluralism and worked to express it publicly; a more objective and comprehensive examination of Buchan's life is required.[28] Ultimately, the problem with Henshaw's account is that it reproduces historical racial exclusions. Henshaw discusses how Buchan, during his time as Canada's governor general, celebrated a variety European cultures, but he chooses not to discuss how Buchan ignored non-European cultures and held them to be inferior. In so doing, Henshaw hides the exclusion of peoples racialized as non-white; thus, they have been twice erased: first in history and again in the present. This happens more broadly within the scholarship on the development of cultural pluralism in Canada: in seeking to celebrate early movements towards tolerance, historians have ignored what made this movement necessary, what it was moving away from, and those it left behind. Early cultural pluralism in Canada excluded African, Asian, and Indigenous cultures, and indeed was only made possible through the processes of colonialism that sought to destroy Indigenous cultures by assimilating

Indigenous peoples to French Canadian or Anglo-Canadian culture (depending on the region). British imperialism was not an endeavour intended to promote cultural tolerance, and Buchan's pluralism was a product of imperialism only insofar as the on-the-ground reality of colonizing a "native" population (racialized as non-white) led him to believe in the necessity of retaining various non-British European colonists, both in South Africa and in Canada.

Political scientist Donald Ipperciel, citing Henshaw's work, has explicitly argued that "Canadian multiculturalism finds its ideological source in a normative multiculturalism characteristic of the third British Empire, also known as the British Commonwealth." From the outset, he claims to be examining the ideological origins of multiculturalism, which he maintains are distinct from its "strictly historical origins." However, he also claims that the British Commonwealth was a distant *cause* of multiculturalism.[29] As such, his work – like Henshaw's before him – seems to fall into the trap of mythologizing as described by Skinner: the assumption that a fully developed ideology (in this case, multiculturalism) somehow always existed in history. Of course, multiculturalism did *not* always exist in history, and it is only possible to argue that it did by examining hypothetical connections between ideas expressed in the past, as opposed to examining the unfolding of historical events in their documented chronological order.

The larger point is this: in theory, Britishness was eventually as expansive as Ipperciel claims. After 1914, "all individuals born in the colonies were considered British, irrespective of their race or ethnic group." Imperial identity was thus apparently raceless and colourblind. (But even this argument has to be qualified, for, as Ipperciel admits, prior to 1914 the term "British" referred only to those racialized as white.) The trouble is that this identity rarely if ever existed in practice: throughout the British Empire, a person's skin colour most often ended up being more important than their citizenship.[30] The settler-colonial liberal order project that was Canada was definitely a racialized project as well, and Canadian history offers many poignant examples showing that the idea of a colour-blind British citizenship is fictive.

One of the most famous examples is that of the "Continuous Journey" clause. In 1907, in the aftermath of the Vancouver Riots, Mackenzie King advised the federal government to limit immigration from both Japan and India. In his estimation, the number of poor and unemployed East Indians in Canada was due to their fundamental incompatibility with Canada's northern climate. Indians were British subjects, but that did not mean that they would be welcomed by other British subjects. Although this presented a legal obstacle, as they could not be banned from immigrating, Canadian politicians quickly came up with a work-around: an order-in-council banning the immigration of those who had not made a continuous journey from the country of their birth to Canada. As most steamships departing India needed to make a stopover in Japan or Hawaii on their way to Canada, this would effectively end Indian immigration. However, a direct voyage was available on a Canadian Pacific Railway (CPR) steamship, so the federal government began negotiating with the company and eventually succeeded in having the trip eliminated. And when the precise wording of the regulation resulted in two Europeans (one from Russia and another from France) being barred entry, it was immediately rewritten to allow immigration officials to exercise their discretion on the point. In 1914, a group of Indians led by Gurdit Singh Sirhali attempted to circumvent the regulation by chartering a steamship, the *Komagata Maru*, to make a direct voyage to Canada. All were refused entry and, after an unsuccessful legal battle, the ship was escorted out of Canadian waters two months after it had arrived.[31]

Even after the Second World War, Canadians expressed a desire to keep people racialized as non-white from immigrating. Prime Minister Mackenzie King's cabinet initially planned to adopt a strict quota system, based on the American model, which would exclude British citizens from colonies and dominions racialized as nonwhite. Even Eurocentric commentators admit that these and other provisions were designed to keep "the country 'British' ... without the need to say so." But given "non-white" British citizens would be excluded, it is more accurate to say that the system was designed to keep the country "white."[32] Within this would-be all-white country, cultural pluralism – with all its limitations – remained ascendant in the years immediately following the end of the Second World War.

### THE RACIAL MOSAIC

For one snapshot, this book ends where it began, at the Lisgar Collegiate Institute's "superlative" thirty-fifth annual concert. Held in mid-February 1947, the concert took place a little over a month

Conclusion 245

Figure 6.1 Unidentified blackface performer, Lisgar Collegiate Institute, 1947.

after National Citizenship Week had ended. When we began, the Girls' Athletic Club had just taken the stage to perform a number entitled "The Canadian Mosaic." Dressed in clothes intended to represent a number of different European countries, the students had performed a variety of folk dances before coming together to dance a Canadian reel. The obvious symbolism of the routine suggests that the theme of unity in diversity, so heavily promoted during the Second World War, had reached and resonated with at least some segments of Canadian society.

Now, as the applause fades and the last of the dancers disappears behind the curtains, another performer takes the stage. Done up in blackface, this student performs a song entitled "Ma Blushin' Rosie." Several acts follow before it is time for the final performance, the Glee Club's blackface minstrel show. The group had been keen to get away from the traditional operettas and, in their words, "everyone favored a minstrel show." Writing for the *Ottawa Journal*, a reporter described the entire stage show as capturing the charm of a bygone era, and the Glee Club's performance in particular as having revived "Southern melodies and wit." Descriptions accompanying the photo coverage noted that the Club had performed "in rhythmic darkey style," and one particular performer was singled out for having played his role of "negro troubadour" with "all the inspired enthusiasm and soulful expression of the old-time minstrels."[33]

This event vividly demonstrates the relationship between cultural pluralism and racism in Canada during the immediate postwar years. The mosaic metaphor, so effectively popularized by Gibbon, provided a discourse that Anglo-Canadians used to describe their country's diversity in favourable terms, and enabled the celebration of non-British, non-French "folk" cultures as harmless traditions that added a splash of colour to the nation. (So, for example, Citizenship Week had also involved plenty of European folk dances: at the ceremony in Victoria, British Columbia, students performed a Dutch folk dance as part of the program, and Ukrainian folk dances were performed at the ceremony in Windsor, Ontario.[34])

But this newfound tolerance, despite its importance, completely failed to address the racism against people racialized as non-white. In this case, people of African descent were treated as a source of amusement ultimately belonging to another time (a "by-gone era") and another place (the American south).[35] The philosophies of cultural pluralism that developed in the interwar period, and further evolved throughout the Second World War, worked to combat racism and prejudice faced by European minority groups but were simultaneously racist towards peoples racialized as non-white. Although this racism often expressed itself through omission and erasure, the limitations of cultural pluralism meant that other expressions of racism, such as denigrating blackface minstrelsy, continued unabated – only now they were performed alongside celebrations of an all-white mosaic.

# Epilogue

## WATSON KIRKCONNELL

What became of the three public intellectuals most responsible for crafting and promoting philosophies of cultural pluralism in interwar Canada? Freed of any official government involvement through his resignation from the Committee on Cooperation in Canadian Citizenship (CCCC) in 1944, Watson Kirkconnell devoted almost all his energies into his campaign against communism.[1] As a result, his involvement with so-called new Canadian literature, which had greatly decreased during the war, stopped almost entirely with the exception of the annual review of "New-Canadian Letters." His upward academic trajectory continued but it must have been somewhat bittersweet, for his appointment to the presidency of Acadia University in 1948 dictated that he rein in his anti-communism. He duly toned down his remarks, and even his research on Communist Russia withered as the more respectable Milton studies gradually became his primary academic undertaking.[2] The move from Hamilton, Ontario, to Wolfville, Nova Scotia, and from professor to administrator influenced Kirkconnell's career in a number of other ways. Despite some initial anxiety about the job, the bump in prestige and salary was certainly welcomed. Acadia was, and remains, one of Canada's most esteemed undergraduate-focused universities. Kirkconnell's starting salary was $6,000 (the equivalent of around $67,000 in 2019) and the university also paid for his housing and utilities. But there were significant drawbacks: rural Wolfville was far removed from the academic and political mainstream, and the duties of administration meant that he had less time for his own research and translation projects.[3]

Several embarrassing incidents in 1959 further damaged Kirkconnell's public reputation: he expelled a student, Robert Fiander, for blasphemy, and shortly thereafter he wrote a letter to the editor of a local paper suggesting that water fluoridation might be a communist plot to weaken Canadians' minds and bodies. The national press picked up on both these stories, which led to much mockery, but Kirkconnell was unrepentant. In his annual report to the Board of Governors, Kirkconnell lumped the Fiander and fluoride fiascos together in a section labelled "The Press Disaster," and wrote that neither "had any business in the press." (This is certainly an odd characterization, given that one began with his ill-advised engagement with the local press.) The result, he concluded, "was most unfortunate for Acadia; but it is difficult to cope with journalistic hijackers."[4] Despite the brave face he put on for his employer, he intentionally sought to keep a lower profile afterwards, even as he clung to the conspiracy theories that had gotten him into such trouble in the first place.[5]

In February 1964, Kirkconnell suffered a heart attack that left him deeply shaken. He attributed it to overwork, which he was certain had killed his father.[6] He recovered and then put things in order at Acadia, officially retiring from the presidency that August. He later wrote to Robert England that he was "supremely happy to be clear of the presidency and its administrative headaches," as they had been "the main reason for my coronary."[7] Faced with his own mortality, he became quite concerned with his legacy, no doubt remembering his recent and embarrassing media coverage. Upon his discharge from the hospital he began work on a collection of poetry and on his memoirs, published at great personal expense as *Centennial Tales and Selected Poems* (1965) and *A Slice of Canada* (1967), respectively.[8] He continued researching, writing, and publishing, finishing a final volume of Milton studies but also delving heavily into local history, until his death on 26 February 1977.[9] His widow Hope Kirkconnell lived for nearly another decade, during which time she stayed in Wolfville and remained a part of the university community. According to the tribute paid to her by J.R.C. Perkin, Acadia's president, she was like a mother to African students and "delighted in her contacts with young people." She died on 9 July 1986.[10]

## ROBERT ENGLAND

After completing his assignment for the Nationalities Branch, England slipped into semi-retirement. From 1944 to 1945, he completed research on veterans' rehabilitation as a Guggenheim Fellow and then settled in to write a manuscript.[11] Soon after, however, additional stints in the civil service called him away from his writing. He worked for three months as an executive assistant to the Department of Veterans' Affairs, and then for another four months as chair of the Department's new Committee on University Requirements. During this period, he also served as a columnist for the *Winnipeg Free Press*, contributing some one hundred articles on veterans' problems and replying to over a thousand letters from veterans. Finally, in 1950, he published the results of his Guggenheim-funded study as *Twenty Million World War Veterans*.[12] For his efforts in laying the foundation for Canada's civil reestablishment program, England was awarded an honorary doctor of laws from the University of Manitoba in May 1948.[13] Despite his professional success, England was soon grappling with personal sorrow: his wife, Amy, fell ill with Parkinson's. Ever a nurse, she diagnosed herself before a doctor confirmed it. The relationship that began with Amy caring for Robert ended with Robert caring for Amy; she died on 4 February 1966.[14]

Two years later, England travelled to Ottawa to represent the Royal Canadian Regiment on the fiftieth anniversary of the 1918 Armistice. On his way back to British Columbia (BC), he stopped in Winnipeg to visit Thelma Thomson, an old friend. Thelma's family had long lived in Winnipeg, though they were Scottish immigrants. Educated at Edinburgh College, Thelma had received high honours and eventually earned a master's degree.[15] In the 1920s, she worked as the assistant superintendent of the women's branch of the Canadian National Railways (CNR) Department of Colonization in London, where she first met Robert England in 1924. She returned to Winnipeg in the 1930s and worked as the registrar of the Medical School at the University of Manitoba. She was also involved with many organizations, including the University Women's Club, the Association for Adult Education, the Local Council of Women, and the Ladies' Alpine Club of Canada. Through their active social lives, Amy England and Thelma had met and become good friends. Thelma also helped with some of

Robert England's projects during that period, such as clerical work for the *Ventures in Citizenship* program.[16]

The two old acquaintances, one a widower and the other unwed, enjoyed each other's company so much that they married on 10 September 1969 in London. They then travelled for a month before settling in Victoria, BC. (Thelma's sister Inga advised the pair that this was to be considered a holiday, for "septuagenarians do not rate a honeymoon.") Writing to Kirkconnell to inform him of the good news, England remarked: "Both of us are very happy, despite the threat of shortened years."[17] The couple eventually sold their home and moved into an intermediate care home, where they enjoyed two walks a day alongside the seashore, moving slowly from bench to bench.[18] This romantic idyll ended with England's death on 14 June 1985. Thelma's health subsequently declined; she died on Christmas Day that same year.[19]

Neither had any children, so the Englands left their estate (valued at over $230,000 in 1985) to the Extension Department at the University of British Columbia (UBC). His will stated that the money was to be used "to cover the whole or part of the cost of a series of lectures or demonstrations or courses every three years ... designed to illustrate recent or experimental methods of education, it being my particular wish that such course should be in the field of disinterested education, being instruction not specifically devoted to the gaining of academic credits or diplomas or degrees or acquirement of professional status." The department in turn established a "Robert England Bequest Fund," which would subsidize programs and services that met two criteria. First, they had to use innovative approaches to the topic or delivery, and second, they had to be in the areas of citizenship education, multiculturalism, or Canadian ethnic heritage.[20]

The bequest funded a variety of events and programming throughout the 1990s. One was a pilot project for cross-cultural diversity training workshops for the UBC faculty and staff.[21] Another was a First Nations Public Education program, proposed by Margaret Stott, which produced a forum about "Native Indian concerns in the context of issues raised during the next [1996] Provincial election campaign." Given that the topics of land claims and self-governance were bound to be hotly debated, Stott felt this was an "educable moment for Native Indian concerns."[22] In light of England's much earlier comments about Indigenous peoples' lack of a right to the land they inhabited, this was a positive (if ironic) turn of events. Even if his own views on Indigenous peoples did not greatly change during his lifetime, owing to the generosity of his bequest, part of England's legacy may be that of helping to educate Canadians about issues facing Indigenous peoples. Unfortunately, it is unclear what has become of the funds that the Englands generously entrusted to UBC.[23]

### JOHN MURRAY GIBBON

Gibbon had been scheduled to retire from his position at the CPR in 1940 but the company asked him to stay on until the end of the war. From that time until his death in 1952, he was the recipient of a number of honours. In 1940, he received an honorary doctor of laws degree from l'Université de Montréal for his promotion of the study of folksong and folklore in Quebec. In 1944 he was made an honorary chief of the Stoney (Nakoda) tribe, and was granted ceremonial dress and the title "Chief Man of Many Sides." The practice of making non-Indigenous people honorary chiefs was well established by this point. According to scholar Courtney Mason, these inductions often happened during "the high-profile Indian Days," and the individuals chosen, "mostly prominent men and women from Calgary's business and political communities, were singled out for their dedication to improving the lives of Nakoda peoples. In some cases, famous celebrities and members of royalty were also given honorary status." He argues that it was more than just recognition of past help, but that it "also established a responsibility to do so in the future." While it is unclear if Gibbon offered further help, he continued to ride with the group for several years afterwards.[24]

In 1945 Gibbon retired and found himself in "a confusing period of change." He quite tellingly characterized it as a "change from office work to work at home," and ensured this was true by accepting a number of writing projects. Regardless, the honours continued to roll in. In 1948, the Composers, Authors, and Publishers Association of Canada lauded him as a "nation builder" in a ceremony attended by Secretary of State Paul Martin Sr, Justice J.T. Thorson, and Leonard Brockington, among other dignitaries. He received similar praise the following year, when the Royal Society of Canada awarded him the Lorne Pierce Gold Medal for his efforts to promote folk arts and for his contributions to mutual understanding between English- and French-speaking Canadians. During this time Gibbon did not weigh in on the ongoing debates about Canadian immigration policy, but instead spent his time writing on an eclectic variety of topics, including the history of nursing, the Victorian Order of Nurses, the canoe, the city of Montreal, and Canadian handicrafts. One brief reprieve was a trip to England as a delegate to the International Folk Music Council Convention, which allowed him to return to Oxford and to reunite with various members of his family.[25]

In 1952 he was back in Canada and hard at work editing his autobiography, but was unable to have it published before he fell seriously ill that May. He nevertheless remained in good spirits and, though unable to write, continued to speak of future writing projects even on his deathbed. His condition deteriorated quickly, and he died on 2 July 1952.[26] Some years later, a coworker suggested that during his life Gibbon had "no friends, just business acquaintances."[27] Whether or not this is true, he most likely formed some of his closest relationships with people in western Canada. It seems that, whether hiking or trail riding, he felt most at peace when in the Rockies. It is therefore fitting that he was buried in Banff, the region he loved so dearly. His widow Nancy lived for another four years; she is buried over three thousand kilometres away, in a cemetery near their Ste Anne de Bellevue home.[28] Outliving them both is the mosaic metaphor, which is with Canadians still.

# Notes

INTRODUCTION

1 Jonas, "Lisgar Collegiate Institute"; "Carries on Tradition at Lisgar Concert," *Ottawa Citizen* (9 February 1947), 9; and "Charm of By-Gone Era Captured at Annual Lisgar Stage Show," *Ottawa Journal* (8 February 1947), 13.
2 As historian Carmela Patrias notes, the terms "preferred" and "unpreferred" were never used in legislation but were used by government officials in correspondence and were commonly expressed in public discourse. Patrias, *Jobs and Justice*, 7.
3 These remarks were made by John Wesley Edwards, a Unionist MP, in the context of a debate on religious schooling. See House of Commons, *Debates* (14 May 1919), 2414.
4 Alerted by an anonymous reviewer (thank you, A1) to a potential source of confusion, I should make it clear at the outset that by using the term "cultural pluralism" I am not invoking theories of pluralism as they have been conventionally developed in other social sciences. Rather, I am specifically referring to the body of thought that developed in Canada during the interwar period. For a helpful primer on the former, see McLennan, *Pluralism*.
5 Trudeau, *Essential Trudeau*, 145–6.
6 Canadian National Railways was created as a Crown corporation in 1919, formed by merging a number of bankrupt and previously nationalized railway companies. In 1960, it was renamed the Canadian National Railway Company, and still later it became referred to as CN. As this book deals with the pre-1960 era, the original pluralized name (abbreviated CNR) is used throughout.

7 Porter, *The Vertical Mosaic*.
8 Or, as he put it elsewhere, biography is at the core of history. Waite, "Books That Have Most Influenced Me," 10; and Waite, "Biography as History." Carl Berger argued that "biography ... is a branch of history but it is not the same thing as history. History deals in generalizations about groups, institutions, and movements in time and is more than a mosaic of lives. Biography deals with the particularities of a human being and seeks to simulate, through narrative, an individual's life." Berger, *The Writing of Canadian History*, 222.
9 Gauvreau, "Not Entirely a Revolution"; and Renders and de Haan, "The Challenge of Biography Studies," 6.
10 Caine, *Biography and History*, 7; and Meister, "The Case for Historical Biography."
11 For an overview of the Canadian context, see Meister, "Historical Biography in Canada."
12 For a discussion, see Lässig, "Biography in Modern History."
13 Tuchman, "Biography as a Prism of History," 133. Alice Kessler-Harris offered a similar metaphor of life as a "lens" and more accurately described her approach as "anti-biography." See her "Why Biography?," 626.
14 Wright, "Biography, and the Writing of History," 354. Emphasis added.
15 Skinner, "Meaning and Understanding in the History of Ideas," 7–12.
16 Ibid., 46, 47.
17 Meister, "Historical Biography in Canada," 34.
18 I am grateful to Lisa Pasolli for her thoughtful critique of the dissertation on which this book is based, which directly informed this brief section.
19 Palmer, "Reluctant Hosts," 95–6; and Bonavia, "Bibliographical Access to Ethno-Cultural Material," 80. Bonavia also listed V.J. Kaye. Kaye, a Ukrainian Canadian, born Vladimir J. Kisilevsky, has already been subject to some historical study but did not significantly contribute to the bureaucracy for multiculturalism, as historian N.F. Dreisziger has called it, until the Second World War. Historian Franca Iacovetta's book *Gatekeepers* deals extensively with the postwar activities of the Citizenship Branch and is based largely on a reading of Kaye's files. However, there is merit to Lee Blanding's critique that the role of Kaye's office gradually diminished and that more attention needs to be given to how the Citizenship Branch evolved over time. See Iacovetta, *Gatekeepers*; Blanding, "Re-branding Canada," 39–44; and Dreisziger, "Bureaucracy for Multiculturalism."
20 Dreisziger, "Kirkconnell and the Cultural Credibility Gap," 94.

21 See for instance Smale, "For Whose Kingdom," esp. 225–43 and 248; Balmer, "Kirkconnell, Watson"; Hoerder, *To Know Our Many Selves*, 198; Clary, "Kirkconnell, Watson"; and Heather J. Coleman, "Watson Kirkconnell," 387.
22 McKay, *The Quest of the Folk*, 58; and Stuart Henderson, "While There Is Still Time," 141.
23 Howard Palmer, "Description of Project," Dr Howard Palmer fonds, box 6, folder 32 ("Elite responses to foreign immigration"), University of Calgary, Archives and Special Collections (UCASC). Palmer intended to write a book on "English-Canadian elite opinion toward immigration and ethnicity in the twentieth century," one that would examine the attitudes of Robert England, J.S. Woodsworth, Nellie McClung, W.L. Mackenzie King, J.W. Dafoe, J.M. Gibbon, and Watson Kirkconnell. England was also the subject of one excellent but overlooked PhD dissertation: Wurtele, "Nation-Building from the Ground Up."
24 For reasons unknown, Isabel Skelton would resign from the CCCC by October 1943. Her replacement (Emily Lynch, a barrister from Windsor, Ontario, about whom little is known) was added around 1944 but the Committee was disbanded shortly thereafter. On the McWilliams see Kinnear, *Margaret McWilliams*; and on the Skeltons, see Terry Crowley's excellent dual biography, *Marriage of Minds*. Information about the CCCC's membership was taken from their meeting minutes, but is also helpfully collated in Caccia, *Managing the Canadian Mosaic in Wartime*, Appendix I, 231–3. For a representative press piece, see "Fosters Racial Understanding," *Globe and Mail* (18 March 1942), 3.
25 Foster, *Our Canadian Mosaic*, 1, 5–6. Press references include the more substantial "Girls of Today Better Than Any World Has Yet Known," *Vancouver Province* (3 April 1927), 16; with passing reference made in the following articles: "Easter Program at McLeod W.M.S.," *Ottawa Citizen* (15 April 1927), 21; "Oratorical Contest Entries Close Dec. 1," *Edmonton Journal* (24 November 1928), 18; and "Women's Club Notes," *Edmonton Journal* (6 March 1930), 17.
26 Gibbon was one of the four founding members of the CAA. The first meeting was originally scheduled to take place at the University Club in Montreal but, as Gibbon later recalled, "to our embarrassment it turned out that apparently 90% of Canadian authors were women," and the Club did not allow mixed gatherings. As such, they were forced to move the event to Royal Victoria College at McGill University. Gibbon, "Scot to Canadian," 2–3, John Murray Gibbon fonds (M454), Whyte Museum of the Canadian Rockies (WMCR).

Women remained a significant force within the organization, though a woman would not be elected president until 1939 (Madge Macbeth), and women faced ongoing prejudice. A comment from acclaimed author Philip Godsell is suggestive: "[Gibbon] started the Canadian Authors Association which was alright untul [sic] it developed into a G...D....hen party." Godsell, letter to Norman [K. Luxton], 5 July 1953, Luxton family fonds, Norman Luxton sous-fonds, LUX/I/H-308, WMCR. For a history of the CAA that pays close attention to gender discrimination, see Doody, "A Union of the Inkpot."

27 The situation was therefore similar in Great Britain as well. England's driver was Mrs Rosemary Henderson of the Women's Transport Service (FANY); see his kind (if somewhat patronizing) letter to her, dated 6 July 1940, found in the Robert England fonds, box 2, folder 2, Library and Archives Canada (LAC) (cited hereafter in the following manner: RE2-2, LAC).

28 Messamore, *Canada's Governors General*, 3.

29 A handful of scholars prefer to call it "Race Critical Theory."

30 See for instance Cheryl I. Harris, "Whiteness as Property"; and López, *White By Law*. Other important texts include Roediger, *The Wages of Whiteness*; Frankenberg, *White Women, Race Matters*; Lipsitz, "The Possessive Investment in Whiteness"; and Jacobson, *Whiteness of a Different Color*. For an excellent and accessible overview of the field's development, see Baird, "The Invention of Whiteness."

31 See for instance Garner, *Whiteness*, 13–14; and Applebaum, "Critical Whiteness Studies."

32 Garner, *Whiteness*, 1.

33 Jackson and Weidman's *Race, Racism, and Science* offers a helpful and accessible overview of the development of race science. See also Meister, "Young Watson Kirkconnell."

34 Zach, *Philosophy of Science and Race*, 9. Italics removed.

35 Kidd, *The Forging of Races*, 54, 75. He also contends "race slavery was in theory nothing of the sort, but rather the enslavement of pagans, who happened to be black" – or, he neglects to say, Indigenous.

36 The essential history of the discipline remains Marvin Harris, *The Rise of Anthropological Theory*. See also Baker, *From Savage to Negro*, esp. 87–100.

37 Banton, "Historical and Contemporary Modes of Racialization," 55.

38 Banton, *The Idea of Race*, 5. See also Marvin Harris, *Rise of Anthropological Theory*, 93–8.

39 Banton, *The Idea of Race*, 5. As the nineteenth century progressed, European hierarchies thus drew on notions of religion, civilization, or race, and oftentimes a combination: these different ways of evaluating people groups and nations were not always running in opposition to one another, or even parallel to each other, but often intersected.
40 For an excellent overview, see Kidd, *The Forging of Races*, 3–18. On the return of race science in the present day, see Saini, *Superior*.
41 See Mills, "Multiculturalism as/and/or Anti-Racism?"
42 Garner, *Whiteness*, 10 and chap. 4.
43 Deniker, *The Races of Man*, xv; and Stocking, "The Persistence of Polygenist Thought," 62.
44 Ripley, *The Races of Europe*, especially the table found on 121; and Spiro, *Defending the Master Race*, 93. See also Painter, *The History of White People*, esp. chap. 15.
45 Grant, *The Passing of the Great Race*; and Spiro, *Defending the Master Race*, 157–8, 161. With the resurgence of the far right, Grant is being discussed once again. See for instance Serwer, "White Nationalism's Deep American Roots."
46 The term Anglo-Saxon is used to refer to a number of Germanic peoples who arrived in what are now the British Isles in the fifth century. In many instances in this book, the people using the term meant it as a synonym for "British," though some intended it to carry the weight of this supposedly racial lineage.
47 Spiro, *Defending the Master Race*, 102–3. Emphasis in the original.
48 Ibid., 157.
49 Kevles, *In the Name of Eugenics*, ix.
50 Spiro, *Defending the Master Race*, 118.
51 Pearson, *Life, Letters, and Labours of Francis Galton*, IIIA, 348, quoted in Kevles, *In the Name of Eugenics*, 3.
52 Kevles, *In the Name of Eugenics*, 13.
53 Bashford and Levine, *Oxford Handbook of the History of Eugenics*. Eugenics is an understudied area in Canadian history; Strange and Stephen note that in spite of "the vigor and wide appeal of eugenics in Canada, historians were slow to chart its past. Angus McLaren's *Our Own Master Race*, published in 1990, remains the sole overview." See their "Eugenics in Canada."
54 Kevles, *In the Name of Eugenics*, 21, 57–76, 85. This biological determinism influenced thinking about race and immigration as well, and some parallels between positive and negative eugenics and immigration policy

can be identified, such as the idea that superior races ought to be encouraged to immigrate and that inferior races ought to be deported and kept out.
55 Spiro, *Defending the Master Race*, 138. Emphasis in the original.
56 Dyer, *White*, 3.
57 Jacobson, *Whiteness of a Different Color*, 6.
58 Kolchin, "Whiteness Studies," 155.
59 See for example Roediger, *The Wages of Whiteness*; and Ignatiev, *How the Irish Became White*. For critiques, see Arnesen, "Whiteness and the Historians' Imagination"; and Kolchin, "Whiteness Studies."
60 Garner, *Whiteness*, 2.
61 Satzewich, "Whiteness Limited." Burkowicz provides many examples of the varied ways in which Slavs were racialized in Canada, but the work is rather preoccupied with sociological theories and pays insufficient attention to change over time. Burkowicz, "Racialization of Slavs."
62 Jacobson, *Whiteness of a Different Color*, 6 (italics in the original), 40.
63 Ibid., esp. 13–14, 38–45, 91–3, 201–2.
64 For a succinct overview of settler colonialism in Canada that points to the present-day ramifications of this past, see Green, "Toward a Detente with History."
65 Veracini, *Settler Colonialism*, quotes at 6 and 8. The importance on labour depends on the specific historical context; see for instance Perry, *Colonial Relations*, 67, 146.
66 Canadian Historical Association, "Canada Day Statement: The History of Violence against Indigenous Peoples Fully Warrants the Use of the Word 'Genocide,'" 30 June 2021, https://cha-shc.ca/news/canada-day-statement-the-history-of-violence-against-indigenous-peoples-fully-warrants-the-use-of-the-word-genocide-2021-06-30.
67 McKay has since begun referring to the process as one of "liberal settler colonialism." See his "The 'Morals of Genealogy.'" On liberalism as an essentially contested concept, see Pitts, "Free for All." On the liberal order framework, see McKay, "Liberal Order Framework," quote at 621; McKay, *Rebels, Reds, Radicals*, 59; Constant and Ducharme, *Liberalism and Hegemony*; and the "Forum" in *The Underhill Review* (Fall 2009), http://www3.carleton.ca/underhillreview/09/fall/content/contents.htm. See also Barrington Walker, "Development of a White Canada," 49.
68 For discussions of the exclusions baked into liberalism, see Mehta, *Liberalism and Empire*; Mehta, "Liberal Strategies of Exclusion"; and, on the relationship between liberalism and racism, see Mills, "Multiculturalism as/and/or Anti-Racism?"; FitzGerald and Cook-Martín,

*Culling the Masses*, 6–7, 144; and the "Symposium" in *Ethnic and Racial Studies* 38, no. 8 (2015): 1285–1327.
69 Valerie Knowles, *Strangers at Our Gates*, 14, 19; and Belmessous, "Assimilation and Racialism," 328.
70 James W. St G. Walker, *Racial Discrimination in Canada*, 8; see also James W. St G. Walker, *Black Loyalists*, 42.
71 James W. St G. Walker, *Racial Discrimination in Canada*, 14; and James W. St G. Walker, *"Race," Rights, and the Law*, 13. Of course, its spread across Canada was neither instantaneous nor uniform. As historian Max Hamon has shown, Métis identity – at least in the period he studied – was not defined by race; community, kinship, and religion were far more important. He also points out that the Métis complicate the divisions between the now-reified categories of "Indigenous" and "Settler." Hamon, *Audacity of His Enterprise*, esp. 22, 29, and 270.
72 On settler colonial narratives, see Veracini, *Settler Colonialism*, chap. 4; and on imagining the nation, see Benedict Anderson, *Imagined Communities*.
73 See Brantlinger, *Dark Vanishings*; and, on the Canadian context, Francis, *Imaginary Indian*, esp. chapters 2 and 3.
74 For an expansive overview of Canadian immigration policy, see Kelley and Trebilcock, *Making of the Mosaic*.
75 Ibid., 94–9; and Roy, *A White Man's Province*, esp. chap. 3.
76 Kelley and Trebilcock, *Making of the Mosaic*, 94–9; and Avery, *Reluctant Host*, 50. See also Roy, *The Oriental Question*; and Ward, *White Canada Forever*.
77 Lord Durham, *Report on the Affairs of British North America*, 7. Unfortunately, scholars have yet to explore how Durham likely defined the term so central to his argument. Some have argued that Durham used the term strictly to mean "nationality," without biological connotations, but historians recognize that more biological understandings of race began to spread in the 1840s, and Durham's own usage suggests a certain amount of essentialism. One of the few brief comments on the subject is found in Knight, *Choosing Canada's Capital System*, 351 n23. See also Nish, *Racism or Responsible Government*, 1–5.
   The early historiographical consensus was that Durham was a racist, but this view was challenged by Ajzenstat, *Political Thought of Lord Durham*. She argues that Durham was a mainstream liberal concerned with equality, liberty, and self-government, one who felt unassimilated French Canadians could not enjoy liberty on equal footing with English Canadians. Despite determining that her argument "warrant[ed] a

rebuttal," political historians have yet to deliver it. Rutherdale, review of *The Political Thought of Lord Durham*.
78 Bellay, "The Image of the French Canadian 'Race.'"
79 This was exemplified in the founding of Halifax and in Lord Bathurst's efforts to prevent American settlement; see Valerie Knowles, *Strangers at Our Gates*, 28–9, 51–2.
80 Kelley and Trebilcock, *Making of the Mosaic*, chap. 3; and Valerie Knowles, *Strangers at Our Gates*, chap. 4. As Veracini puts it, "settlers are made by conquest *and* by immigration." *Settler Colonialism*, 5.
81 Kelley and Trebilcock, *Making of the Mosaic*, 113–23, quote at 122. On Sifton's attitudes towards various people groups, see Hall, *A Lonely Eminence*, 68.
82 Kelley and Trebilcock, *Making of the Mosaic*, 64, 113–15.
83 Ibid., 134; and Canada, *The Immigration Act*, S.C. 1910, c.27, s.38(c). In one case, native-born Canadian and British workers "called themselves 'white men' to distinguish themselves from the southern and eastern Europeans they worked with." Palmer, *Patterns of Prejudice*, 59.
84 Quoted in Kelley and Trebilcock, *Making of the Mosaic*, 133.
85 Quoted in Martynowych, "Canadianizing the Foreigner," 36.
86 House of Commons, *Debates*, 12 April 1901.
87 Canada, *The Immigration Act*, S.C. 1910, c.27, s.38(c).
88 Scott, "Immigration and Population," quote at 531 (emphasis added), quoted in Eyford, *White Settler Reserve*, 44. Note that throughout the essay Scott refers to both "the white race" (531) and "the white races" (571).
89 Young, *Postcolonialism*, 19–20.
90 For an interesting case study, see Eyford, *White Settler Reserve*, esp. 45–7, 96–9, 104, 114, and 136.
91 See for instance F.G. Griffin, "What Type of People Is Our Melting Pot Going to Produce? Will Semi-Asiatic New-Comers Defy Fusion and Swamp Us?" *Winnipeg Evening Tribune* (23 February 1924), 28; and Grant, "Americans of Nordic Origin," 4.
92 McLaren, *Our Own Master Race*, esp. 46, 61–2, 87, 92–3.
93 Berger, *The Sense of Power*, esp. 117–19, 171–3, 227–32. More recently, Mann's comparative history of multiculturalism in Canada and Australia repeatedly refers to "British race patriotism" (without ever defining it), but never to racism. Mann, *The Search for a New National Identity*.
94 Daniel Coleman, *White Civility*, chap. 1.
95 McKay and Bates, *In the Province of History*, 9–10, 378.

Notes to pages 27–31

96 Patrias, *Jobs and Justice*, 3–15, quotes at 6 and 10. For a distilled version, see "Race, Employment Discrimination, and State Complicity."
97 Patrias, *Jobs and Justice*, 131, 112.
98 Gibbon, *Canadian Mosaic*, chap. 19 is entitled "Cement for the Canadian Mosaic." This cement, he wrote, consisted primarily of agencies and voluntary organizations that worked to integrate immigrants.
99 It is worth noting, however, that such critiques are overwhelmingly made by non-historians. For one response to such critics, see Coombs, "In Defence of (Canadian Academic) History."
100 However, I try to avoid using such terms (e.g., black/Black or white/White) to begin with, instead using the phrase "of African/Asian/European descent." There are several reasons for this decision. One is that language around race continues to shift, making the use of such terms at times anachronistic. For example, most people of African descent during the period under study would have self-identified as "negro," yet today this term is widely considered derogatory. Similarly, while most of their contemporaries who were racialized as white would have confidently affirmed their whiteness, most would have identified first and foremost as "Anglo-Saxon" or even "British." Second, in addition to being a presentist intervention, I believe that using such terms can be an act of continued and uncritical racialization, one which I very much wish to avoid. See "Note on Usage," in Jacobson, *Whiteness of a Different Color*, ix–x; Hoyt Jr, *Arc of a Bad Idea*, xv; and Gilroy, *Against Race*, esp. 32–41.
101 Day, *Multiculturalism*, 6. Italics in the original.
102 Millar, "Canada's Myth of Multiculturalism."

CHAPTER ONE

1 Kirkconnell, "A Sensible Census," 1, 6. His concern about the racial composition of the country, the demographic shift from rural to urban, and the decline in family size also led him to further correspondence with the Dominion Statistician. See Kirkconnell, letter to R.H. Coats, 30 November 1920; and R.H. Coats, letter to Kirkconnell, 3 December 1920, Watson Kirkconnell fonds, box 28, folder 74, Esther Clark Wright Archives at Acadia University (cited hereafter in the following style: WK28-74, ECWA). See also Beaud and Prévost, "Immigration, Eugenics and Statistics," which notes Coats's sympathies with the eugenics movement and his belief in race as a biological reality; and Boyd, Goldmann, and White, "Race in the Canadian Census."

2 T.J. Begley, letter to R.H. Coats, 22 November 1920, WK28-74, ECWA.
3 As an adult he went by Watson, but in his youth he gave his name as "T. Watson Kirkconnell."
4 Kirkconnell, *Twilight of Liberty*, 73. Note Kirkconnell's expansive definition of Anglo-Saxon; the community he describes could equally be deemed "Anglo-Celtic."
5 Kirkconnell, *Headmaster*, 11–13, 155; and Gaffield, *Language, Schooling, and Cultural Conflict*, 19, but see also 31–85. Cf. James Allison, letter to Watson Kirkconnell, 18 March 1936; and Kirkconnell, letter to James Allison, 21 March 1936, WK5-35, ECWA.
6 Kirkconnell, *Headmaster*, 46, 135; and Kirkconnell, *Slice*, 84, 120.
7 Kirkconnell, *Headmaster*, 49–59; and Kirkconnell, *Slice*, 8–9.
8 O.R.B. Club, *Lindsay Past and Present*, np. They added, "Labour troubles are practically unknown in Lindsay," despite the fact that the town was home to some active socialists. See McKay, *Reasoning Otherwise*, 37–40.
9 Haudenosaunee Confederacy, "Cayuga"; and Abler, "Cayuga."
10 On the history of Port Hope, see Craick, *Port Hope Historical Sketches*; "Hope," in *Encyclopedia of Ontario*; and Municipality of Port Hope, "The History of Port Hope." The website www.porthophistory.com contains collected census data and some helpful links.
11 Quoted in Miller, *Compact, Contract, Covenant*, 90.
12 M. Martin, "Ganaraska History."
13 On residential schools, see Milloy, *A National Crime*; and Miller, *Shingwauk's Vision*.
14 Kirkconnell also went by Little Elk, or Deerfoot. His brother Walter was known as Bald Eagle, and their friends (the "Braves") included Grey Wolf, Thunder Bull, Little Oak, Howling Coyote, Minnehaha, and Hiawatha. See Kirkconnell, "Diary" (1904–07), 2–12, WK2-6, ECWA. See also his "In Perpetuum, Frater …" in Kirkconnell, *Tide of Life*, 18. Historian Sharon Wall suggests that the popularity of "playing Indian" at camp can be attributed to the antimodernist impulse in Ontario during the period. See her "Totem Poles, Teepees, and Token Traditions."
15 Berger, *The Sense of Power*, 1–12.
16 Ibid., 9, 115.
17 Ibid., 116–17. See also Page, "Canada and the Imperial Idea," 39.
18 Page, "Canada and the Imperial Idea," 33.
19 Stamp, *The Schools of Ontario*, 93. See also Moss, *Manliness and Militarism*, 107; and Pass, "School Flags and Educational Authority," 323–4.
20 Berger, *The Sense of Power*, 233.

21 See Pass, "School Flags and Educational Authority," 324; and Morton, "The Cadet Movement," 63. Kirkconnell was involved in some sports as a youth; see Kirkconnell, "Diary T.W. Kirkconnell" (1913–1914), 1, 7, 10, WK2-9, ECWA; Kirkconnell, *Slice*, 133; and Kirkconnell, "Diary Watson Kirkconnell" (1911–1912), np, WK2-6, ECWA. On his involvement in cadets, see Kirkconnell, *Headmaster*, 122, 124; Kirkconnell, *Slice*, 10, 85, 97–8, 133; Kirkconnell, "Diary Watson Kirkconnell" (1911–1912), np, WK2-6, ECWA; and Kirkconnell, "Diary T.W. Kirkconnell" (1913–1914), 1, WK2-9, ECWA.

22 See for instance Mangan, *The Imperial Curriculum*.

23 Kirkconnell, *Slice*, 8; and Judith Woodsworth, "The Undoing of Babel," 17. James B. Snelson's annotated bibliography runs to 1,800 items. See Perkin and Snelson, *Morning in His Heart*. This work is divided into two parts; the first is Perkin's biographical sketch of Kirkconnell and the second is Snelson's annotated bibliography. The latter is cited hereafter as Snelson, "Bibliography," followed by either the page number or the page and item number.

24 See Queen's University, *Calendar of the Faculty of Arts* (1913), 80; Neatby, *Queen's University*, 286; and Maxwell Cohen, "Kirkconnell – Man of Letters," *Winnipeg Free Press* (12 August 1939), 3. Cf. Kirkconnell, *Slice*, 146.

25 Kirkconnell, *Slice*, chap. 2 and appendix I; E.S. Craig, letter to Kirkconnell, 17 June 1921, WK41-18; and E.I. Carlyle, letter to Kirkconnell, 23 November 1923, WK41-18, ECWA.

26 Kirkconnell, *Slice*, 11, 35; see also 331–3, 344–9. In 1908, Kirkconnell began studying Latin and French, to which he added Greek and German. He would later repeatedly lament that he felt this was several years too late and that the delay was the chief reason he did not become a linguist. Ibid., 9, 34.

27 Kirkconnell, *Slice*, 35.

28 He subscribed to *La Presse* to keep his French in shape, scribbled Greek verse in class, sent postcards to his siblings in French and Latin, and handed in an exercise for his French class with quotations in Hebrew, Latin, Greek, and Spanish. (This particular Professor saw the humour in it, and upped the ante by returning it with criticism "in Scandinavian and Arabic.") See Kirkconnell, "Diary T.W. Kirkconnell" (1913–1914), 5, 9, 26, WK2-9, ECWA; and "Tit for Tat," *Queen's Journal* (28 January 1915), 2.

29 See for example "A.M.S.," *Queen's Journal* (8 November 1915), 1, 5; W.G.M., "The Yellow Peril," ibid. (23 October 1913), 1, 5; "Upcoming Events," ibid.

(10 December 1915), 1; "Q.U.M.A.," ibid. (13 December 1915), 1; "Coming Events," ibid. (17 December 1915), 1; "University Sermon," ibid. (20 December 1915), 1; and [untitled], ibid. (7 January 1915), 5. See also Kirkconnell, "Diary T.W. Kirkconnell" (1913–1914), 42, WK2-9, ECWA.

30 "A.M.S.," *Queen's Journal* (8 November 1915), 1, 5.

31 W.G.M., "The Yellow Peril," *Queen's Journal* (23 October 1913), 1, 5. Kirkconnell did attend some YMCA meetings, but even if he did not attend this particular lecture he nevertheless would have been exposed to its message – given that it appeared on the front page of the *Journal*, which he faithfully read. See Kirkconnell, "Diary T.W. Kirkconnell" (1913–1914), 11, 37, WK2-9, ECWA. Visiting speakers gave similar messages, such as Rev. John MacKay's 1915 address which also called for the restriction of Asian immigration. See "Upcoming Events," *Queen's Journal* (10 December 1915), 1; "Q.U.M.A.," ibid. (13 December 1915), 1; "Coming Events," ibid. (17 December 1915), 1; "University Sermon," ibid. (20 December 1915), 1. Kirkconnell also independently discussed topics such as "the Hebrews and Orientals as immigrants & people" at the "Mission Study Class" that he attended. Kirkconnell, "Diary T.W. Kirkconnell" (1913–1914), 15, 25, 33, WK2-9, ECWA.

32 See "Dr. Zwemer at Queen's," *Queen's Journal* (19 February 1914), 1; "Q.U.M.A.," ibid. (10 January 1916), 2; and [untitled], ibid. (7 January 1915), 5.

33 "The Rough Element," *Queen's Journal* (6 December 1915), 2. No female candidates were elected to the Alma Mater Society (AMS) until the First World War, and it was not until 1917 that the *Queen's Journal* had a female editor on staff. Neatby, *And Not to Yield*, 299, 301, 303.

34 He similarly enjoyed Stephen Leacock's speech on how to make education more attractive, which seemed to fixate on women's bodies. Kirkconnell, "Diary T.W. Kirkconnell" (1913–1914), 27–31, WK2-9, ECWA; and Kirkconnell, *Slice*, 21. Morison's speech was controversial and provoked much debate; see for instance "Faculty Notes: Arts," *Queen's Journal* (1 December 1913), 5; "Professor Morison on Co-Education," ibid., 4, 8; [untitled], ibid. (1 December 1913), 7; ibid. (4 December 1913), 2, 5; ibid. (11 December 1913), 6; and "Faculty Notes: Arts," ibid. (8 January 1914), 3.

35 Kirkconnell, "Diary T.W. Kirkconnell" (1913–1914), 38–41, WK2-9, ECWA.

36 Kirkconnell, *Slice*, 32–3, 41, 192 ("gnawed"), 197, 189–92.

37 Kirkconnell, "The Rush Defended," 1–2.

38 Leonard, *Illiberal Reformers*, 114.

39 This phrase is taken from Nic Clarke, *Unwanted Warriors*. See Kirkconnell, *Slice*, 99, 120–1; and Thomas Kirkconnell, letter to Watson, 21 January 1917, WK3-12, ECWA. For a comprehensive look at internment in Canada, see Kordan, *No Free Man*; and for Kirkconnell's recollections, see his "When We Locked Up the Fritz"; *Kapuskasing*; and *Slice*, 99–106. On the lack of fitness in Internment Operations, see Morton, "Sir William Otter and Internment Operations," 48, 51; and Kordan, *No Free Man*, 136–7.
40 See the image in Perkin and Snelson, *Morning in His Heart*, 49; and in Kirkconnell, *Hungarian Helicon*, iv.
41 Kirkconnell, *Slice*, 369–70.
42 Ibid., 259, but also 99–106.
43 Kordan, *No Free Man*, 131, 269; Kirkconnell, "When We Locked Up the Fritz," 20; and Kirkconnell, *Kapuskasing*, 5–6. Kordan does not define race, racism, or racialism in his work.
44 Kirkconnell, letter to his parents, 9 June 1918, WK3-10, ECWA. Cf. Kirkconnell, *Slice*, 30.
45 Kirkconnell, letter to his father, 24 November 1918, WK3-10, ECWA; Thomson, *Heredity*, iii; and Kevles, *In the Name of Eugenics*, 89, 317 n38. See also Bowler, "From Science to the Popularization of Science."
46 When Kirkconnell was demobilized he had to ship home at least ten boxes of books. Thomas Kirkconnell, letter to Watson, 13 July 1919, WK3-10, ECWA.
47 Grabovac, "Preserving the Great White North," 120.
48 Spiro, *Defending the Master Race*, 350.
49 Goethe, "Beware Race Mixtures," *The Globe* (9 June 1926), 4; and Goethe, "Race Admixture An Evil," *The Globe* (10 June 1926), 4.
50 C.M. Goethe, "Immigration," *Ottawa Journal* (13 November 1924), 6; and Goethe, "The Immigration Problem," *The Winnipeg Tribune* (26 November 1927), 29.
51 Thomas Allison Kirkconnell, letters to Watson, WK3-12, ECWA, dated as follows: 27 January 1917; 3 May 1917; 17 March 1918; 3 May 1919; and 23 December 1919.
52 Thomas Allison Kirkconnell, letters to Watson, WK3-12, ECWA, dated 6 May 1917 and 27 January 1917; and Watson Kirkconnell, letter to his parents, 15 April 1917, WK3-10, ECWA. There are a number of works on Mendel, but for his theory's application to eugenics, see Kevles, *In the Name of Eugenics*, 41–4.
53 Kirkconnell, letter to his father, 24 November 1918, WK3-10, ECWA. In America, philology played an important role in the politics of "Indian removal." See Harvey, "Philology, Indian Removal, and Race Science."

54 See Darnell, *Edward Sapir*; Stocking, *Race, Culture, and Evolution*; and Stocking, *A Franz Boas Reader*.
55 Kirkconnell, *Slice*, 30–1.
56 Jackson and Weidman, *Race, Racism, and Science*, 135. As they put it: "Taken together, these ideas represented a radical departure from nineteenth-century evolutionism, even if Boas himself was formed in that mould and it was really his students who fulfilled his radical suggestions." On the battle between Boas and Madison Grant, see Spiro, *Defending the Master Race*, esp. chap. 12.
57 Kirkconnell, *Slice*, 15; Kirkconnell, "Personal Diary Private Watson Kirkconnell" (1919–1921), entry for 16 October 1919, WK2-9, ECWA; and Max Pemberton, *The Journalism Course*, in WK3-4, ECWA. On Pemberton, see Hilliard, *To Exercise Our Talents*, 23–9.
58 Kirkconnell, "Anglo-Canadian Futurities," WK4-23; and Kirkconnell, letter to the Sub-Rector of Lincoln College, 15 October 1921, WK41-18, ECWA. He likely began in late 1919; in *A Tale of Seven Cities*, 8, he recounted writing his "first book" during the winter of 1919–20.
59 Physiognomy was particularly useful as a way of visually identifying specific typologies. Galton, for one, engaged with the work of Herbert Spencer and was keen to use photography to identify "the true physiognomy of a race." Galton, *Inquiries into Human Faculty and its Development* (1883), quoted in Allan Sekula, "The Body and the Archive," 44 (but see esp. 37–54). See also Edkins, *Face Politics*, 102–9.
60 Kirkconnell, *Slice*, 7, 30. He had taken updated measurements at the request of his friend, R. Ruggles Gates, a race scientist who remained stubbornly racist (and anti-Semitic) even after his theories had been discredited after the Second World War. See Gates, letter to Kirkconnell, 21 September 1957, WK34-14, ECWA; Kirkconnell, letter to Gates, 24 September 1957, WK34-14, ECWA; and Kirkconnell, letter to Gates (and enclosed diagram), 29 October 1959, WK34-14, ECWA.
61 Kirkconnell, "Personal Diary Private Watson Kirkconnell" (1919–1921), entries for 2 September 1919 and 21 October 1919, WK3-9, ECWA. Kirkconnell was apparently already familiar with phrenology, as he noted that the "system and technology" of Professor Young in Montreal were nearly identical to those of a Dr Katherine Blackford.
62 Kirkconnell, "Personal Diary," 28 October 1919, WK2-9, ECWA. Here is a clear example of racialization, as he referred to the thoroughly British Cockneys as if they were a separate race. Note also his physical descriptions, in clinical terminology, of his fellow soldiers in Kirkconnell,

"Personal Diary Private Watson Kirkconnell" (1919–1921), entries for 9 September 1919, WK2-9, ECWA.
63 Kirkconnell, "Futurities," 1–9. Pagination added.
64 Aside from a narrower definition of *genius*, synonymous with *intelligence*, racial theorists also used it in a broader sense. Stocking explains that races were "often thought of as supraindividual entities which had a common 'genius' or 'soul.'" See his *Race, Culture, and Evolution*, 65.
65 Kirkconnell, "Futurities," 1–9.
66 Here Kirkconnell followed Moore, *The Clash*, 4.
67 Kirkconnell, "Futurities," 1–6.
68 Kirkconnell, "Futurities," 1.
69 However, climate did present a problem for colonization. As he argued: "the [United Empire] Loyalists who went to Nova Scotia and Ontario proved one of the finest stocks of the country and gave Canada many outstanding statesman. Those of the very same stock who chose the West Indies instead of Canada are now the decadent 'white trash' of the Bahamas and Barbadoes. They are outside of the natural habitat of their race, and cannot compete in sub-tropical agriculture with other races." Kirkconnell, "Futurities," 13–14.
70 Kirkconnell, "Futurities," 31–4. He also warned against one-child families, on the grounds that the child was overindulged and thus became selfish, ignorant, and prone to "psychic (and consequently physical) damage." They were also obsessed with their mothers and in their teenage years would develop same-sex interests. If this stage were not outgrown, Kirkconnell warned, it gave rise to "homosexual offences, which are thus not the perversion of a normal adult but the result of arrested development."
71 Kirkconnell, "Futurities," 30, 40.
72 McLaren, *Our Own Master Race*, 19–22.
73 Kirkconnell, "Futurities," 36–9.
74 McLaren, *Our Own Master Race*, 9–10.
75 See for example Kirkconnell, letter to his mother, 5 December 1917; Kirkconnell, letter to dad & mother, 22 October 1917; Kirkconnell, letter to dad & mother, 23 December 1917, WK3-10; and Thomas Kirkconnell, letter to Watson, 30 December 1917, WK3-12. Some of this correspondence has recently been cited by Kevin Anderson, "The Cockroaches of Canada"; and Kevin Anderson, *Not Quite Us*. See also Kirkconnell, *Headmaster*, esp. 11–12, 30, and 68–69.
76 Kirkconnell, "Futurities," 43. This differed from Grant, who argued that Canada was "handicapped by the presence of an indigestible mass of

French-Canadians" who were "largely from Brittany and of Alpine origin." Grant, *Passing of the Great Race*, 53, 72.
77 Kirkconnell, "Futurities," 43, 46.
78 His list also included "Hindus." His anti-Semitic ideas were sourced from Woodruff, *Expansion of Races*, 226–41, 381–2; and Fraser, *The Conquering Jew*. On anti-Semitism among eugenicists, see McLaren, *Our Own Master Race*, 78. Though his early anti-Semitism has gone unnoticed, Kirkconnell's later stance has been questioned. See Lipinsky, "Watson Kirkconnell and the Canadian Jewry."
79 Kirkconnell, "Futurities," 47–8.
80 Ibid. An excellent discussion of the long history of the "climatic argument" can be found in Chopra, *Almost Home*, 101–111; see also Winks, *The Blacks in Canada*, 296; and Shepard, *Deemed Unsuitable*.
81 Kirkconnell, "Futurities," 19. Cf. Young, *Colonial Desire*.
82 Kirkconnell, "Futurities," 63.
83 Ibid., 54. See also his note on "Race Suicide" in WK16-10, ECWA. His stance also meant that mission work could be abandoned; there was no point in Anglo-Saxons sacrificing their lives "carrying Christianity to races who have no intention of adopting it."
84 Kirkconnell, "Futurities," 54, 57–8; and Kirkconnell, *Twilight of Liberty*, 73.
85 Kirkconnell, *Slice*, 31. On Paudash, see Benns, "Remembering the 'Gentle Sniper.'"
86 Kirkconnell, "Stone Age Annals of Victoria County," 1, 8–9. Emphasis added. In later bibliographies, he would give the article the more academic and less sensational title "The Amerindian Archaeology of Victoria County." See Snelson, "Bibliography," 107 n177, 108 n183.
87 Kirkconnell, "Stone Age Annals." It is particularly ironic that Kirkconnell does not thank Paudash in the article, all while claiming the land is "ours," given that Paudash would go on to point out errors in the original treaties that would necessitate further treaty-making in the region (see See R. v. Howard [1992]). Instead, Kirkconnell parlayed this research – along with an article on the cephalic index – into a membership in the Royal Anthropological Institute in 1926, his application having been endorsed by race scientist and lifelong racist R. Ruggles Gates. Kirkconnell, *Slice*, 198; Kirkconnell, letter to Gates, 19 October 1926, Reginald Ruggles Gates papers (GB0100 KCLCA K/PP65), 7/5, King's College London Archives; see also his membership application held by the Royal Anthropological Institute (RAI). Thanks to the RAI for providing me with a copy of the latter.

88 Kirkconnell, *Victoria County Centennial History*, 122–35, hereafter cited as VCCH. The book mentions Paudash in passing; see 133.
89 Kirkconnell, VCCH, 9, 10, and chap. 8, "Annals of the Red Man." The heading is intriguing, given that the French were the first settlers in the region. Note also Kirkconnell's use of the past tense – for example, he writes that the Mississaugas "were a tall race" (133).
90 Ibid., 5–6.
91 Ibid., VCCH, 179. Kirkconnell's later comments about Indigenous peoples were imbued with an increased sense of amazement at the sheer timescale involved; see Kirkconnell, *Slice*, 31–2; and Kirkconnell, "Legs to Walk and Eyes to See," typescript, WK29-1, ECWA.
92 Kirkconnell, *Slice*, 134. Given Kirkconnell's love of British imperialism it is fitting that what enabled him to study at Oxford was an Imperial Order Daughters of the Empire (IODE) overseas scholarship. See Pickles, *Female Imperialism and National Identity*, esp. 116–17.
93 Currie, "The Arts and Social Studies," 124–5; and Kirkconnell, *Slice*, 15–21. Kirkconnell later claimed that he was "particularly impressed with the intellectual quality of [his] new Chinese and Hindu colleagues," but, even if true, these impressions were not recorded at the time nor did they perceptibly influence his writings. Kirkconnell, *A Tale of Seven Cities*, 9.
94 Kirkconnell, *Slice*, 122; and "Report of the Examiners," 88, FA 4/11/2/3, Oxford University Archives. The initial draft is not extant, but a glimpse at his essential economic thesis is found in Kirkconnell, "Mechanism and Meliorism." Thanks to Michael Couchman for obtaining a copy of this article for me.
95 See Kirkconnell, *Slice*, 259; the relevant correspondence in WK41-18, ECWA; and Kirkconnell, *International Aspects of Unemployment*, hereafter cited as IAU. The London firm also shopped for an American publisher for the work and eventually found one: Henry Holt and Company, of New York. In March 1923, IAU was included in a list of eight works pitched to Elliott Holt, and was described as a "good book and worth your consideration." Holt accepted and published the book. See Stanley Unwin, letter to Elliott Holt, 5 March 1923, Archives of Henry Holt & Co., box 2, folder 4, Rare Books and Special Collections, Princeton University. However, the book was not immediately commercially successful. Having paid £50 towards its publication, Kirkconnell earned only £6 in royalties on sales of 607 copies by the end of 1923. See "Authors Accounts ledger" (1923), 602, Records of George Allen & Unwin, University of Reading Special Collections (hereafter URSC).

96 Kirkconnell, *IAU*, 39–45; "Prophesied Big Immigrant Rush May Not Come," *Calgary Herald* (14 September 1916), 12; and "Electric Industry and Immigration," *The Gazette* (15 November 1916), 6.
97 Welshman, *Underclass*, 15, 17, 26, and 40.
98 Kirkconnell, *IAU*, 80.
99 Ibid., 95–6. His book can be considered yet another in a line of books expressing racial pessimism during this period; see Brantlinger, *Dark Vanishings*, 191.
100 Kirkconnell, *Slice*, 121. This paragraph is based on my analysis of thirty-one reviews of the book: one from France, two from Australia, three from unidentifiable sources, three from America, four from Canada, and eighteen from the United Kingdom. In terms of reception, two were negative, three were neutral, four were descriptive, and the remaining twenty-two were positive (though only twelve of this group can be considered critical reviews). Nearly all are found in WK4-30, ECWA.
101 Ivanhoe [Alex J. Musgrove], "Civilization's Only Hope Is Internationalism," *Winnipeg Tribune* (16 April 1923), 4 ("prophet"); [untitled, unsigned review], *The Spectator* (18 May 1923), 22 ("profuse"); and "The Break-Down of Industrialism," *Saturday Night* (1923).
102 Chester Lloyd Jones, untitled review of *IAU* in *Ex Libris* 1, no. 1 (February 1924): 243–4 ("mildly"); and "Diagnosing Unemployment," *The Challenge* (6 April 1923): 23–4 ("thorough-going" and "coolie").
103 See for instance "Co-operate or Perish," *The Friend* (30 March 1923; "surely underestimate[es] ... our ignorance of what is due to nature and what to nurture"); "Unemployment and its Remedies," *The Economist* (17 March 1923; "he perhaps exaggerates the influence of heredity"); and R.M. MacIver, "Economics," *Canadian Forum* 37 (October 1923): 24 ("it is far too sweeping to dismiss [significant demographic changes] as due to 'Neomalthusianism'").
104 "'A Sick Civilization': Cerebral Decay and the Elimination of the Unfit," *The Western Daily* (9 April 1923).
105 Ivanhoe, "Civilization's Only Hope is Internationalism"; and "A Reader's Notes," *Manitoba Free Press* (25 September 1923), 1. Decades later, Kirkconnell felt the need to defend the book, and suggested that his "very real sympathy with human distress was secondary to an intellectual interest in the analysis of a complex problem. My diagnosis of the malady was that of the medical school clinic and not that of a man whose family has known disease." Kirkconnell, *Slice*, 121.
106 Moore, *The Clash*, 60–1, 64–65.
107 Avery, *Reluctant Host*, 269 n108.

108 Roy, *The Oriental Question*, 32 and 250 n17; House of Commons, *Debates*, 8 July 1924; and ibid., 1 March 1927.
109 Wesley College merged with Manitoba College to become United College in 1931, and in 1967 it received its charter and became the University of Winnipeg. Kirkconnell, *Slice*, 135; Riddell, letter to Phelps, 17 August 1922, MSS 134 (Arthur Phelps fonds), box 2, folder 2, University of Manitoba Archives (UMA); and Riddell, telegrams to Phelps, 21, 22, and 23 August 1922, MSS 134, box 1, folder 19, UMA. See also Phelps, "Professor Kirkconnell's Book."
110 Kirkconnell, *Slice*, 259; *Twilight*, 74; and *European Elements*, 4.
111 Loewen and Friesen, *Immigrants in Prairie Cities*, 37–8; and Kirkconnell, *Slice*, 297. On Winnipeg during the period prior to Kirkconnell's arrival, see also Korneski, *Race, Nation, and Reform Ideology*.
112 Kirkconnell, *Slice*, 135, and also 36. For a student's reflections on Kirkconnell's teaching during this period, see Duckworth, *One Version of the Facts*, 23, 24, and 29. The success of the book was surely the result of the publisher's efforts; see the promotional pamphlet in WK4-28, ECWA, and the clippings of reviews in WK4-29, ECWA.
113 A glimpse at this milieu is found in Martens, *Over Canadian Trails*, chap. 3; and Xiques, *Margret Laurence*, 107–9. Doody remarks: "There appears to be no rhyme nor reason as to whether it is spelt 'Authors Association' or 'Authors' Association.' Even on official C.A.A. letterhead the apostrophe disappears and reappears seemingly randomly over the years." Doody, "A Union of the Inkpot," 2 n1.
114 The story of Isabel's death is told in Kirkconnell, *Slice*, 55–6; and retold at length in Perkin, "There Were Giants on the Earth in Those Days." See also the brief notice of her death in the *Winnipeg Free Press* (20 July 1925), 5. The children were named after their grandfathers. See Kirkconnell, letter to Arthur Phelps, 4 August 1925, MSS 134, box 2, folder 2, UMA. A glimpse into his time living in residence can be found in his satirical poems from the period, published in *Vox Wesleyana*, the student newspaper. See Kirkconnell, *Slice*, 21; and Snelson, "Bibliography," 117 n255.
115 Kirkconnell, *The European Elegies*; and Kirkconnell, *Slice*, 57–8. For a critical evaluation, see Judith Woodsworth, "The Undoing of Babel." She notes that the translation work he did without any "advice or assistance [from] experts in the various foreign languages he tackled," and overall "the reactions from quite different quarters [we]re quite positive, although they do not constitute nearly as unanimous a chorus of approval as Kirkconnell later claimed." Regarding the figure of fifty languages, she

remarks that some are earlier versions of the same languages and that others can be considered dialects.
116 Kirkconnell, "The Epilogue to Dramatis Personae," 218. Here Kirkconnell is supposedly discussing Robert Browning, but the parallel with his own life is suggestive.
117 Kirkconnell, "A Scotch-Canadian Discovers Poland," 57.
118 Kirkconnell, *European Elegies*, 11.
119 Ibid., 12.
120 Kirkconnell, "Demos and Apollo: An address delivered before the national convention of the CAA, at Ottawa, July, 1927" (manuscript), WK27-18, ECWA. Kirkconnell had been appointed the National Secretary of the CAA in 1925 for a two-year term. See his "Academic Record" (1938), WK7-7a, ECWA; and Kirkconnell, *Slice*, 292.
121 Historian Ryan Eyford argues that, with the case of Icelandic people specifically, their isolation could be used to argue for or against their racial fitness. While Kirkconnell saw isolation as beneficial for a race, commentators in the late-nineteenth century argued that it had left Icelanders backwards and undeveloped. While this argument was initially used against the early Icelandic immigrants when they encountered difficulties, it was quickly put to rest with the ascendancy of racial theories that stressed the superiority of Nordic races. Eyford, *White Settler Reserve*, 29–31.
 This particular section of the book is convincing, however, the broader argument that Icelanders were actively cultivating "white racial identities" is open to the critiques made of many whiteness studies, in that it is more argued that demonstrated (21). Indeed, the book provides no evidence that Icelanders adopted a discourse of race nor that they self-racialized as white. In one instance in which they sought to position themselves as superior than their Indigenous neighbours, they invoked not the language of race but rather of civilization (63 and 136, both citing the same primary document). However, one intriguing but underdeveloped theme was the degree to which Icelandic immigrants understood the treaties that the state was entering into with Indigenous peoples in the region. The book relates at least one example in which Icelanders drew upon the Indigenous peoples' knowledge of the monarch in order to intimidate them, ordering them to perform a certain task "in the name of their great mother, the Queen" (114). On this relationship, see for instance Carter, "Your Great Mother Across the Salt Sea."
122 Kirkconnell, "Demos and Apollo," 2, 3, 13.
123 Kirkconnell's continued belief in hereditarianism led him to publish on the subject of eugenics as late as 1927 but, though privately endorsing

sterilization measures into the 1930s, he did not become involved in any eugenic campaigns nor did he weigh in on Manitoba's heated 1933 sterilization debate. See Kirkconnell, "Mendelism and the Cephalic Index"; "Research into Canadian Rural Decay"; and letter to Gates, 2 January 1934, WK59-8, ECWA.

124 Kirkconnell, "The Genius of Slavonic Poetry." See also the draft in WK27-19, ECWA; and "Proceedings and Members of the Modern Language Association (1928)." For similarly essentialist appraisals, see Kirkconnell, "Ukrainian Poetry"; "Hungary's Linguistic Isolation"; "New Canadians from Hungary"; and "Introduction," in *Hungarian Helicon*, xxxi. The latter two cite Morant, *The Races of Central Europe* (1939).

125 Kitzan, "The Fighting Bishop," 10–12, 16–21; and Kitzan, "Preaching Purity in the Promised Land."

126 Kitzan, "Fighting Bishop," 71–5. According to one estimate, in the summer of 1928 alone Lloyd sent seventy thousand letters! Little wonder some critics called him a "National Nuisance." See "Ukrainian Pastors Protest Anglican Bishop's Stand," *Winnipeg Tribune* (23 July 1928), 3.

127 Kirkconnell, "Western Immigration," 706–7. Also reprinted in Palmer, *Immigration and the Rise of Multiculturalism*, 56–7.

128 It is difficult to determine Lloyd's conception of race. He sometimes drew on biological notions of race, quoted approvingly a professor who warned against the mixing of superior and inferior races, and spoke out against the "mongrelisation" of Canada. He also praised Frank Oliver for bringing in "English-speaking and Scandinavian immigrants," which suggests that he too was influenced by a racism that revered Nordic races. However, his repeated efforts to "train" foreigners to become moral, sober, Protestant Canadians suggests that he believed that European immigrants could improve, despite their racial differences. Kitzan, "Fighting Bishop," 36, 39, 47–51, 81–4, 91.

129 Kirkconnell, "Western Immigration," 706, 707. Emphasis added.

130 Ibid. See also Dreisziger, "Kirkconnell and the Cultural Credibility Gap," 93–4.

131 Kirkconnell, "Western Immigration," 707.

132 Quoted in FitzGerald and Cook-Martín, *Culling the Masses*, 145, table 4.1.

133 Kelley and Trebilcock, *The Making of the Mosaic*, 538 n224; and Beaud and Prévost, "Immigration, Eugenics and Statistics," 15.

134 Craig, *Racial Attitudes in English-Canadian Fiction*, 70, 72, 72 n31.

135 Kirkconnell had also considered as titles "The Greatness of Europe" and "The Creative Continent." See Kirkconnell, letter to J.M. Dent and Sons,

2 May 1928, WK5-12, ECWA; and Kirkconnell, letter to Ms. Davidson, 26 October 1928, WK5-12, ECWA.
136 Kirkconnell, *The European Heritage*, v.
137 Ibid., 1.
138 Ibid., 2–3, 4.
139 Kirkconnell, "Futurities," 48. The Jewish population figure is taken from Trachtenberg, "The Jewish Community of Winnipeg."
140 Kirkconnell, *European Heritage*, 69, 66.
141 Dreisziger, "Kirkconnell and the Cultural Credibility Gap," 91. For a more critical take, see Kevin Anderson, *Not Quite Us*, 108.
142 The spacing before the punctation is in the original. "The European Heritage by Watson Kirkconnell," unsigned and undated review, J.M. Dent & Sons Records (hereafter "Dent Records"), 1834–1986 (#11043), subseries 1.1.2 (Other Authors), folder 1740, Louis Round Wilson Special Collections Library, University of North Carolina at Chapel Hill; and Davidson, letter to Kirkconnell, 22 March 1929 (and enclosed copy of the "Reader's Report"), WK5-12, ECWA; and J.M.R., "Canned Culture," *The Cambridge Review* 51, no. 1265 (6 June 1930): 478, a copy of which can be found in WK77-12, ECWA.
143 See for instance Kirkconnell, "Proletarian Poetry"; and Kirkconnell, "Poetry and National Life."
144 Kirkconnell, "Translations From Greek Poets"; "The Greek Epigram"; "Founder of Modern Slovak Literature"; "Poems From the Danish"; "The Patriarch of Western Letters"; "Poems from Twelve Languages (Translated by Watson Kirkconnell)"; and "Karel Čapek and R. U. R." His translations notably did not include many French authors.
145 Palmer, "Reluctant Hosts," 81–118.
146 Dreisziger, "Kirkconnell and the Cultural Credibility Gap," 94; Bonavia, "Access to Ethno-Cultural Material," 80; and Perkin, "There Were Giants," 109 ("father").
147 Kirkconnell, *Slice*, 93. Eight different programs were issued throughout the festival; see Snelson, "Bibliography," 335–7 n1768.
148 Cf. Lipinsky, "The Agony of Israel," 60.
149 Kirkconnell, *Slice*, 35; Kirkconnell, *Elegies*, 12; and Judith Woodsworth, "The Undoing of Babel," 16. See also Dreisziger, "Kirkconnell and the Cultural Credibility Gap," 91.
150 Kirkconnell, *Slice*, 60, 115–16 n246. Even this trial was a large undertaking. As he wrote to an acquaintance at the time: "My waking hours seem pretty well monopolized by my baby boys and my 'Outline of European Poetry.'" From this, it seems that he was now caring for his children at

least part of the time. Kirkconnell, letter to Dr MacMechan (1 August 1927), WK30-42, ECWA. See also his boastful memo to Phelps in WK5-9, in which he compares his larger task to that of Alexander Pope. On the periodical, see the entry in the Modern Magazines Project Canada, https://web.archive.org/web/20171121045418/http://modmag.ca/whm/.
151 Kirkconnell, letter to F. P. Grove, 22 March 1929, MSS 002, box 2, folder 6, UMA.
152 Kirkconnell, *North American Book of Icelandic Verse*. In his poem "Intolerance," published the same year, Kirkconnell suggested that both linguistic intolerance and notions of race had divided humanity and led to deadly conflicts. Kirkconnell, *Tide of Life*, 66.
153 Indeed, he would later speculate to Grove that perhaps he would have to settle for "posthumous recognition" but that in the end the "mountain will, I am confident, come to Mahomet." Kirkconnell, letter to F. P. Grove, 18 May 1929, MSS 002, box 2, folder 6, UMA.
154 See Kirkconnell, "Towards a National Literature," typescript; Kirkconnell, "Icelandic-Canadian Poetry"; and Wilson MacDonald, letter to Kirkconnell, 5 February 1935, WK30-32, ECWA.
155 Kirkconnell, "Polish Miscellany"; and Aunt Ella [Watson], letter to Watson Kirkconnell, 28 August 1935, WK28-85, ECWA. Emphasis in the original.
156 Iacovetta, *Gatekeepers*, 78.
157 Kirkconnell, letter to Grove, 18 May 1929, MSS 002, box 2, folder 6, UMA. In this letter he wrote that he was prepared to "postpone having a home of my own in order that my savings and energy may go into launching the scheme." If worst came to worst, he was prepared to "plod ahead and try peddling a volume at a time. But that would probably mean absentee paternity for a while longer, and flesh and blood protest." All adjusted figures in this work were calculated using the Bank of Canada's inflation calculator, www.bankofcanada.ca/rates/related/inflation-calculator/.
158 Perkin, *Morning in His Heart*, 21; and "Winnifred Hope Kirkconnell (25 August 1900 – 9 July 1986): A Tribute by J. R. C. Perkin" (Wolfville Baptist Church, 12 July 1986), 2, a copy of which can be found in 88-16 (IN-17), Watson Kirkconnell papers, series 3, file 1, University of Winnipeg Archives (UWA). Sadly – and tellingly – more information about Hope is found in the eulogy that Perkins authored than in her husband's memoir.
159 Kirkconnell, *Slice*, 60–1; and Kirkconnell, "A Canadian Meets the Magyars," 2. In the latter, he recalled that 1930 also saw two more of his publishers, Graphic and Ariston, go bankrupt. In 1931, he privately

remarked: "Only a miracle, moreover, will by 1932 have restored my finances from the ravages of the Carrier debacle." Kirkconnell, letter to Howard Angus Kennedy, 14 February 1931, WK30-43, ECWA.
160 Nayar, *Colonial Voices*, 18. Italics removed.
161 J.S. Woodsworth, *Strangers Within Our Gates*. On this work, see McKay, *Reasoning Otherwise*, 378–84; and Daniel Coleman, "J.S. Woodsworth and the Discourse of White Civility." See also J.S. Woodsworth, Introduction to *Bi-Lingual Schools in Canada*, by C.B. Sissons, 3–6. When examining Woodsworth's book, it is important to remember that some sections of it (such as the one on Ukrainians) were written by journalist Arthur R. Ford.
162 Kirkconnell, *Slice*, 75. His strategy was to write the Consulates of the various countries and inquire if they were aware of any poetry written in Canada by people of that nationality, though very often the officials replied that they were unaware of any such writing. See the letters in WK30-5, ECWA.
163 Kirkconnell, "Hungary's Linguistic Isolation," 99.
164 See for example Kirkconnell, "A Scotch-Canadian Discovers Poland." Note also the fishing metaphor in *Slice*, 75, in which he is the lone diver to discover the greatest variety of first-class seafood (New Canadian literature) while the fishermen on the surface content themselves with only two species of small but abundant fish (French and English Canadian literature). Here is a clear suggestion that so-called new Canadian cultural works are to be "discovered" and translated for anglophone Canadians' consumption.
165 Kirkconnell, letter to the editor of the *Dalhousie Review*, 1 January 1934.
166 Kirkconnell, "Ukrainian Canadiana"; and Kirkconnell, letter to the Editor of *Canadian Forum*, 11 November 1933, WK28-84, ECWA. The contents of Bobersky's library were later donated to the Oseredok Ukrainian Cultural and Educational Centre (UCEC) in Winnipeg. The UCEC cautions that the size of the library should not be exaggerated as at that time several Ukrainian Canadian reading halls or national homes in Canada would have had substantially larger libraries. Oseredok UCEC, correspondence with the author, 1 February 2018. On Bobersky's activities in Canada, see Gerus, "Ukrainian Diplomatic Representation in Canada."
167 Kirkconnell, *Slice*, 76–7.
168 Kirkconnell, *North American Book of Icelandic Verse*, 1–5.

169 Kirkconnell also used the tapestry as a metaphor for language itself, "into which the individual and the nation weave their deepest and most significant thoughts and emotions." Kirkconnell, "Hungary's Linguistic Isolation," 92. Others applied the metaphor in unlikely places. For instance, Gibbon's friend Frederick Niven would later write that the tapestry metaphor came to mind when he read *Canadian Mosaic*; see Niven, "Dominion Tapestry," *The Sunday Times* (6 March 1939), 7.

170 Kirkconnell, "New Canadians in Manitoba," typescript [1932?], WK28-72, ECWA. This piece was originally prepared as a chapter for an edited volume being planned by Robert Watson, although it appears it was never published. See the relevant correspondence and enclosures in the same file. Kirkconnell's racial essentialism led him to some conclusions that are now rather humorous, such as his assessment of Frederick Philip Grove's "brooding intensity" as "peculiarly Scandinavian," in light of the fact that the fellow in question later turned out to be a German man born Felix Paul Greve.

171 See for example the *Manitoba Poetry Chapbook*, which he edited.

172 Kirkconnell, "Towards a National Literature," typescript.

173 Kirkconnell, "Icelandic-Canadian Poetry," 331. He maintained that Icelandic was the most important of the third Canadian poetry.

174 Ibid., 344. He made similar remarks in "Ukrainian Poetry in Canada," 146. In 2016, there were 101,795 Canadians of Icelandic descent, over 1,400 of whom spoke Icelandic. This information taken from Statistics Canada, *Canada [Country] and Canada [Country]* (table), Census Profile, 2016 Census.

175 Kirkconnell, "The First Magyar-American Poet," 1. A copy can be found in WK41-7, ECWA.

176 Kirkconnell, *Canadian Overtones*. Of all Kirkconnell's efforts to draw attention to the artistic works of new Canadians, Dreisziger dubbed this work the "most substantive." Similarly, Snelson described the book as "the first study in Canadian multiculturalism." Dreisziger, "Kirkconnell and the Cultural Credibility Gap," 91; and Snelson, "Introduction," in *Morning in His Heart*, 71. Kirkconnell described it as "Pioneer work in unearthing, evaluating, and translating the foreign-language literature of Canada." See his "Academic Record," 6, in WK7-7a, ECWA.

177 Ewach, letter to Kirkconnell, 14 and 16 June 1933, WK6-3, ECWA.

178 Kirkconnell, *Canadian Overtones*, 4.

179 Ibid., 4.

180 Ibid., 4. His critique of the exclusive interest in folk cultures was perhaps written in relation to the CPR folk festivals organized by Gibbon, of which he had formerly approved. See Kirkconnell, "Western Immigration," 708.
181 Kirkconnell, *Canadian Overtones*, 6.
182 Kirkconnell, *Flying Bull*, 158–61. This vision Kirkconnell would repeat in a great number of future texts. See for instance Kirkconnell, "Canadians All," 20–1; and Kirkconnell, "Introduction," in *The Polish Past in Canada*, 11.
183 Kirkconnell, *Canadian Overtones*, 5.
184 Sarath, *Musical Theory Through Improvisation*, 308. Italics in the original. As for the origins of this metaphor, recall that Kirkconnell had devoted some time to the study of music; see *Slice*, chap. 8, esp. 86–7.
185 Snelson, in *Morning in His Heart*, 71, wondered what was the reaction to this volume, and apparently it was not all positive. One reviewer, writing in *The Slavonic Review*, remarked: "in a trenchant preface he puts up a plea, which has something pathetic for all its restraint and eloquence, for the due recognition of [this poetry]." However, they added that Canadians were nevertheless indebted to him for the "pearls" he had found. N.B.J., "Canadian Overtones," 729–30.
186 Kirkconnell, *Canadian Overtones*, 4–6.
187 Kirkconnell, *Titus the Toad*, 58–9. On the illustrator, see the untitled and undated note in Clarke, Irwin & Company Limited fonds, RC0076, box 1, file 6, William Ready Division of Archives and Research Collections, McMaster University Library (ARCMUL).
188 Perkin, *Morning in His Heart*, 51–2.
189 Kirkconnell, "Western Immigration," 707.
190 Kirkconnell, "The Priest's Tale of the Red River Tragedy," in *The Flying Bull*, 138–47. "Indian" and "Eskimo" stories supposedly form the basis for a number of poems in the volume (see for example ibid., 13, 28, and 40).
191 In his memoirs, he clearly states that the poem was concerned with "the problem of atavism in the French-Indian cross." Kirkconnell, *Slice*, 49.
192 Kirkconnell, "The Seven Oaks Massacre," in *Centennial Tales and Selected Poems*, 40.
193 Austin, *Fear of a Black Planet*, 38–40.
194 Kirkconnell, "New Canadians in Manitoba," typescript [1931–32], WK28-72.
195 ("On peut adjouter du même la poésie qui se mèle dans le folklore des races sauvages indigènes.") Kirkconnell, "La Jeune Poésie Française au Canada," typescript [1931], WK28-82, ECWA. This was later published,

although I have been unable to locate a copy; see Snelson, "Bibliography," 121 n289.
196 Kirkconnell, "The Literature of the New-Canadians," 57.
197 Kirkconnell, "Towards a National Literature," 14, typescript, WK28-83, ECWA. See also his "Towards a National Literature," *Author's Bulletin* (May 1932): 23–4.
198 Kirkconnell, "Manitoba Symphony," in *Manitoba Essays*, 8 and 9. An earlier section worries: "The latest census shows the Anglo-Saxons / Not half our population, and their births / So few they'll vanish in a century." Ibid., 6.
199 Census data cited in Miller, *Skyscrapers Hide the Heavens*, 314.
200 Kirkconnell, "Thoughts for Dominion Day," 2–4. Note also in this article his early critique of the Aryan race theories of Nazi Germany.

CHAPTER TWO

1 Palmer, "Interview with Robert England" (typescript), 39, Howard Palmer fonds, box 5, folder 28, University of Calgary, Archives and Special Collections (cited hereafter in the following manner: HP5-28, UCASC). Palmer's formulation of the question appears odd, as in the written version of the paper in question the author did not quote this early section on "eugenic types" but rather the later section on "stockbreeders"; see Keyfitz, "The Descendants of English Speakers," 67.
2 I began working from what appeared to be latest revision of the transcripts of this interview. However, I later decided to listen to the original interviews, as the finding aid stated that there were nine audiocassettes. Part of this no doubt stemmed from the biographer's romantic impulse to know their subject as well as possible, by hearing their voice, while another part was the historian's fear of leaving good evidence under an unturned stone. Then came the bad news: eight of the nine cassettes were completely blank. The ninth, however, contained just over twenty minutes of the interview and, in a fortunate twist of fate, the section preserved was most germane to my thesis. When I began listening, I immediately realized that the transcript deviated significantly from the actual interview. In this instance, the transcript reads "Physical, I mean physical"; however, in the recording England can be heard to say "Physical, physical in the main." All such amendments I have placed in brackets. See Palmer, "Interview with Robert England" (typescript), quote at 83–4, HP5-28; and the unlabelled tape in HP3-29, UCASC.
3 Earlier in the interview he had discussed his frustration with the Canadian census for treating ethnicity as patrilineal, arguing that the

mother's lineage was just as important. See Palmer, "Interview with Robert England" (typescript), 39.
4 Little wonder that England did not subscribe to the belief that Nordics were superior, given that he understood himself to be a member of a different European race. Palmer, "Interview with Robert England" (typescript), 85–6. Here the transcript reads "Catholic" groups, although he clearly says "Celtic." The phrase "God has written a line of his thought on the cradle of each race," which England frequently quoted, is attributed to Italian politician and revolutionary Giuseppe Mazzini.
5 For genealogical information, consult RE6-15, LAC.
6 England, *Memoirs*, 5; England, letter to Jindra Kulich (Director, Centre for Continuing Education, UBC), 14 July 1982, Continuing Education fonds, box 7, file 15, University of British Columbia Archives (cited hereafter in the following manner: CE7-15, UBCA), emphasis in the original; and Barnes, "Living, Learning, Remembering." For some recollections from his childhood, see England, "Irish Memories."
7 England, *Memoirs*, 7. Such internationally best-selling novels "promoted a version of Canadian identity that championed a link between Anglo-Saxon imperialism and Christianity." Cabajsky, "Canada," 139. See also Karr, *Authors and Audiences*, esp. chap. 5.
8 England, *Memoirs*, 3 and 7.
9 Ibid., 9. After moving to Canada, he was surprised to find that some schoolchildren read the same textbooks he had used back in Ireland. According to historian of education Kerry Alcorn, the man responsible, Egerton Ryerson, felt that the use of American textbooks was "anti-British and unpatriotic," and so implemented the use of the *Irish Readers*. "Though neither English nor Canadian in origin, these pro-imperial volumes were a positive alternative, believed Ryerson, to anything coming from the United States." Alcorn, *Border Crossings*, 23.
10 England, *Memoirs*, 10–11; J. A. Davidson, letter of reference for Robert England, 4 May 1914, in RE1-2; the matriculation certificates in RE8, LAC; the Irish census for 1911, http://www.census.nationalarchives.ie/pages/1911/Armagh/Portadown_Urban/Bridge_Street/299330/; and "Passenger Lists: 1865–1935," RG76-C, roll T-4721, LAC.
11 England did not provide a date in his memoirs, but he appears on a passenger list as having arrived in New York on 24 October 1914; see "Passenger Lists: 1865–1935." He had only passed the matriculation examination for the University of Durham on 6 July and for the University of Belfast on 14 October; see both certificates in RE8, LAC (this oversized box is not subdivided into folders).

12 He appeared in the 1916 census as living in Last Mountain, Saskatchewan and gave his occupation as minister. See "Census returns for 1916 Census of Prairie Provinces," 19, RG31 C-1, Statistics of Canada fonds, T-21937, LAC. According to his *Memoirs*, 27, he lived in southern Saskatchewan and stayed with a farm family.
13 On his time in the military, see England, *Memoirs*, 11–12, 182–9; and England, *Recollections of a Nonagenarian*.
14 England, *Memoirs*, 12–15; and Roe, "Teachers and Schools," 22.
15 England, *Memoirs*, 7, but see also 12 and 185; and the medical history found in his military files, http://www.bac-lac.gc.ca/eng/discover/military-heritage/first-world-war/personnelrecords/Pages/item.aspx?IdNumber=379700.
16 England, *Recollections of a Nonagenarian*, np ("the amazing variety of recruits of so many ethnic groups. Germans from Lunenburg [Nova Scotia], Slavs, French, Italians, from all of North America"); Palmer, "Interview with Robert England" (handwritten notes), 6, HP5-23, UCASC; and Thelma and Bob [England], letter to Marie and Jean [Lanctôt], 8 September 1938, MG31 E71, vol. 47, fonds Jean-Baptiste Lanctôt, LAC. Italics added. (*Pro patria*, a Latin phrase meaning "for one's country," was the official motto of the Royal Canadian Regiment, or RCR, with which he fought.)
17 Clendenan, "Guardians of the Future," 832.
18 England, *Memoirs*, 12–15, 28; and Palmer, interview with England (typescript), 11, HP5-28, UCASC. "I had lived on farms, I had worked on farms and except for the war injury I probably would have continued as a farmer." Details on his injuries can be found in his military records. See also his remarks in "Ethnic Settlers in Western Canada," 22, an earlier draft of which can be found in RE5-1, LAC.
19 England, *Memoirs*, 129.
20 Ibid., 12, 130. See also W. Foran, telegraph to Robert England, n.d., in RE1-1, LAC.
21 For a brief overview of the author's life and work, see McAlpin, "(John) Herbert Quick."
22 England, *Memoirs*, 16–17, quote at 47; Palmer, interview with England (handwritten notes), 3, HP5-23, UCASC.
23 Clendenan, "Guardians of the Future," 832.
24 England, *Memoirs*, 12, 35, 174–5; Melis, "J.T.M. Anderson"; and Pitsula, *Keeping Canada British*, 215. On the discontinuation of the directorship, see "Will the Good Work Go On?", *Saskatoon Daily Star* (12 October 1922), 4.
25 England, "First Quarterly Report. Masonic Scholarships – 1922"

(Confidential; 31 July 1922), 9 (pagination added), RE5-24, LAC; and "A Bit of Biography" [summary of a radio talk, c.1938], RE4-3, LAC.
26 Palmer, interview with England (typescript), 2–3, HP5-28, UCASC; and Foght, *A Survey of Education*. England's marked-up copy can be found in RE9-7, LAC. On the Foght report, see Alcorn, *Border Crossings*, chap. 5, esp. 92 and 104–7.
27 England, *Memoirs*, 18.
28 Clendenan, "Guardians of the Future," 832; and Daniel Coleman, *White Civility*, 10. A teacherage is a house that is provided for a teacher by the school.
29 Clendanen, "Guardians of the Future," 832.
30 Roe, "Teachers and Schools," 9, 22–5. This scene is shown at the end of the "Nation Builders" film (see n34, below). See also "Forms Scout Troup Among Ruthenians," *The Leader-Post* (12 April 1921), 8.
31 England, "Hafford School Sports," 11,16. The government apparently approved of such extracurricular activities; the "Nation Builders" film declared that Boy Scots was the "greatest 'get together' movement in the world and is supported by people of every race and creed." See also Woodger, "Whiteness and Ambiguous Canadianization."
32 "New Canadian School Problems Are Discussed," *Star-Phoenix* [Saskatoon] (1 April 1921); 5. While he did not speak of it until years later, lice was a problem that the school faced: "we got lice in our heads too, but with coal-oil and clippers and prison hair-cuts we won that fight." England, "Ethnic Studies in Western Canada," 22.
33 England, *Memoirs*, 18–20. "This visit across northern Saskatchewan with Dr. Anderson gave us a glimpse of the conditions confronting his work, conditions he hoped to change along the lines of the Foght Report," he wrote. See also "Social and Personal," *The Leader-Post* (3 September 1921), 6. On the importance of cleanliness to social reformers during this era, see Valverde, *Light, Soap, and Water*.
34 Examples of the press coverage include "Teacher of New Canadians Gets a Degree," *Saskatoon Daily Star* (3 June 1921), 17; and ibid., *Star-Phoenix* (4 June 1921), 33. Perhaps as a result, he was asked to give a number of speeches. See for instance England, *Memoirs*, 22; England, "How the Teacher's Lot May Be Improved"; and "Noted Speakers Will Attend Convention of Saskatchewan Education Association Here," *The Leader-Post* [Regina] (5 March 1921), 2; and "New Canadian School Problems Are Discussed," *Star-Phoenix* [Saskatoon] (1 April 1921); 5. Finally, the Englands and their school appeared in a documentary film entitled "Nation Building in Saskatchewan: The Ukrainians" (1921), which can be

found at LAC (R15332-0-8-E). On the film, see Zaporzan and Klymasz, *Film and the Ukrainians in Canada*, 3–5; Petty, "(Re)Visioning Histories," esp. 327–31; and Hewitt, "Policing the Promised Land," 316.

35 Pitched as a war memorial, the program was intended to promote nation building in rural Saskatchewan by recruiting prospective teachers and providing $300 in financial assistance to enable them to complete their professional training at the Normal School in Saskatoon. In return, the teachers were required to teach for one school year in a rural district. Set up with $20,000 in contributions from Freemasons in the province, the program ran for only two years (1922 and 1923). Copies of the correspondence relating to England's educational certification can be found in RE1-2, LAC, while the certificate itself is found in RE8, LAC. On the program, see England, *Central European Immigrant in Canada* (hereafter cited as CEIC), appendix A; Weir, "Introduction," in ibid.; and England, *Memoirs*, 22–4. It is unclear whether England was a Mason at this time; however, he did join the Canada Lodge in Britain when he moved there in 1925. See Willis C. Cooper (Secretary, Canada Lodge), letter to England, 30 October 1950, and the attached demit, in RE1-4, LAC.

36 See England, *Memoirs*, 15–16; and, for some of the books he was reading during this period, his correspondence with the librarian of the Provincial Normal School, in RE5-23, LAC.

37 England, *Memoirs*, 47.

38 England's letters of reference for the scholarship (written by O.D. Skelton and W.A. Carrothers) can be found in the RE1-2, LAC. The scholarship had been introduced in 1919 and was intended to be a memorial for the Canadian soldiers who died in France during the Great War; see the provincial Department of Education's *Annual Report*, 21–2. The scholarship appears to still be on the books but it has not been awarded for decades.

39 England, *Memoirs*, 24–5; Palmer, interview with England (handwritten), 5, HP5-23, UCASC ("evangelist"); and England, "Reminiscences of a Pioneer," 23 ("crusader"). It is unclear what other positions he had been offered, with the exception of the Hafford Mission, but it is worth noting that he was the highest paid of the Masonic Scholarship Teachers. See the "Masonic Scholarship Students Definitely Placed," copies of which are found in RE5-23, LAC. He was paid $1,500 (or the equivalent of around $22,000 in 2019), while the next highest received $1,300.

40 England, "First Quarterly Report," 32 and 31.

41 Ibid., 4 and 10. Emphasis in the original.

42 Ibid., 8. Emphasis in the original.

43 Ibid., 7–8. Emphasis in the original.

44 Ibid., 10.
45 Ibid., 30–1. Cf. England, *Memoirs*, 24.
46 Ibid., 9, 10, and 32.
47 Reid, "Saskatchewan Liberal Machine," 27 and 38.
48 Palmer, "Responses to Foreign Immigration," 110.
49 Pitsula, *Keeping Canada British*, 168–72; England, "First Quarterly Report," 20; and England, "How the Teacher's Lot May Be Improved" (typescript), 2, 9, RE5-23, LAC. His use of the term race up to this point was remarkably elastic, writing in this address that "a new race of teachers" was springing up.
50 England, *Memoirs*, 21; and England, "First Quarterly Report," 8, 25.
51 Kyba, "Anderson, James Thomas Milton"; and England, *Memoirs*, 176.
52 England, *Memoirs*, 25 and 28.
53 Kyba, "Anderson, James Thomas Milton"; Pitsula, *Keeping Canada British*; and England, *Memoirs*, 176–7.
54 England, "Address; Luncheon by Alumni to Graduates," 2, RE4-8, LAC; and England, *Memoirs*, 25.
55 England's later explanation that he "had come across Le Play a great deal in the sociology of the period" seems unlikely. So far as I can determine, none of the introductions to sociology on his reading list made any reference to Le Play. McDougall's book seems to be the only link, and in it he argued that the work of the Le Play school was "entirely ignored by the other French sociologists and anthropologists. It is seldom referred to by them, and outside France it has not received the attention it deserves." McDougall, *The Group Mind*, 232. In 1970, Le Play's biographer concluded that "there is not much evidence that he was widely read, or that his work was closely followed up," although a decade later another scholar argued that his work was taken up in North America by such figures as Leon Gérin, the so-called "father of Canadian sociology." Palmer, "Interview with Robert England" (typescript), 2, HP5-28, UCASC; Brooke, *Le Play*, 135; and Silver, "Introduction," in Le Play, *On Family, Work, and Social Change*, 124.
56 McDougall, *The Group Mind*, 231. While *The Group Mind* was poorly received by his peers, some Canadians engaged with it; see for instance Moodie, "McDougall's Conception of the Group Mind." On McDougall, see his "William McDougall"; Drever, "McDougall, William"; and Farr, "The Social Psychology of William McDougall." Farr ends by noting that *The Group Mind* may have influenced Hitler. In fact, the far right continued to utilize McDougall's work through the end of the 1990s; see for instance Lamb, "Individual & Group Character."

57 ["L'Assimilation des peuples de L'Europe de L'Est – dans la province de Saskatchewan, Canada (particulièrement à l'égard des Ukrainiens)."] All translations are my own. A copy of the thesis, as well as his notes from the period, can be found in RE6-23, LAC. A copy of the "Livre de l'étudient, Université de Paris, 1923–24," which belongs with this material, is found in RE3-24, LAC; a note regarding the defence and written assignments from some of his courses are found in RE4-3, LAC; and other relevant materials are found in RE7-13, LAC. See also England, *Memoirs*, 37; and England, letter to Palmer, 19 August 1978, HP5-24, UCASC. On Le Play, in addition to the works already cited, see Clark, *Prophets and Patrons*, esp. 104–6; and Horne, *A Social Laboratory for Modern France*, esp. 41–5 and 107–9.
58 Clark, *Prophets and Patrons*, 104–6.
59 On Binet, see Kevles, *In the Name of Eugenics*, 76–9.
60 England, "L'Assimilation," 6 ("Frederic Le Play, pour ainsi dire, est à la sociologie ce qui Alfred Binet est à la psychologie"). Pagination added.
61 Despite the yearlong study of Le Play, too much emphasis should not be placed on this or any one thinker in England's intellectual development. Asked in retirement what authors had been most influential on his personal philosophy, England demurred. "I think that I can't say that I've been very devoted to any one person." Palmer, interview with England (typescript), 29, HP5-28, UCASC. England's early interest in Le Play did shape the surveys that were conducted by the Masonic Scholarship teachers, but he described the year in Paris as an opportunity to "re-examine [his] views on the assimilation problem" and would later describe as "naïve" Le Play's faith in "exact factual analysis as a basis for reform" (England, CEIC, vii; and England, *Memoirs*, 37).

Throughout his life England remained ideologically nonpartisan, going so far as to argue: "Ideologies are idols, and it would profit more to bow down to wood or stone." As a result, while he read widely in a variety of disciplines, no single one held sway. "It is not possible to foresee the kind of reaction that any one course of study may produce," he wrote. "My Normal School and teacher training has left me somewhat skeptical of much that passes for pedagogy and educational psychology. My study of socialism and communism and my reading of economics never made me accept with metaphysical awe the invisible hand of laissez-faire myth or on the other hand the tender omniscient mother-state." England, "Address; Luncheon by Alumni to Graduates of University of Manitoba Convocation, May, 1938" (typescript), 3, RE4-8, LAC; and England, *Memoirs*, 38–9. For some of his comments on capitalism and socialism, see his "Gods of the Copybook Headings."

62 England, "L'Assimilation," 7 ("la psychologie-socio-dynamique").
63 England, "First Quarterly Report," 25.
64 England, "L'Assimilation," 7–8 ("Il y a, nous disent les psychologistes, quelques enfants d'une intelligence supérieure et malheureusement quelques-uns d'une intelligence inférieure. Nous apprenons ainsi la force du facteur de l'hérédité. Mais, l'homme est presque toujours ce que son milieu social et son hérédité le font. Ce qui est alors le devoir de la psychologie sociale, c'est d'étudier le milieu social"). This belief was long held among Saskatchewan educators, so it is unsurprising that England went on to argue that Binet's studies would be greatly valuable for pedagogy. See "Special Provision Should be Made for Children Possessing High or Subnormal Mentality," *The Leader-Post* (31 March 1921), 2. This article reported on the convention of the Saskatchewan Education Association, at which England spoke. The headline referred to a speech given by Dr J.S. Huff, the provincial commissioner of education, who discussed the high numbers of "apparently defective and hopeless children" and advocated the use of the Binet-Simon intelligence test in schools to identify them.
65 See Clark, *Prophets and Patrons*, 111; and, on the Collège, Bruant, "Le Collège libre des sciences sociales." England read Maroussem, found his works "very suggestive," and cited him in his *thèse* – a wise move, as Maroussem would sit on the jury that examined it. See England, "L'assimilation," esp. 8, 14–15; and the invitation to the thesis defense found in RE6-23, LAC.
66 Goldberg, *The Racial State*, 43; and Daniel Coleman, *White Civility*, 11. Note that Coleman does not use Goldberg's terms, but rather seems to have been more influenced by Mikhail Bakhtin's work on time. For a more detailed explanation, see his "From Contented Civility to Contending Civilities," esp. 231–7.
67 Charles Mills questioned Goldberg's distinction and suggested that historians of racism re-evaluate it, but this re-evaluation has yet to appear. See Pateman and Mills, *The Contract and Domination*, 6. Peter Wade has argued that instead of this binary, it might be more productive to think in terms of "changing constellations and articulations of race-culture hybrids, in which a discourse of culture has always been important ... but in which some reference to nature is also always present, even if only by using racialized phenotype as a cue to discrimination." Wade, "The Presence and Absence of Race," 48. See also Maldonado-Torres, "The time and space of race," esp. 80–1; and Goldberg, "Call and Response," esp. 92–6.
68 England, "L'Assimilation," i. The original reads: "A. General: Chapitres I) La Problème, II) Le Pays (Saskatchewan), III) Le Peuple (Ukrainien), IV)

Les Moyens d'Assimilation (Les Ecoles [sic] rurales) B. Particulier V) Le District (Slawa près de Hafford, Sask.) C. VII) [sic] Conclusion."
69 England, "L'Assimilation," 17–18 ("ni l'anglais, ni le français n'est parlé. Les coutumes, les habitudes, les vêtements, les superstitions, restent les mêmes qu'en Europe. Le problème est d'assimiler tous ces peoples au milieu canadien"), 19 ("[les français et les anglais] se sont réunis pour bâtir une nation").
70 England, *Memoirs*, 20 (food), 27 (did not learn Ukrainian); England, "Pioneer Group Settlers in Western Canada," typescript (1976), 20, RE5-1, LAC; and Palmer, interview with England (typescript), 83, HP5-28, UCASC. Speaking of J.T.M. Anderson's views on assimilation, he remarked: "I remember he would be happy if the young people would get away from the head dress, you know in the old days, the shawl around the head, and I think that was, he was think [sic] that was alright, until he probably found my wife [around Slawa with a shawl around her head. Then he'd probably take a different view!]" However, elsewhere – early on, at least – England expressed his belief that clothing was an element of culture that required assimilating.
71 England, "L'Assimilation," 19–20 ("au sein de l'âme du Canada il y a les rêves indistincts des idéals d'autres nations, enfoncés dans sa subconscience. Rome tomba à cause des barbares au-dehors. Le Canada doit trouver un moyen d'assimiler ses différent peoples du dedans, s'il veut vivre").
72 England, "L'Assimilation," 22 ("écrits dans leur langues natales et cultivent soigneusement l'amour de leur patrie quelquefois vraiment avec un air d'hostilité contre le Canada et les institutions Canadiennes"), 58–9 ("un milieu Canadien, mais en quelque sorte dans un milieu oppose aux ideals du Canada"; see also 52), 24–5 ("gardent la mémoire des autres pays ... Par conséquent, il y a beaucoup de choses à oublier et quelques sacrifices à faire pour que Canada ne manqué pas sa destinée"), 49 ("une preuve de la communication de pensée presque psychique parmi un people de la même race").
73 England, "L'Assimilation," 47 ("Ce type est court[,] épais et trapu plutôt que vice versa, ni beau ni léger dans les mouvements. Le visage st large avec les yeux éloignes l'un de l'autre et les pommelles saillantes; le nez est large et camus plutôt que ciselé et aquilin; le front est renfrogné et l'expression va de la morosité jusqu'à la sérénité mais elle est peu souvent animée ou réjouie. Les yeux sont d'un gris bleuâtre, et les cheveux sont blonds dans l'enfance, si bien qu'ils ne sont jamais tout-a-fait blonds comme ceux des Scandinaves. Avec l'âge les cheveux deviennent châtain

enfonce. Toute la suggestion est celle de force de confiance et d'une certaine lourdeur. Néanmoins l'excitation ou l'émotion éclaire les visages naturellement dénués d'expression").

74 England, "L'Assimilation," 50–1 ("mal instruits[,] ignorants[,] et pauvres. Leur assimilation doit nécessairement prendre beaucoup de temps"; see also 44), 48 ("On peut si demander pourquoi ce people ancien n'a pas joué un rôle important dans l'histoire du monde. C'est peut-être à cause d'un certain manqué d'énergie de solidarité et de chefs. De plus leur développement politique et cultural a été retarde par les invasions de Tartares et Turcs").

75 England, "L'Assimilation," 41 ("est étrangère, et on remarque que cette population augmente toujours"), 43 ("d'autres langues et coutumes au pouvoir"), 65 ("pas impossible que la Canada puisse un jour se trouver en face du même problème – une demande d'autonomie de la part d'une région quelconque. It peut se sauver lui-même maintenant par un politique discrète en cherchant à enseigner à ses peoples de vivre tranquillement ensemble").

76 England, "L'Assimilation," 51 ("C'est bon de de souvenir que la race Slave donna Copernicus, Huss, Comenius, Tolstoy et Pushkin. L'avenir dons dépend de l'éducation").

77 England, "L'Assimilation," 52–3, 60 ("Soit l'anglais soit le français doit être employé partout ... mais il faut un moyen de communication dans une nation"), 63 ("Le Canada, que deviendra-t-il? Une tour de Babel ou une nation?").

78 "These de M. England," RE6-23, LAC ("Comment se fait la concession des terres aux immigrants? ... Les a-t-il prises aux indigènes, les a-t-il achetées?"). As he later put it, "Mainly they were interested in the property question" Palmer, "Interview with Robert England" (typescript), 2, HP5-28, UCASC.

79 Daniel Coleman, *White Civility*, 12, quoting Jennifer Henderson, *Settler Feminism and Race Making*, 18.

80 Palmer, interview with England (typescript), 6, HP5-28, UCASC.

81 For the story of how he got the job, see England, *Memoirs*, 39; and Palmer, interview with England (typescript), 4–7, quotes at 6 and 7, HP5-28, UCASC. For an excellent overview of the railway's activities during this period, albeit with a focus on Alberta, see Dijks, "Rails to 'The Great Inland Empire.'"

82 England, "First Quarterly Report," 9.

83 For some recollections of his time in Europe, see England, "Glimpses of Out-of-Way People and Places."

84 Dolmage, *Disabled Upon Arrival*, 68–9. Perhaps the most information about Baumgartner comes from England: he recounts that Baumgartner had an MA and had graduated from a Swiss polytechnic, farmed in Saskatchewan, and lectured at Queen's (as a member of O.D. Skelton's staff), all before joining the CNR. See England, *Memoirs*, 41.
85 These included economics, as he was elected a fellow of the Royal Economic Society in 1927. See the certificate in RE8, LAC; and J.M. Keynes, letter to England, 31 October 1927, RE1-2, LAC. See also his review of "Emigration from the British Isles."
86 England, *Memoirs*, 45; Palmer, interview with England (handwritten), 5–6, HP5-23, UCASC; and England, "Reminiscences of a Pioneer," 23.
87 England, *CEIC*, 3; and N.F. Dreisziger, "R. England interview 6–7 October [19]84 (part 2)," Nandor Dreisziger fonds, vol. 2, file 28, LAC. "England wrote the book *Central European Immigrant* largely [to] some extent in response to Bishop Lloyd's statements – used a more polemical tone in it[. He] wrote it 'largely in a far more vigorous style than I would normally[.]' Instead of 'abuse' E[ngland] believed in 'cooperation.'" (Strikethrough used here to reflect the original.)
88 These arguments were also published as England, "Continental Immigration"; and England, "British Immigration."
89 Wurtele, "Apostles of Canadian Citizenship," 22; Osborne and Wurtele, "The Other Railway," 125–6; Craig, *Racial Attitudes in English-Canadian Fiction*, 7–8; and Bellay, "Pluralism and Race/Ethnic Relations," 296–310. A more critical take is found in Day, *Multiculturalism*, 153–8.
90 Pittard, *Les Races et l'histoire* (1924). He also consulted Fleure, *The Peoples of Europe*; Pitt-Rivers, *The Clash of Culture*; Lyde, *The Continent of Europe*; and likely Haddon, *The Races of Man*. Palmer, interview with England (typescript), 45, HP5-28, UCASC. Decades later, he would characterize eugenicists such as Madison Grant and Lothrop Stoddard as "stupid Americans" who were influenced by German superiority thinking. Palmer, interview with England (handwritten notes), 1 and 6, HP5-23, UCASC.
91 Pittard, *Race and History*, 3; and Solonari, "In the Shadow of Ethnic Nationalism," 262–3. This definition Pittard quoted from French palaeontologist Marcellin Boule's work *Les Hommes Fossiles* (1920), 322. Boule continues: "[race] can have nothing, and in general has nothing in common with the people, the nationality, the language, or the customs corresponding to groupings that are purely artificial, in no way anthropological, and arising entirely from history, whose actual products they are."

92 England, CEIC, 42 ("Research continues to reveal facts of the Mendelian inheritance of physical characters, the maintenance of types over thousands of years").

93 England, CEIC, 172–3, but see also 64; and Patrias, "Race, Employment Discrimination, and State Complicity," 14.

94 While in Slawa, England had read the works of John Stuart Mill and others. See G.W. Downey, letter to England, 1 August 1922, RE5-23, LAC. For his earlier and dismissive treatment of Indigenous peoples, see England, "The Emergent West," 405, which reads in part: "The simple approach of the Indian to the world about him did not produce any written record worthy of the name of literature. The very essence of Indian culture lies in inactivity."

95 England, CEIC, 190 (but see also 201), 162, 233 n24. This section of his book relied on Pitt-Rivers, *The Clash of Culture*; Malinowski, *Sex and Repression*; and also McDougall, *The Group Mind*. On Pitt-Rivers, see MacKellar and Hart, "Captain George Henry Lane-Fox Pitt-Rivers."

96 England, CEIC, 42, 174. Emphasis added. Foster, in her work *Our Canadian Mosaic* (1926), is believed to be the first Canadian to use this metaphor in regard to Canada's diversity. While it is possible that England had read her work, it seems unlikely as he was in Europe when it was published and he did not cite it. However, it is clear that he encountered it sometime prior to the publication of his next book in 1936, most likely when he moved to Winnipeg. As for the first use by American travel writer Victoria Hayward, it seems extremely unlikely that he would have encountered her work either. See Gibbon, *Canadian Mosaic*, viii–ix; and England, *Colonization of Western Canada* (hereafter cited as CWC), 323.

97 England, CEIC, 183 ("race egalitarian"), 197–8 ("violent rantings"), 198 ("races too diverse"). The latter is a quote from Frank Hankins, "Social Science and Biology," 408–9. For examples of England's reliance on McDougall, see for example ibid., 174, 233 n31. Arthur de Gobineau was a French race scientist.

98 England, CEIC, 193, 199. In an article published that same year, he reiterated this argument: "There are, of course, undesirables in all races." England, "Continental Migration," 727. He made a similar argument in "Canada Seen Through New Eyes," 43.

As for the survey, which England helped design, it asked the Masonic scholarship teachers to "Estimate, where possible, the influence of Race, Heredity and Environment in the following," and then asked for the incidences of insanity, feeble-mindedness, mentally defective children, average mentality, along with examples of "any outstanding racial or national

Notes to pages 109–12

characteristic." It also asked the degree to which "the Slavic temperament" influenced social life, and the extent to which superstition governed the lives of the people. See England, CEIC, 225. He also praised the work of Helen MacMurchy, who was an ardent eugenicist; see ibid., 206, and McLaren, *Our Own Master Race*.

99 England, CEIC, 233 n36; and Spiro, *Defending the Master Race*, 332.
100 England, CEIC, 173. Emphasis in the original.
101 These were the positive, or at least neutral instincts, while others, such as "flight, repulsion, self-assertion, and self-abasement" were rather negative "from the standpoint of citizenship." England, CEIC, 173–4.
102 Note the parallels with common stereotypes about French Canadians during this period.
103 England, CEIC, 174–5,173.
104 Ibid., 175 ("mother-wit"), 165 ("emancipation"), 163–4 (antimodernism), 168 ("moral fibre").
105 England, CEIC, 178–80, 185, 176 ("heritance").
106 J.W. Clipsham, "Choosing Our Immigrants," *The Globe* (4 January 1927), 4; and Clipsham, "Guarding the Canadian Race" ibid. (2 February 1927), 4. As these were letters to the editor, the titles were picked by the paper, and Clipsham argued that the latter was inaccurate as there was no such thing as a "Canadian race."
107 British (non-Nordic) Canadian, "Guarding the Canadian Race," *The Globe* (8 February 1927), 4; and Clipsham, "Guarding the Canadian Race," ibid. (15 February 1927), 4. This argument about the racial origins of the government was not uncommon. In the early 1920s, "Foster's Weekly Weather Bulletin," issued in Washington but reprinted in the *Ottawa Journal*, repeatedly argued that the "great Nordic race controls North America," having "secured a democracy for Canada" and produced most of the presidents, soldiers, and military officers in the United States. "Foster's Weekly Weather Bulletin," *Ottawa Journal* (3 November 1923), 3; and ibid. (8 March 1924), 24.
108 British (non-Nordic) Canadian, "Guarding the Canadian Nation," *The Globe* (23 February 1927), 4; Clipsham, "Canada Needs Nordics," ibid. (7 March 1927), 4; and Citizen L.C., "Nordic Races," ibid. (2 March 1927), 4. See also the interchange between Grateful, "The 'Canadian Nation,'" *The Globe* (9 February 1927), 4; and E.G. Reburn, "Who Are The Nordics?" *The Globe* (12 February 1927), 4.
109 Berta Hamilton, letter to England, 20 December 1929; and Hamilton, letter to England, 20 January 1930, RE3-5, LAC. In his interview with Palmer, and after a long discussion about the eugenics question (quoted at

the beginning of this chapter), England claimed that he was never happy with any of the writing that he had done under stress, and that both books were written when he "was terribly busy. I was businessman, commanding an organization with little leisure," adding, "I've always been very dissatisfied with the *Central European Immigrant*; it's [terribly] weak in spots, [it was a hurried job]." "Interview with Robert England" (typescript), 13, HP5-23, UCASC; and "Interview with Robert England" (typescript), 86–7, HP5-28, UCASC.

110 R.J.C.S., "The Central European Immigrant in Canada" (book review), *Scientific Agriculture* 11 (May 1930): 627–8; and "The Central European Immigrant in Canada," *The Empire Review* (May 1930): 378–9.

111 "The Central European Immigrant in Canada," *Times Literary Supplement* (24 April 1930), 355.

112 "England R.: The Central European Immigrant in Canada" (book review), *Journal of the Canadian Bankers' Association* 37 (1929–30): 202–4; and William J. Rose, "The Central European Immigrant in Canada," *The Canadian Student* 12, no. 4 (March–April 1930), 185. See also A.R. Randall-Jones, "Our Migrants," *Saturday Night* (1 February 1930), 9–10, which described the book as a defense of "the stranger within our gates hailing from central Europe."

113 The clipping is found in RE3-6, LAC, but lacks the date and page number.

114 A.R. Milne, letter to the editor, 1 April 1930, RE3-5, LAC.

115 Palmer, "Interview with Robert England" (typescript), 13, HP5-23, UCASC; and "Interview with Robert England" (typescript), 86–7, HP5-28, UCASC.

116 England, *Memoirs*, 50 and 61–2. For further documentation, see Black, letter to England, 2 December 1929, RE1-2, LAC; England, telegram to Black, n.d. [December 1929], RE1-1, LAC; and Black, letter to England, 30 December 1929, RE1-2, LAC. For a glimpse into his thoughts on returning, see England, "Canada Seen Through New Eyes."

117 England, "Racial Groups in Western Canada," 15.

118 Ibid. He would repeat these lines in "Some Personal Views on the Future of Western Canada," 16.

119 England, *Memoirs*, 55; "Encouragement to Rural Communities," *The Gazette* (14 May 1930), 13.

120 A detailed analysis of the competitions is found in Wurtele, "Nation-building from the Ground Up," chapters 7 and 8.

121 Osborne, "Constructing the State," 187.

122 England, "Use of Group Consciousness," 263 and 266.

123 Ibid., 263. A lightly revised version of this article appeared as the ninth chapter in CWC, followed by a chapter on "Some Results and Observations." The section that these chapters form is entitled "An Experiment in Nation Building."

124 England, "Use of Group Consciousness," 262; and Palmer, [undated, untitled transcript of an interview with England] 7, HP5-23, UCASC. "Palmer: The purpose wasn't simply to promote assimilation then. / England: This was concerned as an agricultural department with encouraging better breeding and better farming. / Palmer: But the idea behind it was also to kind of improve the image of the central European? / England: Yes." Contrasting these competitions with the CPR folk festivals (discussed in the following chapter), the CNR was focused on the progress of "racial settlements" whereas the CPR was more concerned with ensuring goodwill between these settlements. On the project's press coverage, see England, CWC, 329 (Appendix IV).

125 Palmer, "Interview With Robert England" (typescript), 11–12, HP5-28, UCASC; and England, *Memoirs*, 61. For an early example, see England, "Review of *Wheat*."

126 England, CWC, 7. The book ran to over 300 pages with appendices, and England himself recognized that the "historical and descriptive sections of this effort may be criticized as working over ground that in parts may be familiar to some" (12). For a look at England's economic thought at the end of 1935, see his "The Apathetic Fallacy," which called for increased consideration of human factors in economics. It demonstrates the continuities of his thought, with a few minor changes. For instance, he critiqued intelligence testing as over-simplistic, warned against the dangers of nationalism, affirmed the importance of "crowd psychology," reiterated the value of Le Play's study and the family as a unit of analysis, and critiqued modernity. The article also demonstrated a continued belief in the power of race, as he wrote of racial stocks and their idiosyncrasies and defined tradition as "the transmitted record of race memory" (442, 444, and 449). He would repeat many of these themes in his article, "The Switch-Back Decade," 78–86.

127 Alan Anderson, "Ethnic Bloc Settlements"; and Swyripa, *Storied Landscapes*, 94.

128 Eyford, *White Settler Reserve*, 61–4.

129 Maroussem, *Les enquêtes*, 245, quoted in England, "L'assimilation," 20–1 ("Non assimilée, la colonie populaire est un 'kyste', qui peut amener aux époques de troubles les pires complications"); England, CEIC, 115; and England, CWC, 10–11.

130 Wurtele, "Nation-Building from the Ground Up," 250–2.
131 I am grateful to A1 for drawing out the implications of this point and for this particular phrasing. The "abdication" remark comes from Valerie Knowles, *Strangers at Our Gates*, 141.
132 Dijks, "Rails to 'the Great Inland Empire,'" 49–50.
133 England, "Land Settlement in Northern Areas of Western Canada," 586. As historians have shown, deportations from Canada prior to the Second World War were not always legal and were often used to target leftist immigrants. The essential work on the subject remains Roberts, *Whence They Came*.
134 England, CWC, 297 ("racial heritage"), 303–5. This was most clearly expressed some years earlier; see his "Contribution of Rural Minded Peoples," (typescript), 7, RE4-1, LAC; and England, "How Canada is Building a Community of Peoples." The bibliography in his *Memoirs* erroneously states that the former appeared in the *Proceedings* of the American Railway Development Association in 1930, and the latter in the *Proceedings* of the Conference on Social Work (Minneapolis, 1931), but neither were published as cited.
135 England, CWC, 105; and Palmer, interview with England (typescript), 2–5, quote at 2, HP5-23, UCASC. Of course, he neglected to mention that his opinion on these settlements had radically changed with time.
136 England, CWC, 50, 66, 108, 173, 198, 207.
137 Ibid., 224–5 (Slavs); 226 (Germans); 269 (Hungarians); 250, 254, 262, 264 (Scandinavians).
138 Ibid., 273–4 (Jews), 269–70 (Mormons), and 276 (Chinese and African). These passages were taken from an earlier piece; see England, "Racial Groups in Western Canada," 11, where he included religious groups such as the Mennonites, explaining that they were of "Teutonic origin." The article was a condensed version of an address he gave to the Provincial Homemakers' Convention. "Entertaining Program Presented at Opening Homemakers' Session," *Star-Phoenix* (21 June 1933), 8.
139 England, CWC, 149, "Appendix B," 310–11, 276 ("peculiar type"). For the history of African Canadians in Alberta, see Palmer and Palmer, "The Black Experience in Alberta" and Vernon, *The Black Prairie Archives*; and for history of Chinese Canadians on the prairies, see Marshall, *Cultivating Connections*.
140 England, CWC, 284, 287, 290.
141 Ibid., 279, 291. These comments are repeated in his "Some Personal Views on the Future of Western Canada," 15.

142 For a critical analysis of the Commission, see Haque, *Multiculturalism Within a Bilingual Framework*; and Schrenk, "Directed Cultural Change and Imagined Communities."
143 England, CWC, 231 ("artificial"), 161 ("atavism"). Elsewhere he would continue to flirt with the idea of atavism; see for example England, "The Switch-Back Decade," 85.
144 England, CWC, 161–2. He had been making this argument for several years; see his 1931 article "How Canada Is Building a Community of Peoples," 57; and his "Glimpses of Europe in Western Canada," 19. Several papers noted the latter; see "Canadian Geographical," *The Gazette* (23 July 1932), 20; and "Here and There," *Edmonton Journal* (20 July 1932), 4.
145 England, CWC, 135, 151–2, 302.
146 *Winnipeg Tribune* (4 December 1930), 3; and England, "Contribution of Rural Minded Peoples" (typescript), 3, RE4-1, LAC. A year later, when giving an overview of the Canadian population, he claimed that it was made up "roughly of twenty-eight per cent French Canadians, fifty-five per cent Anglo-Saxon, and minor groups such as the German nearly four per cent, the Scandinavian two per cent, Central European four per cent and the balance aboriginal Indian, Southern Europeans, Hebrews, etc." – again erasing the presence of Canadians of Asian and African descent. England, "How Canada is Building a Community of Peoples," 50.
147 Young, *The Ukrainian Canadians*. Cf. Swyripa, *Ukrainian Canadians*, 45–53.
148 England, Review of *The Ukrainian Canadians*, 209. Despite keeping a meticulous record of all his published works, this one item does not appear on any of the bibliographies he released. This leads me to conclude its omission was intentional, likely because of these remarks. See his *Bibliography of Robert England*; "Reminiscences of a Pioneer," 8–33; and *Memoirs*, 201–5.
149 *Report on the Work of the Canadian Institute of International Affairs, 1933*, 10–14. England made only passing mention of the conference in his *Memoirs*, 62, but for some recollections, see Holland, *Remembering the Institute of Pacific Relations*, 14–16.
150 England, "Canadian Immigration Policy," 15, RE4-1, LAC. In a paper given the year prior, he made similar arguments against "pseudo scientific propaganda against supposedly inferior races." England, "How Canada is Building a Community of Peoples," 50.
151 Smith's study simultaneously confirmed the existence of racism (in one

passage he argued that cultivating a new spirit towards immigrants ought to begin with Canadian children who "are overfond of the derisive salutations, 'Sheeny! Chink! Dago!'") and absolved Canadians of it by claiming that their opposition to "the Oriental" was "not racial, nor social, nor religious, but economic." W.G. Smith, *A Study in Canadian Immigration*, quotes at 382 and 174. However, as Riggins points out in his rather laudatory biographical sketch, Smith also wrote of the Church's need to "arouse a sentiment favouring race equality before the law." W.G. Smith, *Building the Nation* (1922), 158, quoted in Riggins, "A Square Deal for the Least and the Last," 213.

152 Emphasis in the original, as underlining. The paper appeared only in the *Canadian Delegation Papers Prepared for the Banff Conference*, which was no doubt prepared for internal use only, and where it was the only such paper marked "Not for Publication." As such, it does not appear in the published version, *Canadian Papers, 1933*; nor in Lasker and Holland, eds., *Problems of the Pacific, 1933*. In a speech back in Winnipeg, England emphasized only that Japan's expansionism posed a threat. "Sees Japan's New Move As Danger to Great Britain," *Winnipeg Free Press* (27 September 1933), 7.

153 W.W. Swanson, review of *The Colonization of Western Canada*, by Robert England, *American Economic Review* 26, no. 4 (December 1936): 746–8. See also David C. Lamb, "A Cradle of Canada," *The Listener* (6 May 1936), supplement, xv; K.M.H., "Settlement in the West," *Winnipeg Free Press* (29 April 1936), 13; W.N. Sage, "Canadian Prairies Pass in Review," *The Province* [Vancouver] (24 April 1937), 40; and R.P. "The People of the Prairies," *Winnipeg Evening Tribune* (29 April 1936), 13.

154 S.W.A, review of *The Colonization of Western Canada*, by Robert England, *Geography* 21 (December 1936): 313.

155 G.E. Britnell, review of *Group Settlement*, by C.A. Dawson, *The Colonization of Western Canada*, by Robert England, and *The Colonization of Canada*, by D.C. Harvey, *Canadian Historical Review* 18, no. 1 (March 1937): 71–3.

156 W.B. Hurd, review of *Group Settlement*, by C.A. Dawson, and *The Colonization of Western Canada*, by Robert England, *The Canadian Journal of Economics and Political Science* 2, no. 4 (November 1936): 574–6. The following year, Hurd expressed his concerns in an article entitled "Decline of the Anglo-Saxon Canadian."

157 England, CEIC, 162–3; and England, "Contribution of Rural Minded Peoples," 7. "If [internal] colonies are to be successful," he added, "there must be a racial, a social, or a religious link to make rural life agreeable."

158 England, "Transportation and Agriculture," 4 ("if the territory [the Department] serves continues to be attractive to settlers then there is some justification for maintenance of the service already being given [to settlers] by the railway").
159 Gibbon, *Canadian Mosaic*.

CHAPTER THREE

1 "The Fly Leaf," *Globe and Mail* (27 May 1939), 25; and "Gov. General's Literary Awards Are Announced," *The Ottawa Citizen* (29 April 1939), 33. As for the connection to King George, Gibbon shrewdly sent two copies of the book to Buckingham Palace – one for the king, and one for his private secretary. He received a reply from the assistant private secretary, who remarked: "I am commanded by the King to thank you sincerely for the copy of the book ... In view of His Majesty's forthcoming visit to Canada, he is greatly interested in this study of the racial origins of the Canadian people." Gibbon then began to make discreet inquiries as to whether or not he could use the letter for publicity purposes, this perhaps being his intent all along. He eventually received word that one sentence ("In view of ...") could be used for newspaper paragraph but not in display advertising. It thus appeared in at least four newspapers in Canada. See the relevant correspondence in "Gibbon, John Murray," folder 643, series 1.1, Dent Records; and, for example, "Royal Appreciation," *The Gazette* (25 March 1939), 27.

2 The metaphor may have begun to catch on after the radio series, as early as mid-February, when the Vancouver Folk Festival Society was established and began planning a presentation entitled "Canadian Mosaic." The following month, a writer in the *Winnipeg Free Press* described the metaphor as "apt." See "Canadian Mosaic," *Vancouver Daily Province* (14 February 1938), 4; and A.A.A. "Our Festival Adjudicators," *Winnipeg Free Press* (19 March 1938), 16.

Early references after the book's publication include Francis H. Stevens, "Winnipeg Mosaic," *Winnipeg Free Press* (7 December 1938), 3; Nellie McClung, "The Year Goes Out," *The Leader-Post* (31 December 1938), 4; House of Commons, *Debates* (24 January 1939), 296; "Mayhew Spans Canada in Day," *The Victoria Daily Times* (28 February 1939), 1; "S. Bronfman Lauds Policy of Britain," *The Montreal Gazette* (7 August 1939), 11; "Monday Club Meeting," *The Ottawa Journal* (14 November 1939), 8; "Club Events," *Winnipeg Free Press* (17 February 1940), 12; "Athenaeum Club," *The Ottawa Journal* (24 February 1940), 10;

"Chalmer's Y.P.U. Enjoys Review," *The Windsor Star* (24 April 1940), 24; "Elmwood School Takes Steps to Accommodate Refugees," *The Ottawa Journal* (13 June 1940), 8; "Provincial Homemakers Hear Stretch of Work by 425 Clubs," *The Leader-Post* (21 June 1940), 7 ("Canada's nationality problem"); "Here East Meets West," *Nanaimo Daily News* (16 November 1940), 1; and "Scotland's Share in Building Canada Extolled by Pastor," *The Ottawa Citizen* (3 December 1941), 11. Such evidence confirms Ian McKay's assertion that "without Gibbon, the now all-pervasive metaphor of Canada as a cultural mosaic might have died an obscure death as an American writer's deceit." McKay, *The Quest of the Folk*, 57; cf. Daniel Coleman, *White Civility*, 266 n10.

3  Such groups included Canadians of French, Jewish, and Ukrainian descent. See "Help Them to Be Good Canadians," *The Winnipeg Tribune* (25 January 1939), 13; "College Plans Series," *The Montreal Gazette* (27 January 1940), 14; and "Ukrainian Women Given Splendid Reports on War Work During 1941," *Star Phoenix* (6 January 1942), 6;

4  "Gibbon, John Murray," in *Encyclopedia of Literature in Canada*; Coleman, *White Civility*, 182; Bonavia, "Bibliographic Access to Ethno-Cultural Material," 80; and Palmer, "Reluctant Hosts," 81–118. Craig, *Racial Attitudes in English-Canadian Fiction*, 46, wrote that Gibbon "took a great deal of interest in what is now called multiculturalism."

5  This sketch relies primarily on Gibbon, "Scot to Canadian"; and de Silva, *A History of Sri Lanka*. In "Scot to Canadian," Gibbon suggested that his father "was largely responsible for the introduction of tea into this island, importing Tamil labour from India" (2). However, the historiography either does not mention William Gibbon or does not substantiate his son's claim.

6  Perry, *Colonial Relations*, 64–5, 234. "People of colour" is often used to refer to all people racialized as non-white but, despite its general acceptance within the academe, it is a remarkably problematic term. For one discussion, see Bannerji, *The Dark Side of the Nation*, chapter 1.

7  Gibbon, "Scot to Canadian," 2–3. As a young man, he did not seem to hold the separation against them, later writing that his father had always been good to him and that his mother was sweet and longsuffering. Transcript of a letter from Gibbon to Nancy (Anne Fox), 8 August 1894. Original in possession of Joan Gibbon Vaughan.

8  Gibbon, "Scot to Canadian," 2–3.

9  He took classes in took classes in Latin, Greek, English, logic, and moral philosophy. Gibbon, "Scot to Canadian," 3–4; and Robert Gordon College Archives, correspondence with the author, 21 March 2019.

10 For instance, in his correspondence with Nancy, his girlfriend and future wife, young Gibbon repeatedly used the phrase "work like a nigger." Decades later, this phrase had changed to "work like a slave." (Nancy's legal name was Anne but she was known to her family as Nancy. As such, I have referred to her by this preferred name throughout.) Gibbon, "Scot to Canadian," 33–4; Gibbon, letter to Nancy (Anne Fox), [15 August 1894]; Gibbon, letter to [Anne Fox], 22 August 1894 (originals in possession of Joan Gibbon Vaughan); and Gibbon, letter to Barbeau, 19 March 1928, Marius Barbeau fonds, box b197, folder 22, Canadian Museum of History Archives (cited hereafter in the following manner: MB197-22, CMHA).

11 Gibbon, "Scot to Canadian," 3–6; and Gibbon, "Aberdonian to Canadian," 245. For his recollections of Mackenzie, in addition to his memoirs see Gibbon, letter to Nancy (Anne Fox), 8 August 1894, original in possession of Joan Gibbon Vaughan.

12 Gibbon, "Scot to Canadian," 37.

13 In some ways his education followed in his older brother's footsteps. William, who was five years older, had been educated at Gordon's College, then at Aberdeen, and finally at Trinity College, Oxford. See Class Attendance Register (Arts, Science and Divinity), 7, MSU 7, University of Aberdeen, Special Collections (UASC); and Student Register (Faculty of Arts), 243, MSU 1, UASC; "William Duff Gibbon (1880–1955)"; and Gibbon, "Scot to Canadian," 3–11a. (The unfinished manuscript is inconsistently numbered, with numerous inserted pages being marked "a," "b," and so on.) Gibbon later drew on his experiences at King's College when crafting his first novel, *Hearts and Faces*.

14 Gibbon, "Scot to Canadian," 12–21, quote at 14a; and Gibbon, journal entry dated 26 January 1896. Original in possession of Joan Gibbon Vaughan.

15 Transcriptions of journal entries dated 9 and 16 February 1896. Original in possession of Joan Gibbon Vaughan. Gibbon did join the regiment; see Gibbon, "Scot to Canadian," 15. On the college that Anne attended, see Adams, *Somerville for Women*.

16 Mackenzie had come to the city in 1893, taken over the editorship of the paper four years later, and reached out to Gibbon as he needed to replace his former assistant, the well-known novelist Eden Phillpotts. Gibbon, "Scot to Canadian," 18 and 22–5, quote at 22a; and "News Notes," *The Bookman* (April 1911), 3. During this period Gibbon contributed poems, children's stories, and the occasional article to the paper, although it is difficult to determine the extent contributions. In 1897, a poem appeared in

*Black and White* under the initials "J.M.G." An additional three poems and two articles bearing the same initials appeared between then and 1901. However, during the same time a poem, two short stories, and two articles bore his name.

17 Gibbon, "Scot to Canadian" (alternative draft), 30. In the autobiography he downplayed his initial zeal for the movement, dismissing Fabians as "armchair Socialists"; see page 14a of the original draft.

Copies of the consistently cited version of his autobiography are held at Exporail and at the Whyte Museum. However, additional drafts have recently been donated by the family to the latter and are currently unprocessed. This material includes the original version of the aforementioned draft, in two binders (labelled Section I and II), an additional binder containing a similar draft (labelled, probably posthumously, "Addenda"), and an additional pile of loose manuscript pages, which I refer to as the "alternate draft." All references are to the original, unless otherwise noted.

18 Gibbon, "Scot to Canadian," 15a, 28. Gibbon did not talk about his family at any length in his autobiography, and the first mention of Nancy comes in a brief passage recalling his time at Oxford. His account of the marriage in the manuscript is equally sparse, and Anne remains unnamed throughout. ("About this time I found myself a bride, marrying the English girl with whom I had played tennis at Göttingen, and whom I had haunted at a distance in a Canadian canoe," he wrote, adding in a scrawled afterthought that the two had many tastes in common, including music.)

19 Gibbon, "Scot to Canadian," 29–30.

20 This prescription was quite convenient, to say the least. In his unpublished memoirs, Gibbon admitted he had been reading with fascination many books about Morocco, Algiers, and Tunis, and at the time had just finished Robert Hitchen's novel, *The Garden of Allah* (1904), with its descriptions of "dancing girls, radiant with gold earrings and dresses of gold tissue covered with coins of gold, interspersed with lumps of coral." But, he quickly added, "I had a wife of whom I happened to be very fond, so that dancing girls were not much in my line." However, he very intentionally travelled alone so there is no way to know how far out of line they really were. See Gibbon, "Scot to Canadian," 16 and 30; Gibbon, *Conquering Hero*, 57; and Sandwell, "John Murray Gibbon," 599.

21 Gibbon, "Scot to Canadian," 33–4. Emphasis in the original, as underlining.

22 Ibid.

23 Gibbon turned up at the meeting in Trafalgar Square attired in a tall silk hat and frock coat. According to Gibbon's later account, Cameron

planned to offer him £300 per year but, seeing his stylish attire, decided that £360 would be more appropriate. Gibbon, "Scot to Canadian," 38, 74, and 100; and *John Murray Gibbon: Chief 'Man of Many Sides'*, np. The latter is the printed proceedings of his retirement party.

24 Gibbon, "Scot to Canadian," 40–58.
25 Gibbon, "Scot to Canadian," 38–55, quotes at 47 and 55. Books he read included MacKenzie, *Voyages from Montreal* (1801); and Selkirk, *Observations on the Present State of the Highlands of Scotland* (1805).
26 Gibbon, "Scot to Canadian," 56, 52, 54. He had also become interested in handicrafts, having witnessed an exhibition at the Chateau Laurier, and both Canada and its handicrafts remained on his mind after his return to London. For instance, embarking on a tour of European CPR offices (much like Robert England had with the CNR), he was taken by the peasant life, costume, and art on display in Scandinavia, and wondered whether anything was being done in Canada "to keep alive the traditions of the Swedes in their new homes in Western Canada." Ibid., 43 and 59.
27 Gibbon, "Scot to Canadian," 60. These sales were primarily in Great Britain; Gibbon later claimed the sales in Canada were intentionally suppressed by the Canadian publisher contracted for distribution, as they had just released their own two-volume book on the subject. See Gibbon, letter to Peggie Blackstock (of J. M. Dent), 12 March 1952, John Murray Gibbon fonds (M454, unprocessed material), WMCR; and *The Scotsman in Canada*, 2 vols. (Toronto: Musson, n.d. [1911]).
28 Gibbon, *Scots in Canada*, 135.
29 Ibid., 82, 89, but see also 21, 30, and 50.
30 Ibid., 23. This legacy was noted at the beginning and end of the book (9 and 162).
31 Ibid., 108. "It is at this point that the inevitable Scot appears upon the scene," he wrote, describing when the first Scottish men appear in the Hudson's Bay Company records.
32 Gibbon, "Scot to Canadian," 60.
33 Two of the books Gibbon read prior to his departure were Hearn's *Glimpses of Unfamiliar Japan* and *Japan: An Interpretation*. See Gibbon, "Scot to Canadian," 73–4; also "C.P.R. Publicity," *London Standard* (28 August 1913), 1; and "Mr. Murray Gibbon," *National Post* [Toronto] (30 September 1913), 24, reprinted from the *London Financier*.
34 Gibbon, "Scot to Canadian," 84; and "Passenger Lists, 1865–1935," RG 76-C, Department of Employment and Immigration fonds, Roll T-4854, LAC; and Regehr, "Shaughnessy, Thomas George."
35 Gibbon, "Scot to Canadian," 45, 85, 87.

36 Ibid., 86. A story from the day of their arrival illustrates how lurid stories about Indigenous people had already reached the children. Gibbon was waiting at the dock to meet his family. His daughter Ann was misbehaving and so had been confined to her cabin, but her father spotted her and told her to come out. "I'm too scared, the Indians will scalp me," she replied. Ann Faith Shepard, "Grand Old Man of the West: Memories of My Father, John Murray Gibbon," 1, John Murray Gibbon fonds (M454, unprocessed material), WMCR.

37 In this case, pleasure most often came in the form of visits to symphony orchestras and concerts with like-minded American passenger agents. Gibbon, "Scot to Canadian," 89–90, 93a, 94.

38 Marginal comment on an annotated table of contents for "Scot to Canadian," appended to a letter from Henry Button to John Gibbon, 23 September 1952, John Murray Gibbon fonds (M454, unprocessed material), WMCR; and Kines, "Chief-Man-of-Many-Sides," 15–16.

39 Gibbon, letter to Anne, 22 August 1894 (emphasis in the original). Transcribed by Virginia Glover; original in possession of Joan Gibbon Vaughan. Of course, this quote raises interesting questions about his sexuality. In the same letter, moreover, he relayed that one former friend had written him "a most pathetic letter telling me he loved me with more than brotherly love. He said that sometimes he could have fallen on my neck and kissed me. I got awfully sick at this and wrote back saying I would have kicked him if he had." He added that he hated when men were "nauseously affectionate" with one another, and that he had warded off another fellow who had tried to embrace him. Gibbon further explored ideas about gender in his novel *Pagan Love*, in which the main character disguises herself as a man.

40 "Social and Personal," *The Leader-Post* (13 July 1923), 6. It was after this fateful trip that he organized the Trail Riders of the Canadian Rockies group.

41 MacTavish, "Apostle of Silence," 29.

42 Gibbon, "Scot to Canadian," 70.

43 Gibbon refused to divulge any of this information during his lifetime. When preparing his autobiography, he told his publisher: "I find it hard to put in more personal family anecdotes for domestic reasons." A co-worker similarly recalled that Gibbon did not talk about early life or family with anyone. However, this information was kindly shared with me by his relatives (conversation with Fiona Gibbon-Taillefer, Alexa Wilson, and Virginia Glover, 5 October 2019). See [Phil Gibbon,] untitled notes of an interview with Bill MacFarlane, 23 March 1985; and Gibbon, letter to Miss Peggie Blackstock (of J.M. Dent and Sons), 12 March 1952, both in

John Murray Gibbon fonds (M454, unprocessed material), WMCR. Gibbon's second son, John, struggled with similar mental health issues. See Stouck, *As For Sinclair Ross*, 183–4, 266–7.

44 Liz [Elizabeth Blackley (Deane)], letter to Phil [Gibbon], 27 October [198?], John Murray Gibbon fonds (M454, unprocessed material), WMCR. Emphasis in the original.

45 Gibbon, "Scot to Canadian," 88. Despite his astute business sense, he was not above repeating stereotypes about French Canadians, such as the following remark made in an address to the Royal Society of Canada: "Now, as you know, there is no race suicide among the French Canadians, and so the mother who has her lifetime to sing seventeen babies to sleep is not likely to forget the songs." Gibbon, "Music of the People."

46 Ibid., 100 and 102–3; Gibbon, "Aberdonian to Canadian," 248; "Hearts and Faces," *The Bookman* [London] 50 (July 1916), 114; "Hearts and Faces," *Windsor Star* (1 June 1916), 4; "A Novelist's New View of New York," *New York Times Book Review* (21 May 1916), 79; "Runs Railroad…" *Winnipeg Evening Tribune* (20 May 1916), 4.

47 Gibbon, "Scot to Canadian," 87 and 104; and Schwartz, "University Club of Montreal." See also Robertson, "Sir Andrew Macphail and the Pen and Pencil Club." Gibbon was made a member of the Pen and Pencil Club on 13 November 1915. Although the minutes for 1914–30 appear to be missing, see the list of members found in *Pen & Pencil Club 1890–1959*. The earliest evidence of his participation among their files is Gibbon, letter to K.R. McPherson, 22 March 1916, P139, Pen and Pencil Club of Montreal fonds, A5, McCord Museum Archives.

48 Gibbon, "Scot to Canadian, 85, 96, and 97."

49 "Prophesied Big Immigrant Rush May Not Come," *Calgary Herald* (14 September 1916), 12. The editors of the paper concurred with at least some of his arguments; see "A New Point," *Calgary Herald* (14 September 1916), 6.

50 "Electric Industry and Immigration," *The Gazette* (15 November 1916), 6; and "Better System of Immigration Must Be Introduced Now," ibid. (28 September 1917), 13. In fact, the Canadian population had climbed to only 8.7 million by 1921, reaching 10.3 million a decade later, and would not reach 15 million until the 1950s.

51 Gibbon, "A Secular Bible for New Canada."

52 Gibbon, letter to John Lane, 30 November 1917, JL 7/101915-1933, Bodley Head Ltd Archive, URSC. I would like to thank Virginia Glover, Alexa Wilson, Fiona Gibbon Taillefer, Joan Gibbon Vaughan, and Penguin Random House for permission to view these files.

53 It is unclear to what monument Gibbon is referring. Gibbon, "Where Is Canadian Literature," 336–7, 339, 340. See also "War Will Waken Our Literature," *The Gazette* (30 November 1917), 5; Lucian [S. D. Scott], "The Week-End," *The Province* (16 February 1918), 4; and F.P., "The World's Window," *Vancouver Daily World* (21 February 1918), 6.

54 Gibbon, "Where Is Canadian Literature," 339. His use of the term race during this period was elastic; elsewhere in the article he wrote that poets were "a race apart" (336). A fuller discussion of Gibbon's involvement with the CAA is beyond the scope of this chapter; see instead Doody, "A Union of the Inkpot"; Harrington, *Syllables of Recorded Time*; and Parker, "Authors and Publishers on the Offensive." For Gibbon's recollections, see his "Pages from an Informal History"; and "Scot to Canadian," 109–11.

55 Gibbon, "The Coming Canadian Novel." This paper was read before the Royal Society of Canada by W. Lawson Grant two months prior to its publication. See "Annual Sessions of the Royal Society," *The Ottawa Citizen* (12 May 1919), 8; and also "The Canadian Bookman," *The Gazette* (3 May 1919), 18. On the theme of colonial maturation in Gibbon's novels, see Daniel Coleman, *White Civility*, chap. 5.

56 The CPR put their weight behind wartime xenophobia by refusing to hire German Canadians. They also attempted to benefit financially from the results, as they saw prisoners of war as a cheap labour pool and petitioned the government (sometimes successfully) for permission to employ them. See MacKinnon, "Canadian Railway Workers and World War I," 227; and Kordan, *No Free Man*, 205 and 207.

57 Gibbon, "The Foreign Born," 334.

58 Ibid., 348–51, 339.

59 Ibid., 350–1.

60 Ibid., 339, 347.

61 Transcripts of letters from Gibbon to Miss [Anne] Fox, 13 September 1983, 18 December 1893, and 22 August 1894. Originals in possession of Joan Gibbon Vaughan.

62 Gibbon, "The Friends of Dreyfus," 3–4.

63 Gibbon, *The True Annals of Fairyland*.

64 Gibbon, *The Conquering Hero*, 105–6 and 148; and Craig, *Racial Attitudes in English-Canadian Fiction*, 46–7.

65 See for instance "Mr. Gibbon Once More," *The Gazette* (16 October 1920), 19. A publisher's advertisement for the book published in the newspaper a month later provided extracts of positive reviews from a variety of American and Canadian periodicals, including *Saturday Night* and the

*New York Times*. See *The Gazette* (20 November 1920), 17. There were, of course, some dissenting voices, such as "The Conquering Hero," *Canadian Bookman* (December 1920): 50–2. In any case, by 1922 Gibbon was successful enough to warrant hiring a literary agent in England (though from the preceding correspondence, it seems they may have been hired in part to handle copyright difficulties). Gibbon, letter to John Lane, 9 November 1922, JL 7/101915-1933, Bodley Head Ltd Archive, URSC.

66 This does not explain how a paper Gibbon authored came to be read before the society some three years prior. Was he seeking a fellowship at that time? See Gibbon, "Scot to Canadian," 125; and "Annual Sessions of the Royal Society," *The Ottawa Citizen* (12 May 1919), 8.

67 Gibbon, "Scot to Canadian," 125–6. The papers he would be required to write, he remarked, would involve "research rather than creative effort," which would be a new endeavour for him, but he was undaunted. "Research, after all, was a form of travel or mental exploration of a subject," he wrote, "and my private library was lined with books on social history. As for song, I had found a delightful resort for research in the New York Public Library."

68 Gibbon, "European Seeds in the Canadian Garden," 119, 127, and 129. See also Ivanhoe [Alex J. Musgrove], "European Seeds in Canada," *The Winnipeg Tribune* (31 December 1923), 4.

69 Gibbon, "Canadian Letters and the New Canadian."

70 Ibid.

71 Stuart Henderson, "'While There Is Still Time,'" 147.

72 Gibbon, "Canadian Letters and the New Canadian." See also "'New Canadians' Their Name, Not 'Foreigners,'" *Star Phoenix* (23 November 1923), 5. In his autobiography, Gibbon proudly declared that this address "helped to stir up sympathy for the New Canadians in Ontario where such sympathy was needed." Gibbon, "Scot to Canadian," 126.

73 His acre-large sunflower patch in Alberta, grown to provide winter food for his blue-ribbon stock, led to him being dubbed "The Sun-Flower King of Windermere." See "Flower-Lovers Meet," *The Gazette* (16 November 1916), 7; and W.T. Allison, "Literary Notes," *The Victoria Daily Times* (1 October 1923), 4.

74 Ellis, *The Problem of Race-Regeneration*, 71, quoted in Turda, *Modernism and Eugenics*, 7; and Dyck, *Facing Eugenics*, 6. But Gibbon had long been skeptical of the emphasis placed on heredity, at least in relation to some diseases. Transcript of a letter from Gibbon to Nancy (Anne Fox), 8 August 1894. Original in possession of Joan Gibbon Vaughan. ("I suppose you have read the 'Heavenly Twins' by this time. There's a good deal

of psychology in it, but I think what is said there about Heredity is exaggerated a good deal.")

75 Craig, *Racial Attitudes in English-Canadian Fiction*, 30, 46; and Gibbon, *Drums Afar*, 71. See also George Elliott Clarke, "Liberalism and Its Discontents."

76 Gibbon, *The Conquering Hero*, 135–7.

77 "Book Birth Control," *The Gazette* (14 December 1922), 2; Gibbon, "Birth Control for Authors," 603; and *The Ottawa Citizen* (15 December 1922), 24. See also "Says Too Many Novels Written," *Victoria Daily Times* (14 December 1922), 19; "Author Would Restrict Production of Novels," *The Leader-Post* (15 December 1922), 2; and "A Ministry of Literature," *Ottawa Citizen* (16 January 1923), 16, reprinted from the *Vancouver World*. See also Gibbon, "Music of the People."

78 "Immigrants Not a Menace to Culture," *The Gazette* (25 February 1924), 5; and "Europeans' Part in Cultural Life," ibid. (3 April 1924), 10. The Baron de Hirsch Institute is one of the oldest Jewish social service organizations of its type in Canada and dates to 1863, while the Temple Emanu-El is a major Reform synagogue that was founded in 1882.

79 Gibbon told the anecdote in *Mosaic*, x; again in "Scot to Canadian," 42, 141; and mentioned it in passing in "Your Theme is Your Author," 4–5. His interest in the *French Songs of Old Canada*, illustrated by W. Graham Robertson, seems to have been initially more aesthetic than academic. "I had bought the book because of the illustrations which were so attractive that I had them framed in upright panels, using them as decorations for my study," he later confessed. Gibbon, "Scot to Canadian," 42.

80 Gibbon, "Scot to Canadian," 141. For a recent biography of Foster, see O'Connell, *Life and Songs of Stephen Foster*.

81 Barbeau, Gascoigne, Kennedy, and Seath, *Chansons of Old French Canada*. On Gascoigne, see Gray, *No Ordinary School*, esp. 1–42 and, on Seath, 82.

82 Gibbon, "Scot to Canadian," 141–2; "Two Million Dollar Fire in Chateau Frontenac at Quebec," *The Gazette* (15 January 1926), 1; and "Start Work Today on Damaged Wing," *The Gazette* (16 January 1926), 6. On the reopening, see "Press Party at Quebec," *The Gazette* (7 June 1926), 3; "Open New Wing of Chateau Frontenac," *The Ottawa Citizen* (7 June 1926), 7; and H. W. Pepper, "Improvement In Construction," *The Gazette* (8 January 1927), 36.

83 Gibbon, "Scot to Canadian," 141–2. The CPR ran ads in American newspapers, which read in part: "And now, Quebec is singing in the sun. A *chanson*, surely, for the folk are French, and this is New World

Normandy." This ad appeared in such papers as *The Philadelphia Inquirer* (13 June 1926), "Society and Resorts," 9; and *The Baltimore Sun* (6 June 1926), part 1, section 3, 17. Some of the editors did run features on the hotel in the days that followed; see for example "Rebuilt Wing of Chateau Frontenac at Quebec Opens; Many New Features Added," *The Brooklyn Daily Eagle* (13 June 1926), Section F ("Resorts and Travel"), 1. For a detailed look at the Quebec festivals, see Sheedy, "Performing the Canadian 'Mosaic.'"

84  Gibbon, "Scot to Canada," 143; and Gibbon, *Canadian Folk Songs*.
85  Gibbon, *Canadian Folk Songs*, viii–xiv (quote at xiv).
86  Barbeau, review of *Canadian Folk Songs*, 145–6. Italics in the original. Cf. Boddington, review of *Canadian Folk Songs*; and "Shorter Notices," *The Saturday Review* (22 January 1927), 130.
87  Gibbon, *Canadian Folk Songs*, ix and x; "Scot to Canadian," 144; and *Canadian Folk Songs*, rev. ed.
88  In 1928, Gibbon warned Barbeau: "If we exceed our appropriation anything like the extent we did last year, this will mean the end of our Festivals." It is unclear if the two stayed on budget, but a month later Gibbon noted that the bill for fees and expenses for musicians and performers alone had reached $100,000 – "Pray for me!" Gibbon added (jokingly, as he was areligious). This amounts to the equivalent of just under $1.5 million in 2019. See Gibbon, letter to Barbeau, 5 March 1928, MB197-22, CMHA; and Gibbon's annotations on the "Price of Series of Subscription Tickets," enclosed with a letter to Barbeau dated 5 April 1928, MB197-23, CMHA.
89  See for instance Stuart Henderson, "While There Is Still Time," 165 n1, 168 n29.
90  In May 1927, for instance, Luxton wrote Gibbon with some suggestions for publicizing the event. Gibbon replied that they were already printing a poster to promote the event but that he would keep the idea in mind for the following year. Gibbon, letter to Luxton, 25 May 1927, LUX/I/A-156, WMCR.
91  Bart Robinson, *Banff Springs*; and Mason, *Spirits of the Rockies*, 79–95, quote at 93. See also Clapperton, "Naturalizing Race Relations [*sic*]," 349–79; and Luxton, *Banff*. For a brief overview, see also Meister, "The Canadian Mosaic, Archival Silences, and an Indigenous Presence in Banff," *ActiveHistory* (18 August 2020), http://activehistory.ca/2020/08/the-canadian-mosaic-archival-silences-and-an-indigenous-presence-in-banff/.
92  Barbeau, *Indian Days in the Canadian Rockies*; see also the following letters, all in MB197-19, CMHA: Gibbon, letter to Barbeau, 11 December

1922; copy of a letter from Gibbon to Max Enos, 15 December 1922; Gibbon, letters to Barbeau, 8 February, 3 May, and 8 May 1923; and Gibbon, copies of letters to Eayrs, 1 and 3 May 1923. Barbeau clearly learned more about the Nakoda than he did about the actual event; he later wrote to Gibbon, asking if the Banff-based Indian Days were held annually in Windermere. See Barbeau, letter to Gibbon, 27 May 1926, in ibid. For an excellent analysis of the book and its broader context, see Dawn, *National Visions, National Blindness*, chap. 5.

93 While Gibbon never shied away from controversy, believing it to help publicity, I have found no evidence to suggest that was the intention with these events. (See for instance Gibbon, letter to Hugh R. Dent, 3 February 1932, "Gibbon, John Murray," folder 643, series 1.1, Dent Records, in which he remarks about another project: "Controversy will help in the publicity.")

94 "Eighteen Hundred Attend Opening of Mountain Highway," *Calgary Daily Herald* (3 July 1923), 6; "Kootenay Indians Entertain Tourists With Gay Pageant," *The Leader-Post* (4 July 1923), 9; "Banff-Windermere Highway Stands As a Monument to Memory of Those Men Who First Conceived It and Those Who in After Years Did the Work," *The Calgary Daily Herald* (7 July 1923), 5; and "Indians Celebrate Opening Banff-Windermere Road," *The Interior News* (31 October 1923), 5.

95 Gibbon, "Scot to Canadian," 145–6.

96 See the *General Programme* (1927), copy found in MB346-14, CMHA. The Wendat singers included "Caroline Groslouis, M.D. Groslouis, Albert Sioui, Alice Sioui, Mde. Abraham Sioui, Michel Sioui, [and] Mme. Vincent." Untitled memo dated 30 May 1927, MB346-11, CMHA.

97 For a brief overview of de la Vérendrye's life and work see Klassen, "The Complicated Case of Juliette Gaultier."

98 An ad with this title appeared in papers in at least eight different American states between March and April 1927.

99 Gibbon, "Scot to Canadian," 144–7; and "Folk Songs of New France Resound in Halls of Chateau," *The Gazette* (21 May 1927), 3.

100 "Le festival de la chanson canadienne attire à Québec des milliers de touristes," *La Presse* (21 mai 1927), 31, 75. See also "M. E.-W. Beatty, président du C.P.R., décide que le festival se répètera en mai 1928 et offer $3,000 en prix," *La Presse* (23 mai 1927), 5.

101 "Le 'Festival de la Chanson,'" *Le Devoir* (24 mai 1927), 2. A graduate of the Institut grégorian in Paris, Lapierre was at that time the organist for the Saint-Jacques church and the director of the Montreal conservatory. See Huot, "Eugène Lapierre."

102 Gibbon, "Scot to Canadian," 147; and "Quebec Festival of Folk Song and Music Is Success," *The Gazette* (23 May 1927), 6.
103 Gibbon, "Scot to Canadian," 147.
104 Gibbon, "Aberdonian to Canadian," 247. Cf. Gibbon, "From Scot to Canadian," 149. By late October 1927, the CPR had already planned to hold a number of festivals the following year, including one at Quebec and Banff, one at Winnipeg, and a Sea Music Festival at Vancouver, all of which came to fruition. See Gibbon, letter to Barbeau, 26 October 1927, MB197-21, CMHA.
105 Pierre V.R. Key, "Pierre Key's Music Article," *The Birmingham News* (29 May 1927), 48; and Marius Barbeau, letter to Gibbon, 3 January 1928, MB197-22, CMHA. Barbeau was referring to Oscar Thompson, "New Festival Turns Spotlight on Canadian Folk Art," *Musical America* (28 May 1927): 3 and 19. A copy is held in MB347-17, CMHA; my thanks to Benoît Thériault for locating it for me.
106 Gibbon, copy of a letter to Dr W.H. Collins, 20 January 1927 ("wider interest"), MB197-22, CMHA; Gibbon, letter to Barbeau, 15 April [1928] ("only a necessary evil"), MB197-23, CMHA; and Gibbon, letter to Barbeau, 4 January 1928 ("certainly poor"), MB197-22, CMHA.
107 Copy of a letter from Gibbon to Juliette Gaultier, 21 March 1928, MB197-22, CMHA.
108 Gibbon, "Scot to Canadian," 151-2; and Daniel Coleman, afterword to *The Foreigner*, 278, citing Karr, *Authors and Audiences*, 28.
109 Gibbon, "Scot to Canadian," 148, 150-5; and Gibbon "Music of the People" ("not very flattering"); see also Gibbon, *Canadian Mosaic*, 192 and 276-8.
110 Daniel Coleman, afterward to *The Foreigner*, 279.
111 Chicanot, "Homesteading the Citizen," 94.
112 "Folk Song Concerts in connection with the New Canadian Folk-Song Festival," *Winnipeg Tribune* (15 June 1928), 21.
113 Gibbon, "Aberdonian to Canadian," 246 ("fascinating"); and Gibbon, "Canadian Letters and the New Canadian." His interest in Japan had not abated in the 1920s; see "Spoke on Japanese Art," *The Gazette* (5 December 1923), 6. He would later take a "delightful trip" to West Indies; see Gibbon, letter to Hugh Dent, 3 February 1932, "Gibbon, John Murray," folder 643, series 1.1, Dent Records.
114 On the history of African Canadian train porters, see Calliste, "Sleeping Car Porters in Canada"; Calliste, "Blacks on Canadian Railways"; Fingard, "From Sea to Rail"; Grizzle, *My Name's Not George*; and

Mathieu, *North of the Color Line*, quote at 10–11. See also Winks, *The Blacks in Canada: A History*, 423–7.

115 In his advice to young advertisers, Gibbon recommended they keep pace with the news and with social trends by subscribing to magazine digests, listening to the radio, and going to the movies twice a week. Gibbon, *If I Were a Young Man Entering Advertising*, 12–13 (a copy of which is held at the WMCR); and conversation with Fiona Gibbon-Taillefer, Alexa Wilson, and Virginia Glover, 5 October 2019.

116 "I regret I have nothing more constructive to offer," he added. Gibbon, letter to Marius Barbeau, 27 October 1933, MB197-24, CMHA. The script in question was likely a draft of "North Woods Adventure" (1933), prepared by Barbeau and Nora Stirling, and Gibbon was referencing O'Neill's 1920 play "The Emperor Jones."

117 Janet E. McNaughton, one of the first to study Gibbon, noted in an important footnote that his work "was limited to promoting the cultures of European ethnic groups; he never dealt with Asians or non-European peoples," but she did not try explain this limitation. Henderson remarks that none of Gibbon's festivals or writings mentioned non-Europeans, while Coleman maintains that, due to his place of birth, Gibbon's exclusion of Asians was "more likely a conscious than an unconscious decision." See McNaughton, "John Murray Gibbon and the Inter-War Folk Festivals," 67 n2; Stuart Henderson, "While There Is Still Time," 165 n4; and Daniel Coleman, "Woodsworth and the Discourse of White Civility," 240 n14. Gillian Mitchell writes: "Gibbon and his colleagues were no radicals, and it appears that the concerts were in some ways as problematic as they were positive, at least with hindsight. For example, neither Asian nor Native Canadian cultures were featured at the concerts." However, the latter claim is clearly erroneous. Gillian Mitchell, *North American Folk Music Revival*, 48.

118 Stuart Henderson, "While There Is Still Time," 158.

119 Gibbon, "Foreign Born," 334; and Gibbon, "European Seeds," 126.

120 Stuart Henderson, "While There Is Still Time," 158.

121 Ibid., 165 n4. "African- and Asian-Canadians were to be seen as anomalies, or at least without an essential Folk that could be compared with the European version," he suggests.

122 Gibbon was not the only high-ranking figure in the CPR who was fascinated by Asian cultures, or at least aspects of them: Sir William Van Horne, the former company president, assembled what at least one critic considered the finest collection of Japanese ceramics in the world. Ron

Notes to pages 164–8

Graham, *Obsession*, 92; and Valerie Knowles, *William C. Van Horne*, chap. 9.
123 Bun, *Smoke and Fire*, 2; and Sabourin and Lambert, "Montréal's Chinatown." See also Madokoro, "On Racism and Taxation."
124 Thompson, "Cultivating Narratives of Race, Faith, and Community."
125 Winks, *The Blacks in Canada*, 320–6; and Mathieu, *North of the Color Line*, esp. 156–84, quotes at 169–70.
126 See for instance James W. St G. Walker, *"Race," Rights, and the Law*, 124–37.
127 Mathieu, *North of the Color Line*.
128 Gillian Mitchell, *North American Folk Music Revival*, 47; Backhouse, *Colour-Coded*, 186, citing the Montreal *Daily Star* (1 October 1921); and Pitsula, *Keeping Canada British*. According to the latter, some urban iterations of the Klan in America were similarly concerned with southern and eastern European immigrants (15–16). The newest work on the subject is Bartley, *The Ku Klux Klan in Canada*.
129 "Picturesque Scene Marks First Western Canadian Handicrafts Exhibition," *Winnipeg Free Press* (20 June 1928), 2. Original reads "arouses."
130 For a list of the festivals, see Stuart Henderson, "While There Is Still Time," 165 n1; and Neilson, "Branding of a Northern Nation," 127–44, appendix 3.
131 Gibbon, "Music of the People." See also "Revival of English Folk Songs Is Seen," *The Gazette* (2 November 1929), 29.
132 Perhaps at the advice of some of the individuals he consulted, Gibbon set the membership fee at $2 so that the guides would be able to join. Gibbon, "Scot to Canadian," 56–7, 60–6, 115–16, and 129–32; and "Trail Riders of the Canadian Rockies," http://trailridevacations.com/.
133 Gibbon, "Scot to Canadian," 131. Pierre-Jean de Smet was a Belgian-born, nineteenth-century Jesuit missionary to Native Americans who spent some time in the Canadian Rockies.

Charles Doolittle Walcott would later become the honorary president of the order. His butler was a man named Arthur Brown, who was classified by the American Census as mulatto. Brown, whose father had been enslaved, worked as a messenger with the U.S. Geological Survey, but had formerly worked on a dining car and at the White House. According to Walcott's daughter Helen, due to his participation in the research, including sawing fossils out of shale, he was considered a "scientist" by the "colored folk in Washington." Brown travelled with the Walcott family as "nurse, cook, general guardian, and friend" and was called "Doc" by the children. Walcott's biographer strenuously denies that Walcott was racist, writing "race simply seems never to have been a concern to Walcott." He adds that, "although Arthur was called the cook, in the field he was the camp manager and the one who made it possible for the geologists to work" and Walcott "trusted him implicitly." Gibbon's identification of Brown as a mere "butler" may have been due to his own preconceptions but it is equally possible that he was basing this on Brown's apparel, as he was expected to always dress the part. In Washington, at least, Brown dressed in uniform when acting as chauffeur before changing into butler's garb when serving food, leading Helen to exclaim that as a child it was "a constant miracle that he could change his clothes so fast!" Brown disappeared from the record in 1928; the family later hired another African American man, Alfonso Jones, as a chauffeur. See Yochelson, *Smithsonian Institution Secretary*, 521-2 and, on their time in the Rockies, 406-13; and "Notables Embark On Opening Ride Up Rocky Trail," *The Gazette* (22 July 1924), 11.

134 Gibbon, "Aberdonian to Canadian," 246.
135 Gibbon, "Scot to Canadian," 136-8.
136 Bart Robinson, *Banff Springs*, 99. See also Jessup, "Tourist Landscape in Western Canada."

CHAPTER FOUR

1 Dreisziger, "The Rise of a Bureaucracy for Multiculturalism." See also Pal, "Identity, citizenship, and mobilization; Pal, *Interests of State*; and Caccia, *Canadian Mosaic in Wartime*.
2 Gibbon, "Scot to Canadian," 164-72, quotes at 164 and 172. Gibbon's missteps during this time may have helped Beatty's decision; see Potter, "Britishness, the BBC, and the Birth of Canadian Public Broadcasting," esp. 86-7; Gibbon, "Radio as Fine Art"; and Gibbon, "Scot to Canadian," 171-2.
3 Bredin, *Leonard Brockington*, 38 and 39. For a more intimate look at his life, see England, *Memoirs*, 170-4.
4 Gibbon, "Aberdonian to Canadian," 248; and Bredin, *Leonard Brockington*, 14 and 25. Nevertheless, Brockington also subscribed to theories of civilizational hierarchy. For instance, in a letter to England decades later, he made an offhanded comment about a cousin and his wife who were "devoting their lives to work amongst the backward peoples of Africa." Brockington, letter to England, 5 December 1965, RE1-5, LAC.

5 Gibbon, "Scot to Canadian," 182; and "Gibbon Will Produce Canadian Folk Series," *The Gazette* (30 December 1937), 5. The series featured Ms Frances James (a soprano soloist) and the Toronto Conservatory String Quartet, led by Elie Spivak. The CNR ran similar programming, such as their historical drama series, "The Romance of Canada," designed to "encourage Canadian national consciousness." Osborne, "Non-Preferred People," 100.
6 "Listening In," *Ottawa Citizen* (8 January 1938), 14. A reviewer in *Variety* noted that "while dignified and impressive, Gibbon's appeal is strictly limited from the showmanship or popular viewpoint, although reaching listeners of a kind not attainable through the usual type of radio productions." [Mori] Krushen, "Canadian Mosaic," *Variety* 129, no. 7 (26 January 1938), 33; and R.A. Farquharson, "Canada Speaks – Sotto Voce," *National Post* (12 February 1938), 13, 16.
7 Gibbon, "Scot to Canadian," 182; Gibbon, "Aberdonian to Canadian," 248; and Gibbon, "Your Theme Is Your Author," 5. Only in the latter does Gibbon claim that both publishers were listening; in the former two he lists only McClelland. On *Canadian Mosaic*'s reception, see the previous chapter, above.
8 I.G. "The Genius of an Empire," *Vancouver Sun* (2 December 1938), 2; and England, "Canadian Mosaic," *Winnipeg Tribune* (8 December 1938), 11. See also Jane Spence Southron, "The Racial Groups That Form the Canadian Mosaic," *The New York Times Book Review* (21 May 1939), 3, 18. The phrase "God has written a line of his thought on the cradle of each race" is attributed to Giuseppe Mazzini.
9 Both quoted in Gibbon, "Scot to Canadian," 183. William Lyon Mackenzie was cited as an example of the Scottish influence in Canada; Mackenzie King was likely more pleased that he too was mentioned in the text as a similar example, along with several members of his Cabinet. See *Canadian Mosaic*, 107–9, 113.
10 Gibbon, *Canadian Mosaic*, 3. Emphasis added.
11 Here Gibbon diverged from some of his peers. Kirkconnell, for instance, argued that "a Canadian race ... is an improbability even after another thousand years ... diverse elements cannot be easily blended into a common type." He continued: "even if every young Canadian were to marry someone unlike him in racial type, the ultimate result would not be the establishment of some sort of general Canadian average." Instead, descendants would "regularly segregate out," thus perpetuating "ancestral types in proportions prescribed by the so-called Mendelian laws of heredity." Kirkconnell, "Race and Nationality," 5.

12 Gibbon, *Canadian Mosaic*, vii, viii.
13 As Daniel Coleman puts it, "all of its tiles will be various shades of white." See his "Discourse of White Civility," 233; and Gibbon, *Mosaic*, xii. A page before, Gibbon remarked: "For various reasons, it was decided to confine this survey to the European racial groups in Canada." For an accessible overview of the Indigenous history of the land that became Canada, see Dickason with McNab, *Canada's First Nations*, esp. chap. 4.
14 Gibbon, *Mosaic*, 413. Emphasis added.
15 Helen Creighton, letter to Henry Button, 14 February 1938, Helen Creighton fonds, MG1, vol. 2811, folder 162, Public Archives of Nova Scotia (PANS). Fan mail from across Canada is found in ibid., vols 2797 and 2818.
16 For his rationale, see England, *Memoirs*, 65; and Manitoba Association for Adult Education, "Minutes of a luncheon meeting held in the Hudson's Bay dining room on Friday, May 15th, 1936," RE1-11, LAC.
17 The Community Progress Competitions had also resulted in further education work. The CNR had worked with western universities and provincial governments to supplement the competitions with "short courses in community progress and Canadian citizenship for delegates from Eastern settlements." England and John MacKay, principal of Manitoba College, directed the course for their province, and in 1934 England also participated in the inauguration of the Manitoba Association for Adult Education and chaired one of their large public meetings. See England, "Use of Group Consciousness," 260; England, CWC, 165; England, *Memoirs*, 61; and "Courses in Community Progress Launched," *Winnipeg Tribune* (11 February 1931), 16.
18 England, *Memoirs*, chapters 6–7. The late Gordon Selman, who directed the Extension Department after England and who chronicled of the history of adult education, found England's contribution to be valuable. Despite his short tenure, Selman wrote, England "launched several important aspects of the program, set some policies which contributed to future growth, and established important relationships inside and outside the University." Selman, "University Extension 1915–1963," 19; Selman, *Fifty Years of Extension Service*, esp. 10–14; and England, "Forty Years Ago, 1936–1937," 5–16. Cf. the erroneous and vitriolic remarks made by England's successor, Gordon Shrum, in his *Autobiography*, 58.
19 See England, *Memoirs*, 76 and 83; and the correspondence found in RE1-2, LAC. During his first years in BC, England briefly served on the CBC's provincial advisory commission.

20 See England, *Memoirs*, 84; the correspondence and contract with Winnipeg Electric in RE6-9, LAC; and his correspondence with UBC in RE1-2, LAC. Perhaps his two most significant contributions while at Winnipeg Electric were his work organizing transportation for the British royalty during their visit to the city in 1939 and his report on the state of the company, completed just prior to his departure. See the certificates relating to the visit from the Royals in RE8, LAC, and his company report in RE6-10, LAC.
21 On their time in Winnipeg, see England, *Memoirs*, chap. 8.
22 England, *Memoirs*, 90; and A.H. Walls, "Along the Air Waves," *Star-Phoenix* (8 September 1938), 4. Those involved in the direction and production of the series aside from England included John Kannawin, Geoffrey Waddington, Dick Claringbull, and Harry Darracott, England's assistant at Winnipeg Electric.
23 A.H. Walls, "Along the Air Waves," *Star-Phoenix* (18 August 1938), 5; and "Canada's Citizenship New Series of CBC," *Leader-Post* (1 September 1938), 19.
24 England, *Memoirs*, 90; "Saskatchewan Man Directs Program," *Leader-Post* (27 September 1938), 7; and "Radio Programmes," *Winnipeg Free Press* (5 October 1938), 2. Mr Brown was voiced by England, Professor MacAlistair by Harry Darracott, Mr Wood by R. E. "Doc" Guy, and Mr Willoughby by Harry R. Low.
25 See the untitled typescript of the first episode (hereafter cited as "Ventures Script"), 8, RE6-5, LAC. The surviving draft has been marked up, presumably by England, but all quotes are to the original text unless otherwise noted.
26 England, *Memoirs*, 90; and "Radio Programmes," *Winnipeg Free Press* (5 October 1938), 2.
27 A H. Walls, "Along the Air Waves," *Star-Phoenix* (11 October 1938), 5. This was most likely Bernard Bronislaw ("B.B.") Dubienski, a prominent Polish Canadian lawyer. See "Bernard Bronislaw Dubienski (1891–1981)"; and Kirkconnell, *Slice*, 269.
28 "Radio," *The Lethbridge Herald* (15 October 1938), 16.
29 See for instance "Dial Your Favourite Program," *The Vancouver Daily Province* (26 October 1938), 17; and "To Give Broadcast on Naturalization," ibid., 22.
30 In Manitoba, naturalization papers were originally simply mailed to new citizens, but around 1931 the Canadian Club in Winnipeg, of which Dysart was then the president, pushed for a formal ceremony. The Department of State acquiesced, and devised a system whereby the

certificates would accumulate until a sufficient number were ready before a public ceremony, sponsored by the Canadian Club, would be held. See "New Citizens to Be Welcomed at Formal Ceremony," *Winnipeg Free Press* (20 May 1932), 10.

31 A.H. Walls, "Along the Air Waves," *Star-Phoenix* (26 October 1938), 2; "To Give Broadcast On Naturalization," *The Province* (26 October 1938), 22.

32 Denny Brown, "On the Air," *Winnipeg Tribune* (2 November 1938), 2.

33 For his initial plans for each of these programs, see England, letter to Kirkconnell, 20 June 1938, WK27-6, ECWA; see also the introduction to "The Polish Contribution" in RE6-5, LAC. The episode on Jewish Canadians has been discussed in detail by Neary, "The CBC 'Adventures in Citizenship.'"

34 Walls, "Along the Air Waves," *Star-Phoenix* (8 November 1938), 5; ibid. (15 November 1938), 7; ibid. (23 November 1938), 5; ibid. (29 November 1938), 7; ibid. (7 December 1938), 7; Denny Brown, "On the Air," *Winnipeg Tribune* (10 December 1938), 4; and ibid. (21 December 1938), 3.

35 See the untitled introduction in RE6-5, LAC. England often repeated the Lamb quote; see for instance CEIC, 187. The phrase "God has written a line of his thought on the cradle of each race" is attributed to Giuseppe Mazzini.

36 "Ventures in Citizenship," *Stonewall Argus* (7 September 1938), 5; England, *Memoirs*, 90; and "Ventures Script."

37 "Ventures Script," 3.

38 Ibid., 8, and 10–11.

39 Ibid., 4–5.

40 Ibid., 9.

41 Ibid., 11 and 17–18.

42 Ibid., 16.

43 Ibid., 19.

44 A.H. Walls, "Along the Air Waves," *Star Phoenix* (1 November 1938), 2; England, letter to Kirkconnell, 6 June 1938; meeting minutes labelled "'Ventures in Citizenship.' Broadcast No. 6," WK27-6, ECWA; and the memo titled "Broadcast Programme:-Re Ventures in Citizenship," RE6-5, LAC.

45 On the celebrations, see Bhimani, "F.H. Hayward (1872–1954)." Hayward was an important part of a movement towards secular moral and citizenship education in interwar Britain and was also an ardent eugenicist; see his *Education and the Heredity Spectre* (1909); and "A School Celebration for a 'Eugenics Day.'"

46 The script is not found in England's files but was later published by its author under the title "Salute to Pioneers." Kirkconnell, *Twilight of Liberty*, chap. 9.
47 "Radio Programmes," *Winnipeg Free Press* (5 October 1938), 2.
48 Ibid.; A.H. Walls, "Along the Air Waves," *Star-Phoenix* (4 October 1938), 2; and "Radio Review," *The Leader-Post* (26 September 1938), 15.
49 Denny Brown, "On the Air," *Winnipeg Tribune* (17 December 1938), 2. For a glimpse at listener reactions, see the correspondence in RE6-4, LAC.
50 In order to pay for the trip, he raised nearly $500 (the equivalent of nearly $9,000 in 2019) by selling a series of press articles on the European situation to the *Winnipeg Evening Tribune*. Kirkconnell, *Slice*, 63, 175, and 336–9; and Kirkconnell, letter to Payerle, 3 December 1938, WK41-32, ECWA. While they are not grouped together, reference information for these articles can be found in Snelson, "Bibliography," 141–54.
51 Kirkconnell, letter to Payerle, 10 November 1938, WK41-32, ECWA; and Kirkconnell, *Slice*, 176. For contrasting examples of early talks, see "Europe – 1938," *Winnipeg Tribune* (15 October 1938), 6; and "Aileen Garland Heads Teachers," *Winnipeg Tribune* (26 November 1938), 21.
52 Baldwin, letter to Kirkconnell, 24 March [1938], WK6-7, ECWA. Kirkconnell was a founding member of the Winnipeg branch of the Canadian Institute of International Affairs (CIIA), which was formed from the Canadian League there in 1927.
53 In January 1939, with remarkable insensitivity, Kirkconnell mentioned to a friend that in a photo taken during his visit to Europe he looked "like a dying victim of the Dachau concentration camp." Upon returning from the trip, he was diagnosed with an ulcer and put on a diet of milk, later increased to include cream and raw eggs. Deciding that the family could not survive on his salary ($2,800 in 1938, rising to $3,000 the following year, or the equivalent of just over $50,000, rising to just under $54,000, in 2019), he set about drafting a promotional pamphlet that he could use to approach other institutions for a higher paying position. Kirkconnell, letters to Béla Payerle, 3, 10, and 21 November 1938 and 21 January 1939, WK41-32, ECWA; and the salary lists from 19 September and 14 November 1939, "Minutes of the Board of Regents, Executive Committee," series 1, file 1, "1938–Aug. 1939," United College fonds, AC-33-1, University of Winnipeg Archives (UWA). The promotional pamphlet is found in WK7-7a, ECWA.
54 Kirkconnell, letter to Baldwin, 27 March 1939, WK6-7, ECWA.
55 Undated note (1940?) found in WK6-16, ECWA. Original reads "pol. Loyalty."

56 Kirkconnell, "Canada's Minorities and Hitler: No. 1 – The Canadian Germans," *Winnipeg Tribune* (22 November 1939), 6.
57 See the correspondence found in WK6-7, ECWA.
58 Clarke, letter to Kirkconnell, 23 September 1939, WK6-7, ECWA. From their correspondence, it seems that Clarke shared with Kirkconnell not only social conservatism, but also a belief in the racial superiority of Anglo-Saxons and a strong sense of imperialism. See Kirkconnell, *Slice*, 127–8; Macskimming, *The Perilous Trade*, 11–12, 14, 17, 46, and 72; and Panofsky, "A Press with Such Traditions," 13.
59 Later in the work, Kirkconnell would refer to "an old style Frenchman's implacable hatred for Britain" (168).
60 Kirkconnell, *Canada, Europe, and Hitler*, 118 (hereafter cited as CEH). Italics in the original. The phrase is a Biblical reference, specifically to Paul's explanation that though Gentiles were not born God's children they could become "sons by adoption."
61 Kirkconnell, CEH, 201, 203–4.
62 Kirkconnell, "The Twilight of Canadian Protestantism," 2.
63 Kirkconnell, CEH, 188.
64 Ibid., 202.
65 Ibid., 202. Italics added.
66 Sandwell, "Europe in Canada," 2. See also "Canadian Minority Views," *Globe and Mail* (25 November 1939), 8; "Canada Is United As Never Before In Face Of Menace," *Winnipeg Evening Tribune* (2 December 1939), 13; T.A. Whitaker, "A Review of Books," *The Expositor* (2 December 1939); "Hitler Has Brought Unity of All Canada," *The Free Press* [London, ON] (13 December 1939); A.S.P. Woodhouse, "The Plain Man and the War," *University of Toronto Quarterly* 9 (1939–1940): 231–8; and A.E. P[rince], "Canada, Europe and Hitler. By Watson Kirkconnell," *Queen's Quarterly* 47, no. 1 (Spring 1940): 102–3. One negative review came Frank Underhill, see his "Canada, Europe and Hitler," *The Canadian Forum* 19, no. 228 (January 1940): 318–9. Many of these reviews can be found as clippings in WK6-8, ECWA, or in correspondence between Kirkconnell and Oxford University Press in WK6-7, ECWA.
67 See "Thoughts of European-Canadians Analyzed by Watson Kirkconnell Professor of Manitoba University," Quebec *Chronicle-Telegraph*, (20 December 1939); "Canada, Europe and Hitler," Montreal *Daily Star* (9 March 1940); Cloutier, letter to Clarke, 30 November 1939, WK6-7, ECWA; and Clarke, letter to Kirkconnell, 5 December 1939, WK6-7, ECWA.

CHAPTER FIVE

1. Roy, *A White Man's Province*, chap. 8.
2. Lee, "Hemispheric Orientalism," 19-20; and Lake and Reynolds, *Drawing the Global Colour Line*, chap. 7.
3. Price, *Orienting Canada*, 16-21.
4. Ibid., 21, 336 n54; Roy, *A White Man's Province*, 202-4; and Gilmour, *Trouble on Main Street*.
5. King Diaries, quoted in Gilmour, *Trouble on Main Street*, 168.
6. Dreisziger, "Turning Point," 96; Harney, "'So Great a Heritage as Ours'"; and King Diaries, for example 29 March 1938, 1 January 1939, 21 July 1941, and 29 September 1942.
7. Dreisziger, "7 December 1941," 96; and King Diaries, 29 March 1938.
8. Abella and Troper, *None Is Too Many*, 9, 17.
9. Daniel Robinson, "Alien Internment, Arbitrary Detention, and the Canadian State," 7.
10. Dreisziger, "Turning Point," 96.
11. Quoted in Daniel Robinson, "Alien Internment, Arbitrary Detention, and the Canadian State," 10.
12. In the late 1980s, there was a heated debate among Canadian historians as to whether the removal of people of Japanese descent living in British Columbia constituted internment or evacuation. See Adachi, *The Enemy That Never Was*; Halloran, "Ethnicity, the State, and War"; Granatstein and Johnson, "The Evacuation of the Japanese Canadians, 1943"; Roy, Granatstein, Iino, and Takamura, *Mutual Hostages*; and Gregory S. Smith, "The Japanese-Canadians and World War II." On the topic more broadly, see Iacovetta, Perin, and Principe, *Enemies Within*; Auger, *Prisoners on the Home Front*; and Bangarth, *Voices Raised in Protest*.
13. Vancouver *Daily Province* (4 April 1942), cited in Sunahara, *The Politics of Racism*, 89. For a broader examination of the forced sales, see Stanger-Ross and the Landscapes of Injustice Research Collective, "Suspect Properties." See also his edited collection, *Landscapes of Injustice*.
14. Bourrie, "The Myth of the 'Gagged Clam.'"
15. Young, "Making the Truth Graphic," 11.
16. Bredin, *Leonard Brockington*, 44-6; Levine, *King*, 8; and Hutton, "Mr. Brockington."
17. On King and national unity, see Levine, *King*, esp. chap. 9.
18. In the spring of 1940, King turned the BPI over to the newly created Department of National War Services. When the BPI became subject to sustained criticism in the fall of 1942, it was transformed into a new

Wartime Information Board (WIB) that was separated from the DNWS and again answered directly to the prime minister. See Dreisziger, "The Rise of a Bureaucracy for Multiculturalism, 4–5; and Young, "Making the Truth Graphic," chap. 1.
19 Kirkconnell, "War Aims and Canadian Unity: I" and "War Aims and Canadian Unity: II."
20 Kirkconnell definitely was self-aggrandizing and would sometimes inflate his achievements but was not prone to outright inventions. Nevertheless, there is no documentation to substantiate this claim, so it should be taken with a grain of salt. For instance, it is entirely possible that King merely asked Brockington to find someone to begin authoring the types of works that MacNeill had recommended, or that Brockington came up with the idea himself and pitched it to the prime minister. Kirkconnell, *Slice*, 275; and Kirkconnell, letter to Brockington, 1 April 1940, WK48-20, ECWA.
21 Kirkconnell, letter to W.H. Clarke, 23 February 1940, WK6-15, ECWA; and Clarke, letter to Kirkconnell, 6 March 1940, WK6-15, ECWA. See also the following letters, all in WK48-20, ECWA: Kirkconnell, letter to Brockington, 1 April 1940; Brockington, letter to Kirkconnell, 10 April 1940; Kirkconnell, letter to Brockington, 18 May 1940; Brockington, letter to Kirkconnell, 22 May 1940.
22 Kordan and Luciuk, "A Prescription for Nationbuilding," 85.
23 Dreisziger, "Rallying Canada's Immigrants," 183. See also Prymak, *Maple Leaf and Trident*, 35–54.
24 Hinther, "Generation Gap," 27.
25 See Kordan, *Canada and the Ukrainian Question*, 12–18; Dreisziger, "Rallying Canada's Immigrants," 183; and Prymak, *Maple Leaf and Trident*, 35–54.
26 Clarke, letters to Kirkconnell dated 6 March 1940 and 13 March 1940, both in WK6-15, ECWA.
27 Kirkconnell, letter to W.H. Clarke, 23 February 1940, WK6-15, ECWA; and Kirkconnell, *Slice*, 274.
28 Mandryka, *Ukrainian Question*. Other Ukrainian reviewers were more sympathetic; see for instance Davidovich, review of *The Ukrainian Question*; Gerald Sandford Graham, "North America and the War"; and, for a recent reappraisal, Swripa, *Ukrainian Canadians*, 134–35 n63. See also Prymak, *Maple Leaf and Trident*, 38–9; and Momryk, "Surveillance of the Ukrainian Community," esp. 100–1. Kirkconnell's reaction was uncharacteristic: dismissing Mandryka's work as "violent and partisan," he chose to ignore it; the two would later resolve their differences.

Kirkconnell, letter to Roman Lapica, 10 June 1940, WK6-15, ECWA; and the correspondence found in WK44-35, ECWA.
29 Clarke, letter to Kirkconnell, 6 March 1940, WK6-15, ECWA; Kirkconnell, letter to Clarke, 8 March 1940, WK6-15, ECWA; and Kirkconnell, *Slice*, 275. Honoré Ewach, née Onufrij Ivakh (1900–1964), immigrated to Canada at age nine. His parents were farmers but he left the farm, studied at and graduated from the University of Manitoba, and spent much of his adult life as the associate editor of a *Ukrainian Voice* (Winnipeg). A published author of poetry and prose, his works included a novella about life in Canada (written in Ukrainian; an English translation was published posthumously), and, with Paul Yuzyk, a Ukrainian grammar. His involvement with this pamphlet saved Kirkconnell from making some further errors; see for instance Ewach, letter to Kirkconnell, 25 April 1940, WK6-15, ECWA.
30 Kirkconnell, *Our Ukrainian Loyalists*, 23; and Kirkconnell, *Ukrainian Canadians and the War*, 2–4, 30.
31 Kirkconnell, *Ukrainian Canadians and the War*, 8, 9, 25.
32 Ibid., 28–9.
33 Ibid., 29; and McKay, "The Liberal Order Framework," 625.
34 Kordan, *Canada and the Ukrainian Question*, 33; and Momryk, "Surveillance of the Ukrainian Community," 102–3.
35 "Professor Kirkconnell to Leave City for East," *Winnipeg Tribune* (14 June 1940), 13; and "Watson Kirkconnell Goes East," ibid. (15 June 1940), 6; and Kirkconnell, *Slice*, 228 ("ulcer"; see also 137); see also the following documents in United College fonds, AC-33-1, series 1, file 2, UWA: Minutes of a meeting held 7 October 1940, "Appendix A: Principal's Report"; Minutes of a meeting held 10 June 1940, Appendix B, "Re: Watson Kirkconnell"; and minutes of a meeting held 3 July 1940, Appendix A, "Resolution of the Board of Regents, United College re Watson Kirkconnell." A few years later, Kirkconnell remarked to Phelps, "I have been pretty healthy since I came east and the tooth of financial worry stopped gnawing at my duodenum." Letter to Phelps, 10 January 1943, WK33-33, ECWA. Information about his salary taken from Kirkconnell, letter to James Mess, 8 February 1941, WK48-22, ECWA.
36 Kirkconnell, *Slice*, 269–70; "Authors' Association Gathers in Honor of Dr. and Mrs. Kirkconnell," *Winnipeg Tribune* (3 July 1940), 4; "Ukrainians Pay Tribute to Watson Kirkconnell," ibid. (5 July 1940), 7; "Mrs. J. H. Riddell Is Hostess At Tea For Mrs. Kirkconnell," ibid. (9 July 1940), 8; and "Winnipeg Poles Honor Professor Kirkconnell," ibid.

(19 July 1940), 5. Kirkconnell's radio address on the eve of his departure is a useful summary of his opinions on the war and on "non-Anglo-Saxon" Canadians at the time. See "Farewell to the West," typescript, WK27-24, ECWA; and "Coming and Going," *Winnipeg Tribune* (27 July 1940), 2.

37 Kirkconnell, letter to Prof. Seton-Watson, 10 April 1942, WK33-70, ECWA; and Kirkconnell, *Slice*, 270.

38 Kirkconnell, "The Canadian Amalgam." See also Louis Adamic, letter to Kirkconnell, 15 July 1941, WK29-3, ECWA; and the manuscript in WK4-11, ECWA. For similar statements from the same period, see Kirkconnell, "Twilight of Canadian Protestantism"; and Kirkconnell, "Canada and Immigration."

Kirkconnell was seemingly unaware of how tone deaf the article came across, especially when it was reprinted, with a few minor additions, in the *Jewish Year Book* under the title "Canada, a Multi-National State." Despite his Jewish audience, he opened by remarking that it would be advantageous to view "the Jewish question (so far as there is one)" from a point of view of national diversity, which would reveal that it was only "one element in the wider problem of national integration." Kirkconnell, "Canada, a Multi-National State," 97; see also the correspondence between Kirkconnell and R. Grossman, in WK47-4, ECWA. Cf. Lipinsky, "The Agony of Israel," 64–5 and 71 n30.

39 Kirkconnell, "Democracy for Canada," 206. This article is the summary of an address delivered to the Public School Department of the Ontario Educational Association, 24 April 1941.

40 Dreisziger, "Bureaucracy for Multiculturalism," 11–12, 27 n40; and Philipps, "Tour in Western Canada, November–December 1941," Murray S. Donnelly fonds (MSS SC 47), box 1, folder 1, University of Manitoba Archives (UMA). Dreisziger clarifies that while the report is dated 1941, the trip occurred the previous year.

41 Kirkconnell, *Slice*, 276. See also Gerus, "Ethnic Politics in Canada"; *Kordan*, "Ukrainian Canadians and the Second World War"; and Dreisziger, "The Achievement of Ukrainian-Canadian Unity."

42 Dreisziger, "Bureaucracy for Multiculturalism," 28 n46; and N.F. Dreisziger, "R. England interview 6–7 October [19]84," Nandor Dreisziger fonds (R11951-49-9-E), vol. 2, file 28, LAC.

43 Dreisziger, "Bureaucracy for Multiculturalism," 13, citing a memo from Thomas Davis. The precise sequence of events is unclear, as the printed version of the speech did not suggest the creation of such a committee as in Kirkconnell's earlier newspaper article; see his *European Elements in Canadian Life*. However, Kirkconnell did widely circulate the address,

sending copies to Brockington and Skelton among others. See Brockington, letter to Kirkconnell, 25 November 1940, WK48-20, ECWA; and Skelton, letter to Kirkconnell, 30 November 1940, WK48-20, ECWA.

44 Belcourt, "Report Made for the Director of Public Information: On the available talent among new Canadians and the advisability of making use of this talent in a series of Radio broadcasts," 3 December 1940, WK6-21, ECWA.

45 Both Kirkconnell and England had a hand in its launch. See Lash, letter to England, 25 June 1941, RE1-3, LAC; England, "Report on the Reorganization of Nationalities Branch, Department of National War Services," 14, Department of Citizenship and Immigration fonds (RG25), vol. 13A, LAC; England, *Memoirs*, 135; and Kirkconnell, *Slice*, 176.

46 House of Commons, *Debates* (7 March 1941), 1334; ibid. (5 November 1941), 4102; and Lash, letter to 'Friends,' 20 February 1941, WK6-21, ECWA.

47 "Judge Davis, or Lash, or both, would see General Crerar about the twelve army officers who would speak for their representative nationality groups. As for the Anglo-Canadian spokesman, I think that was left to the originating stations in each case." Kirkconnell, letter to Darracott, 27 February 1941, WK48-21, ECWA. For excerpts of some soldiers' addresses, see Gibbon, *The New Canadian Loyalists*, 16, 24–5, 29, 36, and 37–8.

48 "Radio News," *Montreal Gazette* (26 February 1941), 2; and Denny Brown, "On the Air," *Winnipeg Tribune* (26 February 1941), 2.

49 "Ukrainians Attest Loyalty to Canada," *Winnipeg Tribune* (27 February 1941), 12; and "The Ukrainians Speak to the Nation," *The Leader-Post* (1 March 1941), 11.

50 "Battle for Freedom," *Times Colonist* (13 March 1941), 7.

51 "King Says World Liberty at Stake," *Winnipeg Tribune* (22 May 1941), 2.

52 Irene Baird, "What Really Matters," *Vancouver Sun* (24 March 1941), 4. Baird was a left-leaning columnist, novelist, and later a civil servant. On her life, Sangster, *The Iconic North*, chap. 5.

53 Reid Forsee, letter to Kirkconnell (and enclosed copy of announcements), 17 February 1941, WK6-20, ECWA. According to one article, the radio series was written and directed by John Kannawin, who also was involved in the production of *Ventures in Citizenship*. See the *Star-Phoenix* (31 March 1941), 4.

Kirkconnell had developed the title a year prior and used it for a brief article in the Isaac Newton High School yearbook. In it, his emphasis on the importance of unity above diversity is clear. "Let me urge, in the first place, that we all think of ourselves primarily as Canadians," he wrote, adding: "The future culture of the Canadian nation will be all the righter if we can tolerantly cherish, until they blend, all of the national traditions of our manifold nationalities." Using a unique (if mixed and somewhat off-putting) metaphor, he declared every European nation to be "a living omelette of scrambled races ... [with] no specific racial characteristics transmitted to all its colonists everywhere" (20). I would like to thank Debbie Houle, librarian at Isaac Newton High, for providing a scan of the yearbook entry.

54 See the following letters, all in WK6-21, ECWA: Kirkconnell, letter to Lash, 12 March 1941; Lash, letter to Kirkconnell, 13 June 1941; and Claude Melançon, letter to Kirkconnell, 8 July 1941.

55 Kirkconnell, *Canadians All*, 4.

56 Ibid., 5–20. See for instance Kirkconnell, CEH; Kirkconnell, "War Aims and Canadian Unity"; and Kirkconnell, *European Elements in Canadian Life*, among others. As for the list of prominent figures from each racial background, Kirkconnell sent a form letter to their consulates; see twelve such letters in WK6-21, ECWA. The rest of the information was gleaned from Belcourt, "Report Made for the Director of Public Information."

57 Kirkconnell, *Canadians All*, 8.

58 Ibid., 11–19, quotes at 11 and 17. Emphasis in the original.

59 Ibid., 21; and Herbert, letter to Kirkconnell, 11 April 1940, WK6-21, ECWA.

60 Daniel Coleman, "Woodsworth and the Discourse of White Civility," 228; Day, *Multiculturalism*, 8, 116, and 127–34, esp. 131; and J.S. Woodsworth, *Strangers Within Our Gates*, 8–9. Levantines referred to people from the Eastern Mediterranean including Greeks, Turks, Armenians, and Syrians. By "Indian," Woodsworth meant the Indigenous peoples of North America.

61 Day, *Multiculturalism*, 161–2 and 190. Day's critique of *Canadians All* is flawed as he was unaware that there were two editions and that he was analyzing the second, revised edition.

62 Herbert, letter to Kirkconnell, 11 April 1941, WK6-21, ECWA.

63 In the process of researching *Canadians All*, Kirkconnell did write the consul general of China in Ottawa to request information on "Canadians of Chinese origin who have distinguished themselves in professional life, the arts, literature, or in any other way," but there is no record of a reply. Kirkconnell, letter to the Consul General of China, 11 March 1941, WK6-21, ECWA.

64 Belcourt, "Report Made for the Director of Public Information," 1, WK6-21, ECWA.
65 Ibid., 2. Emphasis added.
66 Lash, letter to "Friends," 20 February 1941, WK6-21, ECWA.
67 Herbert, letter to Kirkconnell, 7 April 1941, WK6-21, ECWA; and Young, "Making the Truth Graphic," 438.
68 Belcourt, "Report Made for the Director of Public Information," 3.
69 In preparing to write the section on the Jews, Kirkconnell had consulted the Canadian Jewish Congress. See Kirkconnell, *Slice*, 273; Oscar Cohen, letter to Kirkconnell, 20 March 1941, WK6-21, ECWA; and Cohen, letter to Kirkconnell, 7 April 1941, WK6-22, ECWA.
70 Herbert, letter to Kirkconnell, 7 April 1941, WK6-21, ECWA.
71 Kirkconnell, "Canada and the Refugees"; "The Agony of Israel"; *CEH*, 157; and *Slice*, 272–4. As he later complained to Claris Silcox, the director of the Canadian Conference of Christians and Jews, "if one ventures to mention the fact of any Jewish contact with Communism, the unfailing response is a universal roar of 'anti-Semitism.'" Kirkconnell, letter to Silcox, 22 November 1944, WK47-6, ECWA.
72 Kirkconnell, *Canadians All*, 5–6.
73 Horsefield, letter to the Director of the Bureau of Public Information, 21 July 1941, WK6-21, ECWA.
74 Herbert, letter to Kirkconnell, 30 July 1941, WK6-21, ECWA. Kirkconnell later claimed that a total of 396,000 copies of the booklet were distributed, although by 1942 only 232,000 English and 64,000 French copies had been printed. Kirkconnell, *Slice*, 176; House of Commons, *Debates* (14 May 1942), 2417; and ibid. (15 February 1943), 397.
75 See the following letters, all in WK6-21, ECWA: Herbert, letter to Kirkconnell, 13 July 1941; Herbert, letter to Kirkconnell, 17 September 1941; O.H. Walby, letter to the Director of Public Information, 30 July 1941; Horsefield, letter to the Director of the Bureau of Public Information, 21 July 1941; and Kirkconnell, letter to Herbert, 20 September 1941. Cf. House of Commons, *Debates* (14 May 1942), 2417.
76 See the following letters, all in WK6-21, ECWA: Rev. Alex W. Robertson, letter to Kirkconnell, 22 July 1941; Rev. R.M. Dickey, letter to Kirkconnell, 19 July 1941; Robert Kyle, letter to Kirkconnell, 3 May 1941; Kirkconnell, letter to Mrs McLarty, 16 March 1943; and Prof. B. Ifor Ivans, letter to Kirkconnell, 15 June 1941.
77 Ayque de Meira, letter to Kirkconnell, n.d. [1942], WK40-2, ECWA; see also the following letters, all in WK6-21, ECWA: Mrs Albert Fix, letter to Kirkconnell, 23 July 1941; A.E. Fisk, letter to Kirkconnell, 5 August 1941;

Victoria Babich, letter to Kirkconnell, 27 January 1943; Pauline Donalda, letter to Kirkconnell, 19 October 1941; Richard Beck, letter to Kirkconnell, 25 August 1941; Professor B. Ifor Ivans, letter to Kirkconnell, 15 June 1941; and Muriel McLarty, letter to Kirkconnell, 12 March 1943, 3.
78 See the following letters, all in WK6-21, ECWA: Kirkconnell, letter to E.S. Deacon, 22 November 1941; Mrs Frank Murchie, letter to the Director of National War Services, 3 July 1941; Kirkconnell, letter to Mrs Frank Murchie, 19 July 1941; A.P. Turner, letter to the Director of Public Information, 26 July 1941; Dr W.P. Percival, letter to Herbert, 25 July 1941; and Kirkconnell, letter to Herbert, 14 August 1941. Kirkconnell described Percival's letter as "priceless" but there is no record of Kirkconnell's reply.
79 House of Commons, *Debates*, (14 May 1942), 2417; ibid. (18 May 1942), 2537–9; ibid. (15 February 1943), 397; ibid. (17 April 1944); and ibid. (27 April 1944), 2398, 2407–11, 2416–18, and 2422–3.
80 Kirkconnell, *Our Ukrainian Loyalists*; and Kordan, "Soviet-Canadian Relations," 11, citing G. de T. Glazebrook, memo to N. Robertson, 25 June 1943, RG25, G1, vol. 1896, file 165, Part III, LAC. "It would be hard to imagine anything less helpful than the line he is taking," Grazebrook remarked. Fred Rose, a member of the Communist Party (and later Labor-Progressive Party) made a similar suggestion the following year. "I should think that article 39-A of the defence of Canada regulations is a good article with which to deal with Mr. Watson Kirkconnell." House of Commons, *Debates* (27 April 1944), 2408.
81 Kirkconnell, *Slice*, 276. See also "Russia Is Imperative To Stable Peace Hope, Joseph Davies Declares," *Globe and Mail* (23 June 1943), 1; and "Kirkconnell Hits Canadian Communists," ibid., 27.
82 Kirkconnell, letter to Mr. [W.F.] Sutherland, 12 August 1943, WK33-59, ECWA ("rampage"); and G. Jones, letter to Kirkconnell, 11 February 1944, WK60-22, ECWA. See also Kirkconnell, letter to Capt. G.W. McCracken, 12 August 1943, WK33-59, ECWA.
83 Kirkconnell, *Slice*, 322; and the registration certificate dated 10 May 1945, WK4-20, ECWA.
84 Elliott, letter to Gibbon, 10 April 1941, Macmillan Company of Canada fonds, RC0071 (hereafter "Macmillan fonds"), box 96, file 1, William Ready Division of Archives and Research Collections, McMaster University Library (ARCMUL). The company showered him with praise, writing that they would be proud to have his name and its prestige associated with the series. Letters to Gibbon, 18 April and 2 May 1941, in ibid. For Gibbon's recollections, see "Scot to Canadian," 185.

85 Gibbon, *The New Canadian Loyalists*, 3–5; Norman Knowles, *Inventing the Loyalists*; Gibbon, letter to Mr Henderson, 3 July 1941, Macmillan fonds, box 96, file 1, ARCMUL; and G.E. Rogers, letter to Gibbon, 7 July 1941, Macmillan fonds, box 96, file 1, ARCMUL.
86 Gibbon, *The New Canadian Loyalists*, 9.
87 Ibid., 9, 18, 34; and James W. St G. Walker, *The Black Loyalists*. The term "Black Loyalists" has been vigorously contested, see Cahill, "The Black Loyalist Myth"; and James W. St G. Walker, "Myths, History and Revisionism." Some have even described the Loyalist movement using Gibbon's preferred metaphor; see for instance Magee, *Loyalist Mosaic*.
88 The pamphlet's "racialist overtones and assimilationist impulses" are noted in Mackey, *House of Difference*, 50–1.
89 Petrowsky, a frequent correspondent of Kirkconnell's, was a well-known Ukrainian Canadian author and artist who became a translator and interpreter for the RCMP before turning to undercover work. See the following letters, all in Macmillan fonds, box 96, file 1, ARCMUL: Gibbon, letter to Colin Henderson, 25 June 1941; Gibbon, letter to Henderson, 3 July 1941; Gibbon, letter to G.E. Rogers, 17 July 1941; Gibbon, letter to Elliott, 22 September 1941 (quote from Petrowsky); and Gibbon, letter to Elliott, 27 September 1941.
90 "Literature Owes Much to Press Dr. Murray Gibbon Declares," *The Province* (22 August 1941), 18; see also the following letters, all in Macmillan fonds, box 96, file 1, ARCMUL: Gibbon, letter to Elliott, 22 September 1941; Gibbon, letter to Elliott, 27 September 1941 (and copy of a note from Roberts); Gibbon, letter to Elliott, 30 September 1941; Elliott, letter to Gibbon, 1 October 1941; Gibbon, letter to Elliott, 7 November 1941; Elliott, letter to Gibbon, 11 November 1941 (and enclosure; a translated copy of one review). See also "A Salute to New Canadians," *Montreal Gazette* (30 September 1941), 8; "New Books," *National Post* (4 October 1941), 4; "Tribute to New Canadians," *Globe and Mail* (9 October 1941), 6; "Would Recognize New Canadian Loyalists" (1 November 1941), 54; "New President At St. Andrews" *Star-Phoenix* (11 September 1942), 9; "St. Andrew's Group Enjoys Program," *Windsor Star* (7 October 1942), 15; and "St. Andrew's W.M.S.," *Ottawa Citizen* (19 March 1943), 5.
91 King Diaries, 11 June 1941, quoted in Bertram, "New Icelandic Ethnoscapes," 106.
92 In 1942, the CCCC consisted of H.F. Angus, C.H. Blakeny, Maj. J.S.A. Bois, Jean Bruchési, Donald Cameron, Dr S.D. Clark, Robert England, J.M. Gibbon, Watson Kirkconnell, Margaret McWilliams, George W. Simpson,

and Isabel Skelton. On its history, see especially Caccia, *Canadian Mosaic in Wartime*; Pal, *Interests of the State*; Pal, "The Nationalities Branch in World War Two"; and Dreisziger, "Bureaucracy for Multiculturalism."

93 Caccia acknowledged the trend even while continuing it; see her *Canadian Mosaic in Wartime*, esp. 5–7 and 68–89; Kristmanson, *Plateaus of Freedom*, esp. 1–48; Kordan, *Canada and the Ukrainian Question*; Patrias, *Jobs and Justice*, 157–82; Dreisziger, "Bureaucracy for Multiculturalism," 10–12; and Dreisziger, "The Achievement of Ukrainian-Canadian Unity," 326–41.

94 Bangarth, review of *Managing the Canadian Mosaic in Wartime*, 184.

95 [Simpson,] "Memorandum on the Establishment of a Committee on Cultural-Group Cooperation to Advise the Minister of National War Services," copy found in WK48-22, ECWA; and "Summary of discussion of the first Meeting of the Committee on Co-operation in Canadian Citizenship ..." (10 January 1942), copy found in WK48-22, ECWA. Emphasis in the original, as underlining. The decision to exclude Canadians of Asian descent was deliberate but perhaps belated, given that Angus had been considered for the Committee precisely because of his expertise on "the Japanese-Canadian minority in British Columbia." See "Memorandum for the Prime Minister" (11 March 1941), MG26, J4, vol. 242, page C163381, LAC. Further details about Angus are found in Ward, *White Canada Forever*, 140.

Years later, when interviewed by Howard Palmer, England was defensive about the exclusion of Asian Canadians from the activities of the Nationalities Branch, arguing variously that Japanese Canadians were outside their purview, that late-comers were considered enemy aliens, that Chinese numbered only in the hundreds, and that the war in China was "confused." Palmer, interview with England (typescript), 59–60, HP5-28, UCASC.

96 "Summary of discussion of the fourth meeting of the Committee on Co-operation in Canadian Citizenship..." (25–26 November 1943), marked "Draft," pp. 3–4, George W. Simpson fonds, MG7 (hereafter "Simpson fonds"), box 1, file 9, University of Saskatchewan Archives (USA); and Paul Poremsky, "A Ukrainian Speaks," *The Gazette* [Montreal] (8 November 1943), 8.

97 "Summary of a Discussion of the first Meeting of the Committee on Co-operation in Canadian Citizenship held ... January 10th, 1942," 2–3, WK48-22, ECWA; and "Summary of a discussion of the third meeting ..." (23 September 1942), 5–6, Simpson fonds, series 1, box 1, file 9, USA.

98 Gibbon, "Part of a Three Year Plan," in which he compared the project to the existing the Everyman's Library Series published J.M. Dent. His plan for the Carnegie funding was not unthinkable in this period; see Brison, *Rockefeller, Carnegie, & Canada*.
 99 Copy of a letter from Mitchell to Gibbon, 15 June 1942, WK33-52, ECWA.
100 "Summary of a Discussion of the first Meeting...," 3.
101 Kirkconnell, "Report on Literary Aspects of the projected 'Legacy of Literature Library,'" n.d. [March 1942?], WK33-54, ECWA.
102 "Committee on Co-operation in Canadian Citizenship: Summary of a discussion of the second meeting ..." (11 March 1942), Department of National War service fonds (RG44), vol. 36, file "Committee on Cooperation in Canadian Citizenship," LAC.
103 Kirkconnell, letter to Simpson, 17 March 1948, WK33-51, ECWA; and Gibbon, letter to Simpson, 13 March 1942, WK33-51, ECWA.
104 Gibbon, telegram to Kirkconnell, 10 November 1942, WK33-30, ECWA; and "All Germans Foes U.S. Author Holds," *Montreal Gazette* (10 November 1942), 9. See also Gibbon, *Brahms and Schuberts' Songs Transplanted*; and Gibbon, "Scot to Canadian," 192–3.
105 Interview with Murray and Frances Adaskin (9 November 1972), S1/70, WMCR (transcription by the author); and Lazarevich, *Musical World*, 83–4.
106 Gibbon, letter to Kirkconnell, 20 January 1942, WK33-50, ECWA.
107 Kirkconnell, letter to Simpson, WK33-51, ECWA. "Send to Coventry" is an idiom meaning to deliberately ostracize someone; "contumely" refers to harsh treatment stemming from contempt. The irony of Kirkconnell, the author of *Canadians All*, opposing discrimination in a government publication was apparently lost on all involved.
108 Gibbon, letter to Kirkconnell, 19 March 1942, WK33-51, ECWA.
109 See the following letters all in WK33-51, ECWA: Simpson, letter to Kirkconnell, 19 March 1942; Kirkconnell, letter to Gibbon, 24 March 1942; Gibbon, letter to Kirkconnell, 26 March 1942; Gibbon, letter to Kirkconnell, 27 March 1942; and copy of a letter from Simpson to Gibbon, 25 March 1942.
110 Section II of the RSC was limited to scholars of English Literature, History, and Archaeology. See Gibbon, letter to Kirkconnell, 20 April 1942, and enclosure, "A Secular Bible for a New Canada," WK33-51, ECWA; and the following documents all in WK33-52, ECWA: Gibbon, letter to Kirkconnell, 26 March 1942; copy of a letter from Gibbon to Simpson, 27 March 1942; Gibbon, letter to Simpson, 1 April 1942; Gibbon, letter to Kirkconnell, 15 April 1942; copy of a letter from Simpson to Gibbon, 13

April 1942; Kirkconnell, letter to Gibbon, 17 April 1942; and Gibbon, letter to Kirkconnell, 19 May 1942. According to his letter of 20 April 1942, Gibbon initially considered titling the talk "a Secular Bible for New Canadian Loyalists."

111 "A Secular Bible for a New Canada," WK33-51, ECWA.
112 Blaming a group for its supposed inferiority complex while not discussing the prejudice they faced was an unfortunate habit of Gibbon's, one especially seen in his treatment of women. In a later address to the RSC on "Women as Folk-Song Authors," he confidently declared: "the trouble with women is that they have, or at least used to have, an inferiority complex." In the case of New Canadians, however, he did more frequently comment on the prejudice they faced. See Gibbon, "A Secular Bible for New Canada," 93; "Women as Folk-Song Authors," 53; *Mosaic*, 276–7; and *The New Canadian Loyalists*, 4.
113 Gibbon, "Secular Bible," 94, 96, 98.
114 Ibid., 94, 96. For a summary of the talk in the press, see [William A. Deacon,] "Uniting Canada's Minority Races by Translating Great Literature," *Globe and Mail* (30 May 1942), 9. Gibbon was buoyed by this article, repeatedly mentioning it to Kirkconnell (see the letters dated 11 and 17 July 1942 in WK33-53, ECWA).
115 Button, letter to Kirconnell, 2 February 1941, WK33-50, ECWA.
116 Gibbon, letter to Kirkconnell, 17 July 1942; and copy of a letter from Gibbon to Brockington, 22 June 1942, WK33-53, ECWA.
117 Innis, letter to Kirkconnell, 28 July 1942; and Innis, letter to Kirkconnell, 11 August 1942, and enclosed "Instructions to the Committee on the Murray Gibbon proposals," WK33-53, ECWA.
118 Gibbon, letter to Kirkconnell, 18 December 1942, WK33-32, ECWA; Kirkconnell, letter to Gibbon, 23 December 1942, WK33-32, ECWA; Kirkconnell, *Slice*, 307–8; and the following letters, all in WK33-52, ECWA: Simpson, letter to Kirkconnell, 12 June 1942; Kirkconnell, letter to Simpson, 17 June 1942; Simpson, letter to Kirkconnell, 21 June 1942; Gibbon letter to Kirkconnell, 23 June 1942. In November, Kirkconnell provided a brief update on the project to the CCCC; see "Summary of a discussion of the third meeting ...," 5.
119 "Bishop White's enthusiasm for the Chinese classics ought to add a valuable ingredient to our mixture." Kirkconnell, letter to Gibbon, 3 June 1943, WK33-54, ECWA.
120 "Report of a Special Committee of Section II, Royal Society of Canada," n.d. [4 May 1943], WK33-54, ECWA. One notable aspect of the "Report"

is its insistence on the necessity of a Humanities Research Council. On its formation, see Kirkconnell, *Slice*, chap. 18.

121 Gibbon, letter to Kirkconnell, 1 June 1943, WK33-54, ECWA; and Gibbon, letter to Kirkconnell, 7 June 1943, WK33-54, ECWA.

122 "Summary of discussion of the fourth meeting," 6, Simpson fonds, box 1, file 9, USA. In his memoirs, Kirkconnell claimed that he completed the readers; see *Slice*, 307–8.

123 "Advisory Committee on Co-operation in Canadian Citizenship (Nationalities Branch)," 5 and 20–1, Simpson fonds, box 1, file 9, USA.

124 This is not to suggest that Canada's actions during the Second World War were comparable to the Nazis, but rather to acknowledge the international spread of race science. While the two countries had radically different policy outcomes, both were based on ideas about race that were more similar than is perhaps comfortable for us to recognize. Germany had certainly developed its own canon of scientific racist tracts but Hitler's close advisors had read Madison Grant and Arthur de Gobineau, the only two non-German authors on the Nazi Party's official list of recommended works on human heredity. Hitler wrote to Grant that his book, *The Passing of the Great Race*, was "his Bible," though Grant's biographer suggests Hitler probably "absorbed Grant secondhand, through the works of German eugenicists influenced by Grant." Spiro, *Defending the Master Race*, chap. 14 (quotes at 357).

125 C.H. Payne, letter to Robert England, 29 March 1944, RE3-1, LAC.

126 England, memo to Deputy Minister [Payne], 15 May 1944, RE3-1, LAC.

CONCLUSION

1 Some of this research was presented as "'Chasing More Precise Details': Canadian Multiculturalism in the 1970s" (Paper, Between Postwar and the Present Day conference, University of Guelph, 6–8 May 2021).

2 Caccia, *Canadian Mosaic in Wartime*, chap. 8; and Pal, *Interests of State*, 72–7.

3 England, "Report on the Reorganization of Nationalities Branch, Department of National War Services," 3, 9, 11–12, RG26, vol. 13A, LAC. His report is also neatly summarized in Pal, *Interests of the State*, 75–7.

4 England later claimed that his report provided the inspiration for Martin's bill, though it appears Martin gave him no credit. England, "Reminiscences of a Pioneer," 28; and England, *Memoirs*, 142. In the editor's introduction to the former, Howard Palmer declared that

"England was also the principal author of the first Canadian Citizenship Act (1947)." Cf. Paul Martin, "Citizenship and the People's World." England's claim appears to be based on the account of John Bobbins; see his letter to England, 16 January 1948, RE1-3, LAC. Gibbon similarly claimed that his *Mosaic* was an inspiration; see "Scot to Canadian," 184.

5 House of Commons, *Debates* (22 October 1945), 1337; ibid. (2 April 1946), 502 ("objective"); and Chapnick, "Canadian Citizenship in History," 444.

6 "Proud, Historic Ceremony as New Citizens Take Oath," *Ottawa Citizen* (4 January 1947), 29. The "Text of the Prime Minister's Speech" can be found on the same page. Information about the broadcast and the Citizenship Branch's sponsorship of the ceremony is taken from Jack Strickland, "I Am a Canadian," *The Vancouver Daily Province* [Saturday Magazine section] (4 January 1947), 1; and details of the rehearsal are found in "Participants Briefed in Citizenship Ceremony," *Ottawa Citizen* (3 January 1947), 12.

7 House of Commons, *Debates* (1 May 1947), 2644–7.

8 FitzGerald and Cook-Martín, *Culling the Masses*, 7 and 144. Their broader argument, that there is no inherent relationship between liberalism and racism, has rightly been critiqued by a number of scholars; see esp. the articles in Bulmer and Solomos, eds., "Symposium."

9 At times, this argument has even made its way into the popular press; see for instance Doug Saunders, "Canada's mistaken identity," *Globe and Mail* (26 June 2009), https://www.theglobeandmail.com/news/world/canadas-mistaken-identity/article787370/. In addition to the scholarship referenced below, I should also add mention of Shaw and Smith, "Lady Aberdeen." I arrived at the article too late to incorporate it into this discussion, but would like to thank Lee Blanding for bringing it to my attention.

10 Careless, "'Waspishness' and Multiculture in Canada," 301. This is a revised version; in the introduction to the volume, Careless mentions that this particular essay was first read before the Royal Society of Canada and published that same year in the proceedings. See Careless, "Waspishness and Multiculture." All references are to the former. I would like to thank A2 for pushing me to examine Careless's argument.

11 Careless, "'Waspishness' and Multiculture in Canada," 297.

12 Carter, *Imperial Plots*.

13 Valerie Knowles, *Strangers at Our Gates*, 95 ("Not infrequently, employment ads in western newspapers included the words 'No English Need Apply'").

14 Schwinghamer, "The Colour Bar at the Canadian Border"; and Statistics Canada, "150 Years of Immigration in Canada."
15 Kirkconnell was what he called a "fourth generation Canadian," whose great-grandparents emigrated from Scotland in 1819. His deep and lifelong belief in hereditarianism drove him to, later in life, meticulously trace his family lineage back to his earliest ancestors in Scotland and thoroughly examine each branch of the family tree for any undesirable traits or illnesses. It is unclear how he was able to determine if any of his ancestors had such traits over the previous seven centuries, but he nevertheless proudly declared that he had "found no skeletons in any ancestral Kirkconnell cupboard." Yet his insistence on the perfection of his family line required him to ignore his own physical health and one of his children's mental health. (In the 1940s, James Kirkconnell was diagnosed with schizophrenia. He eventually spent eight weeks in a mental hospital, received electric shock treatment, and was then declared cured. After a brief stint in journalism he went on become a successful advertising executive with the Toronto-based firm Vickers and Benson.) See Kirkconnell, Day Planner, entries for 27, 29, 30 November and 1 and 2 December, 1945, WK1-6, ECWA; Kirkconnell, letter to Béla Payerle, 13 March 1946, WK41-33, ECWA; and Kirkconnell, *Slice*, 4, 7, 123 n1. His genealogical works include *Kirkconnell Pedigree*; *Climbing the Green Tree and Other Branches*; and *Medieval Mosaic*.
16 Daniel Coleman, *White Civility*, 17–19.
17 Marion and Kirkconnell, *The Quebec Tradition*. He would later argue, "I have done my share in interpreting the literature of Quebec to the rest of Canada ... but have always felt, since I settled in Winnipeg in 1922, that the European-Canadians were even more in need of an interpreter." Kirkconnell, letter to George Drew, 28 December 1964, WK58-28, ECWA.
18 Henshaw, "British Imperial Origins of Canadian Multiculturalism"; McKay and Swift, *Warrior Nation*, esp. 4, 16–18, 59–61, 271. And then there is Gorman's sympathetic portrayal of Buchan as a moderate imperialist with "an ecumenical understanding of race and a Romantic conservatism," who developed an idea of imperial citizenship. He further implies that those who accuse Buchan of being racist (which he no doubt was) are simply intemperate. Gorman, *Imperial Citizenship*, esp. chap. 3. See also Galbraith, "Maligning a Model Governor-General."
19 Works denouncing Buchan include Gina M. Mitchell, "John Buchan's Popular Fiction"; Magubane, *The Making of a Racist State*; and McKay and Swift, *Warrior Nation*; while works lauding him include Henshaw,

"British Imperial Origins of Canadian Multiculturalism"; and Galbraith, *Model Governor General*.

20 See for instance Boyd, "First-degree racism and snobbery with violence." Cf. John Roger Clarke, "John Buchan's Uncollected Journalism," 134–5.

21 This point is made by neoconservative scholar Richard Kimball, though he excuses Buchan's early anti-Semitism on the grounds that "nearly everyone in his society was." See Kimball, "Catching up with John Buchan." Defences like these were dismissed by the late critic Christopher Hitchens, who remarked: "It's not merely that anti-Jewish clichés occur in [Buchan's] books; it's that they occur so frequently." Hitchens, "Great Scot." Most recently, Freeman-Maloy has noted that Buchan "gradually recast Jews as worthy settlers for Palestine. Yet in his writings, the image of the Jew as useful settler was slow to eclipse that of the Jew as oriental subversive." See his "Remembering Balfour," 10.

22 See Galbraith, "Maligning a Model Governor-General"; and Galbraith, letter to the editor of the *Literary Review of Canada*, in which he maintains that "the high death rates for blacks (and Boer women and children) in refugee camps [sic] ... came down from a range of 20–34 percent to 3–6 percent in the first seven months that Buchan was administering them."

23 Buchan, *The African Colony*, 75; and Freeman-Maloy, "Remembering Balfour," 7.

24 Buchan, *Sick Heart River*, 167; and Buchan, "Down North," 16; both quoted in Hutchings, "Teller of Tales."

25 The text of the speech can be found in "Tweedsmuir Is Received With Loyal Homage," *Montreal Gazette* (25 November 1935), 2; it was later published in Buchan, *Canadian Occasions*. This speech is quoted by some of Buchan's other boosters; see for instance Ipperciel, "Britannicité et multiculturalism canadien," 292.

26 Henshaw, "British Imperial Origins of Canadian Multiculturalism," 191.

27 Henshaw's later argument, that Buchan "rejected the racial conception of empire," is entirely at odds with this reality. Further, while Henshaw does not discuss skin colour, Buchan showed no such hesitation and racialized people and people groups as "black" or "white." Henshaw, "British Imperial Origins of Multiculturalism," 208; and, for some examples of his racializing impulse, Buchan, *The African Colony*, 40 and 67.

28 For instance, Henshaw argues that Gibbon "followed, quoted, and might even have been partially inspired by Buchan." While no evidence is cited for this claim, it seems to be based on the fact that in *Canadian Mosaic*, Gibbon quoted the passage in which Buchan uttered his now famous line, "You will all be better Canadians for being also good Ukrainians."

However, as chapter 3 has made clear, Gibbon developed his philosophy of cultural pluralism independently, that is, without Buchan's influence. Further, Gibbon's unpublished autobiography reveals that he met Buchan while the two were studying at Oxford and instantly disliked him. According to Gibbon, Buchan attended Brasenose College, which considered itself "extremely select, and my recollection of John Buchan was that he wished to be listed as among the chosen people." He also recalled that Buchan "already had written a novel, and liked to make it known he was writing another, by having his manuscript conspicuously displayed on a reading desk in the middle of his room." See Henshaw, "British Imperial Origins of Canadian Multiculturalism," 205; Gibbon, *Canadian Mosaic*, 307; and Gibbon, "Scot to Canadian," 13. The discrepancy between these accounts has previously been noted by Neilson, "The Branding of a Northern Nation," 135.

Henshaw also writes that Buchan "may have" read and been influenced by Watson Kirkconnell. Though he did not cite any sources, there is some scant but tantalizing evidence to support this claim. In 1936, Kirkconnell, ever the self-promoter, had sent a number of his books to the new Governor General, including the biography of his father, *A Canadian Headmaster*, and "very precious books of poems," which may have included *Canadian Overtones*, the work which laid out most explicitly Kirkconnell's philosophy of cultural pluralism. In early June Kirkconnell received a glowing reply from John Buchan's sister, Anna (who was visiting Canada at the time). She thanked him for the books and informed him that she and her mother had read *Headmaster*, that her brother was next in line to read it, and that they had been reading selections from it aloud in their drawing room. Kirkconnell must have kept the family on his mailing list, for a year later, in a letter marked personal, John Buchan thanked Kirkconnell for the copy of his eugenically tinged poem, "Manitoba Symphony." The brief note added that Buchan had read it "with great enjoyment" and hoped to meet Kirkconnell on his next trip to Winnipeg. See Anna Buchan, letter to Kirkconnell, 2 June 1936, WK60-9, ECWA; and Lord Tweedsmuir, letter to Kirkconnell, 31 December 1937, WK60-9, ECWA.

29 Ipperciel, "Britannicité et multiculturalism canadien," a revised and translated version of appeared as "Britishness and Canadian Multiculturalism." Quote is from the latter, at 54. Emphasis added.
30 One of Ipperciel's primary sources, writing in 1926, admitted that the principle was not universally applied; Alfred Zimmern, a professor of international relations, remarked that while the "established British

principle in regard to racial distinctions is one of complete equality," it had been "very difficult, and in some cases impossible, to apply literally." Zimmern continued on to place the blame on "complex local conditions in certain territories" and then very quickly moved to "concentrate on the question of principle." Zimmern, *The Third British Empire*, 84. Cf. Ipperciel, "Britannicité et multiculturalisme canadien," 302 n25.

31 There is a large and growing literature on this history and the Komagata Maru incident specifically, but see especially Dhamoon et al., eds., *Unmooring the Komagata Maru*; Johnston, *The Voyage of the Komagata Maru*; and Gilmour, *Trouble on Main Street*.

32 Stevenson, *Building Nations From Diversity*, 166. For context, see Benner, "Stevenson Stripped of Emeritus Status."

33 "A Citizen Camera Goes to Lisgar's Annual Concert," *Ottawa Citizen* (18 February 1947), 13; Hugh Dempsey, "The Concert," in *Vox Lycei* (1947), 44 ("superlative"); and Sheila Lamke, "Glee Club," *Vox Lycei* (1947), 43. The Glee Club had renamed themselves "Curly's Pop-over Minstrels" for the occasion. Listing the performers, Dempsey joked: "You mean to say you couldn't see past that stove polish?"

34 See "First Citizenship Certificates Given at Impressive Ceremony in Armories," *Victoria Daily Times* (11 January 1947), 8; and "Great Throng Attends Citizenship Week Ceremony," *Windsor Daily Star* (11 January 1947), 5.

35 Lisgar Collegiate was not exceptional in staging such a performance; rather, such racism was common in Canadian society throughout this period. Minstrel shows in particular were performed by touring groups from the 1870s through the 1920s, after which they were largely replaced by amateur minstrel shows. These shows continued through the 1950s, with some instances occurring into the early 1960s. On the history of minstrelsy and blackface in Canada, see Thompson, "Blackface Minstrelsy as Canadian Tradition"; Nicks and Slonioswki, "Entertaining Niagara Falls"; and Le Camp, "Racial Considerations of Minstrel Shows." On contemporary Canadian blackface, see Howard, "On the Back of Blackness"; and "A Laugh for the National Project." Elaine Keillor briefly mentions blackface in her history of music in Canada, but I strongly disagree with her argument that "in communities where no one knew a Black resident, the mask of blackface allowed criticism of local politics and foibles without racist intent." Keillor, *Music in Canada*, 163–4.

EPILOGUE

1 The historiography of the Cold War has often painted a caricatured and one-dimensional portrait of Kirkconnell, dismissing him as a "intolerant ... self-righteous ideological zealot," with little or no attempt to understand or contextualize his thought, much less document his activities, associates, and their influence in Canadian society. However, on some counts Kirkconnell, who had access to and an understanding of Russian sources, was no doubt correct about the Soviet Union. Whitaker and Marcuse, *Cold War Canada*, 278. See also Baillargeon, "The CBC and the Cold War Mentality," esp. 49–52, 55, 59, 101, and 123 n5; Whitaker, "Official Repression of Communism," 165 n63; Maurutto, "Private Policing and Surveillance of Catholics," 130, 134; and Cavell, "Cultural Production of Canada's Cold War," 18, 28 n15. A slight revision to this trend was found in Whitaker and Hewitt, *Canada and the Cold War*, 44–6; see also Heath, "Watson Kirkconnell's Covert War against Communism."
2 As he later recounted, the university's "Board of Governors intimated ... that a less frequent and belligerent part in political controversy was expected from presidents than from professors." Kirkconnell, "A Scotch-Canadian Discovers Poland," 70; and Kirkconnell, *Slice*, 329.

His contribution as a Miltonist lay in cataloguing and translating select analogues of Milton's major poems. His friend A.S.P. Woodhouse first suggested the project in 1934, and Kirkconnell worked it at sporadically from then until his death, ultimately publishing three volumes: *The Celestial Cycle*; *That Invincible Samson*; and *Awake the Courteous Echo*. On the project, see Kirkconnell, *Slice*, chap. 17 and p. 378; and, for a more critical discussion, von Maltzahn, "Milton and the Deist Prelude to Liberalism."
3 See for instance Kirkconnell, letter to Rupert C. Lodge, 6 December 1947, WK3-25, ECWA, in which he wrote: "I really have been having some moments of stage fright over the whole business, but the optimistic letters of friends are helping to keep up my morale. But I have uneasy feelings that all the congratulations are flowers around the horns of the sacrificial ox." Information about his salary and benefits is found in meeting minutes for 18 May 1947, Acadia University Board of Governors fonds, 1900.034, box 3 (pages 482–7 of the bound volume), ECWA. I would like to thank the Board of Governors of Acadia University for permission to access and quote from these minutes. On the reception to Kirkconnell's appointment, see the letters and clippings in WK3-25, ECWA.
4 The Board of Governors must have forgiven him but there is no record of any discussion in their meeting minutes. See [Kirkconnell], "President's

Report to the Board of Governors, May 19, 1959," 6, Acadia University Board of Governors fonds, 1900.034/430, box 6, file 398, "Minutes (15 May 1959) with attachments," ECWA. I would like to thank the Board of Governors of Acadia University for permission to access and quote from these minutes. On the Fiander case, see Abramson et al, "The Fiander Fiasco"; and for the broader context of the fluoride debate, Carstairs and Elder, "Debating Water Fluoridation."

5 Responding to a request for information about fluoride in 1975, he relayed that after having merely written a "very brief critical letter" he found himself "savagely attacked by the media, in Halifax and Toronto, as a feeble-minded menace to public health." He then provided the name of what he felt was the best book on the subject, and closed by asking not to be publicly quoted on the subject. See Stanley Meister, letter to Kirkconnell, 26 March 1975, WK59-25, ECWA; and Kirkconnell, letter to Stanley Meister, 29 March 1975, WK59-25, ECWA.

6 Thomas had retired but, on the spur of the moment, accepted a call for an emergency teaching replacement and had driven a hundred miles to the new school where the next morning he suffered a stroke. Kirkconnell, *Headmaster*, 150–2.

7 Kirkconnell, letter to England, 30 March 1967, WK59-1, ECWA.

8 He was hurt to have not been mentioned in the most recent edition of the *Literary History of Canada* ("my poetry is not even mentioned while every piddling little free-verse poetaster in the country is given the red carpet treatment," he complained) and so was motivated to put out this final collection of poetry at his own expense in order to "put a neglected old man on the record." Kirkconnell, letter to Angus Munro, 29 April 1966, WK13-4, ECWA ("piddling"); Klinck, *Literary History of Canada*; and Kirkconnell, letter to Ruth DonCarlos (Trade Editor at Clark, Irwin, & Company), 10 March 1966, WK13-4, ECWA ("neglected"). As for the cost, he estimated that even if all two thousand copies of *Centennial Tales* sold, it would still have cost him about $3,000 to have the book published (which equates to approximately $23,000 in 2019).

9 See Snelson, "Bibliography," for details.

10 "Winnifred Hope Kirkconnell," 1, 88-16 (IN-17) Watson Kirkconnell papers, series 3, file 1, University of Winnipeg Archives (UWA).

11 However, he was distracted from this work by environmental factors. He had bought a house in what he believed was a peaceful place, Patricia Bay on Vancouver Island, but was soon disillusioned. As a colleague humorously described the situation, he soon found that "ten thousand planes roared over his head night and day" and so in 1948 he and his wife

Notes to pages 249–50    339

removed to Comox, British Columbia (they would move to Victoria in 1954). Corbett, "Robert England," 22.

12  This sketch taken primarily from England, *Memoirs*, chapters 10 and 11; and England, "Account of Work and Research" (Guggenheim application 1950), 6pp. I would like to thank the John Simon Guggenheim Memorial Foundation for making a copy of England's applications available to me. (England successfully applied for a fellowship in 1944, unsuccessfully for a publication subvention in 1949, and unsuccessfully for a second fellowship in 1950.) For a list of England's publications during this period, see the bibliography in his *Memoirs*, 201–5.

13  "Four to Receive Honorary Degrees from University," *Winnipeg Tribune* (14 May 1948), 1l; and England, *Memoirs*, 144.

14  England, *Memoirs*, 190–1; and her obituary in the *Times Colonist* [Victoria] (7 February 1966), 20.

15  This sketch drawn primarily from England, *Memoirs*, 193–4; and her obituary, a copy of which is found in Jean-Baptiste Lanctôt fonds, MG31 E71, vol. 47, LAC; as well as the following newspaper articles: "City News in Brief," *Victoria Daily Times* (10 August 1907), 5; "Lady Wins Honors," ibid. (28 July 1908), 5; "Attains Her M.A.," *Vancouver Sun* (24 July 1913), 6; "Local Briefs," *Winnipeg Tribune* (3 November 1926), 6; "Association for Adult Education Hears Reports," ibid. (16 June 1936), 4; "Mrs. Clifton Graban is Elected Preident of Local Council of Women," ibid. (22 April 1938), 13; and "Personal Notes," *Victoria Daily Times* (28 July 1947), 8.

16  England, letter to Kirkconnell (and enclosed marriage announcement), 17 July 1969, WK59-1, ECWA. Dedicating his memoirs to her in 1980, he described Thelma as a "friend of half a century." England, *Memoirs*, v.

17  England, letter to Kirkconnell, 17 July 1969, WK59-1, ECWA. Getting married at that age, England later remarked, might be seen as "either poignant or preposterous," but he was pleased that the photographs of the event instead portrayed it as an occasion "marked by dignity, happiness, and splendid hope." England, *Memoirs*, 195.

18  Thelma and Bob [England], letter to Jean and Marie [Lanctôt], 15 August 1981, Jean-Baptiste Lanctôt fonds, MG31 E71, vol. 47, LAC.

19  See Robert England's obituary in the *Times Colonist* (17 June 1985), 25; and R. Treloar, letter to Mrs Jean B. Lanctôt, 10 January 1986 (with attached obituary), Jean-Baptiste Lanctôt fonds, MG31 E71, vol. 47, LAC.

20  "Notes from PD Meeting – December 4/85"; Last Will and Testament of Robert England, 23 May 1980; Extra-Sessional Studies, memorandum "Re: The Robert England Fund," 12 October 1993, all in CE33-28, UBCA.

I would like to thank UBC for allowing me to access and quote from these records, with special thanks to archivist Erwin Wodarczak for all his help.

21 Vera Wojna and Gail Riddell, "Memorandum Re: Funding Support For Training Workshops in Cross-Cultural Diversity for Faculty and Staff at U.B.C.," 15 July 1991, in CE33-28, UBCA.

22 See Kenneth Slade, letter to Margaret Stott, 27 August 1992, CE33-28, UBCA; and Marcie Powell, "Application for Project Funding from the Robert England Fund," 9 April 1991, CE33-28, UBCA. The fund also supported the writing and publication of a book on adult education for citizenship in Canada, and a feasibility study to develop an English as a second language (ESL) training program. See Jinda Kulich, memorandum to Gordan Selman, 26 September 1989, CE32-29, UBCA; and Kulich, memo to Lyn Howes, 13 July 1989, CE32-29, UBCA. The former was published by Gordon Selman as *Citizenship and the Adult Education Movement in Canada*.

23 Archival references to the bequest end in the early 1990s. I requested further information from UBC but they were unable to locate any documents that would shed light on what became of the fund (correspondence with the author, 19 January 2021).

24 Mason, *Spirits of the Rockies*, 120–1.

25 Gibbon, "Scot to Canadian," 188, 194, 196–200, 204; *John Murray Gibbon: Chief 'Man of Many Sides'*; and *Tribute to a Nation Builder*. See also Gibbon, "Handicraft among the Anglo-Canadians"; "Canadian Handicraft Old and New"; "Canada's Million and More Needlecraft Workers"; "Handicraft in Canada"; *Our Old Montreal*; *The Victorian Order of Nurses for Canada*; *The Romance of the Canadian Canoe*; and, with Mary Matthewson, *Three Centuries of Canadian Nursing*.

26 Information about his final days is taken from correspondence between his family and Marius Barbeau, found in MB197-25, CMHA, specifically John Gibbon, letter to Barbeau, 5 June 1952; John Gibbon, letter to Barbeau, 18 June 1952; and Anne Gibbon, letter to Barbeau, 19 June 1952.

Family members give the cause of death as lung cancer, no doubt caused by his habit of chain-smoking. Conversation with Fiona Gibbon-Taillefer, Alexa Wilson, and Virginia Glover, 5 October 2019. Two of his contemporaries, Murray and Frances Adaskin, recalled Gibbon's unique smoking habits. Apparently, Gibbon always had a cigarette in the side of his mouth which he never touched. Instead, it just sat there burning down as he talked, covering his vest with ash, which Gibbon left undisturbed, and as soon as the cigarette went out he would replace it with a fresh one. Interview with Murray and Frances Adaskin (9 November 1972), S1/70,

WMCR. (Transcription by the author.) Similarly, collaborator Ernest MacMillan recalled that during his time at the CPR Gibbon always appeared "through a haze of cigarette smoke" (though the rest of his comment – "he was a devotee of the weed *in those days*" – suggests that Gibbon may have kicked the habit by 1946). See *Tribute to a Nation Builder*, 14. Emphasis added.

27 [Phil Gibbon,] untitled notes of an interview with Bill MacFarlane, 23 March 1985, John Murray Gibbon fonds (M454, unprocessed material), WMCR.

28 "Trail Riders Pay Tribute to Dr. John Murray Gibbon," *Crag and Canyon* (1 August 1952), 1; and "Mrs. J. M. Gibbon," *Montreal Gazette* (6 November 1956), 37. Gibbon was further commemorated in 1955 when the Historic Sites and Monuments Board of Canada installed a bronze plaque in his honour on a granite monument located on the grounds of the Banff School of Fine Arts. The unveiling ceremony was sponsored by the Canadian Authors Association and drew some 500 attendees. See "Hundreds Pay Tribute to Canadian Author at Outdoor Ceremony Sunday," *Crag and Canyon* (12 August 1955), 1.

As for Anne, she had organized one of the first school libraries in Quebec and worked as the Librarian in the Macdonald High School for over two decades. She was also involved with a variety of community organizations including the IODE and the Ladies' Musical Club, and sang in the United Church choir. Her most extensive volunteer work, however, was with the St Anne de Bellevue branch of the Victorian Order of Nurses, where she eventually served as president and then honorary president. For her contributions to community life she was awarded the King George V Silver Jubilee Medal in 1935. (This information gleaned from her obituary as well as from various social columns in the *Montreal Gazette* and the *Ottawa Journal*.)

# Bibliography

ARCHIVAL SOURCES

*Acadia University, Esther Clark Wright Archives (ECWA)*
Board of Governors fonds 1900.034
Watson Kirkconnell fonds 1977.001

*Canadian Museum of History (CMHA)*
Marius Barbeau fonds

*King's College London Archives*
Reginald Ruggles Gates papers GB0100 KCLCA K/PP65

*Library and Archives Canada (LAC)*
Fonds Jean-Baptiste Lanctôt R6007-0-1F, MG31-E71
Nandor Dreisziger fonds R11951-0-1-E
Robert England fonds R5347-0-1-E, MG30-C181

*McCord Museum Archives*
Pen and Pencil Club of Montreal fonds P139

*McMaster University Library, William Ready Division of Archives and Research Collections (ARCMUL)*
Clarke, Irwin & Company Limited fonds RC0076
Macmillan Company of Canada fonds RC0071

*Oxford University Archives*
Examiners' Records

*Princeton University Library, Department of Rare Books and Special Collections, Manuscripts Division*
Archives of Henry Holt & Co. Co100

*Public Archives of Nova Scotia (PANS)*
Helen Creighton fonds MG1 Volumes 2790-2845

*University of Aberdeen, Special Collections (UASC)*
Student Register (Faculty of the Arts) MSU 1
Class Attendance Register (Arts, Science and Divinity) MSU 7

*University of British Columbia Archives*
Continuing Education fonds

*University of Calgary, Archives and Special Collections (UCASC)*
Dr Howard Palmer fonds UARC 2001.007

*University of Manitoba Archives (UMA)*
Arthur Phelps fonds MSS 134
Murray S. Donnelly fonds MSS SC 47

*University of North Carolina at Chapel Hill, Louis Round Wilson Special Collections Library*
J.M. Dent & Sons Records 11043

*University of Reading, Special Collections (URSC)*
Bodley Head Ltd Archive JL
Records of George Allen & Unwin AU

*University of Saskatchewan Archives (USA)*
George W. Simpson fonds MG7

*University of Winnipeg Archives (UWA)*
United College fonds AC-33-1
Watson Kirkconnell papers 88-16 (IN-17)

*Whyte Museum of the Canadian Rockies, Archives and Special Collections (WMCR)*
John Murray Gibbon fonds M454
Luxton Family fonds LUX
Whyte Museum Oral History Programme collection S1

Bibliography 345

PRIMARY AND SECONDARY SOURCES

Abella, Irving, and Harold Troper. *None Is Too Many: Canada and the Jews of Europe, 1933–1948.* Toronto: University of Toronto Press, 1983.

Abler, Thomas S. "Cayuga." In *The Canadian Encyclopedia.* Toronto: Historica Canada, 6 June 2011, http://www.thecanadianencyclopedia.ca/en/article/cayuga.

Abramson, Zelda, Nora Allen, Vicki Archer, Jessica Bundy, Kate Darymple, Kayleigh James, Suleiman Semalulu, and Elise Snow-Kropla. "The Fiander Fiasco: A Case Study of Student Judicial Processes at Acadia University, 1959." Unpublished case study, Acadia University, 2018.

Adachi, Ken. *The Enemy That Never Was.* Toronto: McClelland & Stewart, 1976.

Adams, Pauline. *Somerville for Women: An Oxford College, 1879–1993.* Oxford: Oxford University Press, 1996.

Ajzenstat, Janet. *The Political Thought of Lord Durham.* Montreal and Kingston: McGill-Queen's University Press, 1988.

Alcorn, Kerry. *Border Crossings: US Culture and Education in Saskatchewan, 1905–1937.* Montreal and Kingston: McGill-Queen's University Press, 2013.

Anderson, Alan. "Ethnic Bloc Settlements." In *The Encyclopedia of Saskatchewan,* https://esask.uregina.ca/entry/ethnic_bloc_settlements.jsp.

Anderson, Benedict. *Imagined Communities: Reflections on the Origins and Spread of Nationalism.* Rev. ed. London and New York: Verso, 2006.

Anderson, Kevin. "'The Cockroaches of Canada': French-Canada, Immigration and Nationalism, Anti-Catholicism in English Canada, 1905–1929." *Journal of Religious History* 39, no. 1 (March 2015): 104–22.

– *Not Quite Us: Anti-Catholic Thought in English Canada Since 1900.* Montreal and Kingston: McGill-Queen's University Press, 2019.

Applebaum, Barbara. "Critical Whiteness Studies." *Oxford Research Encyclopedia, Education* (2016), doi:10.1093/acrefore/9780190264093.013.5.

Arnesen, Eric. "Whiteness and the Historians' Imagination." *International Labor and Working Class History* 60 (Fall 2001): 2–32.

Auger, Martin. *Prisoners of the Home Front: German POWs and 'Enemy Aliens' in Southern Quebec, 1940–46.* Vancouver: UBC Press, 2005.

Austin, David. *Fear of a Black Planet: Race, Sex, and Security in Sixties Montreal*. Toronto: Between the Lines, 2013.
Avery, Donald. *Reluctant Host: Canada's Response to Immigrant Workers, 1896–1994*. Toronto: McClelland & Stewart, 1995.
Backhouse, Constance. *Colour-Coded: A Legal History of Racism in Canada, 1900–1950*. Toronto: University of Toronto Press, 1999.
Baillargeon, Philippe. "The CBC and the Cold War Mentality, 1946–1952." MA thesis, Carleton University, 1987.
Baird, Robert P. "The Invention of Whiteness: The Long History of a Dangerous Idea." *The Guardian* (20 April 2021), https://www.theguardian.com/news/2021/apr/20/the-invention-of-whiteness-long-history-dangerous-idea.
Baker, Lee D. *From Savage to Negro: Construction of Race, 1896–1954*. Berkley: University of California Press, 1998.
Balmer, Randall. "Kirkconnell, Watson." In *Encyclopedia of Evangelicalism*, 322. Louisville, KY: Westminster John Knox, 2002.
Balzer, Timothy. *The Information Front: The Canadian Army and News Management During the Second World War*. Vancouver: UBC Press, 2011.
Bangarth, Stephanie. *Voices Raised in Protest: Defending North American Citizens of Japanese Ancestry, 1942–49*. Vancouver: UBC Press, 2008.
– Review of *Managing the Canadian Mosaic in Wartime*, by Ivana Caccia. *Left History* 15, no. 1 (2010): 182–4.
Bannerji, Himani. *The Dark Side of the Nation: Essays on Multiculturalism, Nationalism and Gender*. Toronto: Canadian Scholars' Press, 2000.
Banton, Michael. *The Idea of Race*. Boulder, CO: Westview, 1977.
– "Historical and Contemporary Modes of Racialization." In *Racialization: Studies in Theory and Practice*, edited by Karim Murji and John Solomos, 49–68. Oxford: Oxford University Press, 2005.
Barbeau, Marius. Review of *Canadian Folk Songs (Old and New)*, by John Murray Gibbon. *Canadian Historical Review* 8, no. 2 (June 1927): 144–6.
Barnes, Neil H. Review of *Living, Learning, Remembering*, by Robert England. *Studies in Adult Education* 13, no. 2 (October 1981): 150–1.
Barrett, Paul. *Blackening Canada: Diaspora, Race, Multiculturalism*. Toronto: University of Toronto Press, 2015.
Bartley, Allan. *The Ku Klux Klan in Canada: A Century of Promoting Racism and Hate in the Peaceable Kingdom*. Halifax, NS: Formac Publishing, 2020.

Bashford, Alison, and Philippa Levine, eds. *The Oxford Handbook of the History of Eugenics*. Oxford: Oxford University Press, 2010.

Beaud, Pierre, and Jean-Guy Prévost. "Immigration, Eugenics and Statistics: Measuring Racial Origins in Canada (1921–1941)." *Canadian Ethnic Studies* 28, no. 2 (1996): 1–24.

Bellay, Susan. "The Image of the French Canadian 'Race' in English Canada: English Canadian Attitudes Towards French Canada, 1880–1920." MA thesis, University of Manitoba, 1990.

– "Pluralism and Race/Ethnic Relations in Canadian Social Science, 1880–1939." PhD diss., University of Manitoba, 2001.

Belmessous, Saliha. "Assimilation and Racialism in Seventeenth and Eighteenth-Century French Colonial Policy." *American Historical Review* 110, no. 2 (April 2005): 322–49.

Benner, Allan. "Stevenson Stripped of Emeritus Status." *The Standard* [St. Catharines] (15 August 2018), https://www.stcatharinesstandard.ca/news-story/8840868-stevenson-stripped-of-emeritus-status/.

Benns, Roderick. "Remembering the 'Gentle Sniper.'" *MyKawartha.com* (10 November 2009), https://www.mykawartha.com/community-story/3716234-remembering-the-gentle-sniper-/.

Berger, Carl. *The Sense of Power: Studies in the Ideas of Canadian Imperialism, 1867–1914*. 1970. 2nd ed.: Toronto: University of Toronto Press, 2013. Page references are to the 2013 edition.

– *The Writing of Canadian History: Aspects of English-Canadian Historical Writing: 1900–1970*. Toronto: Oxford University Press, 1976.

"Bernard Bronislaw Dubienski (1891–1981)." *Manitoba Historical Society* (9 June 2018), http://www.mhs.mb.ca/docs/people/dubienski_bb.shtml.

Bertram, Laurie K. "New Icelandic Ethnoscapes: Material, Visual, and Oral Terrains of Cultural Expression in Icelandic-Canadian History, 1875–Present." PhD diss., University of Toronto, 2010.

Bhimani, Nazlin. "F.H. Hayward (1872–1954): A Forgotten Educationalist or an Educational Failure? Moral Education and Education for Citizenship in England." MA thesis, UCL Institute of Education, 2015.

Blanding, Lee. "Re-branding Canada: The Origins of Canadian Multiculturalism Policy, 1945–1974." PhD diss., University of Victoria, 2013.

Bonavia, George. "Bibliographical Access to Ethno-Cultural Material." In *The Bibliographical Society of Canada, Colloquium III*, 76–81. Toronto, 1979.

Bourrie, Mark. "The Myth of the 'Gagged Clam': William Lyon Mackenzie King's Press Relations." *Global Media Journal – Canadian Edition* 3, no. 2 (2010): 13–30.

Bowler, Peter J. "From Science to the Popularization of Science: The Career of J. Arthur Thomson." In *Science and Beliefs: From Natural Theology to Natural Science, 1700–1900*, edited by David M. Knight and Matthew D. Eddy, 231–48. Aldershot, UK: Ashgate, 2005.

Boyd, Alan. "First-Degree Racism and Snobbery with Violence." *The Herald* [Scotland] (24 March 1996), https://www.heraldscotland.com/news/12052647.first-degree-racism-and-snobbery-with-violence/.

Boyd, Monica, Gustave Goldmann, and Pamela White. "Race in the Canadian Census." In *Race and Racism: Canada's Challenge*, edited by Leo Driedger and Shiva S. Halli, 33–54. Montreal: McGill-Queen's University Press, 2000.

Brantlinger, Patrick. *Dark Vanishings: Discourse on the Extinction of Primitive Races, 1800–1930*. Ithaca: Cornell University Press, 2003.

Brison, Jeffrey D. *Rockefeller, Carnegie, & Canada: American Philanthropy and the Arts & Letters in Canada*. Montreal and Kingston: McGill-Queen's University Press, 2005.

Brooke, Michael Z. *Le Play: Engineer and Social Scientist. The Life and Work of Frédéric Le Play*. London: Longman, 1970.

Bruant, Catherine. "Le Collège libre des sciences sociales: une université parallèle qui traverse le XXᵉ siècle." *Les Études Sociales* 146, no. 2 (2008): 3–56.

Buchan, John. *The African Colony: Studies in the Reconstruction*. London: Blackwood & Sons, 1903.

– "Down North." Typescript. N.d. [1937?]. Reprinted in two instalments in *John Buchan Journal* 5 (1985): 3–6; and *John Buchan Journal* 6 (1986): 4–8.

– *Canadian Occasions: Addresses by Lord Tweedsmuir*. Toronto: Musson, 1940.

– *Sick Heart River*. London: Hodder & Stoughton, 1941.

– *John Buchan's Collected Poems*. Edited by Andrew Lownie and William Milne. Scottish Cultural Press, 1996.

Bulmer, Martin, and John Solomos, eds. "Symposium: David FitzGerald's and David Cook-Martín's *Culling the Masses: The Democratic Origins of Racist Immigration Policy in the Americas*." *Racial and Ethnic Studies* 38, no. 8 (2015): 1285–1327.

Bun, Chan Kwok. *Smoke and Fire: The Chinese in Montreal*. Hong Kong: The Chinese University Press, 1991.

Burkowicz, Jakub. "Peripheral Europeans: The History of the Racialization of Slavs in Canada." PhD diss., Simon Fraser University, 2016.

Cabajsky, Andrea. "Canada." In *Blackwell Encyclopedia of the Novel*, edited by Peter Logan, 135–44. Oxford: Blackwell, 2011.

Caccia, Ivana. *Managing the Canadian Mosaic in Wartime: Shaping Citizenship Policy, 1939–1945.* Montreal and Kingston: McGill-Queen's University Press, 2010.

Cahill, Barry. "The Black Loyalist Myth in Atlantic Canada." *Acadiensis* 29, no. 1 (1999): 76–87.

Caine, Barbara. *Biography and History.* New York: Palgrave Macmillan, 2010.

Calliste, Agnes. "Sleeping Car Porters in Canada: An Ethnically Submerged Split Labour Market." *Canadian Ethnic Studies* 19, no. 1 (1987): 1–20.

– "Blacks on Canadian Railways." *Canadian Ethnic Studies* 20, no. 2 (1988): 36–52.

Canadian Institute of International Affairs. *Canadian Papers, 1933.* [Toronto:] Canadian Institute of International Affairs, 1933.

– *Canadian Delegation Papers Prepared for the Banff Conference of the Institute of Pacific Relations.* Toronto: Canadian Institute of International Affairs, n.d.

Careless, J.M.S. "Waspishness and Multiculture." In *Preserving the Canadian Heritage*, edited by K.J. Laidler, 141–50. Ottawa: Royal Society of Canada, 1975.

– "'Waspishness' and Multiculture in Canada." In *Careless at Work: Selected Canadian Historical Studies*, 295–307. Toronto: Dundurn, 1990.

Carstairs, Catherine, and Rachel Elder. "Expertise, Health, and Popular Opinion: Debating Water Fluoridation, 1945–80." *Canadian Historical Review* 89, no. 3 (September 2008): 345–71.

Carter, Sarah. "'Your Great Mother Across the Salt Sea': Prairie First Nations, the British Monarchy, and the Vice Regal Connection to 1900." *Manitoba History* 48 (Autumn/Winter 2004–05), http://www.mhs.mb.ca/docs/mb_history/48/greatmother.shtml.

– *Imperial Plots: Women, Land, and the Spadework of British Colonialism.* Winnipeg: University of Manitoba Press, 2016.

Cavell, Richard. "Introduction: The Cultural Production of Canada's Cold War." In *Love, Hate, and Fear in Canada's Cold War*, edited by idem, 3–32. Toronto: University of Toronto Press, 2004.

Chapnick, Adam. "The Gray Lecture and Canadian Citizenship in History." *American Review of Canadian Studies* 37, no. 4 (December 2007): 443–57.

Chicanot, E.L. "Homesteading the Citizen." *The Commonweal* (29 May 1929): 94–5.
Chopra, Ruma. *Almost Home: Maroons Between Slavery and Freedom in Jamaica, Nova Scotia, and Sierra Leone*. New Haven and London: Yale University Press, 2018.
Clapperton, Jonathan. "Naturalizing Race Relations: Conservation, Colonialism, and Spectacle at the Banff Indian Days." *Canadian Historical Review* 94, no. 3 (September 2013), 349–79.
Clark, Terry Nichols. *Prophets and Patrons: The French University and the Emergence of the Social Sciences*. Cambridge, MA: Harvard University Press, 1973.
Clarke, John Roger. "John Buchan's Uncollected Journalism: A Critical and Bibliographic Investigation." PhD diss., University of the West of England, Bristol, 2015.
Clarke, George Elliott. "Liberalism and Its Discontents: Reading Black and White in Contemporary Québécois Texts." *Journal of Canadian Studies* 31, no. 1 (Autumn 1996): 59–77.
Clarke, Nic. *Unwanted Warriors: The Rejected Volunteers of the Canadian Expeditionary Force*. Vancouver: UBC Press, 2015.
Clary, Ian Hugh. "Kirkconnell, Watson." In *Encyclopedia of Christianity in the United States*, edited by George Thomas Kurian and Mark A. Lamport, 3:1283–84. New York: Rowman and Littlefield, 2016.
Clendenan, May. "Guardians of the Future." *Farmer's Advocate and Home Journal* (15 June 1921), 832.
Coleman, Daniel. *White Civility: The Literary Project of English Canada*. Toronto: University of Toronto Press, 2006.
– "From Contented Civility to Contending Civilities: Alternatives to Canadian White Civility." *International Journal of Canadian Studies* 38 (2008): 221–42.
– "J.S. Woodsworth and the Discourse of White Civility." In *Human Welfare, Rights, and Social Activism: Rethinking the Legacy of J.S. Woodsworth*, edited by Jane Pulkingham, 234–56. Toronto: University of Toronto Press, 2010.
– Afterword to *The Foreigner: A Tale of Saskatchewan*, by Ralph Connor, 275–301. Waterloo, ON: Wilfrid Laurier University Press, 2014.
Coleman, Heather J. "Watson Kirkconnell on 'The Place of Slavic Studies in Canada': A 1957 Speech to the Canadian Association of Slavists." *Canadian Slavonic Papers* 58, no. 4 (2016): 386–97.
Constant, Jean-François, and Michel Ducharme, eds. *Liberalism and*

*Hegemony: Debating the Canadian Liberal Revolution.* Toronto: University of Toronto Press, 2009.
Coombs, Adam. "In Defence of (Canadian Academic) History." *Active History* (13 October 2017), http://activehistory.ca/2017/10/in-defence-of-canadian-academic-history/.
Corbett, E.A. "Robert England, M.C., M.A., LL.D." *Food for Thought* (April 1951): 19–22.
Craig, Terrence. *Racial Attitudes in English-Canadian Fiction, 1905–1980.* Waterloo, ON: Wilfrid Laurier University Press, 1987.
Craick, W. Arnot. *Port Hope Historical Sketches.* Port Hope, Ontario, 1901.
Crowley, Terry. *Marriage of Minds: Isabel and Oscar Skelton Reinventing Canada.* Toronto: University of Toronto Press, 2003.
Currie, Robert. "The Arts and Social Studies, 1914–1939." In *The Twentieth Century,* vol. 8 of *The History of the University of Oxford,* edited by Brian Harrison, 109–38. Oxford: Oxford University Press, 1994.
Darnell, Regna. *Edward Sapir: Linguist, Anthropologist, Humanist.* Lincoln: University of Nebraska Press, 2010.
Dawn, Leslie. *National Visions, National Blindness: Canadian Art and Identities in the 1920s.* Vancouver: UBC Press, 2006.
Davidovich, Stepan. Review of *The Ukrainian Question,* by M.I. Mandryka. *International Affairs Review Supplement* 19, no. 2 (1940): 138.
Davis, Wm. L. "De Smet, Pierre-Jean." In *Dictionary of Canadian Biography,* vol. 10. University of Toronto/Université Laval, 1972. http://www.biographi.ca/en/bio/de_smet_pierre_jean_10E.html.
Day, Richard J.F. *Multiculturalism and the History of Canadian Diversity.* Toronto: University of Toronto Press, 2000.
de Smet, Pierre-Jean. *Oregon Missions and Travels over the Rocky Mountains in 1845–46.* 1847.
de Silva, K.M. *A History of Sri Lanka.* Colombo: Vijitha Yaapa, 2005.
Deniker, Joseph. *The Races of Man: An Outline of Anthropology and Ethnography.* New York: Charles Scribner's Sons, 1904.
Department of Education, Province of Saskatchewan. *Annual Report 1919.* Regina: J.W. King, 1920.
Dhamoon, Rita Kaur, Davina Bhandar, Renisa Mawani, and Satwinder Kaur Bains, eds. *Unmooring the Komagata Maru: Charting Colonial Trajectories.* Vancouver: UBC Press, 2019.
Dickason, Olive Patricia, with David T. McNab. *Canada's First Nations:*

*A History of Founding Peoples from Earliest Times*. 4th ed. Toronto: Oxford University Press, 2009.

Dijks, Ineke J. "Rails to 'the Great Inland Empire': The Canadian National Railways, Colonization, and Settlement in Alberta 1925–1930, with Special Reference to the Peace River Region." MA thesis, Department of Geography, Queen's University, 1994.

Dolmage, Jay Timothy. *Disabled Upon Arrival: Eugenics, Immigration, and the Construction of Race and Disability*. Columbus: Ohio State University Press, 2018.

Doody, Christopher M. "A Union of the Inkpot: The Canadian Authors Association, 1921–1960." PhD diss., Carleton University, 2016.

Douglas, Thomas (Lord Selkirk). *Observations on the Present State of the Highlands of Scotland*. 1805.

Dreisziger, N.F. "Watson Kirkconnell and the Cultural Credibility Gap Between Immigrants and the Native-Born in Canada." In *Ethnic Canadians: Cultural and Education*, edited by M.L. Kovacs, 87–96. Regina: Canadian Plains Research Centre, 1978.

– "The Rise of a Bureaucracy for Multiculturalism: The Origins of the Nationalities Branch, 1939–1941." In *On Guard for Thee: War, Ethnicity, and the Canadian State, 1939–1945*, edited by Norman Hillmer, Bohdan Kordan, and Lubomyr Luciuk, 1–30. Ottawa: Canadian Committee for the History of the Second World War, 1988.

– "Tracy Philipps and the Achievement of Ukrainian-Canadian Unity." In *Canada's Ukrainians: Negotiating an Identity*, edited by Lubomyr Luciuk and Stella Hryniuk, 326–41. Toronto: University of Toronto Press and the Ukrainian Canadian Centennial Committee, 1991.

– "7 December 1941: A Turning Point in Canadian Wartime Policy Towards Ethnic Groups?" *Journal of Canadian Studies* 32, no. 1 (1997): 93–111.

– "Rallying Canada's Immigrants Behind the War Effort." In *Forging A Nation: Perspectives on the Canadian Military Experience*, edited by Bernd Horn, 177–95. St. Catharines, ON: Vanwell Publishing, 2002.

Drever, James. "McDougall, William." In *The International Encyclopedia of the Social Sciences*, 9:503–4. New York: MacMillan, 1968.

du Maroussem, Pierre-Robert Planteau. *Les enquêtes: pratique et théorie*. Paris, 1900.

Duckworth, Henry E. *One Version of the Facts: My Life in the Ivory Tower*. Winnipeg: University of Manitoba Press, 2000.

Dyck, Erika. *Facing Eugenics: Reproduction, Sterilization, and the Politics of Reproduction*. Toronto: University of Toronto Press, 2013.

Dyer, Richard. *White*. London and New York: Routledge, 1997.
Edkins, Jenny. *Face Politics*. London and New York: Routledge, 2015.
Ellis, Havelock. *The Problem of Race-Regeneration*. London: Cassell, 1911.
England, Robert. "How the Teacher's Lot May Be Improved." *Saskatoon Daily Star* (4 March 1922).
– "Hafford School Sports." *The Grain Growers' Guide* (16 August 1922): 11, 16.
– "Continental Immigration." *Queen's Quarterly* (Autumn 1929): 719–28.
– "Glimpses of Out-of-the-Way People and Places." *The Queen's Review* (October 1929): 237–42.
– "British Immigration." *Queen's Quarterly* (Winter 1929): 131–44.
– *The Central European Immigrant in Canada*. Toronto: Macmillan, 1929.
– "Canada Seen through New Eyes." *Canadian National Railways Magazine* (January 1930): 26, 43.
– "Review of *Emigration from the British Isles*, by W.A. Carrothers." *The Quarterly Journal of the Royal Economic Society* (March 1930): 126–30.
– "Review of *Wheat*, by W.W. Swanson and P.C. Armstrong." *Queen's Quarterly* (Summer 1930): 593–603.
– "Review of *The Ukrainian Canadians*, by Charles H. Young." *Canadian Historical Review* 12, no. 2 (June 1931): 208–9.
– "A Project in the Use of Group Consciousness as a Lever in Agricultural Development." *Scientific Agriculture* 12 (December 1932): 11–15.
– "Glimpses of Europe in Western Canada." *Canadian Geographical Journal* 5, no. 1 (July 1932): 2–20.
– "Canadian Immigration Policy." Delegation paper. Institute of Pacific Relations 1933. Canadian Institute of International Affairs. Mimeograph.
– "Racial Groups in Western Canada." *The Western Producer* (23 November 1933), 11, 15.
– "The Emergent West." *Queen's Quarterly* (Autumn 1934): 405–13.
– "Transportation and Agriculture." *Actimist* 11, nos 7–8 (July–August 1935): 3–4.
– "Land Settlement in Areas of Western Canada (1925–35)." *Canadian Journal of Economics and Political Science* 1, no. 4 (November 1935): 578–87.
– "The Apathetic Fallacy." *Queen's Quarterly* (Winter 1935–6): 437–50.
– "Some Personal Views on the Future of Western Canada." *The Payroll* 15, no. 147 (June 1936): 13–16.

- "The Switch-Back Decade (1925–35)." *Dalhousie Review* 16, no. 1 (1936): 78–86.
- *The Colonization of Western Canada: A Study of Contemporary Land Settlement 1896–1934.* London: P.S. King and Son, 1936.
- "The Gods of the Copybook Headings." *Canadian Chartered Accountant* 31, no. 5 (November 1937): 346–52.
- *The Threat to Disinterested Education: A Challenge.* Toronto: Macmillan, 1937.
- "Review of *Canadian Mosaic*, by John Murray Gibbon." *The Winnipeg Tribune* (8 December 1938): 11.
- "Civil Re-Establishment in Canada." *Public Welfare Journal* 1, no. 9 (September 1943): 268–79.
- "Your Contribution and Our Debt." *The Fragment* (September 1943).
- *Discharged: A Commentary on the Civil Re-Establishment of Veterans in Canada.* Toronto: Macmillan, 1943.
- "Canada and the Discharged Service Man." *Public Affairs* (Winter 1944): 108–12.
- "Soldier Settlement Policy: The Oldest Rehabilitation Prospectus." *Journal of Land and Public Utility* 20, no. 4 (November 1944): 285–98.
- *Canadian Re-Establishment for Veterans: Supplement to Discharged.* Toronto: Macmillan, 1944.
- *Rehabilitation and Re-Establishment: A Guide to Reading.* Ottawa: Canadian Legion Educational Services, 1944.
- "Canada's Program to Aid Its Veterans." *Annals of the American Academy of Political and Social Science* 238 (March 1945): 95–102.
- "Disbanded and Discharged Soldiers in Canada Prior to 1914." *Canadian Historical Review* 27, no. 1 (March 1946): 1–18.
- *Contemporary Canada: A Mid-Twentieth Century Orientation.* Toronto: The Educational Book Company, n.d. [1949].
- *Twenty Million World War Veterans.* Toronto: Oxford University Press, 1952.
- "Veterans' Rehabilitation." *Encyclopedia Canadiana* (1958), 10:225–9.
- *Bibliography of Robert England: With a Curriculum Vitae & Biographical References Appended.* Victoria, BC: 1965.
- "Ethnic Studies in Western Canada: Reminiscences of a Pioneer." *Canadian Ethnic Studies* 8, no. 2 (1976): 8–33.
- "Forty Years Ago, 1936–1937." In *Former UBC Extension Directors Reminisce, 1936–1976*, 5–16. Vancouver: Centre for Continuing Education, University of British Columbia, 1976.
- *Living, Learning, Remembering: Memoirs of Robert England.*

Vancouver: Centre for Continuing Education, University of British Columbia, 1980.
– *The First World War Recollections of a Nonagenarian of Service in the Royal Canadian Regiment, 1916–1919.* [Victoria?] British Columbia: 1983.
Eyford, Ryan. *White Settler Reserve: New Iceland and the Colonization of the Canadian West.* Vancouver: UBC Press, 2016.
Farr, Robert M. "The Social Psychology of William McDougall." In *Changing Conceptions of Crowd Mind and Behavior*, edited by C.F. Graumann and S. Moscovici, 83–95. New York: Springer, 1986.
Fingard, Judith. "From Sea to Rail: Black Transportation Workers and Their Families in Halifax, c. 1870–1916." *Acadiensis* 24 (Spring 1995): 49–64.
FitzGerald, David Scott, and David Cook-Martín. *Culling the Masses: The Democratic Origins of Racist Immigration Policy in the Americas.* Cambridge, MA: Harvard University Press, 2014.
Fleure, H.J. *The Peoples of Europe.* 1922.
Foght, Harold W. *A Survey of Education in the Province of Saskatchewan Canada: A Report to the Government of the Province of Saskatchewan.* Regina: J.W. Reid, 1918.
Foster, Kate. *Our Canadian Mosaic.* Toronto: The Dominion Council YWCA, 1926.
Francis, Daniel. *The Imaginary Indian: The Image of the Indian in Canadian Culture.* 2nd ed. Vancouver: Arsenal Pulp, 2011.
Frankenberg, Ruth. *White Women, Race Matters: The Social Construction of Whiteness.* Minneapolis: University of Minnesota Press, 1993.
Fraser, John Foster. *The Conquering Jew.* 1915.
Freeman-Maloy, Dan. "Remembering Balfour: Empire, Race, and Propaganda." *Race & Class* 59, no. 3 (2017): 3–19.
Gaffield, Chad. *Language, Schooling, and Cultural Conflict.* Montreal and Kingston: McGill-Queen's University Press, 1987.
Galbraith, J. William. *John Buchan: Model Governor General.* Toronto: Dundurn, 2013.
– "Maligning a Model Governor-General." *Dorchester Review* 3, no. 2 (Autumn/Winter 2013): 103–4.
– [Letter to the editor.] *Literary Review of Canada* (January–February 2014), https://reviewcanada.ca/magazine/2014/01/complicated-ghosts/.
Galton, Francis. *Inquiries into Human Faculty and Its Development.* 1883.
Garner, Steve. *Whiteness: An Introduction.* London and New York: Routledge, 2007.

Gauvreau, Michael. "Re: 'Quiet, and Not Entirely a Revolution,' by Graham Fraser (February 2018)." *Literary Review of Canada* 26, no. 2 (March 2018), 32.
Gerus, Oleh W. "Ethnic Politics in Canada: The Formation of the Ukrainian Canadian Committee." In *The Jubilee Collection Of the Ukrainian Free Academy of Science*s, edited by Alexander Baran, Oleh Gerus, and Jaroslav Rozumnyj, 467–80. Winnipeg: UVAW, 1976.
"Gibbon, John Murray." In *Encyclopedia of Literature in Canada*, edited by William H. New, 433. Toronto: University of Toronto Press, 2002.
Gibbon, John Murray. "The Friends of Dreyfus – Heaven Help Them! A Trip to Rennes and Its Results." *Black and White* (Supplement; 16 September 1899), ii–iii.
– *The Conquering Hero*. New York: Grosset and Dunlap, 1904.
– ed. *The True Annals of Fairyland in the Reign of King Cole*. London: J.M. Dent, 1909.
– *Scots in Canada: A History of the Settlement of the Dominion from the Earliest Days to the Present Time*. London: Kegan Paul, Trench, Trübner and Co., 1911.
– *Hearts and Faces*. Toronto: S.B. Gundy, 1916.
– "Where Is Canadian Literature?" *The Canadian Magazine* 50, no. 2 (February 1918): 333–40.
– *Drums Afar: An International Romance*. Toronto: S.B. Gundy, 1918.
– "The Coming Canadian Novel." *Canadian Bookman* (July 1919): 13–15.
– "The Foreign Born." *Queen's Quarterly* 27, no. 4 (1920): 331–51.
– "Birth Control for Authors." *Literary Review* (14 April 1923): 603.
– "European Seeds in the Canadian Garden." *Transactions of the Royal Society of Canada* (1923): 119–29.
– "Canadian Letters and the New Canadian." In *The Empire Club of Canada Addresses*, 330–42. Toronto, 1923.
– trans. *Canadian Folk Songs (Old and New)*. London and Toronto: J.M. Dent, 1927.
– "The Music of the People." In *The Empire Club of Canada Addresses*, 278–88. Toronto, 1929.
– *Melody and the Lyric: From Chaucer to the Cavaliers*. London and Toronto: J.M. Dent, 1930.
– "Radio as Fine Art." *Canadian Forum* 11 (March 1931): 212–14.
– *Magic of Melody*. London and Toronto: J.M. Dent, 1933.
– *Steel of Empire*. New York: Bobbs-Merrill, 1935.
– *Canadian Mosaic: The Making of a Northern Nation*. London: J.M. Dent, 1938.

- "Pages from an Informal History." *Canadian Author and Bookman* 16 (April 1939): 5–6.
- *The New Canadian Loyalists*. Toronto: Macmillan, 1941.
- "A Secular Bible for New Canada." *Transactions of the Royal Society of Canada* 36 (1942): 93–100.
- "Your Theme Is Your Author." *Canadian Review of Music and Art* (February 1942): 4–5.
- "Canadian Handicraft Old and New." *Canadian Geographical Journal* 26 (March 1943): 130–43.
- "Handicraft Among the Anglo-Canadians." *Culture* 4 (March 1943): 44–47.
- Canada's Million and More Needlecraft Workers." *Canadian Geographical Journal* 26 (March 1943): 144–55.
- "Handicraft in Canada." *School Arts* 43 (April 1944): 260–2.
- *Brahms and Schuberts' Songs Transplanted*. Toronto: Gordon V. Thompson, 1944.
- "Women as Folk-Song Authors." *Transactions of the Royal Society of Canada* 41 (May 1947): 47–53.
- *Our Old Montreal*. Toronto: McClelland & Stewart, 1947.
- *V.O.N.: The Victorian Order of Nurses for Canada 50th Anniversary, 1897–1947*. Montreal: Southam Press, 1947.
- (with Mary Matthewson). *Three Centuries of Canadian Nursing*. Toronto: Macmillan, 1947.
- trans. *Canadian Folk Songs (Old and New)*. Rev. ed. Toronto: J.M. Dent, 1949.
- *Romance of the Canadian Canoe*. Toronto: Ryerson, 1951.
- "From Aberdonian to Canadian." *Aberdeen University Review* 34, no. 106 (Spring 1952): 244–51.

Gilmour, Julie F. *Trouble on Main Street: Mackenzie King, Reason, Race, and the 1907 Vancouver Riots*. Toronto: Allen Lane, 2014.

Gilroy, Paul. *Against Race: Imagining Political Culture Beyond the Color Line*. Cambridge, MA: Belknap Press of Harvard University Press, 2000.

Goldberg, David Theo. *The Racial State*. Malden, MA: Blackwell, 2002.

- "Call and Response." *Patterns of Prejudice* 44, no. 1 (2010): 89–106.

Gorman, Daniel. *Imperial Citizenship: Empire and the Question of Belonging*. Manchester: Manchester University Press, 2007.

Goutor, David. *Guarding the Gate: The Canadian Labour Movement and Immigration, 1872–1934*. Vancouver: UBC Press, 2007.

Grabovac, Ivan. "Preserving the Great White North: Migratory Birds, Italian Immigrants, and the Making of Ecological Citizenship Across the U.S.–Canada Border, 1900–1924." In *American Studies, Ecocriticism, and Citizenship: Thinking and Acting in Local and Global Commons*, edited by Joni Adamson and Kimberly N. Ruffin, 117–30. London and New York: Routledge, 2013.

Graham, Ron, ed. *Obsession: Sir William Van Horne's Japanese Ceramics*. Montreal: Gardiner Museum, 2018.

Graham, Gerald Sandford. "North America and the War: A Canadian View. By Reginald G. Trotter, India. By L. F. Rushbrook Williams, Turkey: The Modern Miracle. By E. W. F. Tomlin, and the Ukrainian Question: Remarks on Prof. Watson Kirkconnell's book, Canada, Europe, and Hitler. By M. I. Mandryka." *Queen's Quarterly* 47, no. 4 (1940): 472.

Granatstein, J.L., and Gregory A. Johnson. "The Evacuation of the Japanese Canadians, 1943: A Realist Critique of the Received Version." In *On Guard for Thee: War, Ethnicity, and the Canadian State, 1939-1945*, edited by Norman Hillmer, Bohdan Kordan, and Lubomyr Luciuk, 101–29. Ottawa: Canadian Committee for the History of the Second World War, 1988.

Grant, Madison. *The Passing of the Great Race: The Racial Basis of European History*. New York: Scribner and Sons, 1916.

– "Americans of Nordic Origin." *Winnipeg Evening Tribune* (22 March 1924), 4.

Gray, Colleen. *No Ordinary School: The Study, 1915–2015*. Montreal: McGill-Queen's University Press for The Study, 2015.

Green, Joyce A. "Toward a Detente With History: Confronting Canada's Colonial Legacy." *International Journal of Canadian Studies* 12 (Fall 1995): 85–105.

Grizzle, Stanley. *My Name's Not George: The Story of the Brotherhood of Sleeping Car Porters in Canada*. Toronto: Umbrella Press, 1998.

Haddon, Alfred C. *The Races of Man*. 2nd ed. 1924.

Hall, David J. *A Lonely Eminence, 1901–1929*. Vol. 2 of *Clifford Sifton*. Vancouver: UBC Press, 1985.

Halloran, Mary S. "Ethnicity, the State, and War: Canada and Its Ethnic Minorities, 1939–45." *International Migration Review* 21, no. 1 (Spring 1987): 159–67.

Hamon, M. Max. *The Audacity of His Enterprise: Louis Riel and the Métis Nation That Canada Never Was, 1840–1873*. Montreal and Kingston: McGill-Queen's University Press, 2019.

Hankins, Frank H. "Social Science and Biology." In *The Social Sciences and Their Interrelations*, edited by William F. Ogburn and Alexander Goldenweiser, 393–413. Boston: Houghton Mifflin, 1927.

Haque, Eve. *Multiculturalism within a Bilingual Framework: Language, Race, and Belonging in Canada*. Toronto: University of Toronto Press, 2012.

Harney, Robert. "'So Great a Heritage as Ours': Immigration and the Survival of the Canadian Polity." *Daedalus* 117, no. 4 (In Search of Canada, 1988): 51–97.

Harrington, Lyn. *Syllables of Recorded Time: The Story of the Canadian Authors Association 1921–1981*. Toronto: Simon and Pierre for the Canadian Authors Association, 1981.

Harris, Cheryl I. "Whiteness as Property." *Harvard Law Review* 106, no. 8 (June 1993): 1707–91.

Harris, Marvin. *The Rise of Anthropological Theory*. Walnut Creek, California: AltaMira, 2001.

Harvey, Sean P. "'Must Not Their Languages Be Savage and Barbarous Like Them?': Philology, Indian Removal, and Race Science." *Journal of the Early Republic* 30, no. 4 (Winter 2010): 505–32.

Haudenosaunee Confederacy. "Cayuga." https://www.haudenosauneeconfederacy.com/the-league-of-nations/.

Hayworth, F.H. *Education and the Heredity Spectre*. 1909.

– "A School Celebration for a 'Eugenics Day.'" *Eugenics Review* 11, no. 2 (1919): 65–9.

Hearn, Lafcadio. *Glimpses of Unfamiliar Japan*. 1894.

– *Japan: An Interpretation*. New York: Macmillan, 1904.

Heath, Gordon L. "Watson Kirkconnell's Covert War against Communism." In *North American Churches and the Cold War*, edited by Paul Mojzes, 64–79. Grand Rapids: Eerdmans, 2018.

Henderson, Jennifer. *Settler Feminism and Race Making*. Toronto: University of Toronto Press, 2003.

Henderson, Stuart. "'While There Is Still Time...': J. Murray Gibbon and the Spectacle of Difference in Three CPR Folk Festivals, 1928–1931." *Journal of Canadian Studies* 39, no. 1 (Winter 2005): 139–74.

Henshaw, Peter. "John Buchan and the British Imperial Origins of Canadian Multiculturalism." In *Canadas of the Mind: The Making and Unmaking of Canadian Nationalisms in the Twentieth Century*, edited by Norman Hillmer and Adam Chapnick, 191–213. Montreal: McGill-Queen's University Press, 2007.

Hewitt, Steve. "Policing the Promised Land: The RCMP and Negative Nation-Building in Alberta and Saskatchewan in the Interwar Period."

In *The Prairie West as Promised Land*, edited by R. Douglas Francis and Chris Kitzan, 313–32. Calgary: University of Calgary Press, 2007.

Hilliard, Christopher. *To Exercise Our Talents: The Democratization of Writing in Britain*. Cambridge, Massachusetts: Harvard University Press, 2006.

Hinther, Rhonda L. "Generation Gap: Canada's Postwar Ukrainian Left." In *Re-imagining Ukrainian Canadians: History, Politics, and Identity*, edited by idem and Jim Mochoruk, 23–53. Toronto: University of Toronto Press, 2011.

Hitchens, Christopher. "Great Scot." *The Atlantic* (March 2004), https://www.theatlantic.com/magazine/archive/2004/03/great-scot/302897/.

Hoerder, Dirk. *To Know Our Many Selves: From the Study of Canada to Canadian Studies*. Edmonton: Athabasca University Press, 2010.

Holland, William Lancelot. *Remembering the Institute of Pacific Relations: The Memoirs of William Lancelot Holland*, edited by Paul F. Hooper. Tokyo: Ryukei Shyosha, 1995.

Horne, Janet R. *A Social Laboratory for Modern France: The Musée Social and the Rise of the Welfare State*. Durham: Duke University Press, 2002.

Howard, Philip S.S. "A Laugh for the National Project: Contemporary Canadian Blackface Humour and Its Constitution through Canadian Anti-Blackness." *Ethnicities* 18, no. 6 (2018): 843–68.

– "On the Back of Blackness: Contemporary Canadian Blackface and the Consumptive Production of Post-Racialist, White Canadian Subjects." *Journal for the Study of Race, Nation, and Culture* 21, no. 4 (2018): 87–103.

Hoyt, Carlos A., Jr. *The Arc of a Bad Idea: Understanding and Transcending Race*. Oxford: Oxford University Press, 2016.

Huot, Cécile. "Eugène Lapierre." In *The Canadian Encyclopedia*. Toronto: Historica Canada, 15 December 2013. https://www.thecanadianencyclopedia.ca/en/article/eugene-lapierre-emc.

Hurd, W.B. "Decline of the Anglo-Saxon Canadian." *Maclean's* (1 September 1937): 13, 45.

Hutchings, Kevin. "'Teller of Tales': John Buchan, First Baron Tweedsmuir, and Canada's Aboriginal Peoples." In *Irish and Scottish Encounters with Indigenous Peoples*, edited by Graeme Morton and David A. Wilson, 341–70. Montreal and Kingston: McGill-Queen's University Press, 2013.

Hutton, Eric. "... And Now, a Few Words from Mr. Brockington." *Maclean's* (15 April 1953): 24, 64–8.

Iacovetta, Franca. *Gatekeepers: Reshaping Immigrant Lives in Cold War Canada*. Toronto: Between the Lines, 2006.

Iacovetta, Franca, Roberto Perin, and Angelo Principe, eds. *Enemies Within: Italian and Other Internees in Canada and Abroad*. Toronto: University of Toronto Press, 2000.

Ignatiev, Noel. *How the Irish Became White*. London and New York: Routledge, 1996.

Ipperciel, Donald. "Britannicité et multiculturalism canadien." *International Journal of Canadian Studies/Revue international d'études canadiennes* nos 45–46 (2012): 277–306.

– "Britishness and Canadian Multiculturalism." In *Bringing Culture Back In: Human Security and Social Trust*, edited by Michael Böss, 54–69. Aarhus, Denmark: Aarhus University Press, 2016.

Jackson, John P., and Nadine M. Weidman. *Race, Racism, and Science: Social Impact and Interaction*. Santa Barbara, CA: ABC-CLIO, 2004.

Jacobson, Matthew Frye. *Whiteness of a Different Color: European Immigrants and the Alchemy of Race*. Cambridge, MA: Harvard University Press, 1998.

Jessup, Lynda. "The Group of Seven and the Tourist Landscape in Western Canada, or The More Things Change ..." *Journal of Canadian Studies* 37, no. 1 (Spring 2002): 144–79.

*John Murray Gibbon: Chief 'Man of Many Sides.'* Montreal, 1945.

Johnston, Hugh J.M. *The Voyage of the* Komagata Maru: *The Sikh Challenge to Canada's Colour Bar*. Rev. ed. Vancouver: UBC Press, 2014.

Jonas, Anna. "175 Years of Excellence at Lisgar Collegiate Institute." *Ottawa Life Magazine* (4 May 2018), http://www.ottawalife.com/article/175-years-of-excellence-at-lisgar-collegiate-institute.

Karr, Clarence. *Authors and Audiences: Popular Canadian Fiction in the Early Twentieth Century*. Montreal: McGill-Queen's University Press, 2000.

Keefer, Janice Kulyk. "From Mosaic to Kaleidoscope." *Books in Canada* 20, no. 6 (September 1991): 13–16.

Kelley, Ninette, and Michael Trebilcock. *The Making of the Mosaic: A History of Canadian Immigration Policy*. 2nd ed. Toronto: University of Toronto Press, 2010.

Kessler-Harris, Alice. "Why Biography?" *American Historical Review* 114, no. 3 (June 2009): 625–30.

Kevles, Daniel J. *In the Name of Eugenics: Genetics and the Uses of Human Heredity*. New York: Knopf, 1985.

Keyfitz, Nathan. "How the Descendants of English Speakers See the Speakers of Other Languages and Their Descendants." In *Multiculturalism as State Policy: Conference Report*, 65–79. Ottawa: Minister of Supply and Services, 1978.

Kidd, Colin. *The Forging of Races: Race and Scripture in the Protestant Atlantic World, 1600–2000*. Cambridge: Cambridge University Press, 2006.

Kimball, Roger. "Catching up with John Buchan." *Fortnightly Review* (2012), http://fortnightlyreview.co.uk/2012/06/catchin-buchan.

Kines, Gary. "Chief Man-of-Many-Sides: John Murray Gibbon and His Contributions to the Development of Tourism and the Arts in Canada." MA thesis, Carleton University, 1988.

Kinnear, Mary. *Margaret McWilliams: An Interwar Feminist*. Montreal and Kingston: McGill-Queen's University Press, 1991.

Kirkconnell, Watson. "The Rush Defended!" *Queen's Journal* (20 November 1917), 1–2.

– "When We Locked Up the Fritz: The First Authentic Story of Our Internment Camps." *MacLean's* (1 September 1920), 20–21, 57–63.

– "A Sensible Census." *Lindsay Post* (6 November 1920), 1, 6.

– "Stone Age Annals of Victoria County." *Watchman-Warder* (23 December 1920): 1, 8–9.

– *Kapuskasing: An Historical Sketch*. Kingston: Jackson Press, 1921.

– *Victoria County Centennial History*. Lindsay: Watchman-Warder Press, 1921.

– "Mechanism and Meliorism." *The Challenge* 2, no. 27 (28 September 1923): 227–8.

– *International Aspects of Unemployment*. London: George Allen & Unwin, 1923.

– "Translations from Greek Poets." *Vox Wesleyana* (December 1924): 11–12.

– "Founder of Modern Slovak Literature." *Manitoban Literary Supplement* (28 October 1925): 1.

– "Mendelism and the Cephalic Index." *The American Journal of Physical Anthropology* (October–December 1925): 443–4.

– "Two Poems from the Danish." *Manitoban Literary Supplement* (5 November 1925): 1.

– "Poems from Twelve Languages (Translated by Watson Kirkconnell)." *Vox Wesleyana* (December 1925): 16–20.

- "The Greek Epigram." *Queen's Quarterly* (January 1925): 225-44.
- "The Patriarch of Western Letters." *Manitoba Free Press* (7 December 1925): 5, 8.
- "The Epilogue to Dramatis Personae." *Modern Language Notes* 41, no. 4 (April 1926): 213-19.
- "Karel Čapek and R.U.R." *Vox Wesleyana* (December 1926): 24-5.
- "Research into Canadian Rural Decay." *Eugenics Review* 18 (April 1926–January 1927): 155-6.
- "Western Immigration." *Canadian Forum* 8 (July 1928): 706-7.
- *The European Elegies*. Ottawa: Graphic Publishers, 1928.
- "The Genius of Slavonic Poetry." *Dalhousie Review* 9, no. 4 (1930): 500-506.
- *The European Heritage: A Synopsis of European Cultural Achievement*. London: J.M. Dent, 1930.
- ed. and trans. *The North American Book of Icelandic Verse*. New York and Montreal: Louis Carrier and Alan Isles, 1930.
- *The Tide of Life and Other Poems*. Ottawa: Ariston, 1930.
- "La poèsie française au Canada." *Journal des Poètes* [Brussels] 2, no. 2 (February 1932).
- "Towards a National Literature." *Author's Bulletin* (May 1932): 23-4.
- ed. *Manitoba Poetry Chapbook*. Winnipeg: Israelite Press for the Canadian Authors' Association, Manitoba Branch, 1933.
- "Icelandic-Canadian Poetry." *Dalhousie Review* 14, no. 3 (1934): 331-44.
- "Ukrainian Canadiana." *Canadian Forum* 14, no. 160 (January 1934): 144-5.
- "The First Magyar-American Poet." *Magyar Usjág* 22, no, 20 (9 March 1934): 1.
- "Ukrainian Poetry in Canada." *Slavonic and East European Review* 13, no. 37 (July 1934): 139-46.
- "Proletarian Poetry, pt. II." *Canadian Spectator* 1, no. 2 (29 November 1934), 5, 7.
- "A Polish Miscellany." *Slavonic and East European Review* 14, no. 40 (July 1935): 1-10.
- "Ukrainian Poetry." *The New Magazine* 1, no. 7 (October 1935): 14-15, 27-9.
- ed. *Canadian Overtones: An Anthology of Poetry Originally Written in Icelandic, Swedish, Norwegian, Hungarian, Italian, Greek, and Ukrainian and now Translated and Edited with Biographical, Historical, Critical, and Bibliographical Notes*. Winnipeg: Columbia Press, 1935.

- *A Canadian Headmaster: A Brief Biography of Thomas Allison Kirkconnell, 1862–1934.* Toronto: Clarke, Irwin, and Company, 1935.
- "Hungary's Linguistic Isolation." *The Hungarian Quarterly* 1, no. 1 (1936): 92–100.
- "Manitoba Symphony." In *Manitoba Essays*, edited by R.C. Lodge, 1–9. Toronto: Macmillan, 1937.
- "Thoughts for Dominion Day." *The Canadian Thinker* 1, no. 4 (July 1937): 2–4.
- "The Literature of the New-Canadians." In *Canadian Literature Today: A Series of Broadcasts Sponsored by the Canadian Broadcasting Corporation*, 57–64. Toronto: University of Toronto Press, 1938.
- "Our Foreign Language Red Press." *Winnipeg Tribune* (18 November 1939), 6.
- "Canada's Minorities and Hitler; Article No. 1 – The Canadian Germans." *Winnipeg Tribune* (22 November 1939), 6.
- *Canada, Europe, and Hitler.* Toronto: Oxford University Press, 1939.
- "Canadians All." In *Newtonian*, 20–1. Winnipeg: Yearbook of the Isaac Newton High School, 1940.
- *European Elements in Canadian Life: An Address Delivered before a Meeting of the Canadian Club at Toronto, Canada, on Monday, November 4, 1940.* N.p.: [1940?].
- *The Ukrainian Canadians and the War.* Toronto: University of Toronto Press, 1940.
- *Titus the Toad.* Toronto: Oxford University Press, 1940.
- *Canadians All: A Primer of National Unity.* Ottawa: Director of Public Information, 1941.
- *Twilight of Liberty.* Toronto: Oxford University Press, 1941.
- "Race and Nationality in Canada." *The Native Son* [National Council Edition] 2, no. 2 (April 1941): 5.
- "Democracy for Canada." *Canadian School Journal* (June 1941): 206.
- "Poetry and National Life." *The Canadian Poetry Magazine* 6, no. 3 (October 1942): 5–6.
- "The Twilight of Canadian Protestantism." *Canadian Baptist* 88, no 23 (1 Dec. 1942): 2.
- *Our Ukrainian Loyalists.* Winnipeg: Ukrainian Canadian Committee, 1943.
- "Canada and Immigration." In *The Empire Club of Canada Addresses*, 374–91. Toronto: T.H. Best, 1944. http://speeches.empireclub.org/60186/data?n=14.
- *A Tale of Seven Cities.* [Hamilton?]: [1948].

- "A Rime of Glooscap." *Dalhousie Review* 30, no. 3 (October 1950): 287–93.
- "Historical Stratification in Canadian Cultures." *International Institute of Differing Civilizations, Record of the XXXVIth Meeting Held in Paris* (1951): 439–46.
- *The Celestial Cycle*. Toronto: University of Toronto Press, 1952.
- *The Kirkconnell Pedigree*. Wolfville: privately printed, 1953.
- *Canadian Toponymy and the Cultural Stratification of Canada*. Onomastica 7. Winnipeg: Ukrainian Free Academy of Sciences, 1954.
- "Silas Rand and Glooscap." *The Acadia Bulletin* (January 1955): 22–7.
- "New Canadians from Hungary." *The Canadian Baptist* (15 January 1957): 6.
- "A Scotch-Canadian Discovers Poland." In *The Polish Past in Canada: Contributions to the History of the Poles in Canada and of the Polish-Canadian Relations*, edited by Victor Turek, 57–70. Toronto: Polish Alliance Press, 1960.
- "Introduction." In *The Polish Past in Canada*, edited by Victor Turek, 1–11. Toronto: Polish Alliance Press, 1960.
- "Religion and Philosophy: An English-Canadian Point of View." In *Canadian Dualism: Studies of French-English Relations*, edited by Wade Mason, 41–55. Toronto: University of Toronto Press, 1960.
- "The Perilous Duty." In *This Is My Concern: A Symposium*, edited by Foster Meharry Russell, 69–71. Coburg, ON: Northumberland Book, 1962.
- *That Invincible Samson*. Toronto: University of Toronto Press, 1964.
- *Centennial Tales and Selected Poems*. N.p.: Published for Acadia University by the University of Toronto Press, 1965.
- *A Slice of Canada ~ Memoirs*. N.p.: Published for Acadia University by the University of Toronto Press, 1967.
- "Leviathan, Behemoth, Kraken." *Transactions of the Royal Society of Canada* 2, no. 4 (June 1968): 161–70.
- *Awake the Courteous Echo*. Toronto: University of Toronto Press, 1973.
- "A Canadian Meets the Magyars." *The Canadian-American Review of Hungarian Studies* 1, nos 1 and 2 (Spring–Fall 1974): 1–11.
- "The Role of the Ethnic Press." In *The Multilingual Press in Manitoba*, 53–9. Winnipeg: Canada Press Club, 1974.
- *The Flavour of Nova Scotia*. Windsor, NS: Lancelot Press, 1976.
- *Climbing the Green Tree and Other Branches*. Wolfville: privately printed, 1976.
- *Medieval Mosaic: A Genealogical Supplement*. Wolfville: privately printed, 1976.

– ed. *Hungarian Helicon*. Calgary: Széchenyi Society, 1985.
Kitzan, Chris. "The Fighting Bishop: George Exton Lloyd and the Immigration Debate." MA thesis, University of Saskatchewan, 1996.
– "Preaching Purity in the Promised Land: Bishop Lloyd and the Immigration Debate." In *The Prairie West As Promised Land*, edited by R. Douglas Francis and Chris Kitzan, 291–311. Calgary: University of Calgary Press, 2007.
Klassen, Judith. "The Complicated Case of Juliette Gaultier de la Vérendrye." *Canadian Museum of History Blog* (17 March 2015), https://www.historymuseum.ca/blog/the-complicated-case-of-juliette-gaultier-de-la-verendrye/.
Klinck, Carl F., ed. *Literary History of Canada: Canadian Literature in English*. Toronto: University of Toronto Press, 1965.
Knight, David B. *Choosing Canada's Capital System: Conflict Resolution in a Parliamentary System*. Ottawa: Carleton University Press, 1991.
Knowles, Norman. *Inventing the Loyalists: The Ontario Loyalist Tradition and the Creation of Usable Pasts*. Toronto: University of Toronto Press, 1997.
Knowles, Valerie. "Ham, George Henry." In *Dictionary of Canadian Biography* 15. University of Toronto/Université Laval, 2005. http://www.biographi.ca/en/bio/ham_george_henry_15E.html.
– *William C. Van Horne: Railway Titan*. Toronto: Dundurn, 2010.
– *Strangers at Our Gates: Canadian Immigration and Immigration Policy, 1540–2015*. 4th ed. Toronto: Dundurn, 2016.
Kolchin, Peter. "Whiteness Studies: The New Study of Race in America." *The Journal of American History* 89, no. 1 (June 2002): 154–73.
Kordan, Bohdan. "*Disunity and Duality*: Ukrainian Canadians and the Second World War." MA thesis, Carleton University, 1981.
– "Soviet-Canadian Relations and the Ukrainian Ethnic Problem, 1939–44." *Journal of Ethnic Studies* 13, no. 2 (Summer 1985): 1–17.
– *Canada and the Ukrainian Question, 1939–1945*. Montreal and Kingston: McGill-Queen's University Press, 2001.
– *No Free Man: Canada, the Great War, and the Enemy Alien Experience*. Montreal and Kingston: McGill-Queen's University Press, 2016.
Kordan, Bohdan, and Lubomyr Luciuk. "A Prescription for Nationbuilding: Ukrainian Canadians and the Canadian State, 1939–1945." In *On Guard for Thee: War, Ethnicity, and the Canadian State, 1939–1945*, edited by Norman Hillmer, Bohdan Kordan, and Lubomyr Luciuk, 85–100. Ottawa: Canadian Committee for the History of the Second World War, 1988.
Korneski, Kurt. *Race, Nation, and Reform Ideology in Winnipeg*,

*1880s–1920s*. Madison, NJ and Teaneck, NJ: Fairleigh Dickinson University Press, 2015.
Kristmanson, Mark. *Plateaus of Freedom: Nationality, Culture, and State Security in Canada, 1940–1960*. Toronto: Oxford University Press, 2003.
Kyba, Patrick. "Anderson, James Thomas Milton (1878–1946)." *Encyclopedia of Saskatchewan*, https://esask.uregina.ca/entry/anderson_james_thomas_milton_1878-1946.jsp.
Lamb, Kevin. "Individual & Group Character in the Social Psychology of William McDougall." *Mankind Quarterly* 39, no. 3 (Spring 1999): 255–308.
[Lambton, John George.] *Report on the Affairs of British North America from the Earl of Durham, Her Majesty's High Commissioner, &c. &c. &c., (Officially Communicated to Both Houses of the Imperial Parliament, on 11th of February, 1839)*. Montreal: 1839. https://archive.org/details/McGillLibrary-rbsc_lc_report-on-affairs-earl_lande00205-16503.
Lake, Marilyn, and Henry Reynolds. *Drawing the Global Colour Line: White Men's Countries and the International Challenge of Racial Equality*. Cambridge: Cambridge University Press, 2008.
Lasker, Bruno, and W.L. Holland, eds. *Problems of the Pacific, 1933: Economic Conflict and Control. Proceedings of the Fifth Conference of the Institute of Pacific Relations, Banff, Canada, 14–26 August, 1933*. Chicago: The University of Chicago Press, 1934.
Lässig, Simone. "Biography in Modern History – Modern Historiography in Biography." In *Biography between Structure and Agency: Central European Lives in International Historiography*, edited by Volker R. Berghahn and idem, 1–26. New York: Berghann Books, 2008.
Lazarevich, Gordana. *The Musical World of Frances James and Murray Adaskin*. Toronto: University of Toronto Press, 1988.
Le Camp, Lorraine. "Racial Considerations of Minstrel Shows and Related Images in Canada." PhD diss., University of Toronto, 2005.
Le Play, Frédéric. *On Family, Work, and Social Change*. Edited and translated by Catherine Bodard Silver. Chicago: University of Chicago Press, 1982.
Lee, Erika. "Hemispheric Orientalism and the 1907 Pacific Coast Race Riots." *Amerasia Journal* 33, no. 2 (2007): 19–47.
Leonard, Thomas C. *Illiberal Reformers: Race, Eugenics & American Economists in the Progressive Era*. Princeton: Princeton University Press, 2016.
Levine, Allan. *King: William Lyon MacKenzie King: A Life Guided by the Hand of Destiny*. Vancouver: Douglas & McIntyre, 2011.

Lipinsky, Jack. "'The Agony of Israel': Watson Kirkconnell and the Canadian Jewry." *Journal of the Canadian Jewish Historical Society* 6, no. 1 (1982): 57–72.

Lipsitz, George. "The Possessive Investment in Whiteness: Racialized Social Democracy and the 'White' Problem in American Studies." *American Quarterly* 47, no. 3 (September 1995): 369–87.

Loewen, Royden K., and Gerald Friesen. *Immigrants in Prairie Cities: Ethnic Diversity in Twentieth-Century Canada*. Toronto: University of Toronto Press, 2009.

López, Ian Haney. *White By Law: The Legal Construction of Race*. New York: New York University Press, 1996.

Luxton, Eleanor G. *Banff: Canada's First National Park: A History and Memory of Rocky Mountains Park*. 2nd ed. Banff, AB: Summerthought, 2008.

Lyde, Lionel W. *The Continent of Europe*. 1913.

MacKellar, Landis, and Bradley W. Hart. "Captain George Henry Lane-Fox Pitt-Rivers and the Prehistory of the IUSSP." *Population and Development Review* 40, no. 4 (December 2014): 653–75.

Mackey, Eva. *House of Difference: Cultural Politics and National Identity in Canada*. Toronto: University of Toronto Press, 2002.

MacKenzie, Alexander. *Voyages from Montreal, on the River St. Laurence, Through the Continent of North America, to the Frozen and Pacific Oceans; in the Years, 1789 and 1793; with a Preliminary Account of the Rise, Progress, and Present State of the Fur Trade of That Country*. [Ed. William Combe]. London, 1801.

MacKinnon, Mary. "Canadian Railway Workers and World War I Military Service." *Labour/Le Travail* 40 (Fall 1997): 213–34.

Macskimming, Roy. *The Perilous Trade: Book Publishing in Canada, 1946–2006*. Rev. ed. Toronto: McClelland & Stewart, 2007.

MacTavish, Netwon. "John Murray Gibbon: Apostle of Silence." *The Canadian Magazine* (February 1925): 11, 29.

Madokoro, Laura. "On Racism and Taxation: Rethinking the Chinese Head Tax, 1885–1923." *Au delà des frontiers: La nouvelle histoire du Canada/Beyond Borders: The New Canadian History* (20 February 2018), https://thenewcanadianhistory.com/2018/02/20/on-racism-and-taxation-rethinking-the-chinese-head-tax-1885-1923/.

Magee, Joan. *Loyalist Mosaic: A Multi-Ethnic Heritage*. Toronto: Dundurn, 1984.

Magubane, Bernard Makhosezwe. *The Making of a Racist State: British*

*Imperialism and the Union of South Africa, 1875–1910*. Asmara: Africa World Press, 1996.

Maldonado-Torres, Nelson. "The Time and Space of Race: Reflections on David Theo Goldberg's Interrelational and Comparative Methodology." *Patterns of Prejudice* 44, no. 1 (2010): 77–88.

Malinowski, Bronislaw. *Sex and Repression in Savage Society.* 1927.

Mandryka, M.I. *The Ukrainian Question*. Winnipeg: Canadian Ukrainian Educational Association, 1940.

Mangan, J.A., ed. *The Imperial Curriculum: Racial Images and Education in the British Colonial Experience*. London and New York: Routledge, 1993.

Mann, Jatinder. *The Search for a New National Identity: The Rise of Multiculturalism in Canada and Australia, 1890s–1970s*. New York: Peter Lang, 2016.

Marion, Séraphin, and Watson Kirkconnell. *The Quebec Tradition*. Montréal: Les Éditions Lumen, 1946.

Marshall, Alison R. *Cultivating Connections: The Making of Chinese Prairie Canada*. Vancouver: UBC Press, 2014.

Martens, Klaus. *Over Canadian Trails: F.P. Grove in New Letters and Documents*. Würzburg, Germany: Königshausen and Neumann, 2007.

Martin, M. "Ganaraska History." http://www.ganaraska.ca/history.htm.

Martin, Paul. "Citizenship and the People's World." In *Belonging: The Meaning and Future of Canadian Citizenship*, edited by William Kaplan, 64–78. Montreal and Kingston: McGill-Queen's University Press, 1993.

Martynowych, Orest T. "'Canadianizing the Foreigner': Presbyterian Missionaries and Ukrainian Immigrants." In *New Soil – Old Roots: The Ukrainian Experience in Canada*, edited by Jaroslav Rozumnyj, 33–57. Winnipeg: Ukrainian Free Academy of Sciences, 1983.

Mason, Courtney W. *Spirits of the Rockies: Reasserting an Indigenous Presence in Banff National Park*. Toronto: University of Toronto Press, 2014.

Mathieu, Sarah-Jane. "North of the Colour Line: Sleeping Car Porters and the Battle Against Jim Crow on Canadian Rails, 1880–1920." *Labour/Le Travail* 47 (Spring 2001): 9–41.

– *North of the Color Line: Migration and Black Resistance in Canada, 1870–1955*. Chapel Hill: University of North Carolina Press, 2010.

Maurutto, Paula. "Private Policing and Surveillance of Catholics: Anti-Communism in the Roman Catholic Archdiocese of Toronto, 1920–1960." *Labour/Le Travail* 40 (Fall 1997): 113–36.

McAlpin, Sara. "(John) Herbert Quick." In *The Authors*, vol. 1 of *Dictionary of Midwestern Literature*, edited by Philip A. Greasley, 424–5. Bloomington: Indiana University Press, 2001.
McDougall, William. *The Group Mind*. Cambridge: Cambridge University Press, 1927.
– "William McDougall." In *A History of Psychology in Autobiography*, edited by Carl Murchison, 1:191–223. New York: Russell and Russell, 1930.
McKay, Ian. *The Quest of the Folk: Antimodernism and Cultural Selection in Twentieth-Century Nova Scotia*. CLS Edition. Montreal and Kingston: McGill-Queen's University Press, 2009.
– "The Liberal Order Framework: A Prospectus for a Reconnaissance of Canadian History." *Canadian Historical Review* 81, no. 4 (December 2000): 617–45.
– *Reds, Rebels, Radicals: Rethinking Canada's Left History*. Toronto: Between the Lines, 2005.
– *Reasoning Otherwise: Leftists and the People's Enlightenment in Canada, 1890–1920*. Toronto: Between the Lines, 2008.
– "Liberal Settler Colonialism, the Nova Scotia Archives, and the North American Ancestor-Hunters, 1890–1980." *Acadiensis* 48, no. 1 (Autumn 2019): 43–89.
McKay, Ian, and Jamie Swift. *Warrior Nation: Rebranding Canada in an Age of Anxiety*. Toronto: Between the Lines, 2012.
McLaren, Angus. *Our Own Master Race: Eugenics in Canada, 1885–1945*. Toronto: McClelland & Stewart, 1990.
McLennan, Gregor. *Pluralism*. Buckingham: Open University Press, 1995.
McNaughton, Janet E. "John Murray Gibbon and the Inter-War Folk Festivals." *Canadian Folklore* 3, no. 1 (1981): 67–72.
Mehta, Uday Singh. "Liberal Strategies of Exclusion." In *Tensions of Empire: Colonial Cultures in a Bourgeois World*, edited by Frederick Cooper and Ann Laura Stoler, 59–86. Berkeley: University of California Press, 1997.
– *Liberalism and Empire: A Study in Nineteenth-Century British Liberal Thought*. Chicago: University of Chicago Press, 1999.
Meister, Daniel R. "Young Watson Kirkconnell and 'Canadian Futurities': Excavating the Early Racial and Political Thought of the Father of Canadian Multiculturalism, 1918–1920." MA Cognate Essay, Queen's University, 2014.
– "The Biographical Turn and the Case for Historical Biography." *History Compass* 16, no. 1 (January 2018), https://doi.org/10.1111/hic3.12436.

- "'Anglo-Canadian Futurities': Watson Kirkconnell, Scientific Racism, and Cultural Pluralism in Interwar Canada." *Settler Colonial Studies* 10, no. 2 (February 2020): 234–56.
- "Historical Biography in Canada: Historians, Publishers, and the Public." In *Different Lives: Global Perspectives on Biography in Public Cultures and Societies*, edited by David Veltman and Hans Renders, 21–40. Leiden and Boston: Brill, 2020.
- "The Canadian Mosaic, Archival Silences, and an Indigenous Presence in Banff." *ActiveHistory* (18 August 2020), http://activehistory.ca/2020/08/the-canadian-mosaic-archival-silences-and-an-indigenous-presence-in-banff/.
- "'Chasing More Precise Details': Canadian Multiculturalism in the 1970s." Paper presented at the Between Postwar and the Present Day conference, University of Guelph, 6–9 May 2021.

Melis, Caroline. "J.T.M. Anderson, Director of Education Among New-Canadians and the Policy of the Department of Education: 1918–1923." *Saskatchewan History* 33, no. 1 (Winter 1980): 1–12.

Messamore, Barbara J. *Canada's Governors General 1847–1878: Biography and Constitutional Evolution.* Toronto: University of Toronto Press, 2006.

Millar, Nzingha. "Canada's Myth of Multiculturalism." *The Coast* (30 June 2017). https://www.thecoast.ca/RealityBites/archives/2017/06/30/canadas-myth-of-multiculturalism.

Miller, J.R. *Shingwauk's Vision: A History of Native Residential Schools.* Toronto: University of Toronto Press, 1996.
- *Compact, Contract, Covenant: Aboriginal Treaty-Making in Canada.* Toronto: University of Toronto Press, 2009.

Milloy, John S. *A National Crime: The Canadian Government and the Residential School System 1879–1986.* 2nd ed. Winnipeg: University of Manitoba Press, 2017.

Mills, Charles W. "Multiculturalism as/and/or Anti-Racism?" In *Multiculturalism and Political Theory*, edited by Anthony Simon Laden and David Owen, 89–144. Cambridge: Cambridge University Press, 2007.

Mitchell, Gillian. *The North American Folk Music Revival: Nation and Identity in the United States and Canada, 1945–1980.* Aldershot, UK: Ashgate, 2007.

Mitchell, Gina M. "John Buchan's Popular Fiction: A Hierarchy of Race." *Patterns of Prejudice* 7, no. 6 (1973): 24–30.

Momryk, Myron. "The Royal Canadian Mounted Police and the

Surveillance of the Ukrainian Community in Canada." *Journal of Ukrainian Studies* 28, no. 2 (Winter 2003): 89–112.

Moodie, Stanley. "McDougall's Conception of the Group Mind." MA thesis, University of British Columbia, 1923.

Moore, William H. *The Clash! A Study in Nationalities*. Toronto: J.M. Dent, 1918.

Morant, Geoffrey. *The Races of Central Europe*. 1939.

Morton, Desmond. "Sir William Otter and Internment Operations in Canada during the First World War." *Canadian Historical Review* (1 March 1974): 32–58.

– "The Cadet Movement and the Moment of Canadian Militarism, 1909–1914." *Journal of Canadian Studies* 13, no. 2 (Summer 1978): 56–69.

Moss, Mark. *Manliness and Militarism: Educating Young Boys in Ontario for War*. Don Mills, Ontario: Oxford University Press, 2000.

Municipality of Port Hope. "The History of Port Hope," http://visitporthope.ca/the-history-of-port-hope.

Nayar, Pramod K. *Colonial Voices: The Discourses of Empire*. Malden, MA: Wiley-Blackwell, 2012.

N.B.J. "Canadian Overtones" (Review). *The Slavonic Review* 14, no. 42 (April 1936): 729–30.

Neary, Peter. "The CBC 'Adventures in Citizenship' Broadcast of 9 November 1938 (*Kristallnacht*)." *Canadian Jewish Studies/Études juives canadiennes* 10 (2002): 109–22.

Neatby, Hilda. *Queen's University, 1814–1914: And Not to Yield*. Montreal and Kingston: McGill-Queen's University Press, 1978.

Neilson, Leighann C. "John Murray Gibbon (1875–1952): The Branding of a Northern Nation." *CHARM Proceedings* (2011): 127–44.

Nicks, Joan, and Jeannette Slonioswki. "Entertaining Niagara Falls, Ontario: Minstrel Shows, Theatres, and Popular Pleasures." In *Covering Niagara: Studies in Local Popular Culture*, edited by Barry Keith Grant and Joan Nicks, 316–41. Waterloo, ON: Wilfrid Laurier University Press, 2010.

Nish, Elizabeth. *Racism or Responsible Government: The French Canadian Dilemma of the 1840s*. Toronto: Copp Clark, 1967.

Novick, Peter. *That Noble Dream: The 'Objectivity Question' and the American Historical Profession*. Cambridge: Cambridge University Press, 1988.

O'Connell, JoAnne. *The Life and Songs of Stephen Foster*. Lanham, MD: Rowman and Littlefield, 2016.

O.R.B. Club. *Lindsay Past and Present: Souvenir of Old Home Week.* Lindsay, ON, 1924.

Osborne, Brian S. "'Non-Preferred' People: Inter-war Ukrainian Immigration to Canada." In *Canada's Ukrainians: Negotiating an Identity*, edited by Lubomyr Luciuk and Stella Hryniuk, 81–102. Toronto: University of Toronto Press, 1991.

– "Constructing the State, Managing the Corporation, Transforming the Individual: Photography, Immigrants, and the Canadian National Railways, 1925–30." In *Picturing Place: Photography and the Geographical Imagination*, edited by Joan M. Schwartz and James R. Ryan, 162–92. London: I.B. Taurus, 2003.

Osborne, Brian S., and Susan E. Wurtele. "The Other Railway: Canadian National's Department of Colonization and Agriculture." In *Immigration and Settlement, 1870–1930*, History of the Prairie West series, edited by Gregory P. Marchildon, vol. 2, 103–27. Regina: Canadian Plains Research Center, 2009.

Page, Robert J.D. "Canada and the Imperial Idea in the Boer War Years." *Journal of Canadian Studies* 5, no. 1 (1970): 33–49.

Painter, Nell Irvin. *The History of White People.* New York: W.W. Norton, 2010.

Pal, Leslie A. "Identity, Citizenship, and Mobilization: The Nationalities Branch and World War Two." *Canadian Public Administration* 32, no. 3 (1989): 407–26.

– *Interests of State: The Politics of Language, Multiculturalism and Feminism in Canada.* Montreal: McGill-Queen's University Press, 1993.

Palmer, Howard. "Responses to Foreign Immigration: Nativism and Ethnic Intolerance in Alberta, 1880–1920." MA thesis, University of Alberta, 1971.

– "Reluctant Hosts: Anglo-Canadian Views of Multiculturalism in the Twentieth Century." In Canadian Consultative Council on Multiculturalism, *Multiculturalism as State Policy: Conference Report*, 81–118. Ottawa: Minister of Supply and Services, 1978.

– *Patterns of Prejudice: A History of Nativism in Alberta.* Toronto: McClelland & Stewart, 1982.

Palmer, Howard, ed. *Immigration and the Rise of Multiculturalism.* Toronto: Copp Clark, 1975.

Palmer, Howard, and Tamara Palmer. "The Black Experience in Alberta." In *Peoples of Alberta: Portraits of Cultural Diversity*, edited by idem, 365–93. Saskatoon: Western Producer Prairie Books, 1985.

Panofsky, Ruth. "'A Press with Such Traditions': Oxford University Press of Canada." *Papers of the Bibliographical Society of Canada* 42, no. 1 (2004): 7–29.

Parker, George L. "Authors and Publishers on the Offensive: The Canadian Copyright Act of 1921 and the Publishing Industry 1920–1930." *Papers of the Bibliographical Society of Canada* 50, no. 2 (2012): 131–85.

Pass, Forrest D. "'Something Occult in the Science of Flag-Flying': School Flags and Educational Authority in Early Twentieth-Century Canada." *Canadian Historical Review* 95, no. 3 (September 2014): 321–51.

Pateman, Carole, and Charles Mills. *The Contract and Domination*. Cambridge: Polity, 2007.

Patrias, Carmela. "Race, Employment Discrimination, and State Complicity in Wartime Canada, 1939–1945." *Labour/Le Travail* 59 (Spring 2007): 9–42.

– *Jobs and Justice: Fighting Discrimination in Wartime Canada, 1939–1945*. Toronto: University of Toronto Press, 2012.

Pearson, Karl. *The Life, Letters, and Labours of Francis Galton*. Cambridge: Cambridge University Press, 1914–30.

*The Pen & Pencil Club 1890–1959*. Montreal, n.d. [1959].

Perkin, J.R.C. "'There Were Giants on the Earth in Those Days': An Assessment of Watson Kirkconnell." In *Canadian Baptists and Christian Higher Education*, edited by George Rawlyk, 89–128. Montreal and Kingston: McGill-Queen's University Press, 1988.

Perkin, J.R.C., and James B. Snelson, *Morning in His Heart: The Life and Writings of Watson Kirkconnell*. Hantsport, NS: Lancelot Press for Acadia University Library, 1986.

Perry, Adele. *Colonial Relations: The Douglas-Connolly Family and the Nineteenth Century Imperial World*. Cambridge: Cambridge University Press, 2015.

Petty, Sheila. "(Re)Visioning Histories: Racism in Early Prairie Cinema." In *Racism, Eh? A Critical Inter-Disciplinary Anthology of Race and Racism in Canada*, edited by Camille A. Nelson and Charmaine A. Nelson, 326–36. Concord, ON: Captus Press, 2004.

Phelps, Arthur. "Professor Kirkconnell's Book, 'European Elegies.'" *Vox* 2, no. 1 (December 1928): 14–15.

Pickles, Katie. *Female Imperialism and National Identity: The Imperial Order Daughters of the Empire*. Manchester: Manchester University Press, 2002.

Pitsula, James. *Keeping Canada British: The Ku Klux Klan in 1920s Saskatchewan*. Vancouver: UBC Press, 2013.

Pitts, Jennifer. "Free for All." *Times Literary Supplement* 5660 (23 September 2011): 8–9.

Pitt-Rivers, G. Henry Lane-Fox. *The Clash of Culture and the Contact of Races*. 1927.
Pittard, Eugene. *Les Races et l'histoire*. 1924.
– *Race and History*. London: Keegan Paul, (1924) 2003.
Porter, John. *The Vertical Mosaic: An Analysis of Social Class and Power in Canada*. 50th Anniversary edition. Toronto: University of Toronto Press, (1965) 2015.
Potter, Simon J. "Britishness, the BBC, and the Birth of Canadian Public Broadcasting." In *Communicating Canada's Past: Essays in Media History*, edited by Gene Allen and Daniel J. Robinson, 78–108. Toronto: University of Toronto Press, 2009.
Price, John. *Orienting Canada: Race, Empire, and the Transpacific*. Vancouver: UBC Press, 2011.
Prymak, Thomas M. *Maple Leaf and Trident: Ukrainian Canadians during the Second World War*. Toronto: Multicultural History Society of Ontario, 1988.
Regehr, Theodore D. "Shaughnessy, Thomas George, 1st Baron Shaughnessy." In *Dictionary of Canadian Biography* 15. University of Toronto / Université Laval, 2005. http://www.biographi.ca/en/bio/shaughnessy_thomas_george_15E.html
Reid, Escott. "The Saskatchewan Liberal Machine before 1929." *Canadian Journal of Economics and Political Science* 2, no. 1 (February 1936): 27–40.
Renders, Hans, and Binne de Haan. "The Challenge of Biography Studies." In *Theoretical Discussions of Biography: Approaches from History, Microhistory, and Life Writing*, edited by idem, 1–10. Leiden: Brill, 2014.
Riggins, Stephen Harold. "'A Square Deal for the Least and the Last': The Career of W.G. Smith in the Methodist Ministry, Experimental Psychology, and Sociology." *Newfoundland and Labrador Studies* 27, no. 2 (2012): 179–222.
Ripley, William Z. *The Races of Europe: A Sociological Study*. London: Kegan Paul, Trench, Trubner and Co., 1899.
Roberts, Barbara. *Whence They Came: Deportation from Canada 1900–1935*. Ottawa: University of Ottawa Press, 1988.
Robertson, Ian Ross. "Sir Andrew Macphail and the Pen and Pencil Club." In *Thinkers and Dreamers: Historical Essays in Honour of Carl Berger*, edited by Gerald Friesen and Doug Owram, 126–43. Toronto: University of Toronto Press, 2011.
Robinson, Bart. *Banff Springs: The Story of a Hotel*, 4th ed. Banff: Summerthought Publishing, 2007.

Robinson, Daniel. "Planning for the 'Most Serious Contingency': Alien Internment, Arbitrary Detention, and the Canadian State 1938–39." *Journal of Canadian Studies* 28, no. 2 (Summer 1993): 5–20.

Roe, Amy J. "Teachers and Schools." *Grain Growers' Guide* (13 September 1922), 22.

Roediger, David. *The Wages of Whiteness: Race and the Making of the American Working Class*. London and New York: Verso, 1991.

Roy, Patricia E. *A White Man's Province: British Columbia Politicians and Chinese and Japanese Immigrants, 1858–1914*. Vancouver: UBC Press, 1989.

– *The Oriental Question: Consolidating a White Man's Province, 1914–41*. Vancouver: UBC Press, 2003.

Roy, Patricia, J.L. Granatstein, Masako Iino, and Hiroko Takamura. *Mutual Hostages: Canadians and Japanese During the Second World War*. Toronto: University of Toronto Press, 1990.

Rutherdale, R.A. Review of *The Political Thought of Lord Durham*, by Janet Ajzenstat. *Canadian Historical Review* 70, no. 2 (June 1989): 259–61.

Sabourin, Diane, and Maude-Emmanuelle Lambert. "Montréal's Chinatown." In *The Canadian Encyclopedia*. Toronto: Historica Canada, 24 March 2013. https://www.thecanadianencyclopedia.ca/en/article/montreals-chinatown.

Saini, Angela. *Superior: The Return of Race Science*. Boston: Beacon Press, 2019.

Sandwell, B.K. "John Murray Gibbon." *Canadian Magazine* (November 1918): 599.

– "Europe in Canada." *Saturday Night* (9 December 1939): 2.

Sangster, Joan. *The Iconic North: Cultural Constructions of Aboriginal Life in Postwar Canada*. Vancouver: UBC Press, 2016.

Sarath, Ed. *Musical Theory Through Improvisation: A New Approach to Musicianship Training*. New York: Routledge, 2013.

Satzewich, Vic. "Whiteness Limited: Racialization and the Social Construction of 'Peripheral Europeans.'" *Histoire sociale/Social History* 33, no. 66 (2000): 271–89.

Schrenk, Lisa. "Directed Cultural Change and Imagined Communities: The Royal Commission on Bilingualism and Biculturalism Encounters the Language Question in Ontario, 1964–1967." MA thesis, Queen's University, 1993.

Schwartz, Susan. "University Club of Montreal Giving Up Its Percy Nobbs-Designed Downtown Digs." *Montreal Gazette* (25 December

2017), https://montrealgazette.com/news/local-news/university-club-of-montreal-giving-up-its-percy-nobbs-designed-downtown-digs.

Schwinghamer, Steve. "The Colour Bar at the Canadian Border: Black American Farmers." *Canadian Museum of Immigration at Pier 21,* https://pier21.ca/research/immigration-history/the-colour-bar-at-the-canadian-border-black-american-farmers.

Scott, William Duncan. "Immigration and Population." In *Canada and Its Provinces: A History of the Canadian People and Their Institutions by One Hundred Associates,* edited by Adam Shortt and Arthur G. Doughty, 7:517–90. Toronto: Glasgow, Brook, and Company, 1914.

Sekula, Allan. "The Body and the Archive." *October* 39 (Winter 1986): 3–64.

Selman, Gordon. "University Extension 1915–1963." *The Journal of Adult Education* 10 (April 1964): 17–25.

– *A History of Fifty Years of Extension Service by the University of British Columbia 1915–1965.* Toronto: Canadian Association for Adult Education, 1966.

Shaw, Amy, and Andrew Smith. "Lady Aberdeen and the British Origins of Multiculturalism in Canada." *British Journal of Canadian Studies* 32, no. 1–2 (2019–20): 3–22.

Sheedy, Erin. "Performing the Canadian 'Mosaic': Juliette Gauthier, Florence Glenn, and the CPR Festivals of Quebec City." MA thesis, University of Ottawa, 2014.

Shepard, R. Bruce. *Deemed Unsuitable: Blacks from Oklahoma Move to the Canadian Prairies in Search of Equality in the Early 20th Century, Only to Find Racism in Their New Home.* Toronto: Umbrella Press, 1997.

Shrum, Gordon. *Gordon Shrum: An Autobiography.* Edited by Clive Cocking. Vancouver: UBC Press, 1986.

Serwer, Adam. "White Nationalism's Deep American Roots." *The Atlantic* (April 2019), https://www.theatlantic.com/magazine/archive/2019/04/adam-serwer-madison-grant-white-nationalism/583258.

Silver, Catherine Bodard. "Introduction." In Frédéric Le Play, *On Family, Work, and Social Change,* edited and translated by Catherine Bodard Silver, 3–134. Chicago: University of Chicago Press, 1982.

Skinner, Quentin. "Meaning and Understanding in the History of Ideas." *History and Theory* 8, no. 1 (1969): 3–53.

Smale, Robert. "For Whose Kingdom? Canadian Baptists and the Evangelization of Immigrants and Refugees 1880 to 1945." EdD diss., University of Toronto, 2001.

Smith, Gregory S. "The Japanese-Canadians and World War II." In *Alien Justice: Wartime Internment in Australia and North America*, edited by Kay Saunders and Roger Daniels, 93–113. Queensland: University of Queensland Press, 2000.

Smith, W.G. *A Study in Canadian Immigration*. Toronto: Ryerson, 1920.

– *Building the Nation*. 1922.

Solonari, Vladimir. "In the Shadow of Ethnic Nationalism: Racial Science in Romania." In *Race Science in Hitler's New Europe, 1938–1945*, edited by Anton Weiss-Wendt and Rory Yeomans, 259–86. Lincoln: University of Nebraska Press, 2013.

Spiro, Jonathan. *Defending the Master Race: Conservation, Eugenics, and the Legacy of Madison Grant*. Lebanon, NH: University Press of New England, 2009.

Stamp, Robert M. *The Schools of Ontario, 1876–1976*. Toronto: University of Toronto Press, 1982.

Stanger-Ross, Jordan, ed. *Landscapes of Injustice: A New Perspective on the Internment and Dispossession of Japanese Canadians*. Montreal and Kingston: McGill-Queen's University Press, 2020.

Stanger-Ross, Jordan, and the Landscapes of Injustice Research Collective. "Suspect Properties: The Vancouver Origins of the Forced Sale of Japanese-Canadian–owned Property, WWII." *Journal of Planning History* 15, no. 4 (2016): 271–89.

Statistics Canada. "150 Years of Immigration in Canada" (29 June 2016). https://www150.statcan.gc.ca/n1/pub/11-630-x/11-630-x2016006-eng.htm.

– *Canada [Country] and Canada [Country]* (table). Census Profile. 2016 Census. Statistics Canada Catalogue no. 98-316-X2016001. Ottawa. Released November 29, 2017. https://www12.statcan.gc.ca/census-recensement/2016/dp-pd/prof/index.cfm?Lang=E.

Stevenson, Garth. *Building Nations From Diversity: Canadian and American Experience Compared*. Montreal and Kingston: McGill-Queen's University Press, 2014.

Stocking, George, Jr. "The Persistence of Polygenist Thought in Post-Darwin Anthropology." In *Race, Culture, and Evolution: Essays in the History of Anthropology*, edited by idem, 42–68. Chicago: University of Chicago Press, 1968.

– *A Franz Boas Reader: The Shaping of American Anthropology, 1883–1911*. Chicago: University of Chicago Press, 1974.

– *Race, Culture, and Evolution: Essays in the History of Anthropology*. Chicago: University of Chicago Press, 1982.

Bibliography 379

Stouck, David. *As for Sinclair Ross*. Toronto: University of Toronto Press, 2005.
Strange, Carolyn, and Jennifer A. Stephen. "Eugenics in Canada: A Checkered History, 1850s–1990s." In *The Oxford Handbook of the History of Eugenics*, edited by Alison Bashford and Philippa Levine, 523–38. Oxford: Oxford University Press, 2010.
Sunahara, Ann Gomer. *The Politics of Racism: The Uprooting of Japanese Canadians During the Second World War*. 2nd ed. Ottawa: Self-published, 2000.
Swyripa, Frances. *Ukrainian Canadians: A Survey of their Portrayal in English-language Works*. Edmonton: University of Alberta Press for the Canadian Institute of Ukrainian Studies, 1978.
– *Storied Landscapes: Ethno-Religious Identity and the Canadian Prairies*. Winnipeg: University of Manitoba Press, 2010.
Thompson, Cheryl. "Cultivating Narratives of Race, Faith, and Community: *The Dawn of Tomorrow*, 1923–1971." *Canadian Journal of History* 50, no. 1 (2015): 30–67.
– "'Come One, Come All': Blackface Minstrelsy as a Canadian Tradition and Early Form of Popular Culture." In *Towards an African-Canadian Art History: Art, Memory, and Resistance*, edited by Charmaine Nelson, 95–121. Concord, ON: Captus Press, 2018.
Thomson, J. Arthur. *Heredity*. New York: Putnam's Sons, 1908.
Trachtenberg, Henry. "The Jewish Community of Winnipeg and the Federal Election of 1935 in Winnipeg North." *Manitoba History* 61 (Fall 2009), http://www.mhs.mb.ca/docs/mb_history/61/jewishcommunity.shtml.
*Tribute to a Nation Builder: An Appreciation of John Murray Gibbon*. Toronto: Composers, Authors, and Publishers Association of Canada, 1946.
Trudeau, Pierre Elliott. *The Essential Trudeau*. Edited by Ron Graham. Toronto: McClelland & Stewart, 1998.
Trudel, Marcel. *Canada's Forgotten Slaves: Two Centuries of Bondage*. Translated by George Tombs. Montreal: Véhicule Press, 2013.
Tuchman, Barbara. "Biography as a Prism of History." In *Telling Lives: The Biographer's Art*, edited by Marc Pachter, 133–47. Philadelphia: University of Pennsylvania Press, 1985.
Turda, Marius. *Modernism and Eugenics*. New York: Palgrave Macmillan, 2010.
Valverde, Mariana. *The Age of Light, Soap, and Water: Moral Reform in English Canada, 1885–1925*. Toronto: University of Toronto Press, (1991) 2008.

Veracini, Lorenzo. *Settler Colonialism: A Theoretical Overview*. [UK]: Palgrave Macmillan, 2010.
Vernon, Karina, ed. *The Black Prairie Archives: An Anthology*. Waterloo, ON: Wilfrid Laurier University Press, 2019.
von Maltzahn, Nicholas. "Milton and the Deist Prelude to Liberalism." In *Milton and Questions of History: Essays by Canadians Past and Present*, edited by Mary Nyquist and Feisal Mohamed, 215–49. Toronto: University of Toronto Press, 2012.
Wade, Peter. "The Presence and Absence of Race." *Patterns of Prejudice* 44, no. 1 (2010): 43–60.
Waite, Peter. "Invading Privacies: Biography as History." *Dalhousie Review* 69, no. 4 (1990): 479–95.
– "The Five History Books That Have Most Influenced Me ..." *Bulletin of the Canadian Historical Association* 26, no. 1 (2000): 10.
Walker, Barrington. "Immigration Policy, Colonization, and the Development of a White Canada." In *Canada and the Third World: Overlapping Histories*, edited by Karen Dubinsky, Sean Mills, and Scott Rutherford, 37–59. Toronto: University of Toronto Press, 2016.
Walker, James W. St G. *The Black Loyalists: The Search for a Promised Land in Nova Scotia and Sierra Leone, 1783–1870*. 2nd ed. Toronto: University of Toronto Press, 1992.
– *Racial Discrimination in Canada: The Black Experience*. Ottawa: Canadian Historical Association, 1985.
– *"Race," Rights, and the Law in the Supreme Court of Canada: Historical Case Studies*. N.p.: Osgoode Society for Legal History and Wilfrid Laurier University Press, 1997.
– "Myths, History and Revisionism: The Black Loyalists Revisited." *Acadiensis* 29, no. 1 (1999): 88–105.
Wall, Sharon. "Totem Poles, Teepees, and Token Traditions: 'Playing Indian' at Ontario Summer Camps, 1920s–1955." *Canadian Historical Review* 86, no. 2 (September 2005): 513–44.
Ward, W. Peter. *White Canada Forever: Popular Attitudes and Public Policy Toward Orientals in British Columbia*. 3rd ed. Vancouver: UBC Press, 2002.
Weir, George. "Introduction." In Robert England, *The Central European Immigrant in Canada*. Toronto: Macmillan, 1929.
Welshman, John. *Underclass: A History of the Excluded Since 1880*. 2nd ed. London: Bloomsbury, 2013.
Whitaker, Reg. "Official Repression of Communism during World War II." *Labour/Le Travail* 17 (Spring 1986): 135–66.

Whitaker, Reg, and Gary Marcuse. *Cold War Canada: The Making of a National Insecurity State, 1945–1957.* Toronto: University of Toronto Press, 1996.
Whitaker, Reg, and Steve Hewitt. *Canada and the Cold War.* Toronto: James Lorimer and Company, 2003.
"William Duff Gibbon (1880–1955)." *The Badsey Society.* https://www.badseysociety.uk/sladden-archive/people/671.
Winks, Robin. *The Blacks in Canada: A History.* 2nd ed. Montreal and Kingston: McGill-Queen's University Press, 1997.
Woodger, Kevin. "Whiteness and Ambiguous Canadianization: The Boy Scouts Association and the Canadian Cadet Organization." *Journal of the Canadian Historical Association* 28, no. 1 (2017): 95–126.
Woodruff, Charles. *Expansion of Races.* New York: Rebman Company, 1909.
Woodsworth, J.S. *Strangers Within Our Gates; or, Coming Canadians.* Toronto: Missionary Society of the Methodist Church, 1909.
– Introduction to *Bi-Lingual Schools in Canada,* by C.B. Sissons, 3–6. Toronto: J.M. Dent, 1917.
Woodsworth, Judith. "Watson Kirkconnell and 'The Undoing of Babel': a Little-Known Case in Canadian Translation History." *Meta: Translators' Journal* 45, no. 1 (2000), 13–28.
Wright, Donald. "His *Macdonald,* My *Creighton,* Biography, and the Writing of History." *Canadian Historical Review* 98, no. 2 (June 2017): 338–55.
Wurtele, Susan E. "'Apostles of Canadian Citizenship': Robert England, the CNR and Prairie Settlement." In *Reflections from the Prairies: Geographical Essays,* edited by H. John Selwood and John C. Lehr, 18–23. Winnipeg: Department of Geography, University of Winnipeg, 1992.
– "Nation-Building from the Ground Up: Immigrants and Their Assimilation in Inter-war Saskatchewan." PhD diss., Queen's University, 1993.
Xiques, Donez. *Margaret Laurence: The Making of a Writer.* Toronto: Dundurn, 2005.
Yochelson, Ellis L. *Smithsonian Institution Secretary, Charles Doolittle Walcott.* Kent, OH: Kent State University Press, 2001.
Young, Charles H. *The Ukrainian Canadians: A Study in Assimilation.* Toronto: Thomas Nelson, 1931.
Young, Robert J.C. *Colonial Desire: Hybridity in Theory, Culture and Race.* London: Routledge, 1995.

– *Postcolonialism: An Historical Introduction*. Malden, MA: Wiley-Blackwell, 2001.
Young, William R. "Making the Truth Graphic: The Canadian Government's Home Front Information Structure and Programmes During World War II." PhD diss., University of British Columbia, 1978.
Zach, Naomi. *Philosophy of Science and Race*. New York: Routledge, 2002.
Zaporzan, Shirley, and Robert B. Klymasz. *Film and the Ukrainians in Canada 1921–1980*. Edmonton: Canadian Institute of Ukrainian Studies, 1982.
Zimmern, Alfred. *The Third British Empire*. Oxford: Oxford University Press, 1926.

# Index

African peoples, 19, 21, 25, 49, 62, 76–7, 107–8, 122–3, 161–5, 168, 238, 240–1, 248, 311–12n133. *See also* Middle Eastern peoples
Anderson, J.T.M, 88–9, 95–6, 146, 222, 287n70
Anglo-Celtic, 46, 57, 238, 262n4
Anglo-Saxon: "civilization," 26, 31, 36, 50, 51, 70, 74, 81, 90, 111, 190–1, 206, 207, 238, 239; definition of, 16, 17, 34, 47–8, 257n46; as racial identity, 62, 77, 80, 83, 110, 125, 150, 167, 194, 216, 219, 226; as racial regime, 19, 24, 26, 31, 36, 37, 41, 45, 46, 48, 49, 50, 58, 79, 84, 102, 115, 116, 120, 121, 123, 150, 165, 189, 190–1, 192, 204, 206, 207, 215, 238, 239. *See also* Britishness; Nordicism; racism
Angus, H.F., 224–5, 328n95
anthropology, 14, 16, 19, 42, 45
antimodernism, 62–3, 110, 149
anti-Semitism, 24, 31, 39, 49, 64, 142, 146–8, 149, 153, 165, 169, 184, 197, 217, 222, 232, 240, 241, 268n78, 325n71, 334n21

Asian peoples, 15, 22–3, 39, 50, 56, 62–3, 124, 162–4, 196, 215, 224, 236, 238, 264n31, 269n93, 324n63, 328n95
assimilation: of immigrants, 3, 31, 38–9, 56, 71–6, 80, 91–2, 94, 97–103, 106–11, 114–25, 138, 145–7, 159, 162–3, 166–7, 176, 182–6, 196–7, 201, 203–4, 206, 215, 221–2, 228–30, 236–8, 241–2, 259n77, 287n70, 293n124; of Indigenous peoples, 20, 21, 36, 157–8, 218, 242–3

Barbeau, Marius, 154–62, 308n92
biography. *See* historical biography
Black, W.J., 104, 105, 114, 115
blackface, 245–6, 336n35
block settlements, 94, 100, 117–20, 122
Bolshevism. *See* communism
Britishness, 23, 38, 47–8, 62, 90, 111–12, 120–1, 149–50, 166–7, 167, 183–5, 190–1, 215, 220–1, 236–44. *See also* Anglo-Saxon
Brockington, Leonard, 172–3, 178, 199, 200, 202, 230, 251, 312n4

Buchan, John, 240–3, 333n18, 334n21, 334–5n28
Bureau of Public Information (BPI), 200, 208, 213–18, 223, 239, 319–20n18

Canadian Authors Association (CAA), 11, 58, 59–60, 72, 127, 222, 227, 255–6n26, 271n113, 341n28
Canadian Broadcasting Corporation (CBC), 28, 171–5, 177–87, 208–13, 227, 230, 235–6, 238, 314n19
Canadianization. *See* assimilation
Canadian National Railways (CNR), 118–19, 253n6, 293n124. *See also* England, Robert
Canadian Pacific Railway (CPR), 5, 10, 118–19, 136–9, 141–2, 148, 154–55, 164–5, 223, 244, 251, 301n26, 304n56, 301n122; porters, 76–7, 161–2, 165. *See also* Gibbon, John Murray
Catholicism. *See* religion
Caucasian, 16–17, 18, 19, 26, 175. *See also* critical race theory; whiteness
census: criticism of, 31–2, 46; definition of race in, 176
Chicanot, Eugene Louis, 161
citizenship: as an ideal, 34, 75, 76, 89–90, 92, 93, 115, 125, 145, 185, 239, 291n101; official citizenship, 93, 94, 181, 197, 235, 243, 331–2n4
Clarke, William (Bill), 189–90, 200–2, 318n58
class, 6, 17, 21, 31, 47, 54, 146, 149, 155

Committee for Cooperation in Canadian Citizenship (CCCC), 10–11, 223–33
communism, 101, 146, 198, 201, 205, 213, 214, 217, 219–20, 223–4, 233, 247, 248, 326n80. *See also* socialism
Connor, Ralph, 86, 160–1
critical race theory, 13–19, 25–8, 99, 103, 105. *See also* race; racialism; racism; whiteness

diversity, metaphors of: garden, 148–53, 169–70; iceberg, 72–3; kaleidoscope, 122; mosaic, 4, 5, 11, 108–9, 127–8, 192, 246, 290n96, 297–8n2, 327n87; omelette, 324n53; overtones, 73–6, 278n4; tapestry, 71–2, 277n69

England, Amy, 87, 89, 91, 96, 100, 104, 113, 178, 249
England, Robert, 5, 9, 10, 11, 28, 29, 81, 82–126, 128, 175, 177–87, 208, 223–4, 225, 231, 234–5, 238, 239, 249–51; and the CCCC, 10–11, 223, 225, 231; *Central European Immigrant in Canada* (1929), 82–3, 106–14; *Colonization of Western Canada* (1936), 116–25; Community Progress Competitions, 114–16; and eugenics, 83, 109; personal life, 84–8, 96, 177–8, 249–51, 338–9n11, 339n17; thesis on the assimilation of Ukrainians (1923), 97–103; *Ventures in Citizenship* (1938), 177–87
England, Thelma, 249–50

eugenics, 16–17, 27, 31, 41, 43–4, 46–51, 52–57, 68, 79–80, 82–3, 102, 109, 151–3, 191–2, 206, 272–3n123, 289n90, 290–1n98, 303n45, 305–6n74, 317n45, 331n124, 338n5. *See also* racism
Ewach, Honoré, 73, 202, 321n29

Fabians. *See* socialism.
First World War, 41–3, 87–8, 142
folk festivals. *See* Gibbon, John Murray
Foster, Kate A., 11, 127
French Canadians, 34, 49, 56, 79–80, 121–2, 141–2, 153–5, 186, 191, 194, 200, 206, 207, 217, 230, 239–40, 291n104, 303n45, 318n59

Gates, Reginald Ruggles, 266n60, 268n87, 273n123
gender and sexuality, 10–11, 20, 32, 34, 40, 41, 48–9, 87, 90, 108, 110, 143, 152, 168, 191, 255–6n26, 264n34, 267n70, 302n39, 330n112
German Canadians, 4, 42, 62, 89, 120, 186, 198, 201, 219, 227–8, 304n56
Gibbon, John Murray, 5, 9, 10, 11, 28, 29, 54, 58, 65, 66, 109, 126, 127–70, 171, 172–7, 180, 192, 219, 220–3, 224, 225–31, 238, 239, 242, 246, 251–2, 301n26, 340n26, 341n26, 341n28; and the CCCC; 10–11, 225–31; and CPR folk festivals, 9, 66, 155–6, 157–64, 165–7, 172, 278n180, 293n124, 306–7n83, 309n104; and eugenics, 151–3; and the garden metaphor, 148–53; and Indian Days, 156–7; and the mosaic metaphor, 10–11, 127–8, 172–7, 297–8n2; personal life, 130–2, 135, 140–1, 252, 300n18, 300n20, 302n39, 302–3n43; and Trail Riders of the Canadian Rockies, 167–9
Gibbon, Nancy (Anne Fox), 133–5, 140–1, 252, 298n7, 299n10, 300n18, 300n20, 341n28
Gibbon, William Duff, 130, 132–5, 298n5, 298n7
Goldberg, David Theo, 99, 286nn66–7
Gordon, C.W. *See* Connor, Ralph
Grant, Madison, 16–17, 56, 289n90, 331n124
Greek Canadians, 39, 47, 49, 65, 101, 144, 149, 187, 214
Grove, Frederick Philip, 58, 67, 277n170

Hayward, F.H., 185, 316n45
Hayward, Victoria, 11, 127
hereditarianism. *See* eugenics
historical biography, 6–7, 254n8
Hungarian Canadians, 120, 202, 205
Hurd, W.B., 125, 176, 296n156

Icelandic Canadians, 67–8, 70, 71–2, 73, 75, 78, 197, 223, 272n121, 277n173
immigration, 19, 22–6, 38–9, 44, 50, 56–7, 62–3, 94, 104–9, 117–25, 142–3, 145–6, 149–50, 165, 189–90, 196, 222, 236, 238, 244, 257–8n54
imperialism, 19–20, 36–7, 236–44

Indigenous peoples, 15, 21, 36, 45, 51–2, 78–9, 83, 108, 123, 136, 145, 158, 159, 160, 162, 168, 176, 182, 206, 215, 218, 231, 250, 278n190, 290n94, 302n36; Algonquin, 51–2; Cree, 61, 77–8; Huron-Iroquois, 51–2; Huron-Wendat, 157; Métis, 77–8, Peigan, 159; Stoney (Nakoda), 156, 251
internment: First World War, 41–3, 101, 145, 203; Second World War, 197–8; of the unemployed, 54–5
Inuit. *See* Indigenous peoples
Italian Canadians, 145–6, 197–8, 227–8

Jacobson, Matthew Frye, 18–19, 23
Jewish peoples, 56, 57, 64, 101, 120, 146, 149, 150, 153, 181, 186, 187, 214, 219, 222, 224–5, 264n31, 274n139, 298n3, 306n78, 316n33, 322n38, 325n69. *See also* anti-Semitism

Kaye, Vladimir J., 207, 254n19
King, William Lyon Mackenzie, 175, 196–202, 212, 220, 223, 234–44, 313n9
Kirkconnell, Bertha Gertrude, 34, 45
Kirkconnell, Hope, 69, 188, 248, 275n158
Kirkconnell, Isabel, 58, 69, 188, 248
Kirkconnell, Thomas Allison, 34, 44, 248, 338n6
Kirkconnell, Watson, 5, 9, 10, 11, 28, 31–81, 186–94, 199–220, 221, 223, 225, 226–8, 230, 231, 233, 238, 239, 247–8, 262n3, 262n14, 263n26, 268n87, 317n53, 320n20, 321n35, 327n71, 333n15, 333n17, 335n28, 338n5, 338n8; and the CCCC, 10–11, 223–4, 225–31; personal life, 58–9, 69, 188, 205, 247–8, 274–5n150, 275nn157–8, 317n53, 325n31, 333n15, 338n8; publications: "Anglo-Canadian Futurities" (1919–20), 46–53; "A Sensible Census" (1920), 31–2, 45–6; *Canada, Europe, and Hitler* (1939), 188–94; *Canadian Overtones* (1935), 73–6, 278n185; *Canadians All* (1941), 208–20; "Celebration of Citizenship" (1938), 181, 185–7, 317n46; *European Elegies* (1928), 58–60, 271–2n115; *The European Heritage* (1930), 63–5; *International Aspects of Unemployment* (1923), 53–7, 269n95, 270n105; *North American Book of Icelandic Verse* (1930), 67–71; *Titus the Toad* (1939), 76–7, 78; *Ukrainian Canadians and the War* (1940), 200–7; *Victoria County Centennial History* (1921), 52–3; "Western Immigration" (1928), 61–3
Ku Klux Klan, 96, 153, 165, 311n128

Leacock, Stephen, 144, 264n34
Le Play, Frédéric, 91, 96–8, 284n55, 285n61

Levantines, 215, 324n60. *See also* Middle Eastern peoples
liberalism, 20, 117, 134, 200, 236
Lindsay (Ontario), 34, 35, 36, 45, 51, 53, 57, 69, 262n8
Lisgar Collegiate Institute, 3–4, 5, 244–6
Lloyd, George Exton, 61–3, 65, 106, 273n126, 273n128, 289n87

MacNeill, J.F., 199–200
McKay, Ian, 20, 72, 204, 258n67, 289n2
McWilliams, Margaret Stovel, 10
Métis. *See* Indigenous peoples
Middle Eastern peoples: Afghans, 204; Albanians, 187; Armenians, 101; Berbers, 204; Persians, 143, 229; Syrians, 144, 187; Tartars, 102; Turks, 102. *See also* African peoples; Jewish peoples
mosaic. *See* diversity, metaphors of
multiculturalism: as an already achieved ideal, 29–30, 65; history of, 8, 9, 29–30, 65, 171, 234, 236–44; policy of, 4–5, 234, 236–44

nationalism, 26, 36, 43, 134, 145, 180, 203, 293n126
Nationalities Branch, 223–31
Nazism, 19, 175–6, 200–1, 204, 214, 216, 217, 220, 232, 331n124
Nordicism, 16–17, 19, 25–6, 44, 46–50, 56, 60–4, 70, 83–4, 107–13, 122–3, 138, 161, 163, 175–6, 186, 191–2, 214, 272n121

Oliver, Frank, 24–5, 94, 273n128

Palmer, Howard, 9, 65, 82–4, 255n23, 279nn1–2, 331–2n4
Philipps, Tracy, 207, 219, 224–5, 233
Polish Canadians, 3–4, 68, 89, 161, 180, 202, 205
Port Hope, 32, 34, 35, 36, 57, 58, 68
Protestantism. *See* religion

Queen's University, 32, 34, 37–41, 50, 87, 88, 116, 289n85

race, 13–19, 21, 23; definition of, 14; history of, 13–15. *See also* racialism; racialization; racism
racialism, 26, 76; definition of, 14. *See also* racialization
racialization, 27, 266n62; definition of, 14. *For specific examples of racialization, see the entries for specific groups of people*
racism, 15–17, 25; definition of, 14, 109; history of, 13–18. *For examples of racism against specific groups, see* African peoples; Asian peoples; Indigenous peoples; Middle Eastern peoples; Slavic peoples. *See also* anti-Semitism
religion, 13, 34, 37, 39, 41, 50–1, 58, 86–7, 91–2, 116, 180–1, 185, 200, 268n83, 280n7, 307n88. *See also* anti-Semitism
Royal Canadian Mounted Police (RCMP), 136–7, 201, 205, 222–3, 224, 327n89

Royal Society of Canada (RSC), 128–9, 225, 228, 230–1, 329n110

Sandwell, B.K., 142, 194
Scandinavian peoples, 3–4, 16, 57, 72, 101, 104, 111, 120, 162–3, 197, 221–2, 273n128, 277n170. *See also* Icelandic Canadians
scientific racism. *See* eugenics; racism
Second World War, 27–8, 195–233
settler colonialism, 6, 12, 19–20, 21–2, 23, 25, 35–6, 51, 103, 108, 119, 135–6, 156, 185–6, 236–7, 243
sexuality. *See* eugenics; gender and sexuality
Sifton, Clifford, 23–5, 117
Skelton, Isabel, 10, 255n24
Skelton, O.D., 10, 38–9, 175, 201, 283n38
Skinner, Quentin, 8, 66, 243
Slavic peoples, 24–5, 31, 39, 42, 47, 57, 61, 62, 72, 101–2, 120, 137, 144, 146, 160, 173, 186, 241, 291n98
socialism, 39, 133–4, 262n8, 285n61, 300n17. *See also* communism

Thorson, Joseph T., 223, 228, 251
Trudeau, Pierre Elliott, 4–5
Tweedsmuir, Lord. *See* Buchan, John

Ukrainian Canadians, 4, 18, 24, 42, 70–1, 73, 88, 89, 92–3, 94–5, 97, 99–103, 118, 123, 137, 146, 160, 200–5, 207, 212, 219–20, 225, 241–2. *See also* Ewach, Honoré; Slavic peoples
United States of America, 13, 15–16, 18–19, 26, 27, 39, 43–4, 63, 64, 73, 98, 107–8, 112, 122–3, 146, 150, 153, 154, 158, 159–60, 162, 165, 196, 220–1, 227, 235, 237, 238, 244, 246, 280n9, 289n90, 311n128

Van Horne, William, 140, 162, 310n122

Weir, George, 95–6, 106
whiteness, 5, 13–19, 23–8, 57–65, 104–5, 107–8. *See also* Anglo-Saxon; Nordicism; race; racism
Winnipeg, 57–8, 64, 66, 77, 122, 160, 182
Woodhouse, Arthur S.P., 230, 337n2
Woodsworth, James Shaver, 70, 113, 146, 214–15, 276n161